3 9153 00941239 8

W9-CCX-832

Latin American Panorama

AN ANTHOLOGY

EDITED BY

Paul Kramer, M.LITT., CANTAB

AND

Robert E. McNicoll, PH.D.

G. P. PUTNAM'S SONS : NEW YORK

 Published simultaneously in Canada by Longmans of Canada Limited, Toronto.

Library of Congress Catalog
Card Number: 68–12100

Printed in the United States of America

Contents

ACKNOWLEDGMENTS

Our warm thanks and appreciation are due to a number of individuals and institutions for making this book possible. We wish specifically to acknowledge our debt to Alfred A. Knopf, Inc., for permission to reprint "The European Background of Brazilian History" by Gilberto Freyre, published in *New World in the Tropics.* We also wish to thank Professor Freyre.

Also, we wish to acknowledge our debt to Dr. Germán Arciniegas for granting us permission to use his portrait of Manuelita Sáenz, originally published in *America Magica,* II (Buenos Aires, Editorial Sudamericana, 1961). Our thanks are also due Miss Felicity Trueblood for her translation of this essay.

We are also very appreciative of the kindness of Miss Margaret Bryce in allowing us to reprint the chapter, "The Relation of the Races in South America," from the book *South America: Observations and Impressions,* by her uncle, the late Lord Bryce. We are indebted to Cornell University Press and Dr. Arthur Whitaker for permission to reprint his "Whose Hemisphere?" from the book *The Western Hemisphere Idea;* also to the Executors of the André Siegfried Estate, Jonathan Cape Ltd., and H. H. and Doris Hemming for permission to reprint the material on Chile from the late Mr. Siegfried's book *Impressions of South America.*

Our special thanks is due to the Macmillan Company and Professor F. S. C. Northrop for permission to reprint the extracts from "The Rich Culture of Mexico," published in his book *The Meeting of East and West.* Dr. Northrop's kindness in approving the manner in which we have abridged his material was very helpful.

We are indebted to Professor Frank Tannenbaum for his permission to use the material on Fidel Castro from his book *Ten Keys to Latin America.* We wish to thank Miss Evelyn P. Stevens and the *Western Political Quarterly* for permission to reprint her article "Mexican *Machismo:* Politics and Value Orientations." Duke University Press kindly granted permission to reprint "Intellectual Origins of Aprismo." Finally, we wish to thank the *Journal of Inter-American Studies* for permission to reprint the following articles: "Some Effects of Population Growth on Latin America's Economy" by Alfonso Gonzalez; "Cuban Students in Politics, 1956–57" by Jaime Suchlicki; and "Power and Social Change in Colombia: The Cauca Valley" by Cole Blasier.

Introduction

The story of the development of Latin America into what it is today is complex. Also, much of the story is unknown, and much of it is misunderstood. For almost 500 years the Hispanic-Mediterranean civilization introduced by the Spanish and Portuguese invaders has sought to impose itself on a vast continent peopled in large part by descendants of those defeated by the original conquerors. This struggle, almost from the beginning, has been complicated by the presence of thousands of Africans, who have flourished in the area of their transplantation to the extent that they predominate in many of the hemisphere's tropical regions. Thus, today Latin America still lacks a single unified structure but has, instead, numbers of civilizations or cultures, coexisting and competing for control within the limits of the modern state.

From the original three races there soon grew a variety of mixed races, which have evolved societies and cultures of their own. Such a situation, in the absence of a popular and widely read literature and terminology, is difficult for an outsider to understand. Its comprehension is even more difficult for the people of the United States. For Latin America's original invaders did not come from our European centers of migration, but from an Hispanic, Mediterranean, and partly African civilization, whose nature and idiosyncrasies, even to this day, are not fully understood. Furthermore, it has been traditionally difficult for British and American writers to be fully objective on the subject of Spain. For many years Catholic Spain was the enemy of Protestant England, and later it was primarily the former colonies of the Spanish Empire that stood in the way of an expansion-minded United States.

Historians and writers, aware of Latin America's complexity, in an effort to simplify and to unify what has never been either simple or unified, have accepted the term "Latin America" to describe the area in the hope that the word "Latin" would provide a rapid understanding of its many peoples. Although it is true that this key is perhaps better than none, the danger of its use is exemplified by what has happened to Latin American history and writing. On the whole, they have restricted themselves to the relatively simple annals of the Creole aristocracy, a Europeanized minority with its satellite groups who have governed the nations of the hemisphere just as their ancestors governed the Indies in the name of Spain and Portugal. Thus, the other elements in the compound of Central and South America have never been fully recorded and analyzed. The general acceptance of the term "Latin" has tended to inhibit a study of just those factors in the other American republics about which we know the least—namely, the story of the confrontation and intermingling of European, native Indian, and African cultures that constitute present-day Latin America.

From the standpoint of a knowledge of the Creole peoples, it is, of course, true, just as it is for our own civilization, that a phrase of Socrates', a speech of Pericles', or the footsteps of an ancient people that crossed the Red Sea out of Egypt are more significant than the philosophical speculations of the Mayas or the statistical work of the Incas. But the loss of knowledge of these ancient peoples, along with our complete ignorance of the servile imports from Africa who have found such a favorable environment in tropical America, renders our knowledge of the area incomplete. We remain mentally remote from the millions of members of the native races of America who are still not incorporated into the life and civilization of their countries, an unintegrated mass of the disinherited, whose future may influence the whole course of Western Hemisphere affairs. Whenever we read, whenever we study "Latin" America, we must therefore remember that the task of the anthropologist, the sociologist, and the archaeologist remains to be completed so that the single strand of understanding we do have may be extended to include knowledge of the greater, though silent, America that constitutes the majority of its population.

Within the limits of what we do know of the subject peoples of Latin America and our larger knowledge of its politically preponderant Latin society, several significant points merit attention. It must be kept in mind that after the discovery of the New World and its subsequent rapid physical conquest by men like Pizarro and Cortez, the paths of European and Latin American history at once diverge. Not only did Latin America immediately begin to develop its own history, so that the men who lived there were confronted with problems for which there were no precedents in Renaissance Europe, but also events and ideas that had profound effects on Europe had often different effects and at times no effect whatever on Latin America.

No European ruler, for example, was ever faced with the problems of Columbus' son, who, as governor of Hispaniola, had to choose between a policy of seeking to ameliorate the condition of the native population or yielding to the demands of the landlords for greater severity in the interest of increased production. And although the intellectual movement that was started by Erasmus to divert the current of European learning from profane into Christian channels took root in Spain with Cardinal Cisneros and was passed on to Latin America, the efforts of Luther to break the chain of European authority at its strongest link failed in the Iberian Peninsula. Latin America was thus denied an experience that had profound and distinguishing effects in other parts of the modern world.

On other occasions, European tumult, both intellectual and political, impinged directly on Latin America. Spain, for example, fought a losing battle to maintain in Latin America a philosophic basis for its concepts of absolutism. But despite opposition from Madrid and the colonial governors, the ideas of the great thinkers of France's Age of Enlightenment prevailed in Latin America to the extent that when, during the first fifteen years of the nineteenth century, Napoleon's struggle to control continental Europe engulfed Spain, these ideas encouraged a revolt which the weakened mother country and its compromised royalties were never strong enough to suppress.

A few years later, however, the opposite was true. The history of the world from 1850 to 1945 is to a significant degree the story of the rapid growth of Prussia, its domination of Europe, and the two great wars that were fought to deny it a preponderance of power. But this protracted and bloody struggle, which absorbed so much of the wealth and energy of the modern world, for all practical purposes passed Latin America by, with the exception of the demand it generated for the area's raw materials. Thus, Latin America today knows nothing of casualty lists from remote battlefields, nor has it experienced the demands of modern total warfare on labor and industrial and technological initiative in order to develop and supply the necessary weapons for victory. In the field of total national mobilization, Latin America lies outside the mainstream.

The same paradox is also true of United States–Latin American relations. Sometimes upheavals and convulsions that have engulfed the United States have been reflected in Latin America, and at other times they have not. The social aspects of the American Revolution, for example, which reduced the political importance of the great landholders in the United States, had no counterpart in Latin America, where land distribution remained relatively unchanged by its subsequent wars of independence. On the other hand, Franklin Roosevelt's New Deal did have effects in Latin America and contained specifically a philosophy that tended to alter the nature of inter-American relations. The degree to which major political, social, economic, and cultural events occurring elsewhere in the world have affected Latin America has not been consistent, and, these inconsistencies have contributed to the area's unique history.

Unfortunately, much of the story of these interrelationships remains to be written or has not been translated into English. There are some segments that are excellently done, however, and since portions of these have not been included in this book, they merit mention. One of the best, for example, is the lifetime work of John Tate Lanning on the nature of the academic culture brought by Spain to the Spanish-American universities. Lanning has also written of the development of this culture in America and the new forces affecting it on the eve of the wars of independence and has compared it with European scholarship at the time of Latin America's political independence. But despite this solid and impressive beginning, we still have few contemporary studies of the nature of present-day academic culture in Latin America and its European and North American ties, both culturally and politically.

Another major area of study concerns the interrelationship, as well as the indigenous nature, of Latin American literature as a cultural force. This is fortunate because a knowledge of Latin American literature is of paramount importance in assessing the mind of the area. In this field the work of Latin American writers, literary critics, and historians has been exceptional. Besides Arciniegas, Pedro Henríquez-Ureña, José Torres-Ríoseco, and Leopoldo Zea have made notable contributions toward the understanding of the Latin American mind. Also, United States scholars have rendered great service. Isaac Goldberg, for example, was the first to consider Latin American literature as something distinct and separate from the mainstream of Spanish creative writing.

But all this has been at best only a beginning, and we will still lack knowledge in depth of the degree of Latin American involvement in the major currents of European and North American affairs and an appropriate degree of distinction between what is nativist and what is imported. There is still much raw data scattered about in Latin America, yet to be examined and studied in such a way as to shed light on the local, as well as the overseas, forces of national development. One reason, as we mentioned earlier, is the existence of so many different societies and cultures. Another reason has been the oligarchic nature of Latin American society. There has always been the persistent belief in this area that when a country is controlled by a few families, there is little to be gained from the written record of their struggles for and with either ideas or power. Of what use the written record when the ruling families all know one another and are often intermarried? Gossip and conversation in such a society transcend a book or an essay in importance and influence. As a consequence, the tumultuous struggles for power or with ideologies in Latin America have never been fully recorded. This attitude has filtered down into other fields of activity and has acted as an inhibiting factor in the recording of human experience.

Also, Western European and American thinking and development have affected our knowledge of Latin America. Europe and America have not always maintained a steady and objective interest in Latin America, and this at times has affected both the quality and the quantity of scholarship. In the earlier period, when Latin American gold and silver utterly changed the economy of Europe, students of European affairs were drawn to an examination of the conditions existing in the sources of this upheaval. As a consequence, a great deal was written about it, and much scholarly work was done. But with the advent of the Industrial Revolution and the failure of Latin America to embrace either its techniques or its philosophy, there developed the feeling in North America and Europe that Latin America was of little interest or importance, that it had developed little of its own for the mind of man. Historical, sociological, and economic interest in Latin America subsided; its archives and statistics were both forgotten and neglected and its own scholars ignored, so that for much of our knowledge of nineteenth-century Latin America we are still dependent on local archives and libraries that have yet to be sifted and correlated.

With the advent of the Spanish-American War, however, a new interest developed. North America began to invest great sums of money, and the investments were followed not only by marines but also by scholars and savants. Bankers and industrialists wanted to know more about the economics and politics of the countries in which they were investing. Students, with careers in Latin America in mind, wished to learn more about the countries in which they planned to spend their adult lives, Government needed to know more about the nature of the states it sought to manipulate. And scholarship, ever sensitive to a need for its talents, sought to meet this demand as best it could. But here, too, an inhibiting factor developed. As the United States became more and more involved in Latin America, its policies became more and more the subject of domestic political debate, so that the exigencies of domestic argument became the inspiration for a great deal of writing. A good portion of the research of this period, therefore, is not completely objective and has a limited value for the student today.

Unfortunately, the same is true of much of the activist research that is now being conducted in Latin America by government and government-subsidized centers for research. The Alliance for Progress and the great amounts of U.S. money involved in the program have created a need for an enormous amount of research to guide those responsible for the program toward prudent decisions. Never before have the sociology, the economy, and the political policy of Latin America been subject to the detailed writing that prevails today. This research has, of course, great value. The alliance would be impossible to administer without it. But it also has a very grave defect in that such research is supplemental to and contributory toward established policy, whose basis cannot be questioned. It is thus, by its nature, involved in and allied to current problems of government administration. This kind of study cannot rise above intrahemisphere preoccupations and go out into the world at large to inquire if there are not alternatives or countertrends that might improve or negate the objectives of the alliance. It cannot, for example, examine the enormous, but now largely forgotten, contribution that the pre-World War II cheap industrial imports from Japan made to the living standards of the west coast of Latin America, because that lies outside the framework of existing policy.

It is with factors such as these in mind that we have made our selection of readings on Latin America, a selection that must be imperfect if only because the sum of our knowledge is imperfect. We have assembled the readings chronologically so that the reader will have a picture of the development of Latin America. Much excellent material has been rejected because of limitations of space and the desire to cover the entire period from the Age of Discovery to Fidel Castro.

At this point, it might be well to mention some of the excellent works that have been omitted. J. Fred Rippy has written authoritatively on U.S.-Latin American relations, Dexter Perkins examined the Monroe Doctrine in detail, and Sylvanus Morley did pioneer work on Mayan civilization. These are just a few examples; there are many others.

We have been influenced in our decisions on what to include in this book by a desire to provide the student and professor alike with a starting point for lively and enlightened seminar discussions, which, when woven together, may form a basis for understanding Latin American development. Thus, science, economics, philosophy, and culture as well as politics and history, have been touched on, and the desire to maintain this breadth of scope has put an added premium on space and forced the exclusion of much good material. Also, we have preferred at times to include a writing by a preeminent mind rather than by an area specialist. For it is our belief that the essays of scholars of the stature of Lord Acton and Carlyle, Professor Northrop and Dr. Freyre must inevitably, because of their quality and impact on the formulation of world opinion, stimulate the reader into thought and discussion about the subjects which they cover. At the same time, however, this formula has been deliberately varied from time to time in the interest of exposing the reader to other types of more specialized regional research.

Because of this, it has been thought best to precede each selection with a brief biography of the author and a short summary of the point of view held by the author. In this way, both the student and the general reader alike may obtain an insight into the personal forces that have combined to create a profound thinker on Latin America, as well as into the forces that have led toward the research on and knowledge of the area. Also, it is believed that the introductory material will assist in the establishment of a point of departure for profitable and enlightening discussion, not only on Latin America itself, but also on the writing on Latin America.

Though all these considerations have been factors in guiding us in our choice of these readings, over and above all of them we have been guided by one conviction alone: that ours is a world which knows the need and feels the duty to make itself a master of earlier times–in this case Latin America's earlier times–and to forfeit nothing of the wisdom of those times. In this way, it is believed, we can help reader and student alike devote the best of his energies toward the detection of error and the recognition of truth in so far as present-day Latin America is concerned.

Selections from *The Conquest of Peru*

By WILLIAM HICKLING PRESCOTT

The division of the soil was renewed every year, and the possessions of the tenant were increased or diminished according to the numbers in his family. . . . A more thorough and effectual agrarian law than this cannot be imagined. . . .

One of the first foreign areas to attract American scholarship was Spain and its colonial history. Three friends and colleagues–Washington Irving, John Lothrop Motley, and William Hickling Prescott–all ventured into this field. Motley's *Rise of the Dutch Republic* dealt with the decline of Spain's predominance in Europe. Irving exploited the Moorish background of Spain with his *Chronicle of the Conquest of Granada* and *Tales of the Alhambra* and was actually working on the conquest of Mexico when he generously gave up the project to Prescott.

Prescott, born in Salem, Massachusetts, in 1796, was of a distinguished and well-to-do New England family. His father was a leading lawyer, and his paternal grandfather, Colonel William Prescott, had led American troops at Bunker Hill. His maternal grandfather was a prosperous Boston merchant and later American consul in the Azores. Prescott's career was planned, and the way to it was clear–to go to Harvard, then to enter his father's law office and succeed to his prosperous practice. He duly entered Harvard in 1811 (at age fifteen) but during the next year there occurred the first of two accidents that completely altered his life. In a juvenile roughhouse in the University Commons at dinner, he was accidentally struck with a hard crust of bread, which destroyed the sight of his left eye. Later, illness so reduced the sight of the remaining eye that he had to give up his legal ambitions.

Though money was no problem, a Calvinistic need to justify his existence led Prescott to decide on literature as a career, and in 1820 he embarked on a course of studies that would have been severe for one with normal vision. Aided by friends who read to him and by paid secretaries, he devoted at least seven hours a day to reading, studying, and writing. In 1824, the second accident that gave him direction took place. Professor George Ticknor of Harvard, who had recently been appointed professor of French and Spanish and was a pioneer Hispanist, read him some of his lectures on Spanish literature. The effect was profound. Prescott employed a teacher of Spanish and immediately began his attack on this field of culture. There followed his three books: in 1836, *The History of the Reign of Ferdinand and Isabella;* in 1843, his masterpiece, *The Conquest of Mexico;* and in 1846, *The Conquest of Peru*. Prescott became internationally famous with the appearance of his first book, which received the plaudits of European scholars for which Americans then so eagerly hoped. Lord Holland pronounced it the most important historical work since Gibbon. Guizot was loud in praise of the book. Translated into several languages, it was the first historical work produced in America to enjoy an international reputation.

The place of both *Conquests* is assured for all time despite the revisions that must be made as a result of modern archaeological and other investigations. Both as a classic of literature and as an inspiring interpretation of the great Andean civilization, *The Conquest of Peru* will continue to be read. This selection was made because it is less known than its companion study of Mexico and because it contains information relevant to contemporary problems of the area. President Belaunde of Peru, for example, has gone back to the Inca land and settlement systems as a basis for modern development and as a guide to a solution of the man/land ratio problem, which the Incas had solved in their own way.

Thus, although agrarian reform as a current social and political problem had no meaning for Prescott, as he sat in Boston, situated on the edge of a sparsely populated North American continent, and as he studied the documents that had been transcribed for him by assistants in Spanish libraries and copies of material from the British Museum, the result remains an inspiration and a guide. The Indian population that Prescott described was conquered but never destroyed, and the system of land tenure introduced by the Spanish conquerors and preserved to this day has failed to afford the growing indigenous population a sufficiently viable economy to promote political stability. Faced with this dilemma, modern statesmen and researchers are returning to an examination of earlier texts for guidance and deeper knowledge. Prescott's was the first of these.

R. E. M.

THE name of Peru was not known to the natives. It was given by the Spaniards, and originated, it is said, in a misapprehension of the Indian name of "river."[1] However this may be, it is certain that the natives had no other epithet by which to designate the large collection of tribes and nations who were assembled under the scepter of the Incas, than that of *Tavantinsuyu*, or "four quarters of the world."[2] This will not surprise a citizen of the United States, who has no other name by which to class himself among nations than what is borrowed from a quarter of the globe.[3] The kingdom, conformably to its name, was divided into four parts, distinguished each by a separate title, and to each of which ran one of the four great roads that diverged from Cuzco, the capital or *navel* of the Peruvian monarchy. The city was in like manner divided into four quarters; and the various races, which gathered there from the distant parts of the empire, lived each in the quarter nearest to its respective province. They all continued to wear their peculiar national costume, so that it was easy to determine their origin; and the same order and system of arrangement prevailed in the motley population of the capital, as in the great provinces of the empire. The capital, in fact, was a miniature image of the empire.[4]

The four great provinces were each placed under a viceroy or governor, who ruled over them with the assistance of one or more councils for the different departments. These viceroys resided, some portion of their time, at least, in the capital, where they constituted a sort of

[1]Pelu, according to Garcilasso, was the Indian name for "river," and was given by one of the natives in answer to a question put to him by the Spaniards, who conceived it to be the name of the country. (Com. Real., Parte 1, lib. 1, cap. 6.) Such blunders have led to the names of many places both in North and South America. Montesinos, however, denies that there is such an Indian term for "river." (Mem. Antiguas, MS., lib. 1, cap 2.) According to this writer, Peru was the ancient *Ophir* whence Solomon drew such stores of wealth; and which, by a very *natural* transition, has in time been corrupted into *Phiru, Piru, Peru!* The first book of the Memorias, consisting of thirty-two chapters, is devoted to this precious discovery.

[2]Ondegardo, Rel. Prim., MS.—Garcilasso, Com. Real., Parte 1, lib. 2, cap. 11.

[3]Yet an *American* may find food for his vanity in the reflection, that the name of a quarter of the globe, inhabited by so many civilized nations, has been exclusively conceded to him.—Was it conceded or assumed?

[4]Ibid., parte 1, cap. 9, 10.—Cieza de Leon, Cronica, cap. 93.

The capital was further divided into two parts, the Upper and Lower town, founded, as pretended, on the different origin of the population; a division recognized also in the inferior cities. Ondegardo, Rel. Seg., MS.

council of state to the Inca.[5] The nation at large was distributed into decades, or small bodies of ten; and every tenth man, or head of a decade, had supervision of the rest–being required to see that they enjoyed the rights and immunities to which they were entitled, to solicit aid in their behalf from government, when necessary, and to bring offenders to justice. To this last they were stimulated by a law that imposed on them, in case of neglect, the same penalty that would have been incurred by the guilty party. With this law hanging over his head, the magistrate of Peru, we may well believe, did not often go to sleep on his post.[6]

The people were still further divided into bodies of fifty, one hundred, five hundred, and a thousand, with each an officer having general supervision over those beneath, and the higher ones possessing, to a certain extent, authority in matters of police. Lastly, the whole empire was distributed into sections or departments of ten thousand inhabitants, with a governor over each, from the Inca nobility, who had control over the *curacas* and other territorial officers in the district. There were, also, regular tribunals of justice, consisting of magistrates in each of the towns or small communities, with jurisdiction over petty offenses, while those of a graver character were carried before superior judges, usually the governors or rulers of the districts. These judges all held their authority and received their support from the Crown, by which they were appointed and removed at pleasure. They were obliged to determine every suit in five days from the time it was brought before them; and there was no appeal from one tribunal to another. Yet there were important provisions for the security of justice. A committee of visitors patrolled the kingdom at certain times to investigate the character and conduct of the magistrates; and any neglect or violation of duty was punished in the most exemplary manner. The inferior courts were also required to make monthly returns of their proceedings to the

[5]Dec. de la Aud. Real., MS.—Garcilasso, Com. Real., Parte 1, lib. cap. 15.

For this account of the councils I am indebted to Garcilasso, who frequently fills up gaps that have been left by his fellow-laborers. Whether the filling up will, in all cases, bear the touch of time, as well as the rest of his work, one may doubt.

[6]Dec. de la Aud. Real., MS.—Montesinos, Mem. Antiguas, MS., lib. 2, cap. 6. —Ondegardo, Rel. Prim., MS.

How analogous is the Peruvian to the Anglo-Saxon division into hundreds and tithings! But the Saxon law was more humane, which imposed only a fine on the district, in case of a criminal's escape.

higher ones, and these made reports in like manner to the viceroys; so that the monarch, seated in the center of his dominions, could look abroad, as it were, to the most distant extremities, and review and rectify any abuses in the administration of the law.[7]

The laws were few and exceedingly severe. They related almost wholly to criminal matters. Few other laws were needed by a people who had no money, little trade, and hardly any thing that could be called fixed property. The crimes of theft, adultery, and murder were all capital; though it was wisely provided that some extenuating circumstances might be allowed to mitigate the punishment.[8] Blasphemy against the Sun, and malediction of the Inca—offenses, indeed, of the same complexion—were also punished with death. Removing landmarks, turning the water away from a neighbor's land into one's own, burning a house, were all severely punished. To burn a bridge was death. The Inca allowed no obstacle to those facilities of communication so essential to the maintenance of public order. A rebellious city or province was laid waste, and its inhabitants exterminated. Rebellion against the "Child of the Sun," was the greatest of all crimes.[9]

The simplicity and severity of the Peruvian code may be thought to infer a state of society but little advanced; which had few of those complex interests and relations that grow up in a civilized community, and which had not proceeded far enough in the science of legislation to economize human suffering by proportioning penalties to crimes.

[7]Dec. de la Aud. Real., MS.—Ondegardo, Rel. Prim. et Seg., MSS.—Garcilasso, Com. Real., Parte 1, lib. 2, cap. 11-14.—Montesinos, Mem. Antiguas, MS., lib. 2, cap. 6.

The accounts of the Peruvian tribunals by the early authorities are very meager and unsatisfactory. Even the lively imagination of Garcilasso has failed to supply the blank.

[8]Ondegardo, Rel. Prim., MS.—Herrera, Hist. General, dec. 5, lib. 4, cap. 3.

Theft was punished less severely, if the offender had been really guilty of it to supply the necessities of life. It is a singular circumstance, that the Peruvian law made no distinction between fornication and adultery, both being equally punished with death. Yet the law could hardly have been enforced, since prostitutes were assigned, or at least allowed, a residence in the suburbs of the cities. See Garcilasso, Com. Real., Parte 1, lib. 4, cap. 34.

[9]Sarmiento, Relacion, MS., cap. 23.

"I los traidores entre ellos llamava *aucaes,* i esta palabra es la mas abiltada de todas quantas pueden decir aun Indio del Pirú, que quiere decir traidor á su Señor." (Conq. i Pob. del Pirú, MS.) "En las rebeliones y alzamientos se hicieron los castigos tan asperos que algunas veces asolaron las provincias de todos los varones de edad sin quedar ninguno." Ondegardo, Rel. Prim., MS.

But the Peruvian institutions must be regarded from a different point of view from that in which we study those of other nations. The laws emanated from the sovereign, and that sovereign held a divine commission, and was possessed of a divine nature. To violate the law was not only to insult the majesty of the throne, but it was sacrilege. The slightest offense, viewed in this light, merited death; and the gravest could incur no heavier penalty.[10] Yet, in the infliction of their punishments, they showed no unnecessary cruelty; and the sufferings of the victim were not prolonged by the ingenious torments so frequent among barbarous nations.[11]

These legislative provisions may strike us as very defective, even as compared with those of the semi-civilized races of Anahuac, where a graduation of courts, moreover, with the right of appeal, afforded a tolerable security for justice. But in a country like Peru, where few but criminal causes were known, the right of appeal was of less consequence. The law was simple, its application easy; and, where the judge was honest, the case was as likely to be determined correctly on the first hearing as on the second. The inspection of the board of visitors, and the monthly returns of the tribunals, afforded no slight guaranty for their integrity. The law which required a decision within five days would seem little suited to the complex and embarrassing litigation of a modern tribunal. But, in the simple questions submitted to the Peruvian judge, delay would have been useless; and the Spaniards, familiar with the evils growing out of long-protracted suits, where the successful litigant is too often a ruined man, are loud in their encomiums of this swift-handed and economical justice.[12]

The fiscal regulations of the Incas, and the laws respecting property,

[10]El castigo era reguroso, que por la mayor parte era de muerte, por liviano que fuese el delito; porque decian, que no los castigavan por el delito que avian hecho, ni por la ofensa agena, sina por aver quebrantado el mandamiento, y rompido la palabra del Inca, que lo respetaven como á Dios." Garcilasso, Com. Real., Parte 1, lib. 2, cap. 12.

[11]One of the punishments most frequent for minor offenses was to carry a stone on the back. A punishment attended with no suffering but what arises from the disgrace attached to it is very justly characterized by McCulloh as a proof of sensibility and refinement. Researches, p. 361.

[12]The Royal Audience of Peru under Philip II—there cannot be a higher authority—bears emphatic testimony to the cheap and efficient administration of justice under the Incas. "De suerte que los vicios eran bien castigados y la gente estaba bien sujeta y obediente; y aunque en las dichas penas havia esceso, redundaba en

are the most remarkable features in the Peruvian policy. The whole territory of the empire was divided into three parts, one for the Sun, another for the Inca, and the last for the people. Which of the three was the largest is doubtful. The proportions differed materially in different provinces. The distribution, indeed, was made on the same general principle, as each new conquest was added to the monarchy; but the proportion varied according to the amount of population, and the greater or less amount of land consequently required for the support of the inhabitants.[13]

The lands assigned to the Sun furnished a revenue to support the temples, and maintain the costly ceremonial of the Peruvian worship and the multitudinous priesthood. Those reserved for the Inca went to support the royal state, as well as the numerous members of his household and his kindred, and supplied the various exigencies of government. The remainder of the lands was divided, *per capita,* in equal shares among the people. It was provided by law, as we shall see hereafter, that every Peruvian should marry at a certain age. When this event took place, the community or district in which he lived furnished him with a dwelling, which, as it was constructed of humble materials, was done at little cost. A lot of land was then assigned to him sufficient for his own maintenance and that of his wife. An additional portion was granted for every child, the amount allowed for a son being the double of that for a daughter. The division of the soil was renewed every year, and the possessions of the tenant were increased or diminished according to the numbers in his family.[14] The same arrangement was observed

---

buen govierno y policia suya, y mediante ella eran aumentados. . . . . . Porque los Yndios alababan la governacion del Ynga, y aun los Españoles que algo alcanzan de ella, es porque todas las cosas susodichas se determinaban sin hacerles costas." Dec. de la Aud. Real., MS.

[13]Acosta, lib. 6, cap. 15.—Garcilasso, Com. Real., Parte 1, lib. 5, cap. 1. "Si estas partes fuesan iguales, o qual fuese mayor, yo, lo he procurado averiguar, y en unas es diferente de otras, y finalm[te] yo tengo entendido que se hacia conforme á la disposicion de la tierra y a la calidad de los Indios." Ondegardo, Rel. Prim., MS.

[14]Ondegardo, Rel. Prim., MS.—Garcilasso, Com. Real., Parte 1, lib. 5, cap. 2. The portion granted to each new-married couple, according to Garcilasso, was a *fanega* and a half of land. A similar quantity was added for each male child that was born; and half of the quantity for each female. The *fanega* was as much land as could be planted with a hundred weight of Indian corn. In the fruitful soil of Peru, this was a liberal allowance for a family.

with reference to the curacas, except only that a domain was assigned to them corresponding with the superior dignity of their stations.[15]

A more thorough and effectual agrarian law than this cannot be imagined. In other countries where such a law has been introduced, its operation, after a time, has given way to the natural order of events, and, under the superior intelligence and thrift of some and the prodigality of others, the usual vicissitudes of fortune have been allowed to take their course, and restore things to their natural inequality. Even the iron law of Lycurgus ceased to operate after a time, and melted away before the spirit of luxury and avarice. The nearest approach to the Peruvian constitution was probably in Judea, where, on the recurrence of the great national jubilee, at the close of every half-century, estates reverted to their original proprietors. There was this important difference in Peru; that not only did the lease, if we may so call it, terminate with the year, but during that period the tenant had no power to alienate or to add to his possessions. The end of the brief term found him in precisely the same condition that he was in at the beginning. Such a state of things might be supposed to be fatal to any thing like attachment to the soil, or to that desire of improving it, which is natural to the permanent proprietor, and hardly less so to the holder of a long lease. But the practical operation of the law seems to have been otherwise; and it is probable, that, under the influence of that love of order and aversion to change which marked the Peruvian institutions, each new partition of the soil usually confirmed the occupant in his possession, and the tenant for a year was converted into a proprietor for life.

The territory was cultivated wholly by the people. The lands belonging to the Sun were first attended to. They next tilled the lands of the old, of the sick, of the widow and the orphan, and of soldiers engaged in actual service; in short, of all that part of the community who, from

[15]Ibid., Parte 1, lib. 5, cap. 3.

It is singular, that while so much is said of the Inca sovereign, so little should be said of the Inca nobility, of their estates, or the tenure by which they held them. Their historian tells us, that they had the best of the lands, wherever they resided, besides the interest which they had in those of the Sun and the Inca, as children of the one, and kinsmen of the other. He informs us, also, that they were supplied from the royal table, when living at court. (lib. 6, cap. 3.) But this is very loose language. The student of history will learn, on the threshold, that he is not to expect precise, or even very consistent, accounts of the institutions of a barbarous age and people, from contemporary annalists.

bodily infirmity or any other cause, were unable to attend to their own concerns. The people were then allowed to work on their own ground, each man for himself, but with the general obligation to assist his neighbor, when any circumstance–the burden of a young and numerous family, for example–might demand it.[16] Lastly, they cultivated the lands of the Inca. This was done, with great ceremony, by the whole population in a body. At break of day, they were summoned together by proclamation from some neighboring tower or eminence, and all the inhabitants of the district, men, women, and children, appeared dressed in their gayest apparel, bedecked with their little store of finery and ornaments, as if for some great jubilee. They went through the labors of the day with the same joyous spirit, chanting their popular ballads which commemorated the heroic deeds of the Incas, regulating their movements by the measure of the chant, and all mingling in the chorus, of which the word *hailli,* or "triumph," was usually the burden. These national airs had something soft and pleasing in their character, that recommended them to the Spaniards; and many a Peruvian song was set to music by them after the Conquest, and was listened to by the unfortunate natives with melancholy satisfaction, as it called up recollections of the past, when their days glided peacefully away under the scepter of the Incas.[17]

A similar arrangement prevailed with respect to the different manufactures as to the agricultural products of the country. The flocks of llamas, or Peruvian sheep, were appropriated exclusively to the Sun and to the Inca.[18] Their number was immense. They were scattered over the different provinces, chiefly in the colder regions of the country, where they were intrusted to the care of experienced shepherds, who conducted them to different pastures according to the change of season. A large number was every year sent to the capital for the consumption

[16]Garcilasso relates that an Indian was hanged by Huayna Capac for tilling a curaca's ground, his near relation, before that of the poor. The gallows was erected on the curaca's own land. Ibid., Parte 1, lib. 5, cap. 2.

[17]Ibid., Parte 1, lib. 5, cap. 1-3.—Ondegardo, Rel. Seg., MS.

[18]Ondegardo, Rel. Prim., MS.

Yet sometimes the sovereign would recompense some great chief, or even some one among the people, who had rendered him a service, by the grant of a small number of llamas—never many. These were not to be disposed of or killed by their owners, but descended as common property to their heirs. This strange arrangement proved a fruitful source of litigation after the Conquest. Ibid., ubi supra.

of the Court, and for the religious festivals and sacrifices. But these were only the males, as no female was allowed to be killed. The regulations for the care and breeding of these flocks were prescribed with the greatest minuteness, and with a sagacity which excited the admiration of the Spaniards, who were familiar with the management of the great migratory flocks of merinos in their own country.[19]

At the appointed season, they were all sheared, and the wool was deposited in the public magazines. It was then dealt out to each family in such quantities as sufficed for its wants, and was consigned to the female part of the household, who were well instructed in the business of spinning and weaving. When this labor was accomplished, and the family was provided with a coarse but warm covering, suited to the cold climate of the mountains–for, in the lower country, cotton, furnished in like manner by the Crown, took the place, to a certain extent, of wool–the people were required to labor for the Inca. The quantity of the cloth needed, as well as the peculiar kind and quality of the fabric, was first determined at Cuzco. The work was then apportioned among the different provinces. Officers, appointed for the purpose, superintended the distribution of the wool, so that the manufacture of the different articles should be intrusted to the most competent hands.[20] They did not leave the matter here, but entered the dwellings, from time to time, and saw that the work was faithfully executed. This domestic inquisition was not confined to the labors for the Inca. It included, also, those for the several families; and care was taken that each household should employ the materials furnished for its own use in the manner that was intended, so that no one should be unprovided with necessary apparel.[21] In this domestic labor all the female part of the establishment was expected to join. Occupation was found for all, from the child five years old to the aged matron not too infirm to hold a distaff. No one, at least none but the decrepit and the sick, was allowed to eat the bread of idleness in Peru. Idleness was a crime in the

[19]See especially the account of the Licentiate Ondegardo, who goes into more detail than any contemporary writer, concerning the management of the Peruvian flocks. Rel. Seg., MS.

[20]Ondegardo, Rel. Prim. et Seg., MSS.

The manufacture of cloths for the Inca included those for the numerous persons of the blood royal, who wore garments of a finer texture than was permitted to any other Peruvian. Garcilasso, Com. Real., Parte 1, lib. 5, cap. 6.

[21]Ondegardo, Rel. Seg., MS.—Acosta, lib. 6, cap. 15.

eye of the law, and, as such, severely punished; while industry was publicly commended and stimulated by rewards.[22]

The like course was pursued with reference to the other requisitions of the government. All the mines in the kingdom belonged to the Inca. They were wrought exclusively for his benefit, by persons familiar with this service, and selected from the districts where the mines were situated.[23] Every Peruvian of the lower class was a husbandman, and, with the exception of those already specified, was expected to provide for his own support by the cultivation of his land. A small portion of the community, however, was instructed in mechanical arts; some of them of the more elegant kind, subservient to the purposes of luxury and ornament. The demand for these was chiefly limited to the sovereign and his Court; but the labor of a larger number of hands was exacted for the execution of the great public works which covered the land. The nature and amount of the services required were all determined at Cuzco by commissioners well instructed in the resources of the country, and in the character of the inhabitants of different provinces.[24]

This information was obtained by an admirable regulation, which has scarcely a counterpart in the annals of a semi-civilized people. A register was kept of all the births and deaths throughout the country, and exact returns of the actual population were made to government every year, by means of the *quipus,* a curious invention, which will be explained hereafter.[25] At certain intervals, also, a general survey of the

[22]Ondegardo, Rel. Seg., MS.—Garcilasso, Com. Real., Parte 1, lib. 5, cap. 11.

[23]Garcilasso would have us believe that the Inca was indebted to the curacas for his gold and silver, which were furnished by the great vassals as presents. (Com. Real., Parte 1, lib. 5, cap. 7.) This improbable statement is contradicted by the Report of the Royal Audience, MS., by Sarmiento, (Relacion, MS., cap. 15,) and by Ondegardo, (Rel. Prim., MS.) who all speak of the mines as the property of the government, and wrought exclusively for its benefit. From this reservoir the proceeds were liberally dispensed in the form of presents among the great lords, and still more for the embellishment of the temples.

[24]Garcilasso, Com. Real., Parte 1, lib. 5, cap. 13–16.—Ondegardo, Rel. Prim. et Seg., MSS.

[25]Montesinos, Mem. Antiguas, MS., lib. 2, cap. 6.—Pedro Pizarro, Relacion del Descubrimiento y Conquista de los Reynos del Perú, MS.

"Cada provincia, en fin del año, mandava asentar en los quipos, por la cuenta de sus nudos, todos los hombres que habian muerto en ella en aquel año, y por el consiguiente los que habian nacido, y por principio del año que entraba, venian con los quipos al Cuzco." Sarmiento, Relacion, MS., cap. 16.

country was made, exhibiting a complete view of the character of the soil, its fertility, the nature of its products, both agricultural and mineral—in short, of all that constituted the physical resources of the empire.[26] Furnished with these statistical details, it was easy for the government, after determining the amount of requisitions, to distribute the work among the respective provinces best qualified to execute it. The task of apportioning the labor was assigned to the local authorities, and great care was taken that it should be done in such a manner, that, while the most competent hands were selected, it should not fall disproportionately heavy on any.[27]

The different provinces of the country furnished persons peculiarly suited to different employments, which, as we shall see hereafter, usually descended from father to son. Thus, one district supplied those most skilled in working the mines, another the most curious workers in metals, or in wood, and so on.[28] The artisan was provided by government with the materials; and no one was required to give more than a stipulated portion of his time to the public service. He was then succeeded by another for the like term; and it should be observed, that all who were engaged in the employment of the government—and the remark applies equally to agricultural labor—were maintained, for the time, at the public expense.[29] By this constant rotation of labor, it was intended that no one should be overburdened, and that each man should have time to provide for the demands of his own household. It was impossible—in the judgment of a high Spanish authority—to improve on the system of distribution, so carefully was it accommodated to the condition and comfort of the artisan.[30] The security of the working classes seems to have been ever kept in view in the regulations of the government; and these were so discreetly arranged, that the most wearing and unwholesome labors, as those of the mines, occasioned no

[26] Garcilasso, Com. Real., Parte 1, lib. 2, cap. 14.

[27] Ondegardo, Rel. Prim., MS.—Sarmiento, Rel., MS., cap. 15.

"Presupuesta y entendida la dicha division que el Inga tenia hecha de su gente, y orden que tenia puesta en el govierno de ella, era muy facil haverla en la division y cobranza de los dichos tributos; porque era claro y cierto lo que á cada uno cabia sin que hubiese desigualdad ni engaño." Dec. de la Aud. Real., MS.

[28] Sarmiento, Relacion, MS., cap. 15.—Ondegardo, Rel. Seg., MS.

[29] Ondegardo, Rel. Prim., MS.—Garcilasso, Com. Real., Parte 1, lib. 5, cap. 5.

[30] "Y tambien se tenia cuenta que el trabajo que pasavan fuese moderado, y con el menos riesgo que fuese posible. . . . . . Era tanta la orden que tuvieron estos Indios, que a mi parecer aunque mucho se piense en ello seria dificultoso mejorarla conocida su condicion y costumbres." Ondegardo, Rel. Prim., MS.

detriment to the health of the laborer; a striking contrast to his subsequent condition under the Spanish rule.[31]

A part of the agricultural produce and manufactures was transported to Cuzco, to minister to the immediate demands of the Inca and his Court. But far the greater part was stored in magazines scattered over the different provinces. These spacious buildings, constructed of stone, were divided between the Sun and the Inca, though the greater share seems to have been appropriated by the monarch. By a wise regulation, any deficiency in the contributions of the Inca might be supplied from the granaries of the Sun.[32] But such a necessity could rarely have happened; and the providence of the government usually left a large surplus in the royal depositories, which was removed to a third class of magazines, whose design was to supply the people in seasons of scarcity, and, occasionally, to furnish relief to individuals, whom sickness or misfortune had reduced to poverty; thus, in a manner, justifying the assertion of a Castilian document, that a large portion of the revenues of the Inca found its way back again, through one channel or another, into the hands of the people.[33] These magazines were found by the Spaniards, on their arrival, stored with all the various products and manufactures of the country—with maize, *coca, quinua,* woolen and cotton stuffs of the finest quality, with vases and utensils of gold, silver, and copper, in short, with every article of luxury or use within the compass of Peruvian skill.[34] The magazines of grain, in particular,

[31]"The working of the mines," says the President of the Council of the Indies, "was so regulated that no one felt it a hardship, much less was his life shortened by it." (Sarmiento, Relacion, MS., cap. 15.) It is a frank admission for a Spaniard.

[32]Garcilasso, Com. Real., Parte 1, lib. 5, cap. 34.—Ondegardo, Rel. Prim. MS.

"E asi esta parte del Inga no hay duda sino que de todas tres era la mayor, y en los depositos se parece bien que yó visité muchos en diferentes partes, é son mayores é mas largos que nó los de su religion sin comparasion." Idem, Rel. Seg., MS.

[33]Todos los dichos tributos y servicios que el Inga imponia y llevaba como dicho es eran con color y para efecta del govierno y pro comun de todos asi como lo que se ponia en depositos toda se combertia y distribuia entre los mismos naturales." Dec. de la Aud. Real., MS.

[34]Acosta, lib. 6, cap. 15.

"No podre decir," says one of the Conquerors, "los depositos. Vide de rropas y de todos generos de rropas y vestidos que en este reino se hacian y vsavan que faltava tiempo para vello y entendimiento para comprender tanta cosa, muchos depositos de barretas de cobre para las minas y de costales y sogas de vasos de palo y platos del oro y plata que aqui se hallo hera cosa despanto." Pedro Pizarro, Descub. y Conq., MS.

would frequently have sufficed for the consumption of the adjoining district for several years.[35] An inventory of the various products of the country, and the quarters whence they were obtained, was every year taken by the royal officers, and recorded by the *quipucamayus* on their registers, with surprising regularity and precision. These registers were transmitted to the capital, and submitted to the Inca, who could thus at a glance, as it were, embrace the whole results of the national industry, and see how far they corresponded with the requisitions of government.[36]

Such are some of the most remarkable features of the Peruvian institutions relating to property, as delineated by writers who, however contradictory in the details, have a general conformity of outline. These institutions are certainly so remarkable, that it is hardly credible they should ever have been enforced throughout a great empire, and for a long period of years. Yet we have the most unequivocal testimony to the fact from the Spaniards, who landed in Peru in time to witness their operation; some of whom, men of high judicial station and character, were commissioned by the government to make investigations into the state of the country under its ancient rulers.

The impositions on the Peruvian people seem to have been sufficiently heavy. On them rested the whole burden of maintaining, not only their own order, but every other order in the state. The members of the royal house, the great nobles, even the public functionaries, and the numerous body of the priesthood, were all exempt from taxation.[37] The whole duty of defraying the expenses of the government belonged to the people. Yet this was not materially different from the condition of things formerly existing in most parts of Europe, where the various privileged classes claimed exemption–not always with success, indeed –from bearing part of the public burdens. The great hardship in the

[35]For ten years, sometimes, if we may credit Ondegardo, who had every means of knowing. "E ansi cuando nó era menester se estaba en los depositos é habia algunas vezes comida de diez años. . . . . Los cuales todos se hallaron llenos cuando llegaron los Españoles desto y de todas las cosas necesarias para la vida humana." Rel. Seg., MS.

[36]Ondegardo, Rel. Prim., MS.

"Por tanta orden é cuenta que seria dificultoso creerlo ni darlo á entender como ellos lo tienen en su cuenta é por registros é por menudo lo manifestaron que se pudiera por estenso." Idem, Rel. Seg., MS.

[37]Garcilasso, Com. Real., Parte 1, lib. 5, cap. 15.

case of the Peruvian was, that he could not better his condition. His labors were for others, rather than for himself. However industrious, he could not add a rood to his own possessions, nor advance himself one hair's breadth in the social scale. The great and universal motive to honest industry, that of bettering one's lot, was lost upon him. The great law of human progress was not for him. As he was born, so he was to die. Even his time he could not properly call his own. Without money, with little property of any kind, he paid his taxes in labor.[38] No wonder that the government should have dealt with sloth as a crime. It was a crime against the state, and to be wasteful of time was, in a manner, to rob the exchequer. The Peruvian, laboring all his life for others, might be compared to the convict in a treadmill, going the same dull round of incessant toil, with the consciousness, that, however profitable the results to the state, they were nothing to him.

But this is the dark side of the picture. If no man could become rich in Peru, no man could become poor. No spendthrift could waste his substance in riotous luxury. No adventurous schemer could impoverish his family by the spirit of speculation. The law was constantly directed to enforce a steady industry and a sober management of his affairs. No mendicant was tolerated in Peru. When a man was reduced by poverty or misfortune (it could hardly be by fault) the arm of the law was stretched out to minister relief; not the stinted relief of private charity, nor that which is doled out, drop by drop, as it were, from the frozen reservoirs of "the parish," but in generous measure, bringing no humiliation to the object of it, and placing him on a level with the rest of his countrymen.[39]

[38] "Solo el trabajo de las personas era el tributo que se dava, porque ellos no poseian otra cosa." Ondegardo, Rel. Prim., MS.

[39] "Era tanta la orden que tenia en todos sus Reinos y provincias, que no consentia haver ningun Indio pobre ni menesteroso, porque havia orden i formas para ello sin que los pueblos reciviesen vexacion ni molestia, porque el Inga lo suplia de sus tributos." (Conq. i Pob. del Piru, MS.) The Licentiate Ondegardo sees only a device of Satan in these provisions of the Peruvian law, by which the old, the infirm, and the poor were rendered, in a manner, independent of their children, and those nearest of kin, on whom they would naturally have leaned for support; no surer way to harden the heart, he considers, than by thus disengaging it from the sympathies of humanity; and no circumstance has done more, he concludes, to counteract the influence and spread of Christianity among the natives. (Rel. Seg., MS.) The views are ingenious; but, in a country where the people had no property, as in Peru, there would seem to be no alternative for the supernumeraries, but to receive support from government or to starve.

No man could be rich, no man could be poor, in Peru; but all might enjoy, and did enjoy, a competence. Ambition, avarice, the love of change, the morbid spirit of discontent, those passions which most agitate the minds of men, found no place in the bosom of the Peruvian. The very condition of his being seemed to be at war with change. He moved on in the same unbroken circle in which his fathers had moved before him, and in which his children were to follow. It was the object of the Incas to infuse into their subjects a spirit of passive obedience and tranquillity–a perfect acquiescence in the established order of things. In this they fully succeeded. The Spaniards who first visited the country are emphatic in their testimony, that no government could have been better suited to the genius of the people; and no people could have appeared more contented with their lot, or more devoted to their government.[40]

Those who may distrust the accounts of Peruvian industry will find their doubts removed on a visit to the country. The traveler still meets, especially in the central regions of the table-land, with memorials of the past, remains of temples, palaces, fortresses, terraced mountains, great military roads, aqueducts, and other public works, which, whatever degree of science they may display in their execution, astonish him by their number, the massive character of the materials, and the grandeur of the design. Among them, perhaps the most remarkable are the great roads, the broken remains of which are still in sufficient preservation to attest their former magnificence. There were many of these roads, traversing different parts of the kingdom; but the most considerable were the two which extended from Quito to Cuzco, and, again diverging from the capital, continued in a southern direction towards Chili.

One of these roads passed over the grand plateau, and the other along the lowlands on the borders of the ocean. The former was much the more difficult achievement, from the character of the country. It was conducted over pathless sierras buried in snow; galleries were cut for leagues through the living rock; rivers were crossed by means of bridges that swung suspended in the air; precipices were scaled by stairways hewn out of the native bed; ravines of hideous depth were filled up with solid masonry; in short, all the difficulties that beset a wild and mountainous region, and which might appal the most courageous engineer of

[40]Acosta, lib. 6, cap. 12, 15.—Sarmiento, Relacion, MS., cap. 10.

modern times, were encountered and successfully overcome. The length of the road, of which scattered fragments only remain, is variously estimated, from fifteen hundred to two thousand miles; and stone pillars, in the manner of European milestones, were erected at stated intervals of somewhat more than a league, all along the route. Its breadth scarcely exceeded twenty feet.[41] It was built of heavy flags of freestone, and in some parts, at least, covered with a bituminous cement, which time has made harder than the stone itself. In some places, where the ravines had been filled up with masonry, the mountain torrents, wearing on it for ages, have gradually eaten a way through the base, and left the superincumbent mass–such is the cohesion of the materials–still spanning the valley like an arch![42]

Over some of the boldest streams it was necessary to construct suspension bridges, as they are termed, made of the tough fibers of the maguey, or of the osier of the country, which has an extraordinary degree of tenacity and strength. These osiers were woven into cables of the thickness of a man's body. The huge ropes, then stretched across the water, were conducted through rings or holes cut in immense buttresses of stone raised on the opposite banks of the river, and there secured to heavy pieces of timber. Several of these enormous cables, bound together, formed a bridge, which, covered with planks, well secured and defended by a railing of the same osier materials on the sides, afforded a safe passage for the traveler. The length of this aerial bridge, sometimes exceeding two hundred feet, caused it, confined, as it was, only at the extremities, to dip with an alarming inclination towards the center, while the motion given to it by the passenger occa-

[41]Dec. de la Aud. Real., MS.

"Este camino hecho por valles ondos y por sierras altas, por montes de nieve, por tremedales de agua y por peña viva y junto á rios furiosos por estas partes y ballano y empedrado por las laderas, bien sacado por las sierras, deshechado, por laspeñas socavado, por junto á los Rios sus paredes, entre nieves con escalones y descanso, por todas partes limpio barrido descombrado, lleno de aposentos, de depositos de tesoros, de Templos del Sol, de Postas que havia en este camino." Sarmiento, Relacion, MS., cap. 60.

[42]"On avait comblé les vides et les ravins par de grandes masses de maçonnerie. Les torrents qui descendent des hauteurs aprés des pluies abondantes, avaient creusé les endroits les moins solides, et s'etaient frayé une voie sous le chemin, le laissant ainsi suspendu en l'air comme un pont fait d'une seule pièce." (Velasco, Hist. de Quito, tom. I, p. 206.) This writer speaks from personal observation, having examined and measured different parts of the road, in the latter part of the last century.

sioned an oscillation still more frightful, as his eye wandered over the dark abyss of waters that foamed and tumbled many a fathom beneath. Yet these light and fragile fabrics were crossed without fear by the Peruvians, and are still retained by the Spaniards over those streams which, from the depth or impetuosity of the current, would seem impracticable for the usual modes of conveyance. The wider and more tranquil waters were crossed on *balsas*–a kind of raft still much used by the natives–to which sails were attached, furnishing the only instance of this higher kind of navigation among the American Indians.[43]

The other great road of the Incas lay through the level country between the Andes and the ocean. It was constructed in a different manner, as demanded by the nature of the ground, which was for the most part low, and much of it sandy. The causeway was raised on a high embankment of earth, and defended on either side by a parapet or wall of clay; and trees and odoriferous shrubs were planted along the margin, regaling the sense of the traveler with their perfumes, and refreshing him by their shades, so grateful under the burning sky of the tropics. In the strips of sandy waste, which occasionally intervened, where the light and volatile soil was incapable of sustaining a road, huge piles, many of them to be seen at this day, were driven into the ground to indicate the route to the traveler.[44]

All along these highways, caravansaries, or *tambos,* as they were called, were erected, at the distance of ten or twelve miles from each other, for the accommodation, more particularly, of the Inca and his suite, and those who journeyed on the public business. There were few other travelers in Peru. Some of these buildings were on an extensive scale, consisting of a fortress, barracks, and other military works, surrounded by a parapet of stone, and covering a large tract of ground. These were evidently destined for the accommodation of the imperial armies, when on their march across the country.–The care of the great roads was committed to the districts through which they passed, and a

[43]Garcilasso, Com. Real., Parte 1, lib. 3, cap. 7.

A particular account of these bridges, as they are still to be seen in different parts of Peru, may be found in Humboldt. (Vues des Cordillères, p. 230 et seq.) The *balsas* are described with equal minuteness by Stevenson. Residence in America, vol. II, p. 222, et. seq.

[44]Cieza de Leon, Cronica, cap. 60.—Relacion del Primer Descubrimiento de la Costa y Mar del Sur, MS.

This anonymous document of one of the early Conquerors contains a minute and probably trustworthy account of both the high roads, which the writer saw in their glory, and which he ranks among the greatest wonders of the world.

of the crimson fringe worn round the temples of the Inca, which was regarded with the same implicit deference as the signet ring of an Oriental despot.[49]

The *chasquis* were dressed in a peculiar livery, intimating their profession. They were all trained to the employment, and selected for their speed and fidelity. As the distance each courier had to perform was small, and as he had ample time to refresh himself at the stations, they ran over the ground with great swiftness, and messages were carried through the whole extent of the long routes, at the rate of a hundred and fifty miles a day. The office of the *chasquis* was not limited to carrying despatches. They frequently brought various articles for the use of the Court; and in this way, fish from the distant ocean, fruits, game, and different commodities from the hot regions on the coast, were taken to the capital in good condition, and served fresh at the royal table.[50] It is remarkable that this important institution should have been known to both the Mexicans and the Peruvians without any correspondence with one another; and that it should have been found among two barbarian nations of the New World, long before it was introduced among the civilized nations of Europe.[51]

By these wise contrivances of the Incas, the most distant parts of the long-extended empire of Peru were brought into intimate relations with each other. And while the capitals of Christendom, but a few hundred

[49]Con vn hilo de esta Borla, entregado á uno de aquellos Orejones governaban la Tierra, i proveian lo que querian con maior obediencia, que en ninguna Provincia del Mundo se ha visto tener á las Provissiones de su Rei." Zarate, Conq. del Peru, lib. 1, cap. 9.

[50]Sarmiento, Relacion, MS., cap. 18.—Dec. de la Aud. Real., MS.

If we may trust Montesinos, the royal table was served with fish, taken a hundred leagues from the capital, in twenty-four hours after it was drawn from the ocean! (Mem. Antiguas, MS., lib. 2, cap. 7.) This is rather too expeditious for any thing but rail-cars.

[51]The institution of the Peruvian posts seems to have made a great impression on the minds of the Spaniards who first visited the country; and ample notices of it may be found in Sarmiento, Relacion, MS., cap. 15.—Dec. de la Aud. Real., MS.—Fernandez, Hist. del Peru, Parte 2, lib. 3, cap. 5.—Conq. i Pob. del Piru, MS., et auct. plurimis.

The establishment of posts is of old date among the Chinese and, probably, still older among the Persians. (See Herodotus, Hist., Urania, sec. 98.) It is singular, that an invention designed for the uses of a despotic government should have received its full application only under a free one. For in it we have the germ of that beautiful system of intercommunication, which binds all the nations of Christendom together as one vast commonwealth.

large number of hands was constantly employed under the Incas keep them in repair. This was the more easily done in a country whe the mode of traveling was altogether on foot; though the roads are sa to have been so nicely constructed, that a carriage might have roll over them as securely as on any of the great roads of Europe.[45] Still, a region where the elements of fire and water are both actively at wo in the business of destruction, they must, without constant supervisic have gradually gone to decay. Such has been their fate under t Spanish conquerors, who took no care to enforce the admirable syste for their preservation adopted by the Incas. Yet the broken portio that still survive, here and there, like the fragments of the great Rom roads scattered over Europe, bear evidence to their primitive grande and have drawn forth the eulogium from a discriminating travel usually not too profuse in his panegyric, that "the roads of the Inc were among the most useful and stupendous works ever executed man."[46]

The system of communication through their dominions was still fu ther improved by the Peruvian sovereigns, by the introduction of pos in the same manner as was done by the Aztecs. The Peruvian pos however, established on all the great routes that conducted to the ca tal, were on a much more extended plan than those in Mexico. along these routes, small buildings were erected, at the distance of l than five miles asunder,[47] in each of which a number of runners, *chasquis,* as they were called, were stationed to carry forward despatches of government.[48] These despatches were either verbal, conveyed by means of *quipus,* and sometimes accompanied by a thr

[45]Relacion del Primer Descub., MS.—Cieza de Leon, Cronica, cap. 3 Zarate, Conq. del Peru, lib. 1, cap. 11.—Garcilasso, Com. Real., Parte 1, li cap. 13.

[46]"Cette chaussée, bordée de grandes pierres de taille, peut être comparée plus belles routes des Romaines que j'aie vues en Italie, en France et en Espa . . . . . Le grand chemin de l'Inca, un des ouvrages les plus utiles, et en n temps des plus gigantesques que les hommes aient exécuté." Humboldt, des Cordillères, p. 294.

[47]The distance between the posthouses is variously stated; most writer estimating it at more than three fourths of a league. I have preferred the au ity of Ondegardo, who usually writes with more conscientiousness and know of his ground than most of his contemporaries.

[48]The term *chasqui,* according to Montesinos, signifies "one that recei thing." (Mem. Antiguas, MS., cap. 7.) But Garcilasso, a better authority f own tongue, says it meant "one who makes an exchange." Com. Real., Pa lib. 6, cap. 8.

miles apart, remained as far asunder as if seas had rolled between them, the great capitals Cuzco and Quito were placed by the high roads of the Incas in immediate correspondence. Intelligence from the numerous provinces was transmitted on the wings of the wind to the Peruvian metropolis, the great focus to which all the lines of communication converged. Not an insurrectionary movement could occur, not an invasion on the remotest frontier, before the tidings were conveyed to the capital, and the imperial armies were on their march across the magnificent roads of the country to suppress it. So admirable was the machinery contrived by the American despots for maintaining tranquillity throughout their dominions! It may remind us of the similar institutions of ancient Rome, when, under the Caesars, she was mistress of half the world.

A principal design of the great roads was to serve the purposes of military communication. It formed an important item of their military policy, which is quite as well worth studying as their municipal.

Notwithstanding the pacific professions of the Incas, and the pacific tendency, indeed, of their domestic institutions, they were constantly at war. It was by war that their paltry territory had been gradually enlarged to a powerful empire. When this was achieved, the capital, safe in its central position, was no longer shaken by these military movements, and the country enjoyed, in a great degree, the blessings of tranquillity and order. But, however tranquil at heart, there is not a reign upon record in which the nation was not engaged in war against the barbarous nation on the frontier. Religion furnished a plausible pretext for incessant aggression, and disguised the lust of conquest in the Incas, probably, from their own eyes, as well as from those of their subjects. Like the followers of Mahomet, bearing the sword in one hand and the Koran in the other, the Incas of Peru offered no alternative but the worship of the Sun or war.

It is true, their fanaticism—or their policy—showed itself in a milder form than was found in the descendants of the Prophet. Like the great luminary which they adored, they operated by gentleness more potent than violence.[52] They sought to soften the hearts of the rude tribes around them, and melt them by acts of condescension and kindness. Far from provoking hostilities, they allowed time for the salutary ex-

[52]"Mas se hicieron Señores al principio por maña, que por fuerza." Ondegardo, Rel. Prim., MS.

ample of their own institutions to work its effect, trusting that their less civilized neighbors would submit to their scepter, from a conviction of the blessings it would secure to them. When this course failed, they employed other measures, but still of a pacific character; and endeavored by negotiation, by conciliatory treatment, and by presents to the leading men, to win them over to their dominion. In short, they practiced all the arts familiar to the most subtle politician of a civilized land to secure the acquisition of empire. When all these expedients failed, they prepared for war.

Their levies were drawn from all the different provinces; though from some, where the character of the people was particularly hardy, more than from others.[53] It seems probable that every Peruvian, who had reached a certain age, might be called to bear arms. But the rotation of military service, and the regular drills, which took place twice or thrice in a month, of the inhabitants of every village, raised the soldiers generally above the rank of a raw militia. The Peruvian army, at first inconsiderable, came, with the increase of population, in the latter days of the empire, to be very large, so that their monarchs could bring into the field, as contemporaries assure us, a force amounting to two hundred thousand men. They showed the same skill and respect for order in their military organization, as in other things. The troops were divided into bodies corresponding with our battalions and companies, led by officers, that rose, in regular gradation, from the lowest subaltern to the Inca noble, who was intrusted with the general command.[54]

Their arms consisted of the usual weapons employed by nations, whether civilized or uncivilized, before the invention of powder–bows and arrows, lances, darts, a short kind of sword, a battle-axe or partisan, and slings, with which they were very expert. Their spears and arrows were tipped with copper, or, more commonly, with bone, and the weapons of the Inca lords were frequently mounted with gold or silver. Their heads were protected by casques made either of wood or of the skins of wild animals, and sometimes richly decorated with metal and with precious stones, surmounted by the brilliant plumage of the tropical birds. These, of course, were the ornaments only of the higher orders. The great mass of the soldiery were dressed in the peculiar costume of their provinces, and their heads were wreathed with a sort

[53]Idem, Rel. Prim., MS.—Dec. de la Aud. Real., MS.
[54]Gomara, Cronica, cap. 195.—Conq. i Pob. del Piru, MS.

of turban or roll of different-colored cloths, that produced a gay and animating effect. Their defensive armor consisted of a shield or buckler, and a close tunic of quilted cotton, in the same manner as with the Mexicans. Each company had its particular banner, and the imperial standard, high above all, displayed the glittering device and the rainbow —the armorial ensign of the Incas, intimating their claims as children of the skies.[55]

By means of the thorough system of communication established in the country, a short time sufficed to draw the levies together from the most distant quarters. The army was put under the direction of some experienced chief, of the blood royal, or, more frequently, headed by the Inca in person. The march was rapidly performed, and with little fatigue to the soldier; for, all along the great routes, quarters were provided for him, at regular distances, where he could find ample accommodations. The country is still covered with the remains of military works, constructed of porphyry or granite, which tradition assures us were designed to lodge the Inca and his army.[56]

At regular intervals, also, magazines were established, filled with grain, weapons, and the different munitions of war, with which the army was supplied on its march. It was the especial care of the government to see that these magazines, which were furnished from the stores of the Incas, were always well filled. When the Spaniards invaded the country, they supported their own armies for a long time on the provisions found in them.[57] The Peruvian soldier was forbidden to commit

[55]Gomara, Cronica, ubi supra.—Sarmiento, Relacion, MS., cap. 20.—Velasco, Hist. de Quito, tom. I. pp. 176–179.

This last writer gives a minute catalogue of the ancient Peruvian arms, comprehending nearly every thing familiar to the European soldier, except fire-arms. —It was judicious in him to omit these.

[56]Zarate, Conq. del Peru, lib. 1, cap. 11.—Sarmiento, Relacion, MS., cap. 60.

Condamine speaks of the great number of these fortified places, scattered over the country between Quito and Lima, which he saw in his visit to South America in 1737; some of which he has described with great minuteness. Mémoire sur Quelques Anciens Monumens du Pérou, du Tems des Incas, ap. Histoire de l'Académie Royale des Sciences et de Belles Lettres, (Berlin, 1748,) tom. II. p. 438.

[57]"E ansi cuando," says Ondegardo, speaking from his own personal knowledge, "el Señor Presidente Gasca passó con la gente de castigo de Gonzalo Pizarro por el valle de Jauja, estuvo alli siete semanas á lo que me acuerdo, se hallaron en ∋deposito maiz de cuatro y de tres y de dos años mas de 15 . hanegas junto al camino, é alli comió la gente, y se entendió que si fuera menester muchas mas nó faltaran en el valle en aquellos depositos, conforme á la orden antigua, porque á mi cargo estubo el repartirlas y hacer la cuenta para pagarlas." Rel. Seg., MS.

any trespass on the property of the inhabitants whose territory lay in the line of march. Any violation of this order was punished with death.[58] The soldier was clothed and fed by the industry of the people, and the Incas rightly resolved that he should not repay this by violence. Far from being a tax on the labors of the husbandman, or even a burden on his hospitality, the imperial armies traversed the country, from one extremity to the other, with as little inconvenience to the inhabitants, as would be created by a procession of peaceful burghers, or a muster of holiday soldiers for a review.

From the moment war was proclaimed, the Peruvian monarch used all possible expedition in assembling his forces, that he might anticipate the movements of his enemies, and prevent a combination with their allies. It was, however, from the neglect of such a principle of combination, that the several nations of the country, who might have prevailed by confederated strength, fell one after another under the imperial yoke. Yet, once in the field the Inca did not usually show any disposition to push his advantages to the utmost, and urge his foe to extremity. In every stage of the war, he was open to propositions for peace; and although he sought to reduce his enemies by carrying off their harvests and distressing them by famine, he allowed his troops to commit no unnecessary outrage on person or property. "We must spare our enemies," one of the Peruvian princes is quoted as saying, "or it will be our loss, since they and all that belong to them must soon be ours."[59] It was a wise maxim, and, like most other wise maxims, founded equally on benevolence and prudence. The Incas adopted the policy claimed for the Romans by their countryman, who tells us that they gained more by clemency to the vanquished than by their victories.[60]

In the same considerate spirit, they were most careful to provide for the security and comfort of their own troops; and, when a war was long protracted, or the climate proved unhealthy, they took care to relieve their men by frequent reinforcements, allowing the earlier recruits to

[58]Pedro Pizarro, Descub. y Conq., MS.—Cieza de Leon, Cronica, cap. 44.—Sarmiento, Relacion, MS., cap. 14.

[59]Mandabase que en los mantenimientos y casas de los enemígos se hiciese poco daño, diciendoles el Señor, presto serán estos nuestros como los que ya lo son; como esto tenian conocido, procuraban que la guerra fuese la mas liviana que ser pudiese." Sarmiento, Relacion, MS., cap. 14.

[60]"Plus pene parcendo victis, quàm vincendo imperium auxisse." Livy, lib. 30, cap. 42.

return to their homes.[61] But while thus economical of life, both in their own followers and in the enemy, they did not shrink from sterner measures when provoked by the ferocious or obstinate character of the resistance; and the Peruvian annals contain more than one of those sanguinary pages which cannot be pondered at the present day without a shudder. It should be added, that the beneficent policy, which I have been delineating as characteristic of the Incas, did not belong to all; and that there was more than one of the royal line who displayed a full measure of the bold and unscrupulous spirit of the vulgar conqueror.

The first step of the government, after the reduction of a country, was to introduce there the worship of the Sun. Temples were erected, and placed under the care of a numerous priesthood, who expounded to the conquered people the mysteries of their new faith, and dazzled them by the display of its rich and stately ceremonial.[62] Yet the religion of the conquered was not treated with dishonor. The Sun was to be worshiped above all; but the images of their gods were removed to Cuzco and established in one of the temples, to hold their rank among the inferior deities of the Peruvian Pantheon. Here they remained as hostages, in some sort, for the conquered nation, which would be the less inclined to forsake its allegiance, when by doing so it must leave its own gods in the hands of its enemies.[63]

The Incas provided for the settlement of their new conquests, by ordering a census to be taken of the population, and a careful survey to be made of the country, ascertaining its products, and the character and capacity of its soil.[64] A division of the territory was then made on the same principle with that adopted throughout their own kingdom; and their respective portions were assigned to the Sun, the sovereign, and the people. The amount of the last was regulated by the amount of the population, but the share of each individual was uniformly the same. It may seem strange, that any people should patiently have acquiesced in an arrangement which involved such a total surrender of property. But it was a conquered nation that did so, held in awe, on the least suspicion of meditating resistance, by armed garrisons, who were

[61]Garcilasso, Com. Real., Parte 1, lib. 6, cap. 18.
[62]Sarmiento, Relacion, MS., cap. 14.
[63]Acosta, lib. 5, cap. 12.—Garcilasso, Com. Real., Parte 1, lib. 5, cap. 12.
[64]Ibid., Parte 1, lib. 5, cap. 13, 14.—Sarmiento, Relacion, MS., cap. 15.

established at various commanding points throughout the country.[65] It is probable, too, that the Incas made no greater changes than was essential to the new arrangement, and that they assigned estates, as far as possible, to their former proprietors. The curacas, in particular, were confirmed in their ancient authority; or, when it was found expedient to depose the existing curaca, his rightful heir was allowed to succeed him.[66] Every respect was shown to the ancient usages and laws of the land, as far as was compatible with the fundamental institutions of the Incas. It must also be remembered, that the conquered tribes were, many of them, too little advanced in civilization to possess that attachment to the soil which belongs to a cultivated nation.[67] But, to whatever it be referred, it seems probable that the extraordinary institutions of the Incas were established with little opposition in the conquered territories.[68]

Yet the Peruvian sovereigns did not trust altogether to this show of obedience in their new vassals; and, to secure it more effectually, they adopted some expedients too remarkable to be passed by in silence.— Immediately after a recent conquest, the curacas and their families were removed for a time to Cuzco. Here they learned the language of the capital, became familiar with the manners and usages of the court, as well as with the general policy of government, and experienced such marks of favor from the sovereign as would be most grateful to their feelings, and might attach them most warmly to his person. Under the influence of these sentiments, they were again sent to rule over their vassals, but still leaving their eldest sons in the capital, to remain there

[65]Sarmiento, Relacion, MS., cap. 19.

[66]Fernandez, Hist. del Peru, Parte 2, lib. 3, cap. 11.

[67]Sarmiento has given a very full and interesting account of the singularly humane policy observed by the Incas in their conquests, forming a striking contrast with the usual course of those scourges of mankind, whom mankind are wise enough to requite with higher admiration even, than it bestows on its benefactors. Sarmiento, who was President of the Royal Council of the Indies, and came into the country soon after the Conquest, is a high authority, and his work, lodged in the dark recesses of the Escurial, is almost unknown.

[68]According to Velasco, even the powerful state of Quito, sufficiently advanced in civilization to have the law of property well recognized by its people, admitted the institutions of the Incas, "not only without repugnance, but with joy." (Hist. de Quito, tom. II. p. 183.) But Velasco, a modern authority, believed easily—or reckoned on his readers' doing so.

as a guaranty for their own fidelity, as well as to grace the court of the Inca.[69]

Another expedient was of a bolder and more original character. This was nothing less than to revolutionize the language of the country. South America, like North, was broken up into a great variety of dialects, or rather languages, having little affinity with one another. This circumstance occasioned great embarrassment to the government in the administration of the different provinces, with whose idioms they were unacquainted. It was determined, therefore, to substitute one universal language, the *Quichua*—the language of the court, the capital, and the surrounding country—the richest and most comprehensive of the South American dialects. Teachers were provided in the towns and villages throughout the land, who were to give instruction to all, even to the humblest classes; and it was intimated at the same time, that no one should be raised to any office of dignity or profit, who was unacquainted with this tongue. The curacas and other chiefs, who attended at the capital, became familiar with this dialect in their intercourse with the Court, and, on their return home, set the example of conversing in it among themselves. This example was imitated by their followers, and the Quichua gradually became the language of elegance and fashion, in the same manner as the Norman French was affected by all those who aspired to any consideration in England, after the Conquest. By this means, while each province retained its peculiar tongue, a beautiful medium of communication was introduced, which enabled the inhabitants of one part of the country to hold intercourse with every other, and the Inca and his deputies to communicate with all. This was the state of things on the arrival of the Spaniards. It must be admitted, that history furnishes few examples of more absolute authority than such a revolution in the language of an empire, at the bidding of a master.[70]

[69]Garcilasso, Com. Real., Parte 1, lib. 5, cap. 12; lib. 7, cap. 2.

[70]Ibid., Parte 1, lib. 6, cap. 35; lib. 7, cap. 1, 2.—Ondegardo, Rel. Seg., MS.—Sarmiento, Relacion, MS., cap. 55.

"Aun la Criatura no hubiese dejado el Pecho de su Madre quando le comenzasen á mostrar le Lenguaque havia de saber; y aunque al principio fué dificultoso, é muchos se pusieron en no querer deprender mas lenguas de las suyas propias, los Reyes pudieron tanto que salieron con su intencion y ellos tubieron por bien de cumplir su mandado y tan de veras se entendió en ello que en tiempo de pocos años se savia y usaba una lengua en mas de mil y doscientas leguas." Ibid., cap. 21.

Yet little less remarkable was another device of the Incas for securing the loyalty of their subjects. When any portion of the recent conquests showed a pertinacious spirit of disaffection, it was not uncommon to cause a part of the population, amounting, it might be, to ten thousand inhabitants or more, to remove to a distant quarter of the kingdom, occupied by ancient vassals of undoubted fidelity to the crown. A like number of these was transplanted to the territory left vacant by the emigrants. By this exchange, the population was composed of two distinct races, who regarded each other with an eye of jealousy, that served as an effectual check on any mutinous proceeding. In time, the influence of the well-affected prevailed, supported, as they were, by royal authority, and by the silent working of the national institutions, to which the strange races became gradually accustomed. A spirit of loyalty sprang up by degrees in their bosoms, and, before a generation had passed away, the different tribes mingled in harmony together as members of the same community.[71] Yet the different races continued to be distinguished by difference of dress; since, by the law of the land, every citizen was required to wear the costume of his native province.[72] Neither could the colonist, who had been thus unceremoniously transplanted, return to his native district. For, by another law, it was forbidden to any one to change his residence without license.[73] He was settled for life. The Peruvian government ascribed to every man his local habitation, his sphere of action, nay, the very nature and quality of that action. He ceased to be a free agent; it might be almost said, that it relieved him of personal responsibility.

In following out this singular arrangement, the Incas showed as much regard for the comfort and convenience of the colonist as was compatible with the execution of their design. They were careful that the *mitimaes,* as these emigrants were styled, should be removed to climates most congenial with their own. The inhabitants of the cold countries were not transplanted to the warm, nor the inhabitants of the warm countries to the cold.[74] Even their habitual occupations were consulted, and the fisherman was settled in the neighborhood of the

[71]Ondegardo, Rel. Prim., MS.—Fernandez, Hist. del Peru, Parte 2, lib. 3, cap.11.

[72]"This regulation," says Father Acosta, "the Incas held to be of great importance to the order and right government of the realm." lib. 6, cap. 16.

[73]Conq. i Pob. del Piru, MS.

ocean, or the great lakes; while such lands were assigned to the husbandman as were best adapted to the culture with which he was most familiar.[75] And, as migration by many, perhaps by most, would be regarded as a calamity, the government was careful to show particular marks of favor to the *mitimaes,* and, by various privileges and immunities, to ameliorate their condition, and thus to reconcile them, if possible, to their lot.[76]

The Peruvian institutions, though they may have been modified and matured under successive sovereigns, all bear the stamp of the same original—were all cast in the same mold. The empire, strengthening and enlarging at every successive epoch of its history, was, in its latter days, but the development, on a great scale, of what it was in miniature at its commencement, as the infant germ is said to contain within itself all the ramifications of the future monarch of the forest. Each succeeding Inca seemed desirous only to tread in the path, and carry out the plans, of his predecessor. Great enterprises, commenced under one, were continued by another, and completed by a third. Thus, while all acted on a regular plan, without any of the eccentric or retrograde movements which betray the agency of different individuals, the state seemed to be under the direction of a single hand, and steadily pursued, as if through one long reign, its great career of civilization and of conquest.

The ultimate aim of its institutions was domestic quiet. But it seemed as if this were to be obtained only by foreign war. Tranquillity in the heart of the monarchy, and war on its borders, was the condition of Peru. By this war it gave occupation to a part of its people, and, by the reduction and civilization of its barbarous neighbors, gave security to all. Every Inca sovereign, however mild and benevolent in his domestic rule, was a warrior, and led his armies in person. Each successive reign extended still wider the boundaries of the empire. Year after

[74]"Trasmutaban de las tales Provincias la cantidad de gente de que de ella parecia convenir que saliese, á los cuales mandaban pasar a poblar otra tierra del temple y manera de donde salian, si fria fria, si caliente caliente, en donde les daban tierras, y campos, y casas, tanto, y mas como dejaron." Sarmiento, Relacion, MS., cap. 19.

[75]Ondegardo, Rel. Prim., MS.

[76]The descendents of these *mitimaes* are still to be found in Quito, or were so at the close of the last century, according to Velasco, distinguished by this name from the rest of the population. Hist. de Quito, tom. I. p. 175.

year saw the victorious monarch return laden with spoils, and followed by a throng of tributary chieftains to his capital. His reception there was a Roman triumph. The whole of its numerous population poured out to welcome him, dressed in the gay and picturesque costumes of the different provinces, with banners waving above their heads, and strewing branches and flowers along the path of the conqueror. The Inca, borne aloft in his golden chair on the shoulders of his nobles, moved in solemn procession, under the triumphal arches that were thrown across the way, to the great temple of the Sun. There, without attendants–for all but the monarch were excluded from the hallowed precincts–the victorious prince, stripped of his royal insignia, barefooted, and with all humility, approached the awful shrine, and offered up sacrifice and thanksgiving to the glorious Deity who presided over the fortunes of the Incas. This ceremony concluded, the whole population gave itself up to festivity; music, revelry, and dancing were heard in every quarter of the capital, and illuminations and bonfires commemorated the victorious campaign of the Inca, and the accession of a new territory to his empire.[77]

In this celebration we see much of the character of a religious festival. Indeed, the character of religion was impressed on all the Peruvian wars. The life of an Inca was one long crusade against the infidel, to spread wide the worship of the Sun, to reclaim the benighted nations from their brutish superstitions, and impart to them the blessings of a well-regulated government. This, in the favorite phrase of our day, was the "mission" of the Inca. It was also the mission of the Christian conqueror who invaded the empire of this same Indian potentate. Which of the two executed his mission most faithfully, history must decide.

Yet the Peruvian monarchs did not show a childish impatience in the acquisition of empire. They paused after a campaign, and allowed time for the settlement of one conquest before they undertook another; and, in this interval, occupied themselves with the quiet administration of their kingdom, and with the long progresses, which brought them into nearer intercourse with their people. During this interval, also, their new vassals had begun to accommodate themselves to the strange institutions of their masters. They learned to appreciate the value of a gov-

[77]Sarmiento, Relacion, MS., cap. 55.—Garcilasso, Com. Real., Parte 1, lib. 3, cap. 11, 17; lib. 6, cap. 16.

ernment which raised them above the physical evils of a state of barbarism, secured them protection of person, and a full participation in all the privileges enjoyed by their conquerors; and, as they became more familiar with the peculiar institutions of the country, habit, that second nature, attached them the more strongly to these institutions, from their very peculiarity. Thus, by degrees, and without violence, arose the great fabric of the Peruvian empire, composed of numerous independent and even hostile tribes, yet, under the influence of a common religion, common language, and common government, knit together as one nation, animated by a spirit of love for its institutions and devoted loyalty to its sovereign. What a contrast to the condition of the Aztec monarchy, on the neighboring continent, which, composed of the like heterogeneous materials, without any internal principle of cohesion, was only held together by the stern pressure, from without, of physical force!— . . .

The New World

BY LORD ACTON

History is often made by energetic men, steadfastly following ideas, mostly wrong, that determine events.

A contemporary of Lord Acton's used to say that however much you knew about anything, Acton was certain to know more. Biographers have told us how Gladstone used to dismiss abstruse points that arose in conversation with the remark "We must ask Lord Acton." Queen Victoria, after Acton's appointment as lord-in-waiting, paid him the supreme compliment of remarking that she wished only that Prince Albert were alive to hear him and talk with him. "To be with Acton," wrote a grateful pupil, "was like being with the cultivated mind of Europe. In the deep tones of his voice, there seemed to sound the accent of history."

This lecture by Lord Acton on "The New World" reflects his position as one of the most erudite men of his time and his astounding mastery of the events and ideology of the period from the Renaissance to the French Revolution. Delivered at Cambridge after his appointment to the chair of modern history in 1895, it was designed primarily for undergraduates and is a demonstration of Acton's conviction that attitudes of mind and thoughts jointly weave the web of history along with events. His final sentence about history and energetic men must rank next to his comment to Bishop Creighton, written in 1887, that "power tends to corrupt and absolute power corrupts absolutely" as among the great truisms uttered by a preeminent Victorian.

John Emerich Edward Dalberg-Acton, first Baron Acton, was born in Naples in 1834. He was the only son of Sir Richard and Marie Louise Pellini de Dalberg Acton. His paternal grandfather had made his career in the service of the King of Naples as Prime Minister during and after the French

Revolution. His maternal grandfather was a noble of the Holy Roman Empire, who served Napoleon and sat as a peer of France and a colleague of Talleyrand's at the Congress of Vienna. His maternal great-uncle had been Archbishop Elector of Mainz, and his wife's family was active in French politics in the first half of the nineteenth century. Acton's stepfather was Lord Granville, several times British Foreign Secretary.

Because of this complex family background, Lord Acton was in every way cosmopolitan. French, German, Italian, and English were the languages of his table. Acton spent the years 1850–1854 in Munich as a private pupil of J. J. I. von Döllinger, one of the most celebrated historians and Catholic theologians of his day. In 1869 Acton was raised to the peerage, and in 1895 he was named regius professor of modern history at Cambridge. He died in Bavaria on June 19, 1902.

Significantly for the present, Acton was probably the first modern historian to appreciate the importance of Communism. He detected the importance of Marx' *Das Kapital,* speaking of the book as the Koran of the new Socialists, and he recognized the difference between the second and first edition—a difference so great that he regarded them as two separate books. Acton's papers reveal that he maintained tabulations on the circulation of the German Socialist papers.

Also important, especially insofar as Latin America is concerned, is that he was a Catholic scholar who fought the adoption of the doctrine of papal infallibility and opposed ultramontanism. Since, today, Latin America is both Catholic and partly Communist, this rare combination in one historian-philosopher, who was singularly free of insularity, gives his work a special flavor.

Although, save for his lecture on "The Rise and Fall of the Mexican Empire" (which appears later in this book) and the lecture on "The New World" (which is reprinted here), he wrote no other articles on Latin America, it was a subject of research for him. References to it appear in his writings and lectures on other subjects.

The pre-Columbian Inca civilization was of special interest to him. In his manuscripts the reflection is recorded that "the Incas had an exact Census, a thing unknown to the Spaniards. It was a system of communistic distribution of land. And the most terrible despotism on earth."

Acton was especially alive to the complexity and differences of classes in Latin America and noted the distinction between Spanish and British colonial policy. "It is the pride of the colonial system of Spain," he wrote, "that it succeeded in preserving . . . the native race . . . whose numbers vastly exceeded that of their masters; a people of mixed blood sprang up between them and thus there were three races separated by a very broad line, and isolated by the pride and jealousy of color." He felt that class distribution in Latin America was "the greatest social inequity that can be conceived."

By the time Acton died in 1902, he had proved that what his friend and tutor Döllinger had said was true–namely, that if Acton did not write a great book before he was forty, he would never do so. Although his production of articles, lectures, essays, letters, and plans was prodigious, he never wrote a book as such. As a consequence, many have thought of him as a "standing riddle," if only because his failure to write a great book was *not* caused by the fact that he was the type of scholar who was so overawed by a multiplicity of facts that he could not deliver a judgment.

However, perhaps no other scholar has had his knowledge so carefully cultivated and diffused. Acton's immense personal library of 60,000 to 70,000 volumes became part of the Cambridge University Library, where his manuscripts and notes, intended for no other eyes than his own, were also preserved. His stature, while alive, was such that many of his letters, written with no expectation of publication, have survived. And all this, as well as his lectures and articles, has been studied and commented on by eminent scholars. Taken together, Acton's works and the scholarly comments thereon have become what can be described only as a "wonderful work of art, such as in all likelihood will never again be witnessed."

P. K.

Greater changes than those which were wrought by governments or armies on the battlefield of Italy were accomplished at the same time, thousands of miles away, by solitary adventurers, with the future of the world in their hands. The Portuguese were the first Europeans to understand that the ocean is not a limit, but the universal waterway that unites mankind. Shut in by Spain, they could not extend on land, and had no opening but the Atlantic. Their arid soil gave little scope to the territorial magnate, who was excluded from politics by the growing absolutism of the dynasty, and the government found it well to employ at a distance forces that might be turbulent at home.

The great national work of exploration did not proceed from the State. The Infante Henry had served in the African wars, and his thoughts were drawn towards distant lands. He was not a navigator himself; but from his home at Sagres, on the Sacred Promontory, he watched the ships that passed between the great maritime centre at the mouth of the Tagus and the regions that were to compose the Portuguese empire. As Grandmaster of the Order of Christ he had the means to equip them, and he rapidly occupied the groups of islands that lie between Africa and mid Atlantic, and that were a welcome accession to the narrow territory of Portugal. Then he sent his mariners to explore the coast of the unknown and dreaded continent. When they reached the Senegal and the Gambia, still more, when the coast of Guinea trended to the East, they remembered Prester John, and dreamed of finding a way to his fictitious realm which would afford convenient leverage for Christendom, at the back of the dark world that faced the Mediterranean.

As the trade of the country did not cover the outlay, Henry began in 1442 to capture negroes, who were imported as slaves, or sold with advantage to local chiefs. In five years, 927 blacks from Senegambia reached the Lisbon market; and, later on, the Guinea coast supplied about a thousand every year. That domestic institution was fast disappearing from Europe when it was thus revived; and there was some feeling against the Infante, and some temporary sympathy for his victims. On the other side, there were eminent divines who thought that the people of hot countries may properly be enslaved. Henry the Navigator applied to Rome, and Nicholas V issued Bulls authorising him and his Portuguese to make war on Moors and pagans, seize their possessions, and reduce them to perpetual slavery, and prohibiting all Christian nations, under eternal penalties, from trespassing on the privilege. He applauded the trade in negroes, and hoped that it would end in their conversion. Negro slavery struck no deep root in Europe. But the delusion, says Las Casas, lasted to his own time, when, half a century after the death of its founder, it began to control the destinies of America.

Henry's brother, the Regent Dom Pedro, had visited the courts of Europe, and brought Marco Polo's glowing narrative of his travels in the Far East, still, in Yule's edition, one of the most fascinating books that can be found. Emmanuel the Great, in the Charter rewarding Vasco da Gama, affirms that, from 1433, the Infante pursued his operations with a view to India. After his death, in 1460, they were carried on by the State, and became a secondary purpose, dependent on public affairs. Africa was farmed out for some years, on condition that an hundred leagues of coast were traced annually. There was a moment of depression, when the Guinea coast, having run eastward for a thousand miles and more, turned south, apparently without end. Toscanelli of Florence was a recognized authority on the geography of those days, and he was asked what he thought of the situation. No oracle ever said anything so wise as the answer of the Tuscan sage. For he told them that India was to be found not in the East, but in the West; and we shall see what came of it twenty years later, when his letter fell into predestined hands. The Portuguese were not diverted from their aim. They knew quite well that Africa does not stretch away for ever, and that it needed only a few intrepid men to see the end of it, and to reach an open route to Eastern Asia. They went on, marking their advance beyond the Congo, and erected crosses along the coast to signify their claim; but making no settlements, for Africa was only an obstruction on the way to the Indies.

Each successive voyage was made under a different commander, until 1486, when the squadron of Bartholomew Diaz was blown offshore, out into the Atlantic. When the storm fell he sailed east until he had passed the expected meridian of Africa, and then, turning northward, struck land far beyond Cape Agulhas. He had solved the problem, and India was within his reach. His men soon after refused to go farther, and he was forced to renounce the prize. On his way back he doubled the Cape, which, from his former experience, he called the Cape Tempestuous, until the king, showing that he understood, gave it a name of better omen. Nevertheless, Portugal did no more for ten years, the years that were made memorable by Spain. Then, under a new king, Emmanuel the Fortunate, Vasco da Gama went out to complete the unfinished work of Diaz, lest Columbus, fulfilling the prophecy of Toscanelli, should reach Cathay by a shorter route, and rob them of their reward. The right man had been found. It was all plain sailing; and he plucked the ripe fruit. Vasco da Gama's voyage to the Cape was the longest ever made till then. At Malindi, on the equatorial east coast of Africa, he found a pilot, and, striking across the Indian Ocean by the feeble monsoon of 1497, sighted the Ghats in May. The first cargo from India covered the expenses many times over. The splendour of the achievement was recognised at once, and men were persuaded that Emmanuel would soon be the wealthiest of European monarchs. So vast a promise of revenue required to be made secure by arms, and a force was sent out under Cabral.

The work thus attempted in the East seemed to many too much for so small a kingdom. They objected that the country would break its back in straining so far; that the soil ought first to be cultivated at home; that it would be better to import labour from Germany than to export it to India. Cabral had not been many weeks at sea when these murmurs received a memorable confirmation. Following the advice of Da Gama to avoid the calms of the Gulf of Guinea, he took a westerly course, made the coast of South America, and added, incidentally and without knowing it, a region not much smaller than Europe to the dominions of his sovereign.

The Portuguese came to India as traders, not as conquerors, and desired, not territory, but portable and exchangeable commodities. But the situation they found out there compelled them to wage war in unknown seas, divided from supports, and magazines, and docks by nearly half the globe. They made no attempt on the interior, for the Malabar coast was shut off by a range of lofty mountains. Their main object was the trade of the Far East, which was concentrated at Calicut, and was then carried by the Persian Gulf to Scanderoon and Constantinople, or by Jeddah to Suez and Alexandria. There the Venetians shipped the products of Asia to the markets of Europe. But on the other side of the isthmus the carrying trade, all the way to the Pacific, was in the hands of Moors from Arabia and Egypt. The Chinese had disappeared before them from Indian waters, and the Hindoos were no mariners. They possessed the monopoly of that which the Portuguese had come to take, and they were enemies of the Christian name. The Portuguese required not their share in the trade, but the monopoly itself. A deadly conflict could not be avoided. By the natives, they were received at first as friends; and Vasco da Gama, who took the figures of the Hindoo Pantheon for saints of the Catholic Calendar, reported that the people of India were Christians. When this illusion was dispelled, it was a consolation to find the Nestorians settled at Cochin, which thus became a Portuguese stronghold, which their best soldier, Duarte Pacheco, held against a multitude. Calicut, where they began operations, has disappeared like Earl Godwin's estate. Forbes, who was there in 1772, writes: "At very low water I have occasionally seen the waves breaking over the tops of the highest temples and minarets." It was an international city, where 1500 vessels cleared in a season, where trade was open and property secure, and where the propagation of foreign religion was not resented.

The Zamorin, as they called the Rajah of Calicut, ended by taking part with the old friends from the Arabian Seas, who supplied his country with grain, against the visitors who came in questionable shape. The Portuguese lacked the diplomatic graces, and disregarded the art of making friends and acquiring ascendency by the virtues of humanity and good faith. When it came to blows, they acquitted themselves like men conscious that they were the pioneers of History, that their footsteps were in the van of the onward march, that they were moulding the future, and making the world subservient to civilisation. They were Crusaders, coming the other way, and robbing the Moslem of their resources. The shipbuilding of the Moors depended on the teak forests of Calicut; the Eastern trade enriched both Turk and Mameluke, and the Sultan of Egypt levied duty amounting to £290,000 a year. Therefore he combined with the Venetians to expel the common enemy from Indian waters. In 1509 their fleet was defeated by the Viceroy Almeida near Diu, off the coast of Kattywar, where the Arabian seaman comes in sight of India. It was his last action before he surrendered power to his rival, the great Albuquerque. Almeida sought the greatness of his country not in conquest but in commerce. He discouraged expeditions to Africa and to the Moluccas; for he believed that the control of Indian traffic could be maintained by sea-power, and that land settlements would drain the resources of the nation. Once the Moslem traders [were] excluded, Portugal would possess all it wanted, on land and sea.

Almeida's successor, who had the eye of Alexander the Great for strategic points and commercial centres, was convinced that sea-power, at six months from home, rests on the occupation of seaports, and he carried the forward policy so far that Portugal possessed fifty-two establishments, commanding 15,000 miles of coast, and held them, nominally, with 20,000 men. Almeida's victory had broken the power of the Moors. Albuquerque resolved to prevent their reappearance by closing the Persian Gulf and the Red Sea. With Aden, Ormuz, and Malacca, he said, the Portuguese are masters of the world. He failed in the Red Sea. When Socotra proved insufficient, he attacked Aden, and was repulsed. There was a disconcerting rumour that no Christian vessel could live in the Red Sea, as there was a loadstone that extracted the nails. Albuquerque succeeded in the Persian Gulf, and erected a fortress at Ormuz, and at the other end of the Indian world he seized Malacca, and became master of the narrow seas, and of all the produce from the vast islands under the equator. He made Goa the impregnable capital of his prodigious empire, and the work that he did was solid. He never perceived the value of Bombay, which is the best harbour in Asia, and did not see that the key of India is the Cape of Good Hope. His language was sometimes visionary. He beheld a cross shining in the heavens, over the kingdom of Prester John, and was eager for an alliance with him. He wished to drain the Nile into the Red Sea. He would attack Mecca and Medina, carry off the bones of the prophet, and exchange them for the Holy Sepulchre. The dependency was too distant and too vast. The dread proconsul in his palace at Goa, who was the mightiest potentate between Mozambique and China, was too great a servant for the least of European kings. Emmanuel was suspicious. He recalled the victorious Almeida, who perished on the way home; and Albuquerque was in disgrace, when he died on his quarter-deck, in sight of the Christian city which he had made the capital of the East.

The secret of Portuguese prosperity was the small bulk and the enormous market value of the particular products in which they dealt. In those days men had to do without tea, or coffee, or chocolate, or tobacco, or quinine, or cocoa, or vanilla, and sugar was very rare. But there were the pepper and the ginger of Malabar, cardamoms in the damp district of Tellicherry; cinnamon and pearls in Ceylon. Beyond the Bay of Bengal, near the equator, there was opium, the only conqueror of pain then known; there were frankincense and indigo; camphor in Borneo; nutmeg and mace in Amboyna; and in two small islands, only a few miles square, Ternate and Tidor, there was the clove tree, surpassing all plants in value. These were the real spice islands, the enchanted region which was the object of such passionate desire; and their produce was so cheap on the spot, so dear in the markets of Antwerp and London, as to constitute the most lucrative trade in the world. From these exotics, grown on volcanic soil, in the most generous of the tropical climates, the profit was such that they could be paid for in precious metals. When Drake was at Ternate in 1579, he found the Sultan hung with chains of bullion, and clad in a robe of gold brocade rich enough to stand upright. The Moluccas were of greater benefit to the Crown than to the Portuguese workman. About twenty ships, of

100 to 550 tons, sailed for Lisbon in the year. A voyage sometimes lasted two years, out and home, and cost, including the ship, over £4000. But the freight might amount to £150,000. Between 1497 and 1612 the number of vessels engaged in the India trade was 806. Of these, ninety-six were lost. After the annexation by Philip II., Lisbon was closed to countries at war with Spain. Dutch and English had to make their own bargains in the East, and treated Portugal as an enemy. Their empire declined rapidly, and the Dutch acquired the islands long before the English succeeded on the mainland of India.

The Portuguese acknowledged no obligations of international law towards Asiatics. Even now, many people know of no law of nations but that which consists in contracts and conventions; and with the people of the East there were none. They were regarded as outlaws and outcasts, nearly as Bacon regarded the Spaniards and Edmund Burke the Turks. Solemn instruments had declared it lawful to expropriate and enslave Saracens and other enemies of Christ. What was right in Africa could not be wrong in Asia. Cabral had orders to treat with fire and sword any town that refused to admit either missionary or merchant. Barros, the classic historian of Portuguese Asia, says that Christians have no duties towards pagans; and their best writers affirm to this day that such calculated barbarities as they inflicted on women and children were justified by the necessity of striking terror. In the Commentaries of the great Albuquerque, his son relates with complacency how his father caused the Zamorin to be poisoned. These theories demoralised the entire government. S. Francis Xavier, who came out in 1542, found an organised system of dishonesty and plunder, and wrote home that no official in India could save his soul. By him and his brethren many converts were made, and as intermarriages were frequent, the estrangement grew less between the races. Just then, the Inquisition was introduced into Portugal, and sent a branch to Goa. One of the governors afterwards reported that it had helped to alienate the natives, whose temples were closed. But the solid structure of Almeida and Albuquerque was strong enough to defeat a second expedition from Egypt, after Egypt had become a province of Turkey, and an Indian war and insurrection. It declined with the decline of Portugal under Sebastian, in the latter part of the sixteenth century, but it perished through its association with Spain, at the hands of enemies not its own, and not from internal causes.

While the Asiatic empire was built up by the sustained and patient effort of a nation, during seventy years, the discovery of the West was due to one eager and original intellect, propelled by medieval dreams. Columbus had sailed both North and South; but the idea which changed the axis of the globe came to him from books. He failed to draw an inference favourable to his design from the driftwood which a tropical current carries to Iceland, and proceeded on the assurance of Pierre d'Ailly and of Toscanelli, that Asia reaches so far east as to leave but a moderate interval between Portugal and Japan. Although he rested his case on arguments from the classics and the prophets, his main authority was Toscanelli; but it is uncertain whether, as he affirmed, they had been in direct correspondence, or whether Columbus obtained the letter and the Chart of 1474 by means which were the cause of his disgrace.

Rejected by Portugal, he made his way into Spain. He was found, starving, at the gate of a Franciscan convent; and the place where he sank down is marked by a monument, because it is there that our modern world began. The friar who took him in and listened to his story soon perceived that this ragged mendicant was the most extraordinary person he had known, and he found him patrons at the court of Castile. The argument which Columbus now laid before the learned men of Spain was this: The eastern route, even if the Portuguese succeed in finding it, would be of no use to them, as the voyage to Cipango, to Cathay, even to the spice islands, would be too long for profit. It was better to sail out into the West, for that route would be scarcely 3000 miles to the extremity of Asia; the other would be 15,000, apart from the tremendous circuit of Africa, the extent of which was ascertained by Diaz while Columbus was pursuing his uphill struggle. The basis of the entire calculation was that the circumference of the earth is 18,000 miles at the equator, and that Asia begins, as is shown in Toscanelli's chart, somewhere about California. Misled by this belief in cosmographers, he blotted out the Pacific, and estimated the extent of water to be traversed at one-third of the reality. The Spaniards, who were consulted, pointed out the flaw, for the true dimensions were known; but they were unable to demonstrate the truths against the great authorities cited on the other side. The sophisms of Columbus were worth more than all the science of Salamanca. The objectors who called him a visionary were in the right, and he was obstinately wrong. To his auspicious persistency in error Americans owe, among other things, their existence.

A majority reported favourably—a majority composed, it would appear, of ignorant men. Years were spent in these preliminaries, and then the war with Granada absorbed the resources and the energies of the Crown. Columbus was present when the last Moorish king kissed the hand of Isabella, and he saw the cross raised over the Alhambra. This victory of Christendom was immediately followed by the expulsion of the Jews, and then the Catholic queen gave audience to the Genoese projector. His scheme belonged to the same order of ideas, and he was eloquent on its religious aspect. He would make so many slaves as to cover all expenses, and would have them baptized. He would bring home gold enough in three years to reconquer Palestine. He had one impressive argument which was not suggested by the situation at Court. Toscanelli had been at Rome when envoys came from the Grand Khan, petitioning for missionaries to instruct his people in the doctrines of Christianity. Two such embassies were sent, but their prayer was not attended to. Here were suppliants calling out of the darkness: Come over and help us. It was suitable that the nation which conquered the Moslem and banished the Jews should go on to convert the heathen. The Spaniards would appear in the East, knowing that their presence was desired. In reality they would come in answer to an invitation, and might look for a welcome. Making up by their zeal for the deficient enterprise of Rome, they might rescue the teeming millions of Farthest Asia, and thus fulfil prophecy, as there were only a hundred and fifty-five years to the end of the world. The conversion of Tartary would be the crowning glory of Catholic Spain.

All this was somewhat hypothetical and vague; but nothing could be more definite than the reward which he demanded. For it appeared that what this forlorn adventurer required for himself was to be admiral of the Atlantic, ranking with the constable of Castile, Viceroy with power of life and death, in the regions to be occupied, and a large proportion of the intended spoil. And he would accept no less. None divined what he himself knew not, that the thing he offered in return was dominion over half the world. Therefore, when he found that this would not do, Columbus saddled his mule and took the road to France. In that superb moment he showed what man he was, and the action was more convincing than his words had been. An Aragonese official, Santangel, found the money, the £1500 required for the expedition, and the traveller was overtaken by an alguazil a couple of leagues away, and recalled to Granada. Santangel was, by descent, a Jew. Several of his kindred suffered under the Inquisition, before and after, and he fortified himself against the peril of the hour when he financed the first voyage of Columbus. Granada fell on the 2nd of January 1492. The Jews were expelled on the 20th of March. On the 17th of April the contract with Columbus was signed at Santa Fe. The same crusading spirit, the same motive of militant propagandism, appears in each of the three transactions. And the explorer, at this early stage, was generally backed by the clergy. Juan Perez, the hospitable Franciscan, was his friend; and Mendoza, the great cardinal of Toledo, and Deza, afterwards Archbishop of Seville. Talavera, the Archbishop of Granada, found him too fanciful to be trusted.

Sailing due west from the Canaries he crossed the Atlantic in its widest part. The navigation was prosperous and uneventful until, changing their course to follow the flight of birds, they missed the continent and came upon the islands. It was the longest voyage that had ever been attempted in the open sea; but the passage itself and the shoals and currents of the West Indies, were mastered with the aid of nautical instruments from Nuremberg, and of the *Ephemerides* of Regiomontanus. These were recent achievements of the Renaissance, and without them the undertaking was impossible. Even with the new appliances, Columbus was habitually wrong in his measurements. He put Cuba 18° too far to the west; he thought San Domingo as large as Spain; and he saw mountains 50,000 feet high in Yucatan. Indeed, he protested that his success was not due to science, but to the study of the prophet Isaiah. Above all things, he insisted that Cuba was part of the Asiatic continent, and obliged his companions to testify to the same belief, although there is evidence that he did not share it.

He had promised Cathay. If he produced an unknown continent instead, a continent many thousands of miles long, prohibiting approach to Cathay, he would undo his own work; the peasants who had exposed his fallacies would triumph in his failure, and the competing Portuguese would appropriate all that he had undertaken to add to the crown of Castile. Without civilisation and gold his discoveries would be valueless; and there was so little gold at first that he at once proposed to make up for it in slaves. His constant endeavour was not to be mistaken for the man who discovered the new world. Somewhere in the near background he still beheld the city with the hundred bridges, the crowded bazaar, the long train of caparisoned elephants, the palace with the pavement of solid gold. Naked savages skulking in the forest, marked down by voracious cannibals along the causeway of the Lesser Antilles, were no distraction from the quest of the Grand Khan. The facts before him were uninteresting and provisional, and were overshadowed by the phantoms that crowded his mind. The contrast between the gorgeous and entrancing vision and the dismal and desperate reality made the position a false one. He went on seeking gold when it was needful to govern, and proved an incapable administrator. Long before his final voyage he had fallen into discredit, and he died in obscurity.

Many miserable years passed after his death before America began, through Cortez, to weigh perceptibly in the scales of Europe. Landing at Lisbon from his first expedition, Columbus, in all his glory, had an audience of the king. It was six years since Diaz proved that the sea route to India was perfectly open, but no European had since set eyes on the place where Table Mountain looks down on the tormented Cape. Portugal apparently had renounced the fruits of his discovery. It was now reported that a Spanish crew had found in the West what the Portuguese had been seeking in the East, and that the Papal privilege had been infringed. The king informed Columbus that the regions he had visited belonged to Portugal. It was evident that some limit must be drawn separating the respective spheres. Rome had forbidden Spain from interfering with the expeditions of Portugal, and the Spaniards accordingly demanded a like protection. On the surface, there was no real difficulty. Three Bulls were issued in 1493, two in May and one in September, admonishing Portuguese mariners to keep to the east of a line drawn about 35° west of Greenwich. That line of demarcation was suggested by Columbus, as corresponding with a point he had reached on 13th September, an hundred leagues beyond the Azores. On that day the needle, which had pointed east of the Pole, shifted suddenly to the west. There, he reckoned, was the line of No Variation. At that moment, the climate changed. There was a smooth sea and a balmy air; there was a new heaven and a new earth. The fantastic argument did not prevail, and in the following year Spain and Portugal agreed, by the treaty of Tordesillas, to move the dividing meridian farther west, about midway between the most westerly island of the Old World and the most easterly island of the New. By this agreement, superseding the Papal award, Portugal obtained Brazil. When the lines of demarcation were drawn in 1493 and 1494, nobody knew where they would cut the equator on the other side of the globe. There also there was matter for later negotiation.

After the fall of Malacca, Albuquerque sent a squadron to examine the region of islands farther east. One of his officers, Serrano, remained out there, and after as many adventures as Robinson Crusoe, he found his way to the very heart of the Moluccas, to Ternate, the home of the clove. In describing his travels to a friend, he made the most of the distance traversed in his eastward course. Magellan, to whom the letter was addressed, was out of favour with his commander Albuquerque, and on his return home found that he was out of favour with King Emmanuel. For the country which had repelled Columbus repelled the only navigator who was superior to Columbus. Magellan remembered Serrano's letter, and saw what could be made of it. He told the Spaniards that the spice islands were so far east that they were in the Spanish hemisphere, and he undertook to occupy them for Spain. He would sail, not east, but west, in the direction which was legally Spanish. For he knew a course that no man knew, and America, hitherto the limit of Spanish enterprise, would be no obstacle to him.

It seemed an apparition of Columbus, more definite and rational, without enthusiasm or idealism, or quotations from Roger Bacon, and Seneca, and the greater prophets. Cardinal Adrian, the Regent, refused to listen, but Fonseca, the President of the Board of Control, became his protector. Magellan wanted a good deal of protection; for his adventure was injurious to his countrymen, and was regarded by them as the intrigue of a traitor. Vasconcellos, Bishop of Lamego, afterwards Archbishop of Lisbon, advised that he should be murdered; and at night he was guarded in the streets of Valladolid by Fonseca's men. Magellan was not the first to believe that America comes to an end somewhere. Vespucci had guessed it; the extremity is marked on a globe of 1515; and a mercantile house that advanced funds is supposed to have been on the track.

Without a chart Magellan made his way through the perilous straits that perpetuate his name in twelve days' sailing. Drake, who came next, in 1577, took seventeen days, and Wallis, one hundred and sixteen.

And then, at Cape Deseado, the unbroken highway to the fabled East, which had been closed against Columbus, opened before him. The Spaniards discovered Cape Horn five years later, but it was doubled for the first time in 1616 by the Dutchman who gave his name to it. From the coast of Chili, Magellan sailed north-west for three months, missing all the Pacific Islands until he came to the Ladrones. He was killed while annexing the Philippines to the Crown of Spain, and his lieutenant Delcano, the first circumnavigator, brought the remnant of his crew home by the Cape. On the 9th of September 1522, thirteen wasted pilgrims passed barefoot in procession through the streets of Seville, not so much in thanksgiving for that which had not been given to man since the Creation, as in penance for having mysteriously lost a day, and kept their feasts and fasts all wrong. Magellan's acquisition of the Philippines lasted to the present year (1899), but his design on the Moluccas was given up. Nobody knew, until the voyage of Dampier, to whom, by the accepted boundary, they belonged; and in 1529 Spain abandoned its claim for 350,000 ducats. The Portuguese paid that price for what was by right their own; for Magellan was entirely wrong both as to the meridian and as to the South American route, which was much the longest, and was not followed by sailors.

For more than twenty years Spain struggled vainly with the West Indian problem. Four large islands and forty small ones, peopled by barbarians, were beyond the range of Spanish experience in the art of government. Grants of land were made, with the condition that the holder should exercise a paternal rule over the thriftless inhabitants. It was thought to pay better to keep them underground, digging for gold, than to employ them on the surface. The mortality was overwhelming; but the victims awakened little sympathy. Some belonged to that Acadian race that was the first revealed by the landfall of Columbus, and they were considered incurably indolent and vicious. The remainder came from the mainland and the region of the Orinoco, and had made their way by the Windward Islands as far as San Domingo, devouring the people they found there. Neither the stronger nor the weaker race withstood the exhausting labour to which they were put by taskmasters eager for gold. Entire villages committed suicide together; and the Spaniards favoured a mode of correction which consisted in burning Indians alive by a slow fire. Las Casas, who makes these statements, and who may be trusted for facts and not for figures, affirms that fifty millions perished in his time, and fifteen millions were put to death.

Without a fresh labour supply, the colony would be ruined. It was the office of the clergy to prove that this treatment of the natives was short-sighted and criminal, and their cause was taken up by the Dominican missionaries. In 1510 the preacher Montesino, taking for his text the words, "I am the voice of one crying in the wilderness," denounced the practice. Their mouthpiece with the Home Government, their immortal mouthpiece with posterity, is Las Casas, whose narrative is our authority. The government was anxious to preserve conquests that began to yield some profit. They appointed Commissions to advise, and followed sometimes one report, sometimes the other, taking generally the line of least resistance. The most important Commission of all, in which Las Casas asserted the duties of Christians and the rights of savages, against Sepulveda, who denied them, never came to a decision.

Failing the native supply, the Spaniards substituted negroes. The slaves forwarded by Columbus had been sent back with tokens of the queen's displeasure, and Ximenes would not permit the importation of Africans. But the traffic went on, and the Indies were saved. Under Charles V. 1000 slaves were allotted to each of the four islands. It did not seem an intolerable wrong to rescue men from the devil-worshippers who mangled their victims on the Niger or the Congo. Las Casas himself was one of those who advised that the negro should be brought to the relief of the Carib, and he would have allowed twelve slaves to each settler. He survived half a century, lived to lament his error, and declared his repentance to the world. He repented from motives of humanity rather than from principle; his feelings were more sensitive than his conscience, and he resembled the imperious Parliaments of George III. which upheld the slave trade until imaginations were steeped in the horrors of the middle passage.

The supreme moment in the conquest of America is the landing of Cortez at Vera Cruz in 1521. He was an insubordinate officer acting in defiance of orders, and the governor of Cuba, in just indignation, despatched a force under Narvaez to bring him back. Cortez came down from the interior to the coast, deprived Narvaez of his command, and took possession of his men. With this unexpected reinforcement he was able to conquer Mexico, the capital of an illimitable empire. There was plenty of hard fighting, for the dominant race about the king was warlike. They were invaders, who reigned by force, and as they worshipped beings of the nether world who were propitiated with human sacrifice, they took their victims from the subject people, and their tyranny was the most hateful upon earth. The Spaniards, coming as deliverers, easily found auxiliaries against the government that practised unholy rites in the royal city. When Mexico fell Cortez sent a report to Charles V., with the first-fruits of his victory. Then, that no protesting narrative might follow and weaken his own, that his men might have no hope except in his success, he took the most daring resolution of his life, and scuttled his ships. Fonseca had signed the order for his arrest, when the most marvellous tale in that sequence of marvels reached his hands, and the disgraced mutineer was found to have added to the Emperor's dominions a region many times vaster and wealthier than all that he possessed in Europe. In 1522 the accumulated treasure which had been extracted from Mexican mines since the beginning of ages came pouring into the imperial exchequer, and the desire of so many explorers during thirty unprofitable years was fulfilled at last.

Cortez was not only the most heroic of the Conquistadors, for there was no lack of good soldiers, but he was an educated man, careful to import the plants and quadrupeds needed for civilisation, and a statesman capable of ruling mixed races without help from home. From the moment of his appearance the New World ceased to be a perplexing burden to Spain, and began to foreshadow danger and temptation to other nations. And a man immeasurably inferior to him, a man who could not write his name, whose career, in its glory and its shame, was a servile imitation, almost a parody, of his own, succeeded thereby in establishing a South American empire equal to that of Cortez in the North. One of the ships sailing from the islands to the isthmus carried a stowaway hidden in a cask, whose name was Balboa, and who discovered the Pacific.

The third name is Francisco Pizarro. He stood by and listened while a native described a mighty potentate, many days to the south, who reigned over the mountains and the sea, who was rich in gold, and who possessed a four-footed beast of burden, the only one yet encountered, which was taken at first for a camel. He waited many years for his opportunity. Then, with 168 armed men, and with aid from an associate who risked his money in the business, he started for the Andes and the civilised and prosperous monarchy in the clouds, which he had heard of when he was the lieutenant of Balboa. The example of Cortez, the fundamental fact of American history, had shown what could be done by getting hold of the king, and by taking advantage of internal dissension. How much could be accomplished by treachery and unflinching vigour Pizarro knew without a teacher. Whilst he established his power in the highlands under the equator, Almagro occupied the coast in the temperate zone, 1000 miles farther. Together they had conquered the Pacific. Then, as no man had the ascendency of Cortez, the time that succeeded the occupation was disturbed by internal conflict, in which both the conquerors perished. They had done even more for the Spanish empire than their greater rival. There were 4,600,000 ducats in the treasury of the Inca, and he filled his prison with gold as high as he could reach for the ransom which did not save his life. The mines were soon in working order; and, as the expanse of fertile soil was 3000 miles long, it was clear that Peru, added to Mexico, constituted an important factor in European finance.

As time carried away the tumult of conquest, and the evil generation that achieved it, Spanish America became the seat of such abundance and profusion as was not found in any European capital; and the natives, instructed and regulated by the missionaries, were the object of an elaborate protective legislation, which gave reason for attachment to the mother country. The prodigality of nature was too much for tropical society, and it accomplished nothing of its own for the mind of man. It influenced the position of classes in Europe by making property obtained from afar, in portable shape, predominate over property at home. Released from the retarding pressure of accumulated years, it developed towards revolution; and all the colonies founded by the Conquistadors on the continent of America became Republics. These events shifted the centre of political gravity from land to sea. The resources of the ocean world extended the physical basis of modern History; and increase of wealth involving increase of power, depended thenceforward on the control of distant regions. Vasco da Gama created a broad channel for the pursuit of Empire, and Columbus remodelled the future of the world. For History is often made by energetic men, steadfastly following ideas, mostly wrong, that determine events.

The European Background of Brazilian History

BY GILBERTO FREYRE

For eight centuries the Hispanic, or Iberian, peninsula was dominated by Africans. Arabs and Moors left their traces there.

In a search for understanding of the other Americans, we grasp at every familiar concept and well-known name with the hope of finding some key. First, we equate "Latin" America with the better-known "Latin" states of Europe. Then we review our impressions of Spain and Portugal. But this is only a beginning, as our author shows us in this unusual selection. For Portugal is more than an Iberian variant and implies much of Africa and something of the Jews. Its parallel with Russia is also interesting in that, like Russia, Portugal has been the meeting place of two continents and shares aspects of both. Thus, we find that the racial democracy that typified Renaissance Portugal was transported to Brazil, where new racial elements were added to the African and Semitic elements that had been commingled in the mother country. The Portuguese legend of the *moura encantada,* for example, which attributes to the brown Moorish girl unexcelled beauty and sexual attractiveness and which has evolved out of centuries of contact between Europeans and Africans in Portugal has had its effect on the racial evolution of Brazil. Also, the unique size of Brazil, which is itself half a continent, and its wide variations of climate and geography have been factors in the evolution of its distinctive and fascinating New World culture.

No writer has done more to introduce Brazil to North Americans than Gilberto Freyre, who is a product of inter-American education and can thus present Brazil in terms of United States backgrounds and ways of thought. Dr. Freyre was born in Recife in 1900 and was educated at Baylor

University, from which he received an A.B. degree in 1920, and at Columbia University, from which he received a graduate degree in 1922. Technically his field is sociology, which he studied at Columbia, but his intellectual interests range widely from philosophy to folklore and literature. He has been professor of sociology at the Normal School of Pernambuco for many years. He has also been a visiting professor at Stanford; Kings College, London; and the University of Indiana. His writings, which have usually appeared first in Portuguese and later been translated into many languages, comprise a number of classics which have done much to shape the world's view of Brazil. Four of these merit special note: *Sobrados e mucambos,* published in 1936; *Casa grande e senzala,* published in 1937; *Sociologia,* in two volumes, published in 1945; and the work from which the selection presented here was taken: *New World in the Tropics,* published in 1945.

Dr. Freyre's devotion to writing, research, and teaching is unusual for a Latin American of his intellectual reputation. Despite his international education and his knowledge of many languages, he has never allowed himself to be diverted by either politics or diplomacy, as is often the case with intellectuals in the other American republics. Instead, he prefers the quieter atmosphere of academia and directs the studies of a group of promising young scholars who constitute the faculty of the Institute for Educational Research, which adjoins his home in Recife. From this center flow many items of educational research dealing with the school system of Dr. Freyre's native state of Pernambuco.

There are, of course, scholars who dissent from the picture Dr. Freyre gives of colonial Brazil and its institutions, but his work has established a base from which variations in interpretation and emendations may be made without substantially altering the value of his contribution. Particularly for the Anglo-American student, Dr. Freyre's writings give an introduction to and a provocative view of Brazil that are not to be found elsewhere.

R. E. M.

Brazil, which was discovered and colonized by the Portuguese, is sometimes called Portuguese America. As Portuguese America it is generally considered an extension of Europe, and in its main characteristics it remains Portuguese and Hispanic, or Iberian. It is also Catholic, or a branch or variant of the Latin form of Christianity or civilization.

But the facts that its origins are mainly Portuguese or Hispanic and that its principal characteristics are Latin Catholic do not make of Brazil so simple or pure an extension of Europe as New England was of old England and as New England was of Protestant or Evangelical Christianity in North America. For, as everyone knows, Spain and Portugal, though conventionally European states, are not orthodox in all their European and Christian qualities, experiences, and conditions of life, but are in many important respects a mixture of Europe and Africa, of Christianity and Mohammedanism. According to geographers the Hispanic peninsula is a transition zone between two continents; it is a popular saying that "Africa begins in the Pyrenees"–a saying sometimes used sarcastically by Nordics.

For eight centuries the Hispanic, or Iberian, peninsula was dominated by Africans. Arabs and Moors left their trace there. Though some of the modern Spanish and Portuguese thinkers (like Unamuno) would have Spain and Portugal Europeanized with all speed, others (like Ganivet) maintain that Spain and Portugal must look south, to Africa, for their future and for the explanation of their ethos. The same conflict of opinion is to be found among foreign students of Hispanic social history and cultural problems: some–the German, Schulten, for instance–believe that one of the tasks of modern Europe should be to definitely annex Spain to the European system of civilization; while others–the Frenchman, Maurice Legendre, for instance–go so far as to say that the African element is one of the best original ingredients of Spain, not to be repudiated with shame but to be cherished with pride.

Legendre is one of the authors who point out the similarity between the Spanish peninsula and Russia in their being each a transition zone between two continents: *"Elle* [Spain, or Iberia] *est à la rencontre de deux continents comme la Russie."*[1] And not only between two continents, one might add: betwen two climates, two types of soil and vegetation, two races, two cultures, two conceptions of life, two ecological complexes–and between Euro-Africa and Hispanic America.

[1]Maurice Legendre, *Portrait de l'Espagne* (Paris, 1923), p. 49. The situation of the Hispanic peninsula as a transition zone is certainly similar in many important respects to that of Russia, described by Professor Hans Kohn as "a meeting place of the East and the West by her history and by her nature" (*Orient and Occident,* New York, 1934, p. 76).

As in Russia, such antagonistic conditions and conceptions of life as are to be found among Spaniards and Portuguese have not come together without violent conflict. But amalgamation, accommodation, assimilation have been more powerful than conflict. The result is that the Portuguese, like the Spanish and the Russians, are, in more than a cultural and social aspect, a people with the "split" or Dr. Jekyll–Mr. Hyde personality that psychologists have studied in certain individuals, and that sociologists have perceived in certain social groups. In other aspects, however, they are made not only more dramatic but psychologically richer and culturally more complex than simpler peoples by the fact that they have developed a special capacity to maintain contradictions and even to harmonize them. This capacity is now being demonstrated impressively by the Russians; and it has been demonstrated by the Spanish and the Portuguese during the most creative phases of their history, through one or another of the classical methods by which individuals and groups solve their inner conflicts of personality. According to modern American sociologists and social psychologists such solutions are, fundamentally, three: (1) the rejection of one element or interest, usually by repression, and the selection of another, opposing one; (2) the splitting of the personality into two or more divisions, each looking toward some interest or objects; (3) integration, or balance, of contending elements.

If I am not mistaken, each of the three classical solutions could be found as a dominant factor in any of the various phases of the social and cultural development of the Spanish and Portuguese peoples. Of these phases, that which concerns us most directly is the one that immediately preceded the discovery of the American continent and the colonization of it by Spanish and Portuguese. But the truth is that the social and psychological preparation—unconscious preparation—of the Spaniards and the Portuguese for that tremendous task seems to have taken the entire eight centuries of close contact of the Spanish and Portuguese Christians with the Arabs and Moors who dominated the peninsula. For such centuries were not all, or only, centuries of war, conflict, intolerance. As Professor Fernando de los Ríos reminds us, there were epochs of struggle and intolerance but also "marvelous periods of understanding and co-operation." "To stress the latter we have only to remember," he writes, "how in the thirteenth century the three cults–Christian, Moorish and Mosaic–were celebrated in the same temple, the mosque of Santa María la Blanca de Toledo."[2]

On the other hand, the periods of Castilian and orthodox Catholic domination over the so-called "Hispanic totality" seem to illustrate the solution–or attempt at a solution–of co-existent ethnic and cultural antagonisms through rejecting or repressing various elements and selecting one stock or group and one culture or religion as the perfect or orthodox one: the Inquisition was perhaps the most powerful instrument used in Spain and Portugal to accomplish this end. But neither Castilian centralization nor the Inquisition was able to repress differences or entirely neutralize the process of accommodation in the cultural field and the process of amalgamation in the biological and ethnic one. The *mozarabes* (Christians living under Mohammedan rule), the *mudejares* (Moors living under Christian rule) and the *New Christians* (Jews completely or superficially converted to Christianity) had in Spain and Portugal become too powerful, too penetrating, too plastic, too fluid, and too complex to allow Spanish or Portuguese social and cultural life to be controlled by a single, definitive, and clear-cut group considering itself biologically pure (*sangre limpia*) or culturally perfect according to either European or African standards. There were dramatic conflicts between those who had Christianity and Latin as their ideal of perfection and those who were fanatical followers of Mohammed or Moses. But the general result of the long contact of the Spanish and Portuguese peoples with the Arabs, the Moors, and the Jews was one of integration, or balance, of contending elements rather than of segregation, or sharp differentiation, of any of them or violent conflict between them.

The Arabs added to the Spanish and Portuguese languages a rich vocabulary of Arabisms, through which some sociological conclusions may be reached. One of these is that in both languages Arabisms seem to outnumber Latinisms among old scientific and technical terms of importance, related to agriculture and land industries. And some popular expressions, as "to work hard like a Moor," seem to explain why certain parts of the peninsula are considered "fertile soil" by Arabian authors and "arid land" by Christian ones. A significant

[2]Spain in the Epoch of American Civilization," in *Concerning Latin Amreican Culture* (New York, 1940), p. 24.

detail is that in the Portuguese language the word for olive tree, *oliveira,* is of Latin origin whereas the current word for the commercial product of the same tree—*azeite,* oil—is of Arab origin. Other examples might be added to suggest how Arabs and Latins, Christians and Jews, Catholics and Mohammedans have formed the Spanish and Porttuguese culture (for it is really *one* culture composed of various subcultures), the Spanish and Portuguese languages, and the Spanish and Portuguese ethnic types—more or less harmonious, more or less contradictory products of a sort of competitive co-operation between different human (and perhaps ethnic) capacities and culturally diverse specialized talents and antagonistic dispositions.

Regional diversity in peninsular conditions of soil, of geographical situation, and of climate should also be taken into consideration by the student of the European background of Brazilian history, a background that is not purely European but also African; not purely Christian but also Jewish and Mohammedan; not only agrarian (as illustrated by the importance of the farmers in the earlier days of Portugal) but also military) not only industrial (as developed by the Arabs and the Moors) but maritime and commercial (as developed by Nordics and Jews); marked not only by the capacity for hard, continuous, and monotonous work and by the inclination towards sedentary farm life, but also by the spirit of adventure and romantic chivalry. The diversity of physical conditions is only less important in Spanish and Portuguese history than is the dramatic diversity of ethnic and cultural elements as a key to understanding why such tremendous forces for absolute uniformity of culture, character, and life as a violent centralization of political power in Lisbon (or in Madrid), the Inquisition or the Society of Jesus, and as, after the discovery of Brazil, such a brutal and efficient one-man dictatorship as that of the Marquis of Pombal in Portugal, were not able to destroy differences, variety, spontaneous popular vigour among the Portuguese.

These forces for uniformity were probably essential to the development not only of Spain but of Portugal as efficient colonizing powers; but it is certainly a good sign of social vitality in each that neither of them became strictly orthodox or Catholic in the religious and social sense desired by the Jesuits or the Inquisition; that neither of them lost its regional and cultural diversity under the pressure of strongly centralized government. For the preservation of such healthy differences or antagonisms, it was a good thing that the forces for uniformity did not always act together but were sometimes competitive or antagonistic: the Crown against the Church, for instance; the Society of Jesus against the Inquisition. There was a period when the Jews themselves had the Jesuits as their protectors against the powerful Inquisition. And the fact is that, though nominally expelled, the Jews did not disappear from Portuguese life.

As a very competent student of Portuguese cultural history, Mr. Aubrey F. G. Bell, reminds us, Sobieski, a Polish traveller, wrote in 1611: "There are in Portugal very many Jews, so many that various houses in Portugal have a Jewish origin. Although they have burnt and expelled them, many live hidden among the Portuguese."[3] When it became fashionable in Portugal during the seventeenth and the eighteenth centuries for gentlemen to wear glasses in order to look wise and learned, shrewd Sephardic Jews were able to disguise their Semitic noses under spectacles. And Christians and Jews alike seem to have used rings set with precious stones to show their disdain for manual labour—a custom that survived in Brazil. The display of nobility by Portuguese aristocrats, both Christian and Jew–for the Jews in Portugal and Spain were an aristocracy rather than a plutocracy –sometimes assumed grotesque forms, as when three gentlemen formed a partnership in the use of the same silk suit, two of them having to stay at home when the third went out . A traveller tells us of Jewish physicians, disguised as Christians, in Portuguese America in the seventeenth century who prescribed pork so as to lessen the suspicion of the charge of Judaism. And they all were noted for their attention to dress, even when working as carriers or engaging in other humble occupations, like the Sephardic sellers of *"pan de España"* in Smyrna.

Sometimes the King of Portugal himself was the one who protected the Jews of his kingdom against a too strict enforcement of laws against them, laws based on an ideal of religious rather than of racial purity. Such an ideal would have considerable political importance in the foundation and development of Brazil as a politically orthodox colony of Portugal. There was a time in Brazil when friars came to meet new comers in their boats, not to ascertain their nationality or inspect police

[3]*Portugal of the Portuguese* (London, 1915), p. 4.

papers or examines their physical health, but to inquire into their religious health: Were they Christian? Were their parents Christian? How orthodox were they? As immigration authorities at the service of the State as well as the Church, the friars were guarding against the danger, not of contagious disease or of a criminal disposition, but of infidelity or heresy. The heretic was considered a political enemy of Portuguese America: if he was a Jew he had to disguise himself as a New Christian and remain a Jew secretly; if a Protestant, he had to disguise himself as a Catholic. It seems, however, that there was considerable accommodation in the adjustment of such differences as far as the rich Jews were concerned.

The Jews were an important element in Portugal's social and cultural life, not only for their commercial activity and their capacity to establish cosmopolitan contacts for the Lusitanian Christian adventurers when their maritime enterprises began, but for other things as well. One should not forget that for such enterprises the Portuguese were particularly favoured by their geographical situation; or that from their remote beginning they were greatly influenced by the sea. Some authors refer to that portion of the Atlantic Ocean which lies between the west coast of Portugal and a line drawn through the Azores to Madeira as "the Lusitanian Sea"; and Dalgado, a specialist in climatic geography, reminds us of the fact that, taken as a whole, the "Lusitanian Sea" has more currents than any other sea in Europe–a fact that explains, he adds, "the quantity and the variety of fishes to be found in it."[4] Another specialist in the subject, Kohl, more than half a century ago styled Portugal the "Netherlands of the Iberian Peninsula," a comparison likewise made by Fischer, the author of a map showing the configuration of the Hispanic peninsula. Dalgado describes Portugal as "the Western Inclined Plane of the Iberian peninsula, for it is the exposure of the large portion of its surface to the oceanic winds on the western side that gives it its distinctive climate."[5] Not only, one might add, its distinctive climate from the point of view of physical geography, but also its distinctive historical and cultural climate. For the ethnic and cultural history of Portugal, the heterogeneous ethnic composition of its population, and its commercial and urban

[4]D. G. Dalgado, *The Climate of Portugal* (Lisbon, 1914), p. 33.
[5]*Ibid.*, p. 42.

cosmopolitanism in opposition to its agrarian or rural conservatism are all connected with Portugal's being the "Western Inclined Plane of the Iberian Peninsula."

Certain anthropologists consider the Iberians to have been the original inhabitants of the Hispanic peninsula, and some describe them as mongoloid. But so many intruders have settled in Portugal–the Ligurians, the Celts and the Gauls, the Phoenicians, the Carthaginians, the Romans, the Suevi and the Goths, the Jews, the Moors, the Germans, the French, the English–that it would be difficult to find a modern people whose recent and remote ethnic and cultural past is more heterogeneous. It should be added that, before Brazil was discovered and its colonization begun, the population of Portugal had been coloured by the introduction of a considerable number of Negroes,[6] used as domestic slaves, and of some East Indians, noted for their talent as wood-carvers and cabinet-makers.

With such a heterogeneous ethnic and cultural past, the diversity shown by the Portuguese both as anthropological and as cultural types is not surprising. Some students of the Portuguese ethos regard the Phoenicians, the Carthaginians, and the Jews as the source of the spirit of maritime enterprise that flourished in Portugal from the fourteenth to the seventeenth centuries. They also point out that the Romans gave the Portuguese the bony structure of their language and of some of their social institutions; and that the Moors left many a trait of influence, not only in social institutions and in the language, music, and dances of Portugal, but also in its material culture–architecture, industrial technique, cuisine, and popular dress. The presence and influence in Portugal of French and English Crusaders with their spirit of adventure and their disdain for agricultural labour; the presence and influence there of the Jews, with their commercial spirit and (since they were Sephardic Jews) their disdain for all kinds of manual labour and their excessive enthusiasm for the intellectual and bureaucratic professions; the Portuguese victories over the Moors; the conquests of the Portuguese in Asia and in Africa and the opportunity to employ Negroes, East Indians, and Moors to work in the fields and in the manual arts–all these factors seem to have developed in a large part of the Portuguese population the spirit of adventure and the aristocratic

[6]L. S. Silva Rebello, *Memoria sobre a populaçáo e a agricultura de Portugal desde a fundaçáo da monarchia até 1865* (Lisbon, 1865), p. 60.

prejudices that appeared among some of the first men to come from Portugal to America. In Portuguese America these prejudices took the form of love of military action, of show and grandeur, and of bureaucratic occupation or parasitism, along with slave-making activities, first directed again the Indians and later concentrated in the importation of Africans to work on the almost feudal plantations that some Portuguese were able to establish in Brazil. Fortunately for both Portugal and Brazil such acquired tastes did not destroy entirely in the Portuguese of the old, rural stock–in the so-called *portugueses velhos,* who would be the basic human element of the agrarian colonization of Brazil–their traditional love of agriculture. Men like Duart Coelho and the Albuquerques brought from Portugal to Brazil, in addition to the spirit of adventure, a feeling for social continuity and a capacity for long, patient, and difficult labour. They loved trees and rural life. They were, by tradition, gentlemen farmers or planters. Duarte descended from the agricultural nobility of the North of Portugal, as did his wife, Dona Brites, who became the first woman governor in America. From the same region there migrated to Brazil a number of families who followed Duarte and Dona Brites, some related to them. The Portuguese peasants of that region–the North Atlantic region–are generally considered rather dull of intellect, though religious, musical, occasionally gay, patient, and hard-working.

But the Portuguese of the old rural stock who came to Brazil in the sixteenth century would have been incomplete or one-sided without the so-called "enemies of agriculture," whose predominating traits were their spirit of adventure, their love of novelties, their cleverness, their commercial and urban spirit, their genius for trade. The farmers with a deep love for the land and a thorough knowledge of agriculture were sometimes abused or exploited in Brazil by those of their fellow countrymen whose passion was for commercial adventure and for urban life–most of them probably Jews; but this antagonism was, in more than one respect, beneficial to Portuguese America. Urban Jews with a genius for trade made possible the industrialzation of sugar-cane agriculture in Brazil and the successful commercialization of Brazilian sugar.

This antagonism, however, must be regarded by the student of early Brazilian history not only as an evil–for it was an evil–but as a stimulus to differentiation and progress. One of the most capable interpreters of

Portuguese economic history, Senhor Antonio Sergio, has made sufficiently clear that the commercial class in Portugal, the business men of the coast line, became more important than the aristocratic proprietors of the hinterland in shaping, with the King's co-operation, a national, or rather an international, policy that neglected the hinterland to foster maritime adventure. The process has been carefully studied by J. Lucio de Azevedo, the best authority on the economic history of Portugal.[7] I hardly do more than summarize what Sergio suggests and Azevedo explains when I say that the early rise of the commercial classes in Portugal is a fact never to be overlooked by the student of the European background of Brazilian history. As Sergio reminds us, Lisbon became the seaport where the commerce of the North of Europe met that of the South; it was due to this tendency towards maritime commerce and the concentration of attention on the seaports that the problem of peopling the southern part of Portugal, where agriculture has always depended on expensive irrigation, began to be neglected at an early stage. Since the chief aim of European commerce at this time was, as everyone knows, the acquisition of oriental products, the Portuguese business men of Lisbon, some of them Jews or connected with Jews, took advantage of the geographical situation of their town and also of the fact that feudalism was not so powerful in Portugal as in other parts of Europe to become masters of the national policy and to transform it into a bold cosmopolitan, commercial, and at the same time imperial adventure, through scientific and quasi-scientific efforts to discover new routes for commerce, new lands and new markets to be exploited, and pagan populations not only to be converted into Christians but also to be subdued into Portuguese subjects or slaves. The King of Portugal himself became "the Merchant of Merchants" and the state officials also turned traders.[8]

It is well known that in the fourteenth and fifteenth centuries, with the irruption of the Turks into the eastern seaports of the Mediterrean and because of other difficulties, the need for a sea-route to India became acutely felt in Europe. No European nation was in a more advantageous position to solve this grave problem than semi-European Portugal, a nation so precociously maritime and commercial in its

[7]*Epocas de Portugal Economico* (Lisbon, 1929).

[8]Antonio Sergio, *A Sketch of the History of Portugal,* trans. from the Portuguese by Constantino José dos Santos (Lisbon, 1928), p. 88.

political program that, as early as the latter part of the fourteenth century, laws were enacted by King Dom Fernando which gave special protection to maritime commerce and encouraged naval construction; which gave more assistance to such a cause than to the noble proprietors of latifundia, especially of lands regained from the Moors —lands that needed irrigation, then considered a matter of royal aid or something about the economic capacity of the not too wealthy proprietors. It seems that such aid was never given. In not assisting the aristocratic proprietors of latifundia, the kings of Portugal perhaps had in view the definite and efficient development of centralized royal power, which might be endangered by a strong land aristocracy.

The policy of disdain or neglect of the Portuguese hinterland followed by some of the most influential kings of Portugal like Dom Fernando explains why so many noblemen began to come to Lisbon as candidates for government appointments. And, as such, even they grew enthusiastic over maritime adventure, trade, naval construction; they became co-operators, rather than enemies, of the merchant princes of the seaports when the sea-route to India was opened and parts of the East became colonies or semi-colonies of Portugal. Some of these aristocrats went to Brazil, appointed by the Portuguese Crown to high bureaucratic positions or military posts, or sent on special missions that required from them the best of their military experience and of their capacity as leaders. There they encountered such mutually antagonistic but also co-operative forces as the King, the Church, the Jews, the common man, the heretic, and the political or common criminals forced to leave Portugal and go to Brazil.

It seems to me that some authors—Sombart is one of them—overemphasize the importance of the Jews in Portuguese maritime and colonial enterprises, including the development of Brazil as a sugar-producing colony. Nevertheless one should not go to the opposite extreme: that of overlooking the part played by the Jews in the cultural development of Portugal and in the definitely cosmopolitan shape taken by its economic policy after the days of Dom Fernando. For Portuguese kings and Jewish princes of finance understood each other so well that Jews had been royal tax-collectors since the early days of the Portuguese monarchy; and under some of the best kings Sephardic Jews were ministers of finance, royal physicians, royal astrologers. Under Portuguese royal protection Jewish merchants are said to have become proud and conceited; to have adorned their horses with tassels; to have indulged in luxury. And one can imagine what powerful rivals of the Catholic chaplains, confessors, advisers, and educators they became as royal physicians, astrologers, and tax-collectors. For in those days a man's body was becoming again almost as important as his soul, and shrewd astrologers seemed to be able to guide a king or a queen, a prince or a captain, through mysterious regions of this world and of the next–regions entirely unknown to Catholic masters of theology and divinity.

For those who study the history of Portugal from a Brazilian point of view it is interesting to follow Jewish activities in connection with the maritime and commercial enterprises that had sugar-producing in Brazil as their by-product, if not their chief product. From the reign of King Sancho II, who was interested in the development of the Portuguese navy, the Jews were obliged to pay a navy tax: for each ship fitted out by the King they had to provide "an anchor and a new anchor-tow sixty ells long or instead to make a money payment of 60 livres." They controlled, among other branches of commerce, the food supply, and more than once we are reminded by such students of the history of Jewish activities in Portugal as Azevedo that they were accused, with or without reason, of holding up supplies in order to raise prices–a practice not peculiar to Portuguese Jews of the fourteenth and fifteenth centuries.

According to some authors, at the root of the ability of the Portuguese to acclimatize themselves in various parts of the world better than almost any other Europeans, lies the great admixture of the people of Portugal with the Semitic race; and not the Jews alone but the Moors also would have contributed to that special capacity. Against such a generalization there stands a fact of considerable importance: that "New Lusitania"–the north-eastern part of Brazil–was settled mostly by men and women from northern Portugal, a population noted for its Romano-Visigothic blood and "Nordic" characteristics. Such men and women, some of them from the agricultural nobility, could adapt themselves well to the tropical climate of that Brazilian region where sugar-cane was made the basis for a revival of feudal social organization, with Africans as slaves. Perhaps the Portuguese climate itself–a climate more African than European–best explains why the Portuguese adapt themselves better than other Europeans to tropical climates. And one should not forget that, during the first generations of settlers of the tropical parts of Brazil, this adaptation was based on slave work; the Portuguese did not themselves do the hardest work in the fields but had Indians and later Negroes as plantation slaves.

It is to be noted that it was not Brazil that made the Portuguese masters in the art of living and sometimes of fortunes based on slavery: when the colonization of Brazil began, Portugal itself was full of African slaves—though this, of course, was only a miniature of what was to develop in Brazil on a large, almost monumental, scale. But when they reached Brazil, most of the Portuguese already had a love of display and grandeur and a distaste for manual work that are to be explained, in large part, by their having had, for nearly a century, most of their domestic work done by Negro slaves and, for many centuries, some of the most difficult agricultural labour provided by the Moors.

To the Portuguese the Moors had been not only the efficient agricultural workers who knew how to transform arid lands into gardens, as if by a miracle, but a dark race who had not always been the serfs but sometimes were the masters of a large part of the Iberian peninsula. Portuguese of the purest Nordic blood had found in brown Moorish women, some of them princesses, the supreme revelation of feminine beauty. As more than one student of Brazilian history has pointed out—in particular the American Mr. Roy Nash, whose book *The Conquest of Brazil* is one of the best ever written on Brazil from a sociological standpoint—the darker-skinned people had been "the contact of the conquered with their brown-skinned conquerors." And "the darker man was the more cultured, more learned, more artistic. He lived in castles and occupied the towns. He was the rich man and the Portuguese became serfs upon his land. Under such conditions, it would be deemed an honor for the white to marry or mate with the governing class, the brown man, instead of the reverse."[9]

Through the sociological study of the famous Portuguese legend of the *moura encantada,* I reached years ago the same conclusion as Mr. Roy Nash: that the idealization, by the Portuguese people, of the brown woman, or the Moorish girl or woman, as the supreme type of human beauty had probably a very important effect on the direction taken by their relations with Indian (Amerindian) women in Brazil. Mystic,

[9]*The Conquest of Brazil* (New York, 1926), p. 37.

poetical, given to dreams about their past, lovers of beautiful plants as well as of useful and commercial ones, the Portuguese have peopled some of their woods and fountains with fascinating legends of Moorish princesses. The boy who is fortunate enough to discover and treat well the animal or the plant which is only a disguise for some beautiful Moorish princess of the past will marry her and be rich and happy. And in all such stories and legends the Moorish brown girl is regarded as the supreme type of beauty and of sexual attractiveness; the Moors are considered superior, and not inferior, to the purely white Portuguese.

Such legends are still active among the Portuguese peasants, a large majority of whom are illiterate. Portuguese children of all classes grow up under the spell of such non-European or non-"Aryan" legends and myths. One can imagine how active the pro-Moorish legends were among the Portuguese who in the sixteenth century first came into contact with the Indians in America, another brown race. Their historical experience, their folk-lore, their popular literature in prose and verse—all these voices from their past told the Portuguese who first arrived in Brazil that brown people are not always inferior to white people.

Legends are a living force among illiterate peasants like those of Portugal; and legends may express a truth more effective and enduring than some of the ever-changing half-truths by pedants rather than by scholars. Illiteracy among peasants with a rich folk-lore or folk heritage like that of Spain and Portugal does not necessarily mean ignorance but may be intimately connected with wisdom, imagination, and humour. From their legends most of the Portuguese who discovered and colonized Brazil knew that a brown people may be superior to a white people, as the Moors had been in Portugal and Spain; and from their long contact with the Moors, considered in that part of Europe not an inferior but a superior race, the Portuguese assimilated many mores and conceptions: the Moorish ideal of feminine beauty (a fat woman), the Moorish taste for concubinage or polygamy, the tolerance and consideration of both races for mixed-bloods, their conception of domestic slaves as almost a sort of poor relation kept at home. The Portuguese in Brazil retained many marks of Moorish influence in their not too strictly European nor too strictly Christian moral and social behaviour. This was especially true of the common men, though in general it applies to Portuguese of all classes.

I wish to say more about the illiterate peasants of Portugal, to whom Brazil owes so much. Since the early days of the sixteenth century they have been the continuous basic element for the development of a real new culture–not a merely sub-European or colonial one–in that part of the American continent. As James Murphy[10] and more recent foreign observers in Portugal have found out, the illiterate peasants are the flower or the cream of that nation; and from more than one point of view they–and not the noblemen, the bourgeois, the finely educated–have been the flower and the cream of the Portuguese colonization of Brazil.

A number of Brazilian anecdotes and jokes are directed at the Portuguese peasants: about how naïve or rustic they are; how ignorant of technical progress; how stupid or dull some of them are by contrast with other Europeans or with the native or mestizo Brazilian–the *carioca,* the *caboclo,* the *amarelinho* (who is, of course, the supreme hero of many Brazilian stories). In these anecdotes the Portuguese peasant is not necessarily the villain–indeed he never is really the villian. But, being generally represented as stout, naïve, and childlike, and also as sexually potent as primitive men are supposed to be in contrast with the too civilized ones, he is made by Brazilian legend a sort of ridiculous but lovable Falstaff. The caricature merely emphasizes his ignorance in the face of an urban and technical progress which naturally is entirely strange to men from a predominantly pastoral and agricultural country like Portugal.

Since the sixteenth century, Portuguese peasants have brought with them to Brazil a wealth of legends, of incantations, of folk-songs, of popular literature in verse and prose, of popular arts; and it is mainly through them–illiterate peasants and artisans–rather than through the erudite or the learned, that similar popular or folk values from the Indians and the Negroes have been assimilated by Portuguese America and become the source for a new culture: the Brazilian culture.

Some students of modern cultures tend to exaggerate the importance of literacy. Reading and writing are means of communication very useful for industrial civilizations and for merely political forms of democratic organization–though, at that, they are apparently being superseded by the telephone, the radio, and television. Such countries

[10]*Travels in Portugal* (London, 1795).

as China, India, Mexico, and Brazil will probably not have the same need for literacy as a means of achieving modernization as had the vast masses during the nineteenth century and even Soviet Russia at the beginning of this century.

Mr. Aubrey F. G. Bell, who knows Portugal familiarly, writes that "thrice fortunate" are they who "can associate and converse with the Portuguese peasants during the summer *romaria* or village *festa,* or as they sit round the winter fire (*a lareira*), or gather from some great common task, a shearing (*tosquia*) or *esfolhada* (separating the maize cob from its sheath), for they are certain to glean a rich store of proverbs, folklore, and philology," and goes on to state that "it may be said without exaggeration that the Portuguese people, for all its colossal ignorance and lack of letters, is one of the most civilized and intelligent in Europe."[11] In saying this he is paying the greatest tribute that the son of a highly industrial and mechanical civilization such as the British can pay to a people often ridiculed for its backwardness. That this backwardness is no evidence of low intelligence or inferior race is the opinion of the most careful students of the Portuguese people and of Portuguese history.

Noblemen, kings, merchant princes, doctors of philosophy, law, and medicine, priests, Sephardic Jews, scholars, and scientists have contributed brilliantly to the Portuguese colonization of Brazil. But it should be repeated that the most constant creative force in it has probably been the illiterate peasants, some of them men with North African blood: Arabian, Moorish, and even Negro. It is the result of their work that may be presented today to the world as one of the most successful colonizing efforts, not so much of Europeans, but of semi-Europeans, in tropical America.

The Portuguese common man was present in the first Portuguese colonizing efforts in Brazil; a recent careful study of documents of that period has shown that a number of Portuguese founders of *paulista* families in southern Brazil—families later famous for their pioneer work in central, northern, and the extreme parts of southern Brazil—were artisans or peasants. Portuguese artisans seem to have come in a considerable number in the sixteenth century to Bahia, the first town of importance built in Brazil; some of them were paid very high wages.

[11]*Op. cit.,* p. 15.

They soon became numerous in Pernambuco as small-town merchants and artisans, rivals of the second and third generation of descendants of the noblemen and gentlemen farmers from the North of Portugal who, with the help or assistance of rich Jews, had founded the sugar industry in Brazil. Later, in 1620, two hundred Portuguese families arrived in Maranhão from the Azores. In 1626 others came to Pará, and in the eighteenth century a large number established themselves in Rio Grande do Sul. They were not noblemen but peasants and artisans, common men whose mediocre success in agricultural colonization is explained by the fact that the feudal system prevailing in large areas of Portuguese America made it almost impossible for common men to prosper as farmers. If Portuguese agricultural colonists established in Pará (Nossa Senhora do O and other places), in Bahia (Sinimbù Engenho Novo, Rio Pardo), and in Rio de Janeiro did not succeed remarkably as agriculturists, it must be pointed out that even less successful were the Irish peasants established also as farmers in the interior of Bahia and the German families located early in the nineteenth century in the interior of Pernambuco; indeed, these were magnificent failures. But as soon as they were able to escape from a feudal system of land domination in which there was hardly any place for a genuine farmer or an independent agriculturist, most of those Portuguese agriculturists found jobs as artisans or prospered as traders in coast cities, where so many of them have been strikingly successful as merchants and founders of new industries.

In his very interesting *New Viewpoints on the Spanish Colonization of America* Professor Silvio Zavala tells us that Philip II permitted Portuguese farmers to emigrate to Spanish America[12]–perhaps, I venture to suggest, because the conditions were more favourable to farmers in some areas of Spanish America than in most areas of Portuguese America. According to Professor Zavala, colonization of a military character had spread over Spanish America; but a large part of Portuguese America was dominated from the sixteenth to the nineteenth century by a feudal type of colonization even more alien to the ordinary European farmer than was the purely military one. And in both Hispanic Americas, the Portuguese and the Spanish, there

[12]*New Viewpoints on the Spanish Colonization of America* (Philadelphia, 1943), p. 110.

[13]*Ibid.*, pp. 110–111.

developed another type of privileged colonization whose interests did not coincide with those of the ordinary colonists–that of the Jesuits, whose policy it was to segregate the Indians and even to compete agriculturally and commercially with the ordinary colonists through using Indian (Amerindian) labour that most of the civilian community did not obtain so easily or freely as the Jesuits, though it was taxed to support them. Privileged as they were under most of the kings of Portugal and Spain during the most decisive phase of colonization of America, the Jesuits did extraordinarily valuable work in Brazil as missionaries and educators; but their excessively paternalistic and even autocratic system of educating the Indians ran counter to the early tendencies of Brazil's development as an ethnic democracy. This point–so clearly seen, from the Spanish-American democratic point of view, by Las Casas, when he wished to utilize colonization by farmers "who should live by tilling the rich lands of the Indies, lands which the Indian owners would voluntarily grant to them," lands where "the Spaniards would intermarry with the natives and make of both peoples one of the best commonwealths in the world and perhaps one of the most Christian and peaceful"[13]–was also clearly seen, from a Brazilian point of view, by José Bonifacio, leader of the movement for the independence of Portuguese America. He realized the danger of a native policy of isolation like the one followed for some time by the Jesuits in Brazil–danger to the development of Brazil as a democratic community–and he therefore advocated the practice of racial crossing and cultural interpenetration until, under the inspiration of his ideas, a comprehensive plan for dealing with the Indians was adopted by the Emperor of Brazil in 1845. Following a tradition that has its roots in ideas held by the Portuguese kings and statesmen, sometimes in opposition to the Jesuits, the plan included the promotion of intermarriage between the Portuguese and the Indian, of instruction, and of assistance in the form of housing, tools, clothing, and medicine. It also included the right of natives to acquire title to land outside reservations.

If privileged types of colonization have prevented the majority of Portuguese common men who have emigrated to America from becoming conquerors there and owners of virgin areas of good agricultural lands, they seem to have found compensation for this repression of their "possessive" rather than "creative" instincts in their really extraordinary procreative activity as polygamous males. Some of them became famous, like João Ramalho in the sixteenth century, for their many children from Indian women. As such they became the rivals, the equals, sometimes the triumphant competitors of Portuguese *fidalgos,* or noblemen, like Jeronymo de Albuquerque, whose addiction to polygamy marks them as inheriting Moorish rather than European and Christian traditions of sexual morality. Such excesses, profitable to Brazil from the point of view of a purely quantitative colonization, were not always beneficial to the development of a Christian family life in Portuguese America. Against them not only the Jesuits, but Church authorities as well, more than once made their voices heard.

Every student of the social history of Brazil knows that, for an adequate knowledge of this subject (as for that of the social origins and social development of other modern nations), the gathering of sufficient information on the life, the activity, and the influence of the masses of the people is a task still remaining to be done. Information on the basic social and cultural contacts between human groups producing modern civilization is still incomplete. As has been remarked by an American student of social history, Professor Dwight Sanderson, the available sources have often emphasized political structures and documentary evidence, while students of mythology and folk-lore not infrequently go to the other extreme in their evaluation of cultural survivals and of the common people's contributions to the development of modern culture or civilization. Hence the need of a re-study of some problems of European and American history from a sociological standpoint.

Portugal and the Portuguese colonization of Brazil need such a re-study, based on a new evaluating of the Portuguese contribution to modern civilization. This contribution was perhaps made in larger part by the merchant, the missionary, the common man, the intellectual, the scientist, and the woman who followed her husband in his overseas adventures, than by the *conquistador,* the military leader, the statesman, the bishops, or the kings—even though Portugal, in its most creative phase (that is, during the fifteenth and the sixteenth centuries), was remarkable for its far-seeing, energetitc, and capable kings, princes, and statesmen.

During the fifteenth and sixteenth centuries the Portuguese—most of them engaged in trade-enriched European civilization with a number of plants and cultural values and techniques assimilated from Asia and Africa. Portuguese America was also benefited by these, for it was Portuguese merchants who introduced into Europe (or were among the first Europeans to introduce or re-introduce) a taste for the following things: sugar, tea, rice pudding, pepper, and cinnamon; the guinea fowl; the parasol, the umbrella, and the palanquin; porcelain and Arabian tiles; the veranda (of the East Indies); concave roofs, rounded cornices, and pagoda-like summer houses; Chinese gardens and fans; oriental rugs and perfumes. And as early as the sixteenth century the same merchants took to Brazil some of these tastes and luxuries, as well as silks and jewels. They were the pioneers of modern international trade between the orient and the occident, between the Old World and the New.

North Europeans, who have made of the daily bath a supreme technique in modern domestic comfort, scorn the Portuguese peasant for not taking so many baths as they do; but it was Portuguese navigators and traders who were among the first Europeans to bring from the East the almost un-Christian (and certainly un-European) habit of the daily bath–which in Europe was at first, and to some extent is still, a luxury reserved to ladies and gentlmen. Though the Portuguese are ridiculed today for using toothpicks at the dinner table, it was probably a Portuguese who brought from China to Europe the first porcelain for the tea of the sophisticated. The Portuguese were, also, probably the first Europeans to bring, from the East to Europe, East Indian cotton textiles, especially calicoes, thus revolutionizing social habits and cultural behaviour in the European Christian countries. For, as every student of modern European civilization knows, the cheap East Indian cottons increased the use of underclothes, thereby "improving both health and cleanliness."[14] And the Portuguese started yet another social and cultural revolution, this one in the orient, when they introduced into Japan the European Jesuits

[14]Shepard Bancroft Clough and Charles Woolsey Cole, *Economic History of Europe* (Boston, 1941), p. 263. See also Adolphe Reischwein, *China and Europe* (London, 1915), pp. 61–67. James Edward Gillespie, *The Influence of Overseas Expansion on England* (1500–1700) (New York, 1920); Ramalho Ortigão, *O Culto da Arte em Portugal* (Lisbon, 1896); Edgar Prestage, *The Portuguese Pioneers* (London, 1934); and Gilberto Freyre, *O Mundo que o Portugues Creou* (Rio, 1940) also discuss the subject and point out aspects of the Portuguese influence in the social and cultural life of Europe as a result of Portuguese contacts with Africa, the orient, and America.

(including the great Francis Xavier), European muskets, and possibly syphilis.

The Portuguese also made their new colony known in Europe for its beautiful plants like the evening primrose, its useful woods like Brazil-wood and rosewood, its delicious fruits like the pineapple, its fine Bahai tobacco, its Pará or Brazil nuts, its Amazonian rubber, its hammocks made by the Indians, and its plants with medicinal properties like ipecacuanha. Soon after the discovery of Brazil, the Portuguese began to study Brazilian plants and animals, and especially Indian or Amerindian customs and foods with an accuracy that has been praised by modern scientists. They also began to build in tropical America houses of a new type and with extra-European characteristics, houses whose architecture exhibited a combination of Asiatic and African modes with traditional European styles. They began to develop a Luso-Brazilian cookery based on their European traditions adapted to American conditions and resources, and also on their experience with the plants and the culinary processes of Asia and Africa.

The Portuguese are also associated not only with the introduction into or popularization in Europe of Brazilian sugar, under the name of *mascavado* or *muscovado,* but also with the dissemination of the use of tobacco as an aristocratic custom among Europeans. As a result of the use of tobacco–from Brazil and other parts of America–it seems that the Europeans in general, and the Portuguese in particular, began to spit more than before; and it is significant that the English word *cuspidor* comes from the Portuguese verb *cuspir,* to spit. But this is not the only word that has come from the Portuguese, or, through the Portuguese, from East Indian, African, Asiatic, and American languages into the English and other European languages. Numerous words of Portuguese origin indicate how important a part Portugal played in the pioneer days of modern international trade: *bamboo* (the tree), *veranda* (for porch), *caravel* (a type of vessel), *tapioca* (the starch of "mandioca"), *pagoda* (a tower-like structure), *kraal* (a type of African village), *muscovado* (a type of sugar), *cobra* (snake), *cobra-de-capelo* (an East Indian snake), *jararaca* (a serpent), *jacaranda* (Brazilian rosewood), *caste* (a hereditary and endogamous social group), *palanquin* (the Asiatic sedan chair largely used in Brazil), *cashew* or *cajou* (a nut), *jaguar* (a large feline of Latin America), *samba* (an Afro-Brazilian dance), *mango* (an East Indian fruit now very common in Brazil), *Port* and *Madeira* (types of wine), *canja* (a thick soup of chicken and rice, highly praised by Theodore Roosevelt),[15] *cruzado* (a Portuguese coin mentioned by Shakespeare), and *valorization,* a "Portuguesism" in the English language denoting a technique for the commercial protection of a product, a technique used first by Brazilians in connection with their coffee and since then by other peoples in connection with various other commodities. And it is my belief that *pickanniny* comes not from the Spanish, as generally stated by dictionaries and by Mr. H. L. Mencken in *The American Language,* but from the Portuguese word *pequenino. Formosa* (the name of the important island off the coast of China) is also a Portuguese word, not Spanish. These words are a few evidences of Portuguese ubiquity prior to the colonization of Brazil or contemporaneous with it.

In dealing with the European background of Brazilian history from a sociological standpoint, one is led to the somewhat paradoxical conclusion that it was not an entirely European background: it was also Asiatic and African.

[15] *Through the Brazilian Wilderness* (New York, 1914), p. 165. Theodore Roosevelt introduced also into the English language a number of Portuguese-Amerindian names of animals like *tamanduá-bandeira* and *piranha.*

Manuelita Saenz

BY GERMÁN ARCINIEGAS

When Bolívar was out, Manuelita remained as the villa's mistress and señora.

In order to reach an understanding of the mind of Latin America, the study of Bolívar, both in his statements and in his actions, provides much meaningful material. In this effort, as in many others, the Colombian writer Germán Arciniegas has served as an eloquent guide. From his *Green Continent* to his *America Magica,* Arciniegas presents a timeless picture of the men and women of Latin America and the fascinating milieu in which they live out the drama of their lives, dedicated to a set of values and possibly "a tragic sense of life" which are hard for more practical and pragmatic Northerners to understand.

The life of Manuelita Sáenz, who was the Liberator's mistress, reveals Bolívar the man more than his dramatic speeches at the head of his troops. She typifies, too, the Latin American regard for feminine feeling, passion, and determination, even when these are in direct opposition to convention. The same Latin America which at times seems to reduce women to a guarded and secondary role has produced the Manuelitas and the Maria Lynches who have become its heroines. Latin America remains the home of romanticism. It prefers, as heroes, people who live dangerously and are willing to lose all in a gallant gesture. Scholars have attempted to correlate this attitude with the economic and social development of the area and the greater or lesser development of a middle class. Regardless, the example of the Bolívars and the Manuelitas continues to influence modern Latin America despite the gradual changes in its forms of production or the state of its foreign commerce.

Germán Arciniegas' personal experience has equipped him to be a superb interpreter of Latin America to people of other areas because he not only knows his own country, but also has viewed it from afar and has thus acquired perspective. He was born in Bogotá in 1900 and completed his education at the National University of Colombia with degrees both in letters and in law. He served as minister of education of Colombia in 1941 and 1942 and again in 1945 and 1946. Previously he held diplomatic posts in London and Buenos Aires. After leaving the Ministry of Education, he served in Paris and in Rome and is now the Colombian ambassador in Venezuela. He has also served as a foreign correspondent in London of the Colombian daily *El Tiempo,* and he has been a visiting professor in many United States institutions, including Columbia University and Mills College of California, which granted him a doctor's degree, *honoris causa.*

It is, of course, by his writing that he is best known, and through it he has made his most important contribution to inter-American comprehension. In his books he has devoted himself primarily to studies of people and human nature, just as he does in the selection that follows. His writing adds a dimension to this survey of Latin America that could be supplied by scarcely anyone else.

The style of "Manuelita Sáenz," which on first examination, may seem strange to the North American reader, is not atypical of Latin American writers who cultivate what might be called a poetic prose style. This is deliberately used to underline their basic preoccupation with the emotional dimension of their subjects. Essentially pre-Freudian, it retains many of the characteristics of nineteenth-century romanticism and subscribes to the theory that the intuitive, esthetic, and religious nature of man transcends in importance scientific doctrine.

R. E. M.

1

When Bolívar entered Quito in 1822, he had experienced in the previous six months the blackest depths and the most promising glories of his shining life. He had leaped from paradise to the inferno and from the inferno to glory once, twice, three, four, and five times in giddy path, wearing at times his soul in his fist and at others, freeing it as one might a bird from a cage. Behind him was the sum of these ups and downs. Finally, though it was not to be his end, he came upon Quito, which he had never seen, delicious, filled with temptations, a hidden corner of green America which clothed itself against the cold with the stories of already legendary loves.

A few months before, from Cali, Bolívar wrote to "the fussy and more than fussy, beautiful Bernardina," a note which began in this way: "My adored: what love can do! I think only of you. . . ." Within the month, he wrote to Santander, from Popayán: "Smallpox is present, there are daily desertions, veterans flee, there is nothing to sustain the troops, I'm going to suffer, staying here indecently: send *alpargatas,* cartridge belts if there are any, caps for the recruits, and even a dress of coarse cotton cloth; if there are good flints, send them because the ones sent are useless. . . ." Desperate, he threw himself into the war against the people of Pasto. It was to smash himself against the rocks. "They are the most tenacious and obstinant people, and the worst of it is that their country is a chain of precipices." Circumstances were ideal for a man as stubborn as the Liberator. Sunk in these abysses, he soon wrote to the Spanish colonel: "I am returning your communications, so that you will send them to me again with the treatment due me or keep them forever. We have the right to treat all people of Pasto as prisoners of war and to confiscate all their goods, because all of them, without exception, are making war against us. . . . We have the right to treat this garrison with the utmost severity of war and to confine the people in narrow prisons. . . ." Frightening with words and fighting without flints, he insisted upon the stupid Battle of Bombona and won it. The most heroic and least glorious battle, as Mosquera said. But he won it . . . and had to return to the other bank of the Juanambu River. These absurdities made the realists die of fright. Meanwhile, Sucre won the Battle of Pichincha, and Bolívar redoubled the offensive with that literature so very his, the best machete to flash in the sun of America. "How do you want to enter Pasto?" the vanquished governor asked him. And Bolívar: "When the Liberator President of Colombia enters a city as victor, he receives the honors of a Roman emperor." They made arches of triumph for him. The bishop awaited Bolívar in the plaza with pontifical vestments and under the pallium. A *Te Deum* was sung. "From Tulcán to Quito we have marched on flowers. . . ."

Upon entering the streets of Quito, "all the windows and balconies were draped with tapestries and shining among them were the señoras and señoritas, dressed and combed with great elegance." It rained roses, carnations. Six señoritas dressed as nymphs waited for them on the platform of the plaza. Señorita Arboleda arranged Bolívar's crown of laurel. . . . From a balcony a certain lady threw a crown of laurel which hit him on the forehead. With this blow, history was altered. The lady of prodigious aim was Mrs. Thorne. Mr. Thorne had remained in Lima. Mrs. Thorne had arrived from Lima days before, it was said, with the intention of selling a zambo slave, "without vices, public or private illnesses, free from obligation, pledge or mortgage," and besides, 300 yards of damask and 237 cashmere handkerchiefs. It is possible—since everything is possible—that Mrs. Thorne was telling the truth. But it is also possible that she was not. Mrs. Thorne was not a foolish Englishwoman, but rather a brave and astute *Quiteña.* She was able to leave Lima to give herself a vacation from her husband; Mr. Thorne was Anglican and boring, realistic and stupid. It was clearly visible that Mrs. Thorne wished to cast to the air the gray hair she did not have. Life gushed through her pores. She was impetuous youth, passion made flesh and bone. She was lighting a candle in a heavy downpour. She dreamed of a knight of heroic stature. Of . . . Bolívar.

There was a dance that night. The required presentations were made to the Liberator. Almost last was the lady of good aim. This in itself signified a great deal to such a notable soldier as Bolívar. It was easy for him to recognize her. "Mrs. Thorne?" "No, Manuelita: I'm called Manuelita, they call me Manuelita." She could have added: until less than a moment ago she was Mrs. Thorne. It was not necessary. It could be seen in her eyes; they were the flint that makes good sparks.

They danced crazily, desperately. She performed a few *napanga* solos, a dance which the Bishop of Quito had called "The resurrection of the flesh." The English officers watched this resurrection dry-mouthed. Apart from the dance solos, the whole night was Bolívar's. Manuelita with the fighting republican. The indulgent said: She has news from Lima which she will communicate to His Excellency. Those who think other things should be quict. But she, that day, was Bolívar's before the dance, at the dance, and after the dance. Bolívar told himself: *Adiós,* Bernardina! Manuelita: *Chao,* Mr. Thorne!

A year passed. A year of love at full speed. Then, with that adorable misspelling appropriate to her education, the ex-Mrs. Thorne wrote to Dr. Thorne, who from Lima was summoning her to reunite herself with him: "No, no, no more man; by god why make me write breaking my resolution? and *bamos* [*sic*] what do you achieve? nothing except making me suffer the pain of telling you 1,000 times NO. Senor [*sic*] you are excellent, you are inimitable I shall never say anything other than what you are, but my friend to leave you for General Bolívar is something, to leave another husband without your qualities would be *nothing* and do you believe that I after being the mistress of this Senor for 1 year and with the security of possessing his heart would prefer to be the wife of the father, son or holy ghost? *e,* not even the most holy Trinity! and if I am sorry about anything it is that you were not better so that I could still have left you. . . . Enough of jest–formally and without laughing and with all the seriousness, truth, purity of an Englishwoman I say *that I shall never join you again.* You Anglican, and I atheist, the strongest religious impediment is that I love another and not you, don't you see with what formality your unswerving friend thinks. Manuela."

For Bolívar's peace of mind, and perhaps thinking of not confusing orthodox historians a century later, Manuelita added the following to the copy of the lettter she sent Bolívar: "I must warn you that my husband is a Catholic, and I not an atheist, the desire to be without him made me talk like that."

We summarize: Mrs. Thorne is dead! Long live Manuela!

Curtain. End of the first act.

2

No one has said that Manuelita was ugly. She would be prohibited to minors, and that is enough said. So also was her mother, the pretty Joaquina Aispuru, of the best Basque families. Joaquina had the devil inside her body when she made fall into her clutches a gentleman as respectable as Don Simón Sáenz y Vergara, a dignitary of the *uyuntamiento,* young, yes, but the center of a home fashioned as God ordains. As a consequence of the loves of the tempting Joaquina and Don Simón Sáenz, Manuela was born. Joaquina Aispuru's sister, abbess of the Convent of Carmen, took her. The baptismal certificate, if there was one, was written in *letra bastardilla,* italics. The daughter of sin grew up lively and attractive. At seventeen, Manuelita was a beautiful bastard. To protect her from her legacy of the neighbors' tongues, she was confined in the Convent of Santa Catalina. Through those streets passed the royal battalion commanded by the good-looking Captain Fausto de Elhuyar. For some reason he was baptized Fausto by his father, the sage discoverer of tungsten. Fausto saw Manuelita, Manuelita took the bait, and Fausto prevailed upon her to escape from the convent. Manuelita was not timid or candid like Margarita: she simply carried her own little devil within her body. In the convent, scandal. And scandal, also, in Quito. To avoid problems, Manuelita was taken to Panama, where she met Mr. Thorne who fell in love with her, now not in the Spanish style like Elhuyar, but in the English. They were married as God ordains. Thorne conducted her to the altar with an air as paternal as Britannic; he was twenty years older. If Mr. Thorne was not aware of the risks, Manuelita, in due course, opened his eyes with letters such as those we have seen.

From the night Manuelita stole Bolívar in Quito to the night she saved his life in Santa Fe de Bogotá, she must always have terrified the ladies of good society. In the three capitals–in Quito, in Lima, in Bogotá–the señoras shut their windows so as not to see her passing by with soldiers and generals. In Quito she was the one who had abandoned her husband; in Lima, the mistress of Bolívar; in Bogotá, the woman commanding soldiers like a colonel. Juan Bautista Boussingault met Manuelita after the tremendous Peruvian campaigns and the difficult journeys she had made following the footsteps of Bolívar. Boussingault was a youth of twenty-six and even worse: French. Gossip, courtier, lively spirit. He left such moving descriptions of Manuelita that today they produce among historians the same whirlwind that the heroine's presence caused among the ladies of her own time. It could be argued that Boussingault was a sage and no one would deny it, but what is evident, and all assert it, is that in the matter of women he was an expert. The picture he draws of Manuelita in Bogotá serves as much to enlighten us about him as about her: "She did not confess her age. When I knew her, she looked about twenty-nine or thirty; she was in all the splendor of her irregular beauty: a pretty woman, a bit fat, dark eyes, indecisive glance, peaches and cream complexion, black hair. . . . At times a great lady, at times a *napanga.* She danced a minuet or the *cachucha* with equal grace. She possessed a secret charm to make herself adored . . . she smoked gracefully. . . . Her hands were the most beautiful in the world."

For Bolívar, Manuelita was not only the woman with the most beautiful hands in the world, of magnetic amorous attraction; she was also the republican, fierce, astute, implacable, who dressed as a soldier and threatened with the lance. She was the general's *generala.* When Bolívar arrived in Quito, he touched the equatorial line of his historic world. To the north, he had left that half of the map free; the other half, to the south, remained. He would have to dispute with San Martín in Guayaquil to know whose was that glory. And Manuelita, for this, was the fortune-teller who never missed. She knew of the south's intimidations all that women can know who conspire, who are impassioned by a cause, who embrace an idea. The good Mr. Thorne, merchant, businessman, realist, must have contributed not a little to make Manuelita do the opposite, to turn more bellicose, more independent, more warlike. When San Martín entered Lima, he found a city tepid and cautious in its males, ardent and decided in its women. He then created the *Orden del Sol* and rewarded 112 women, tying the sash and presenting the medal himself. In this selection, San Martín made equally haughty countesses and marquises and Manuelita Sáenz, the *Quiteña;* Rosita Campusano, the *Guayaquileña.* In their case, only patriotic women counted. Rosita Campusano was San Martín's Lima peccadillo. Manuelita was to be Rosita's friend . . . who would believe it!

Bolívar was jealous of his glory. Manuelita, zealous of Bolívar's glory. From the instant Manuelita incorporates herself into the Liberator's military train, she is the watchman who sees everything, the agitator who awakes all, she who watches over his sleep, she who follows in his footsteps, she who does not permit anyone to cast the slightest shadow upon him. She complains to him: "I am"–she tells him–"very wild and sick; it is certain that long absences kill love and increase grand passions. . . . General Sandes arrived and did not bring me anything from you. Does it cost you that much to write me? If you have to do violence to yourself, don't do anything. I leave the 1st of December, and I go because you call me, but later don't tell me to return to Quito, I'd rather die than pass for shameless. Manuela." Bolívar, in turn, is not short: "You want to see me, at least with the eyes. I always want to see you and resee you and touch you and feel you and savor you and unite you to me by all contacts. I bet you don't love as much as I do? Well, this is the purest and most cordial truth. Learn to love, and don't run off even with God himself. . . ."

Bolívar and Manuelita went to the war in Peru. The Liberator arrived in Lima first, with Manuelita arriving immediately thereafter. Soon she was in the office, received letters and arranged them, talked with the officers, with the republicans. The ladies who had seen her not too long before as Mrs. Thorne now found in the frantic lover a savage female warrior. The Liberator left for the great campaign in the icy *puna*. "I left Lima," Bolívar wrote to Santander, "to interpose myself between Riva Agüero and the 'goths' of Jauja, because this villain, desperate to triumph, was trying to turn over his homeland to the enemy in order to obtain more profit, though less luster." Manuelita remained in Lima, transformed into a cabinet minister, or better: a *guerrillera* who, from afar, jealously guarded her master. In December, 1823, Bolívar described the landscape to Santander, from Pellasca: "In the middle of the Andes, breathing a foul air they call *soroche,* above the snows and at the side of the vicuñas, I write you this letter which will be frozen if a condor doesn't carry it away and heat it with the sun. . . . The goths are terrible. . . . We shall take up positions in the summits of the Andes." Two days later, he wrote to Torre Tagle: "You now have Peru in internal peace; the addicts of Riva Agüero have disappeared. Immediately, Juan José Santana wrote to Manuela: "I wish to be the first to give you this news: Riva Agüero's faction is now destroyed! We shall soon be in Lima!"

Bolívar could not return to Lima immediately; the campaign had destroyed him. They had to take him to Pativilca, half-dead. There he began to live again. Santana wrote to Manuela: "He is now in a convalescent state. Nevertheless, our journey to Lima will not be so soon. . . . Here we are like a spirit carried off by the devil, dead from heat, from annoyance, and bored. . . ." It was during those days that Bolívar wrote a fantastic letter to his marvelous teacher, the crazy Don Simón Rodríguez. Two weeks passed. In Lima the royalists celebrated the news that Bolívar was dying. Callao rebelled, and its people entered Lima. Among the first on the list of those to be jailed was Manuela. She astutely smelled danger and did not let herself be seized. She packed Bolívar's archives in boxes at full speed, dressed like a soldier, and left in search of her master. Bolívar wrote to Santander: "This world is crumbling." Bolívar wrote to Mariano Necochea: "Callao is lost. Lima is going to be lost. The ships are under enemy batteries. The troops, miserable. . . ." But Bolívar was Bolívar. During those days, Don Joaquín Mosquera arrived to visit him. "I found him," Don Joaquín wrote, "now without the risk of dying from the fever [*tabardillo*] which had passed its crisis, but so frail and emaciated that his appearance caused me very severe pain. He was seated on a poor leather chair, leaning against the wall of a tiny garden, his head bound in a white handkerchief; his pants permitted me to see his bony knees; his legs, thin; his voice, hollow and weak; and his countenance, cadaverous. 'And what do you plan to do now?' I asked. Then, enlivening those hollow eyes and with decisive tone, he answered: 'Triumph! Triumph!' "

And so it was. Improbable as it appears, Pativilca was the waiting room of Junín. To arrive at Junín, Bolívar scaled the Andes, passed once again through that landscape of frost and desolation. Manuelita followed at a distance. She journeyed three hundred kilometers through that inferno of cold where the frost burns. They spent a night together in Huaraz. Then, Bolívar continued ahead. Manuelita, alone, was a Red Cross division. On nearing the plains of Junín, Bolívar told the soldiers some incomprehensible things that drove them mad with the urge to fight. He said to them: "Peru and all America expect from you peace, the child of victory, and even liberal Europe regards you with admiration, because the freedom of the New World is the hope of the universe. . . ." Bolívar was like that: he spoke directly in bronze. The battle came and victory. "The avenging hand of the Incas" was raised. It was the beginning of the liberation of Peru. A fierce joy at the love of victory illuminated Manuela's face. After the victory of Junín came Ayacucho. And it was the freedom of America. Exactly what Bolívar had told the soldiers.

What follows has only a bitter flavor today. When Bolívar received the news of Ayacucho from the lips of Captain Alarcón, who erupted with the cry of Victory! Victory! Victory! in his office, he must have felt, together with the infinite joy of seeing his liberating mission fulfilled, the cruel impression that he was beginning his harsh journey, without hope, of organizing the republics. And concerning this mattter, his doubts were abysmal. In New Granada, Santander was defending civil democracy, the dominion of a representative constitution. He was the man of law, as Bolívar said. Bolívar's friends, his comrades-in-arms, were for military predominance; they wanted a Bolívar omnipotent and theirs, repudiating the idea of congresses. Venezuela was not submitting to the government of New Granada, desiring its own life. Páez was surging up as the great *caudillo* with the legend of the *Queseras del Medio,* which had converted him into the centaur of the Llanos. Could Bolívar remain in Lima on the margin of everything? Gaze from a distance at the bonfire being made of *Gran Colombia?* Live in the villa of La Magdalena, making love to Manuelita? Neither would she permit it! The Liberator, duty-bound, embarked for Guayaquil, more melancholy than resolved. And he began to walk. Toward Bogotá. Toward chance. Manuela saw him leave and did not tell him, "Good-bye," only, "I'll catch up with you very soon." She was like a woman on guard.

3

1827. It is three years after Ayacucho, and the sordid struggle of men has followed the epic poem's faint dawn. Something more. The impassioned struggle of ideas. America was more romantic than Europe. The Liberator arrived in Bogotá bearing the ideas of the constitution he had written for Bolivia—a reactionary constitution, daughter of skepticism, having a life President, aristocratic Senate, discriminatory voting. Bogotá, permeated with the civil spirit of Santander, gave him a reception somewhere between hostile and pedagogic, with floral arches bearing this provocative legend: "Long Live the Constitution!" It was, of course, Santander's civil constitution, not Bolívar's. A month before entering Bogotá, Bolívar had written to Santander from Pasto: ". . . all the peoples of the South have proclaimed me dictator, and have requested the Bolivarian constitution after the dictatorship. I do not think that this constitution is worth a great deal, but I do imagine that it has more solidity than that of Colombia. Those who criticize it are miserable ones who cannot rise to the stature of a legislator; I am not one, but I have more experience and more inspirations than those pygmies. . . . The dictatorship in its omnipotence will fuse all parties and make them enter into silence. Afterward, the national will should be consulted to ascertain what it wishes . . . dictatorship has been my constant authority. . . . This magistracy is republican; it has saved Rome, Colombia, and Peru. Let us suppose that a congress were to meet in January. What would it do? Nothing more than exasperate the existing parties. A congress has never saved a republic."

Also on the road from Quito to Bogotá, Bolívar had written to Manuelita: "My enchanting Manuela: Your letter of the 12th of September has charmed me: all is love in you. I, too, am possessed by this ardent fever that devours us like two children. I, old, suffer the malady that I should already have forgotten. You alone have me in this state. You ask me to tell you that I do not love [*querer*] anyone. Oh, no: *I love* [amar] *no one, I shall love no one.* The altar which you inhabit shall not be profaned by another idol or another image, even of God himself. You have made me a worshiper of beautiful humanity or of Manuela. Believe me: I love you and shall love you alone and no more. Don't kill yourself. Live for me and for you: live to console the unhappy and your lover who sighs *to see you.* I am so tired of the journey and of all the complaints of your land that I don't have time to write you huge letters in tiny handwriting as you wish. But in recompense, if I am not praying, I am eternally meditating all day and the entire night upon your graces and how much I love you, upon my return and what you will do and what I shall do when we see each other again. I can't write anymore with my hand. *I don't know how to write.*"

It was not the time, with everything, for love. More than with the civil ideas of Bogotá, Bolívar was preoccupied with the news of the insurrection in Venezuela, and without delaying in the capital, he organized his journey to Caracas. One thing gave him a sense of security: Peru's fidelity to the constitution of Bolivia. The mails went more slowly than Bolívar. He arrived in Caracas, and the letters reaching him from Peru were two and three months delayed. In February, 1827, he wrote to Fernández Madrid, telling him: "The republics of Peru and Bolivia are tranquil, and according to the latest news I have had from those countries, everything there marches in order and toward tranquillity. Both peoples have adopted the constitution which was presented to them. . . ." Bolívar did not know that a month before, Lima had risen up against him, that Manuelita had been captured and deposited in the Convent of the Nazarenas, that Manuelita, disguised as a soldier, had escaped in order to raise the spirits of her people, that she had been caught once more and plucked from Peru within twenty-four hours and embarked for Guayaquil. While Manuelita was in the Convent of the Nazarenas, it was converted into the counterrevolution's general headquarters; officers entered, Manuela's mail left; the authorities said she was a scurrilous shrew. In reality, never had she lighted a like blaze in a Lima convent.

The journey from Lima to Guayaquil was not a peaceful one for Manuelita. On the ship, she fought with one of the bravest soldiers of the independence, General Córdoba, the man who determined the triumph of Ayacucho with the order the infantry made sweeping: "Soldiers, arms at the ready, pace of victors!" The handsome General Córdoba must have appeared little Bolivarian to Manuelita; Córdoba must have thought that part of Lima's animosity toward Bolívar's generals was one consequence of Manuela's excesses. As they both were soldiers, it took them little time to come to blows.

In Guayaquil, things were no better than in Lima. Manuela was forced to leave on horseback for Quito. From Bogotá, from Caracas, the news arrived with hopeless slowness. She was a wild beast chained in idleness. Or in despair. She did not receive replies from her lover. Finally, she received a letter: "The snows of my years were revived by your kindnesses and graces. Your love gives life which is expiring. I cannot be without you, I cannot voluntarily deprive myself of my Manuela. I haven't as much strength as you not to see you: Even immense distance is hardly enough. I see you even though far from me. Come, come, come soon. Yours in soul. . . ."

Manuelita rode horseback. She was accompanied by Colonel de Marquet and two slaves, two faithful Negroes who never abandoned her: Jonatás and Nathan. Manuelita rode like a soldier, rode for a month and nine days. What it took, at a good pace, to go from Quito to Bogotá.

4

On February 6, 1827, Bolívar wrote Santander a long letter from Caracas, ending with these words: "They write from Bogotá that I don't have two friends in that capital. Infallible proof that, at least, they are working against me, and I can say with frankness that this makes me happy, because it would cost me nothing to rid myself of Colombia." These were the last words in Bolívar's life ever to carry a friendly message to Santander. A short time later, Bolívar learned about Lima and attributed it to Santander. He then ordered Santander: "Do not ever write me again." And they never again corresponded. In a letter to Páez, Bolívar told him: "My ideas regarding Bogotá and what I've told you many times about Santander have finally been realized. The treachery and evil of this man have gone to such an extreme that he has swelled the discord between Venezuelans and Granadians in the Colombian Army of Peru." In Manuelita's jealous and fighting soul, this enmity was transformed into an uncontainable passion. Once arrived in Bogotá, she mounted guard on the palace. That someone would conspire against her hero's glory was to force her to ride with fixed lance. If Santander had fallen into her hands, she would have shot him. She writes Bolívar: what Santander has done "is enough to make us shoot him. Please God that all these malevolent men who call themselves Santander, Padilla, Páez may die. . . . I am always expecting something from the latter, Páez. The day these vile men die will be a great day for Colombia, they and others who are sacrificing you with their evil acts to make you their victim, one day or another. This is the most humane thought, that ten die in order to save millions."

Without an appetite for palace living, Bolívar resided in a villa on the outskirts of Bogotá—something like La Magdalena in Lima—where only his intimates or illustrious visitors went. When Bolívar was out, Manuelita remained as the villa's mistress and señora. The site was stirring and rustic, at the foot of the two hills, Monserrate and Guadalupe, with their white churches at the summit. The villa, low, with galleries extending outward, pleased the officers who walked around, smoking and clinking their spurs. In a small garden, enclosed by large bricks laid like stone, wild and cultivated roses, violets and verbena, and heliotrope sent up a perfume of first love. Pines, cherry trees, myrtles, oaks formed a small forest that would have invited a woman less active than Manuelita to rest. In the middle of the forest could be heard the stream that filled the reservoir, where Bolívar and Manuela took delicious baths in water ice cold. At those times a bath like that and a glass of wine were a pleasure, an invitation to ride horseback, to race across the dusty roads of the Sabana.

One afternoon, when the villa looked like an army camp and Bolívar was away, Manuelita got up a mock tribunal to make Santander the target of all her wrath. A council of war was formed, carnival-style, in which the gestures of the orators took on phantasmagoric reflections in the light of the bonfires, where delicious roasts were being prepared. People had drunk as if at a feast, and the whole process ended with a decree for the firing-squad execution of the "man of law." A general's uniform was stuffed with straw and wool to make a plump doll. A face was made with rags, which they adorned with moustaches of soot. Its hands were gloves stuffed with grass. The officers in Manuelita's retinue followed these deviltries with guffaws and barracks words. The *Quiteña's* eyes flashed sparks in the candlelight. The order to fire was not given by a general; the *generala* gave it. Manuelita enjoyed the proceedings like a madwoman. Except that all those present did not echo her enjoyment. And one, at least, clearly expressed his disgust, the hero of Ayacucho, General José María Córdoba.

Shortly thereafter, Bolívar wrote a letter of reply to Córdoba, in which he told him: "[*Sabe usted que yo lo conozco a usted por lo que no puedo sentirme con lo que usted me dice.*] You know that I know you by what I am unable to feel at what you tell me. Certainly I know, more than anyone, the insanities committed by my friends. By this letter you will see that I don't humor them. I am thinking of suspending the commandant of 'Granaderos' and sending him away from the corps to serve someone else. He alone is guilty. As for the rest of it, he has a legal excuse, I mean to say, that it is not a public crime, but, yes, an eminently stupid and miserable one. . . . Regarding the amiable madwoman, what do you want me to tell you? You know her from past times. I have tried to leave her, but nothing can be achieved against resistance like hers; nevertheless, as soon as this event passes, I am thinking of making the most determined effort to make her go away to her own country or wherever she likes. . . . You, my dear Córdoba, don't have to tell me anything I don't already know, as much concerning the unfortunate event of these crazy ones as respecting the proof of friendship which you give me. I am not weak and don't fear to be told the truth. You are more than right, you are a thousand and one times right, and, therefore, I must be grateful for the warning which must have cost you a great deal to give me, more through delicacy than through fear of bothering me. . . . Tear up this letter as I don't want this miserable document of misery and foolishness to remain in existence. . . ."

5

1828 was a fatal year for Bolívar. The year of the Convention of Ocaña, and the year of the conspiracy. Bolívar's party lost the elections in the capital for the convention. At the head of those elected was Santander, and following were the great men of his persuasion: Azuero, Soto, Gómez. . . . Sadly, the Liberator said that he expected nothing of the convention, that from it would stem civil war. He went to Bucaramanga to follow its results. From the first moment, it could be seen that opinion was against the system which Bolívar praised for Bolivia. Daily he received in the large old house, where he shared the hours of waiting with his aides-de-camp, letters which only made more precise the outlines of the split. Bolívar rode horseback to Girón or Piedecuesta, read Homer and Voltaire, nervously rocked in his hammock. From Bogotá notes reached him from Manuelita. One day he answered her: "I'm going to Bogotá. Now I am not going to Venezuela. Neither do I think I'll pass through Cartagena, and probably we shall see each other very soon. How are you? Don't you like this? Well, friend, this is the way I am who loves you with all my soul." Two months later the Liberator took the road for Bogotá, traveling the route of his setting sun. On reaching Socorro, he was informed of a movement in Bogotá. A junta of notables had been formed to disavow the Convention of Ocaña and had named him dictator. The same day he was informed from Ocaña that the twenty delegates of his party had abandoned the convention, leaving it without a quorum. He spurred his horse and hurried his journey, riding toward dictatorship. He was received by the notables, accepted the dictatorship, and by decree removed Santander from the vice-presidency. He tried to take advantage of the circumstances to issue a provisional constitution, also by decree, "in order to establish," he wrote Páez, "a perpetual system, and not a transitory one like dictatorship." The *civiles* of Bogotá rushed into conspiracy. In less than a month, violence flared.

Now Bolívar lived in the palace, and Manuelita had her rooms half a block away. Boussingault had taken charge of making a portrait of Manuelita, a pastel in the French style. "Manuelita was always conspicuous; in the morning she wore a negligee which did not lack attractiveness. Her arms bare, without care at showing them. She spoke little, smoked gracefully; her aspect was modest. By day, she was in the habit of going out dressed as an officer. At night, she metamorphosed, perhaps under the influence of a few glasses of port. She undoubtedly wore rouge. She dressed her hair artistically. She showed great impetuousness; she was gay, without formal politeness, and at times used slightly bold expressions. Imprudent to an excess, she committed truly reprehensible acts just for the pleasure of doing them. One day, riding through the streets of Bogotá, she saw at a distance an infantry soldier carrying an envelope containing the password stuck in the tip of his gun. To fling herself at a gallop at the poor wretch and take the password from him were a matter of an instant. The soldier fired without wounding her, and she immediately turned around and gave him back the envelope. She loved animals, among them an unbearable bear, who had the privilege of running around the whole house. One morning I arrived to visit Manuelita: as she had not yet arisen, I was forced to go into her bedroom. There I saw a frightening scene. The bear was on top of her, and it had its paws on her breasts. On seeing me enter, Manuelita said to me calmly: 'Don Juan, go to the kitchen, bring a cup of milk, and put it at the foot of the bed: this bear of the devil doesn't want to leave me alone.' I brought the milk. The animal slowly descended from on top of its victim. 'You see,' Manuelita said, showing me her breast, 'I haven't any wound.' One night I went to her house. Manuelita had just finished getting up from the table and received me in her little salon. In the conversation she praised the *Quiteñas*' skill at all kinds of embroidery and to prove it wished to show me an artistically made chemise. Without the least embarrassment and in the most natural way, she caught the chemise she was wearing by its bottom edge and raised it so that I could examine the truly notable work of her female friends. I saw, as is natural, something more than just the embroideries. 'Look, Don Juan, how they are made. *[Hechas al torno]*' 'Done to a turn,' I replied, alluding to her legs. . . ."

On September 25 there was a splendid moon. The streets, paved, wet, brilliant. Downtown, the water pipe which orchestrated with its music the croaking of the frogs. Five blocks from the palace, in the Santa Bárbara quarter, the house of the poet Luis Vargas Tejada. The conspirators were arriving. No one was spying on them, though it was in the air that an attempt against Bolívar's life was inevitable. There were always on those solitary streets types like these, who, muffled in Spanish capes, were going to play cards. Agustín Horment was a blond Frenchman who taught languages and mathematics to Córdoba and who had in his head stories and novels of the French Revolution. Pedro Carjuo, a Venezuelan, was a primitive, elemental bully; he entered the conspiracy through a simple taste for adventure. The Granadians were more men of letters than of arms; they did not know how to fire a blunderbuss or stab with a knife, but they were very much in on the plan to seize the Liberator, impassioned as they were by the law, by Santander's spirit. All later were great patricians: Vicente Azuero, Florentino González, Mariano Ospina. Vargas Tejada, the owner of the house, was also there. He bested the others in talent and madness; he was lyric passion, the man of the theater whose heroic or bantering comedies moved Santa Fe de Bogotá or provided its enjoyment, a romantic poet, pale and spirited. The plan was discussed, and while they waited for the hour of departure to arrive, Vargas Tejada declaimed the famous octave:

> *Si a* BOLÍVAR *la letra con que empieza*
> *y aquella con que acaba le quitamos*
> OLIVA, *de paz simbolo, hallamos*
> *Esto quiere decir que la cabeza*
> *del tirano, y los pies, cortar debemos*
> *si una perfecta paz apetecemos.*

> If from BOLÍVAR the letter with which it begins
> and that with which it ends we take
> OLIVA, of peace, a symbol, we find.
> This is to say that the head
> of the tyrant, and the feet, cut off
> we must if a perfect peace we crave.

The nights in Santa Fe de Bogotá were like glass when the sky was clear, and on September 25 the full moon made the whitewashed houses even whiter, the pines even blacker. The conspirators did not have to take a lantern; hearing alone was sufficient to permit them to move like shadows. They passed the San Agustín bridge. Noisy the river, which at that time was a real river, breaking its water against the rocks. They left behind the Augustine monastery and its gardens. The silhouettes of the arboloco trees and the tops of the cherries stood out from the grounds of great houses. They went up the street leading to the Jesuit monastery. On turning the corner—now it was a matter of 100 yards—they quickened their steps and gripped the handles of their daggers. The guard was scarce. In reality, it sufficed to knock down a few soldiers, take possession of the gate, and the rest was a question of knowing how to conduct themselves. Tie him up, a few thought; arrest him, the others; someone, perhaps, kill him. Carujo, the soldier, was at the head of the conspirators with other soldiers; his role was to break into the front gate. The sentries stopped them with their cries of "Halt!" They did not say it twice; blows and stabs felled them in place. The conspirators were now in possession of the entrance hall. They passed through the inner gate; the palace was theirs. The wet patio seemed like crystal in the moonlight. The cries of victory resounded: "Death to Bolívar! Down with the tyrant! Long live liberty!" The servants were awakened; the dogs barked furiously. Bolívar had his bedroom on the upper floor in the middle of the palace. The conspirators leaped up the wide stone staircase. A young officer, Andrés Ibarra, who in great haste had put on his military jacket, opposes the invaders fiercely. They wound him and he wheels, dripping blood. Carujo kills Colonel William Ferguson with a pistol. The servants shouted for help, and the conspirators answered them with the same cries against the tyrant, for liberty. In five minutes, the palace, which had a patio and corridors like a convent, became a battlefield. One could say that the assailants amused themselves distributing blows and knife wounds, as if they were not in a hurry to reach the Liberator's bedroom. After all, he could now consider himself their prisoner. Finally, they arrived at his bedroom and announced themselves by banging loudly on the door. The door was not opened to them immediately. They banged again and tried to force the leaves of the door, shouting, "Give yourself up! Long live liberty!" The door was opened; Manuelita opened it. She was alone. She detained them imperiously. "What do you want?" "We are looking for Bolívar." "He's not here; look for yourselves!"

The bedroom was small, the furniture sparse. "Where is he?" "Sleeping." "Take us to where he is." "Yes, but on the condition that you don't kill him." "We promise." "Follow me." Manuela quickly arranged her dress, passed her hand through her hair. She wished to go out into the corridors like a lady. But neither did she show the will to delay. They walked through the corridors, climbed, descended. "I thought he was here," "He will be there," "I left him here," "Nevertheless, we shall see. . . ." until they returned to their point of departure. Then, with a smile of triumph she opened the window and told them, the sarcasm in her face shattering them, "He left through here, don't be idiots!" She burst out laughing. "Now, if you feel like it, kill me." The most barbarous advanced, threw her to the floor. "Kill me, cowards," she screamed at them. "Kill a woman."

Manuelita writes: "The 25th at 6 the Liberator sent for me. I answered that I had a pain in my face; he sent another message saying that my illness was less grave than his. . . . When I entered he was in a lukewarm bath; he told me that there was going to be a revolution. . . . He made me read to him during his bath . . . he slept deeply. . . . It would have been about 12 at night when the dogs barked a great deal. . . . Some strange noise could be heard which must have been the clash with the sentries but without firearms. . . . I awakened the Liberator and the first thing he did was take up his sword and a pistol and try to open the door. I stopped him and made him get dressed which he did with great serenity and promptness. He said to me bravo *baya [sic]* well now I am dressed, and what do we do now? . . . Once again he wished to open the door and I detained him. Then it occurred to me what I had heard the general say one day. Didn't you tell Don Pepe Paris that this window was very good for a critical moment like this? You speak well he told me and went to the window, I impeded his flinging himself out of it because people were passing and he did it when there weren't any people and because they were already forcing the door. . . ."

Boussingault recounts that Manuelita told him how she had induced Bolívar to leap through the window and flee: "Imagine, he wanted to defend himself. My God! How amusing: in his nightshirt and sword in hand! Don Quixote in person! If I didn't force him to go through the window, they kill him *[sic.]*"

Faster than the Liberator, the conspirators raced to hide. They disguised their flight with cries of "The tyrant is dead! Long live liberty!" In reality, nothing remained for them but the freedom of flight. At daybreak, the notes of reveille indicated that the revolution was over and Bolívar once again in the palace. Manuelita writes:

"In order not to see Ibarra being treated I went as far as the plaza and there I found the Liberator, on horseback, talking with Santander and Padilla, in the midst of many troops shouting long live the Liberator. When I returned to the house I said to myself: you are the *libertadora* of the *Libertador.*"

6

Manuelita was hardly thirty and had the energy and vitality of twenty-five. She can perform deviltries. She maintains a spirit of coquetry and of struggle. They say that Dr. Chayne has fallen in love with her. She shows the calves of her legs to Boussingault with relish, she organizes a party for the Salto de Tequendama in which after a spectacular fall from a horse—she went dressed as an officer, with false moustaches—then, in full recovery of her feminine charms, she struggles at the edge of the abyss with Dr. Chayne and Boussingault at such risk that it lacks little for the spree to end in the depths of death for the three. One day she is told that they are setting up fireworks in the Plaza Major and that the man in charge will make a caricature of Bolívar appear in colored lights. She at once takes up her lance, mounts a horse, and—a female Quixote—runs her horse wild, attacks the fireworks display, and dashes it to the ground.

Bolívar is forty-five years old and looks sixty. The *libertadora* has saved a liberator who now travels under leaden skies toward his funeral hearse. His shining glory is a torch moving among shadows. The narrow sheath of his body often resounds with the cough tearing out his lungs. All the free world crumbles in his hands. The southern provinces rise up against him; Peru becomes an openly hostile country. He is unloved in New Granada, and from Venezuela they announce they do not wish to see him again. When he mounts his horse, and moves in this death's chess game in leaps of the devil, the flush in his face of copper makes him seem a phantom of madness.

In the villa on the outskirts of Bogotá, Manuelita and "her" Liberator, under pines and cherry trees, move over the naked earth with deafening steps. The cold sun, which leaps among the branches like butterflies of old gold, has the fire of distant glory, of future glory, of the marvelous past when Bolívar loosed his armies, crying in clarion tones: "Charge, charge, we gallop under forests of laurel!" What delicious support for walking through these gardens of sadness was the amorous madwoman's strong arm. They encouraged each other with false offensives. Manuelita talked of hanging Santander, of shooting the conspirators, of crushing the rebels. Bolívar ordered the sergeants to keep his horse ready, his pistols clean, his uniform in order. When he returned to the villa, he dictated letters, many letters, as he did always throughout a life in which he fought as much with the pen as with the sword. On September 25, 1828, Bolívar escapes from the conspiracy; on September 18, 1830, he dies. Between these two dates, Bolívar reflects upon all the melancholy drama.

He wrote his friends:

"Bogotá, October 16, 1828.–The conspiracy is being examined and punished. Fourteen have been executed; among them, General Padilla and Colonel Guerra have been hanged, and more than twenty persons have been confined. . . . Regarding General Santander, I still can't tell you what may result. . . . At the very least, he will be exiled."

"October 23.–At this moment I have received news from Popayán in which they tell me that a Colonel Obando has risen up in the towns of Patía, proclaiming the constitution of Cúcuta. I have to send some reinforcements to pacify Popayán and punish those rebels. I also fear that the Peruvians will take advantage of the occasion to attack our army of the south."

"October 29.–I am thinking of forming a reserve army against Peru."

"October 30.–La Mar has issued a furious proclamation aginst me. I have given command of the south to General Sucre with power to make war or peace and whatever else he finds expedient. Our troops amount to 6,000 veterans capable of resisting Peru."

"February 5, 1829 (from Popayán).–When the people conferred extraordinary powers upon me the republic was not in the horrible situation in which it finds itself now, and yet they recognized that almost absolute power was necessary. . . ."

"June 10 (from Riobamba).–They have called me a tyrant and the sons of our capital have tried to punish me as such. In addition, no one likes me in New Granada and almost all its army officers detest me. . . ."

"August 15 (from Guayaquil).–It seems that I now see unleashed all the inferno of the abominations against me. . . ."

"September 28 (from Babahoyo).–Córdoba is going around like a missionary of division and rebellion. Wherever he passes he leaves everyone scandalized. . . . I am thinking of sending Silva and some corps to the Cauca. I shall go to those infernal places soon, where there is nothing but hate on all sides. . . . I have no one to write for me. I am too lazy to carry on my correspondence in my own hand; neither do I know how to and I tire."

"December 6 (from Popayán).—I have received the letter from you [Dr. de Alamo] about the mines. Abandon my defense and let my enemy and the judge seize my property. I know them. Infamous goth! Don't do anything more in this matter. I shall die as I was born: naked. You have money and will give me something to eat when I don't have anything. I can't go on against the opprobrium this damned cause of the fatherland causes me [*sic*]."

"December 27 (from Buga).—I became very irritated at the lampoons and lewdnesses published in Caracas against my reputation, slandering me with thoughts unworthy of my glory and of a man who bears the title *war to tyrants,* which is the same as *Liberator*. . . . I very much wish to go to Caracas to see what has been decided about my Aroa mines; I don't wish to lose them, ending up in the street an indigent and beggar, after having had enough to eat all my life. Besides, I don't know what I'll use to leave this country the day it becomes necessary. . . ."

"March 8, 1830 (from Fucha).—I am resolved to leave Colombia, to die of sadness and of misery in foreign countries. Ay! My grief cannot be measured, because slander is suffocating me like those serpents of Laocoön."

"May 11 (from Guaduas).—I have finally left the presidency and Bogotá, finding myself now on the way to Cartagena, with the intention of leaving Colombia and living where I can; but since it is not easy to maintain oneself in Europe with little money, when there will be many of the most distinguished subjects of that country *[sic]* who will wish to force me to enter the society of the upper class, and after all I have been the first magistrate of three republics, it will seem indecent that I am going to exist like a *miserable*. . . ."

"May 11 (from Guaduas, to Manuelita).—My love: I am glad to tell you that I am very well and filled with pain at your grief and mine at our separation. Love of mine: I love you very much, but I shall love you more if you will now have more than ever great judgment. Be careful in what you do; if not, you will ruin us both, ruining yourself. I am always your most faithful lover. Bolívar."

7

Seven months later, as Bolívar already lay dying in the villa of San Pedro Alejandrino, in Santa Marta, the officers around him hardly let him breathe, blowing their tobacco smoke in his face. "Go smoke in the corridor," the sick man tells them. And one of the sarcastic officers: "Your Excellency was not bothered by smoke when the one smoking was Manuela. . . ." Amid the blue clouds of tobacco, the Liberator saw his *libertadora* smiling in his imagination, and said simply, "Ah, my Manuela. . . ." He died within a few days, after having said, "If my death contributes to the cessation of parties and the consolidation of the union, I shall go down tranquil to my grave. . . ."

The mails were delayed in arriving in Bogotá. Manuelita awaited news with anguish. Rumors that the Liberator had died were circulating. She mounted her horse and at a gallop descended the stone road which runs from the high plateau to the bottom of the valley where the Magdalena River flows. The hours were like centuries for her. When, now at the banks of the river, they were preparing the raft covered with a shade of palm and the formidable ebony oarsmen were readying themselves to grab the poles and row, row, mail arrived from Santa Marta. It brought a letter for Manuelita from Peru from Lacroix, announcing the death of the Liberator. Sobbing, Manuela once again mounted her horse and with soul rent returned to Bogotá.

With Bolívar dead, New Granada called upon its old President, General Santander, exiled in Europe, to assume charge again of the government. Manuelita awakened his old hatred. Her house became converted into the center of the opposition and conspiracy. She did not hide it. Dissimulation was not exactly her distinctive trait. The government did not think twice about it; Manuelita was deported to Cartagena. From Cartagena she went to Jamaica, as if retracing Bolívar's steps. In Jamaica she found protection precisely in Maxwell Hyslop, Bolívar's friend in the days in which from that same island he wrote the most famous of his political documents: the letter to an English citizen. But Manuelita's eyes returned to her homeland. To the Quito of her infancy, of her first gallant adventures, of her encounter with

Bolívar. After heaven, Quito, and in heaven a tiny rent through which to see Quito. . . . She wrote to President General Flores, her friend. A few months later, Manuelita disembarked in Guayaquil. She went toward Quito, on horseback. She got as far as the little town of Guaranda. Flores was no longer President, and the new government had her detained in Guaranda. Return to Guayaquil. Neither did they wish in Ecuador to let the adorable madwoman arm the powder magazine. Manuela protested, argued, struggled, but finally had to submit. She submitted in Bogotá; she was submitting now in Guayaquil. She had to leave for Peru by boat. For Lima? No. For a minuscule town, a forgotten town, Paita.

If diphtheria had not come, Manuelita would have died a rattan plant, of old age. She spent nineteen years in Paita, where now there was no one against whom to conspire. Sailors arrived, fishermen passed, and she . . . selling tobacco in her shop. Tobacco, sugar loaves, candles. . . . She was a legend cast up upon a lost coast by the tide of life. One day, Guiseppe Garibaldi arrived to see her. Garibaldi knew better than anyone what an American companion is. Another day, Don Ricardo Palma arrived, the foxy compounder of the Peruvian *tradiciones,* who stitched his stories together and made weavings of delicious tangles from them. Another day, a famous madman, who ended like Manuelita running a village store: Don Simón Rodríguez, the Liberator's teacher, the most active and fortunate disciple Rousseau had in the New World, he who led Bolívar to swear in Rome, on the Aventino, to the independence of America. Like Manuelita, Don Simón Rodríguez was out of circulation, and he set himself to selling candles, saying, "If I have not been able to illuminate these Americans with schools, at least I shall help them with candles to give themselves light."

One day she received the news that her husband, James Thorne, had died, murdered. He left a sum of money for Manuela; poor Manuela did not accept it. The only reason for her life was her memories. The major part of them she took to the grave; the flames burned them; they were lost with her letters. The brave Amazon, the violent *apasionada,* the astute fighter, saw the coming of tranquil old age, saw the arrival of quiet death, lighting a cigar when the night fell. A tiny button of red that appeared and disappeared in the shadows. Like her heart.

*The Later American Policy of George Canning**

By H. W. V. TEMPERLEY

But suspicion was everywhere.

Latin American *cognoscenti* have always felt a special reverence for George Canning, the British Foreign Secretary at the time of the enunciation of the Monroe Doctrine by the United States in 1823. Their views toward Canning have been similar to those of the United States toward Chatham, and for the same reason. They have instinctively felt that he was the one European statesman who understood and sympathized with them at the great crisis in their history. To understand something of the Latin American view of their diplomatic history, it is thus important to know something about Canning, especially his activities subsequent to the first pronouncement of the Monroe Doctrine. These were directed at defeating certain claims of the doctrine—namely, those which forbade future colonization of unexplored parts of America to European powers—and the principle which tended to make America a separate world from Europe.

Curiously, it was not until some eighty-five years after the enunciation of the Monroe Doctrine that the complexity of Canning's maneuvers and the forces which he had unleashed regarding the doctrine's early development began to be fully understood. This was largely due to the research of one man, H. W. V. Temperley, the British diplomatic historian who devoted many years of his life to a study of Canning. The results of these efforts were first made evident in the publication of *The Life of George Canning* in 1905, which was followed in 1906 by the publication of the article reprinted in this book. This in turn was amended and expanded in Chapters VI and VII of his book *The Foreign Policy of Canning,* published in 1925.

*Reprinted from *The American Historical Review,* Vol. XI, No. 4 (July, 1906).

Temperley points out that immediately after the Monroe Doctrine was pronounced, Canning went to work, via his representatives in Latin America, subverting the principle which tended to make America a separate world from Europe. He made clear the advantages that the newly created Latin American states would derive from friendly relations with Great Britain and established in the minds of the new leaders the debt they owed England for their independence. Although, despite this policy, the United States eventually established beyond dispute its claim to forbid further European colonization on the American continent, Canning's activities created a tradition among the chancelleries of Latin America to the effect that a European power had as much, if not more, to do with the achievement of their independence than the United States, and, thus, that Europe might at times serve as a convenient counterweight against the claims of the United States to speak for the whole hemisphere.

Harold William Vazeille Temperley was born at Cambridge, England, on April 20, 1879. His father was a gifted mathematician and a fellow and tutor of Queen's College. Temperley entered King's College in 1898, and from the time he won the Members' English Essay Prize at Cambridge in 1901 with his article on "The Office of Prime Minister Under the Hanoverian Dynasty," he was a passionate and devoted historian.

His work in the field of history may be broadly divided into two parts. The first period began in 1905, when at the age of twenty-six, he published his first book, *The Life of George Canning,* and continued until 1925, when his masterpiece, *The Foreign Policy of Canning* appeared. The second part began in 1925 and continued nearly to his death in 1939, during which time his main concern was editing, with G. P. Gooch, the *British Documents on the Origins of the War*. During all this time he continued his association with Peterhouse College at Cambridge—an association which began in 1905 with his appointment as lecturer and assistant tutor. In 1931 a chair of modern history was founded at Cambridge, and Temperley was chosen to fill it.

Temperley was always as passionate a traveler as he was a historian. In 1905 he paid the first of seventeen visits to Serbia. There were also trips to Hungary, Slovakia—then a backward and discontented province of Austria-Hungary—and other parts of the Near East. In 1908 he witnessed the Young Turks' revolution. In 1910 he was in Albania during the revolt against Turkey and was shot at by Albanian Comitadjis. He sampled Macedonia in 1911 and Dalmatia and Bosnia in 1912. Of all this backward area, Serbia attracted him the most, Bulgaria the least. He learned the Serbs' language and wrote a book about them. Temperley's knowledge of the Near East led to a brilliant nonacademic career during World War I. At the outbreak of hostilities he went to the Dardanelles and, on his return, was appointed head of the political sub-section of the intelligence division of the General Staff. In 1918 he served as acting military attaché to the Serbian Army with the rank of major (it was Temperley's boast that during the Salonika offensive he slept in fifty-nine different beds within seventy-six days). During the peace conference he served as a member of the military section of the British delegation and took part in the drawing of the frontier of Czechoslovakia. Temperley was present at the signing of the Versailles Treaty on June 28, 1919, an event he felt to be one of the most memorable of his life.

After the signing of the treaty he returned to the Near East and was in Belgrade from July to October, 1919. Also during this period he went to Montenegro; he was the first Allied officer to see Zog, the future King of Albania. His decorations included the Order of the British Empire, the Order of the Rumanian Crown, the Order of the Serbian White Eagle, the Order of Karageorge, and the Order of Polonia Restituta.

Temperley, as a professor of history at Cambridge University, set standards of scholarship, historical research, and research procedures that still influence British historians. His two great books, *The Foreign Policy of Canning* and *England and the Near East* are classics. The work is done with such thoroughness and perfection that it need not be done again. None of his contemporaries did more to encourage disinterested study and research than Temperley did. Of the historical imagination "without which no true history can exist," he wrote, "the power of discovering and forming a coherent theory out of apparently unrelated scraps of evidence, is one of the greatest an historian can possess. It is a faculty demanding insight of the highest kind, it is a kind of constructive detective work."

Temperley also felt keenly about the use of documents by research students. "It is very dangerous for him," he wrote, "to begin his research with printed selections of summaries of documents printed in books. Here is a pitfall of the largest size . . . they can hardly convey any meaning at all to the apprentice in research. What he wants to do is to learn the detail and routine of a foreign office or a policy or a cartulary or a set of accounts. When he has done this his imagination may be able to fill in the gaps which occur in selected material. It will not do so without training."

Coming from one of the editors of *British Documents on the Origins of the War,* as well as from a distinguished historian and biographer, this advice would appear significant.

P. K.

The figure of Canning has hardly yet emerged from the mists of contemporary eulogy or depreciation. The policy of the man, of whom Lord Acton said "that no English Foreign Secretary *equalled*

Canning," has not yet been fully understood even in its broad outlines. In America the greatness of the man is recognized, but the actual details of his policy are still somewhat obscure. His exact relations and concern with the Monroe doctrine are still not absolutely clear; and if this is the case with regard to that important phase of policy, it is still more the case with regard to his later diplomatic work. The old idea about Canning, expressed and championed by Stapleton, was that he was practically the author and suggester of the Monroe doctrine. The brilliant deductions of Mr. Reddaway, combined with the later research of Mr. W. C. Ford, have done much to define the limits and extent of his contribution to that memorable stroke of policy. It is at least clear that the Monroe doctrine had, in many important respects, been already formulated by American statesmen. Canning admitted the United States to be the leading power in America. Further, he rendered her an essential service in forcing Polignac, by a threat of war on October 9, 1823, to disclaim any idea of French aggression or influence to restore the revolted colonies to Spain. The publication of the presidential message on December 2, 1823, aided Canning materially in his European policy, because the European powers took that message in the sense of an unqualified support of British policy by the United States. But it is now known that Canning disapproved of that part of the presidential message which contained the first statement of the Monroe doctrine, when it announced that the continent of America would in future be closed to colonization by European powers. What is not known is how strong were his feelings on this point, and the means and policy by which he designed to render inoperative this part of the Monroe doctrine.

The object of the present article is to show that the later American policy of George Canning was intended to defeat certain claims and pretensions of the Monroe doctrine. These were the principle which forbade future colonization in America to European powers, and the principle which tended to make America a separate world from Europe. The motives which led Canning to recognize the Spanish-American republics, to send an envoy to the congress of Panama, and to take up a firm attitude on the Oregon question were all influenced and indeed conditioned by this idea. Adams, in formulating the presidential message, had denied the right of any European power to intervene in Spanish America, expressly on the ground of the withdrawal of Americans from European interests. Canning himself asserted the doctrine of non-intervention in the internal affairs of states, and was the great foe of the Holy Alliance, which desired so to intervene. His great fear was that the world would be divided into a league of worn-out governments in Europe and new and vigorous republics in America. He was resolved therefore that England should maintain active political relations between one continent and the other, and thereby be enabled to enact England's favorite political role of arbiter between conflicting claims or pretensions. Hence he was prepared to introduce America into Europe and Europe into America, to deny the exclusive pretensions of the Holy Alliance to intervene in Spanish America, and check the exclusive pretensions of Adams to place his continent in a water-tight compartment and reserve America for the Americans.

Canning's famous boast that he had "called the New World into existence to redress the balance of the Old" has often been misunderstood. A recent writer, Colonel E. M. Lloyd,[1] even professes to doubt whether this was really the cause of recognition. There can however be no question of this, for several memoranda on the subject exist.[2] In them are detailed the inconvenience of the French continuing to occupy Spain:

[1]*Transactions of the Royal Historical Society,* N. S., XVIII. 93 *et seqq.*

[2]Some historians, for example Colonel Lloyd and E. J. Stapleton (*Some Official Correspondence of George Canning,* 2 vols., 1887, I. 213–214), have been misled by the fact that there were three memoranda: (1) A memorandum, apparently written by Canning, but perhaps corrected by Liverpool, indorsed with his approval, and circulated to the Cabinet (about November 30); see Wellington's *Despatches,* N. S., II. 354–358, and Charles D. Yonge, *Life and Administration of Liverpool* (3 vols., 1868), III. 297–304. (2) A memorandum—supplementary and qualifying—circulated in consequence of information received from Granville. It is undated, but must be about December 1–6. (3) A minute, embodying the collective opinion of the Cabinet, laid before the King by Canning on December 14, 1824, together with No. 1. This is in A. G. Stapleton, *George Canning and His Times* (1859), 407–411.

No. 2 is the most interesting, characteristic, and important. It is the memorandum "which enabled us to carry Columbia too [as well as Mexico] at the Cabinet." Canning to Granville, December 17, 1824. It is to be found in Vansittart's papers at the British Museum, Ad. MSS. 31, 237, f. 258. So far as I know, its existence, as well as its substance, have hitherto been unknown and unsuspected. The memorandum is unsigned; the handwriting appears to be Vansittart's, possibly with two corrections by Canning. The general character of the opinions, agreeing precisely with Canning's letters of the time to Granville, leave no doubt that the real author or inspirer is Canning. Mr. F. L. Paxson, in his able work on *The Independence of the South-American Republics* (1903), is quite unaware of the existence of this document, and his knowledge of English records is large.

The great practical question however for us seems to be how, in the event of an actual incorporation of the resources of Spain with those of France such an accession to the power of France can best be counteracted. I have no hesitation in saying this must be by a separation of the resources of Spanish America from those of Spain: and it is (at least in this point of view) a fortunate circumstance that this state of things [*i. e.*, the virtual independence of Spanish America] has already taken place; and that we are in a situation to avail ourselves of it.

This is merely a prosaic version of the famous rhetorical phrase. Canning is looking to America to redress the inequalities of Europe. Though this is of some interest as indicating the real cause of Canning's recognition, our purpose is with the American, not the European aspect of that recognition. Canning goes on to advocate the recognition not only of Buenos Ayres, but of Colombia and Mexico, from two motives. One motive is that Colombia and Mexico have English capital sunk in mining and territorial concerns of a more permanent interest than "mere commercial speculations." Then comes a passage of immense interest and importance:

The other and perhaps still more powerful motive is my apprehension of the ambition and ascendancy of the U[nited] S[tates] of Am[erica]: It is obviously the policy of that Gov[ernmen]t to connect itself with all the powers of America in a general Transatlantic League, of which it would have the sole direction. I need only say how inconvenient such an ascendancy may be in time of peace, and how formidable in case of war.

I believe we now have the opportunity (but it may not last long) of opposing a powerful barrier to the influence of the U[nited] S[tates] by an amicable connection with Mexico,[3] which from its position must be either

[3]Italics my own. Compare with this passage the more unofficial and even more emphatic declaration in the letter of Canning to Frere, January 8, 1825, printed in Gabrielle Festing, *John Hookham Frere and His Friends* (1899), 267–268, and quoted in my *Life of Canning* (1905), 188: "The thing is done. . . . The Yankees will shout in triumph; but it is they who lose most by our decision. The great danger of the time—a danger which the policy of the European System would have fostered, was a division of the World into European and American, Republican and Monarchical; a league of worn-out Gov[ernmen]ts, on the one hand, and of youthful and st[i]rring Nations, with the U[nited] States at their head, on the other. *We* slip in between; and plant ourselves in Mexico. The Un[ited] States have gotten the start of us in vain; and we link once more America to Europe. Six months more—and the mischief would have been done." Almost every word of this is of immense importance.

subservient to or jealous of the U[nited] S[tates]. In point of population and resources it is at least equal to all the rest of the Spanish colonies; and may naturally expect to take the lead in its connections with the powers of Europe. I by no means think it at present necessary to go *beyond the mere relations of amity and commercial intercourse;* but if we hesitate much longer, and especially if our commercial treaty [July 23, 1824] with Buenos Ayres should not take effect, all the new states will be led to conclude that we regret their friendship upon principle, as of a dangerous and revolutionary character, and will be driven to throw themselves under the protection of the U[nited] S[tates], as the only means of security.

The importance of these words is equal to their emphasis, for they form the key to Canning's future American policy. He resumes that line of secret policy, which the younger Pitt had held in reserve, in order to checkmate any pretensions on the part of the United States. In 1790 Pitt had declared the right of England to Nootka Sound, as against Spain. In 1798, before the Spanish colonies revolted, he had coquetted with Miranda[4] the first of Spanish-American liberators. There can be no doubt that in the latter instance Pitt saw the advantage of keeping up an understanding with South America, in order to check any claims or aggressions of the United States. Canning now, and under different circumstances, resumed this policy.[5] He meant to indicate to the South-American states that their true friend was distant England, not the adjacent English-speaking land.

During his later years commercial disputes and disputes about the slave-trade (in the second of which, at least, Canning did his best to conciliate the United States) served to increase irritation, but would not alone have sufficed to change his attitude. Canning had shown toward the United States diplomatists a large-minded tolerance and a frankness very unusual in diplomacy. He had paid the United States the exquisite compliment of saying that England would model her neutrality during the war between France and Spain on the neutrality toward

[4]Paxson, *The Independence of the South-American Republics,* 47.

[5]This policy is indicated, but only indicated, in my *Life of Canning,* 188. At that time I had not sufficient proofs to state it more emphatically. "The recognition was certainly opportune, it bound closer the new States to England, it restrained the pretensions of the Yankees, and preserved Cuba to Spain. The Panama Congress . . . was overshadowed by Canning, and partly through his influence the alliance between the United States and the South American Republics was never formed."

England shown "in the presidency of Washington and secretaryship of Jefferson." Yet American statesmen certainly viewed Canning with undeserved suspicion.[6] The failure of his negotiations with Rush in the September of 1823, and the proclamation of the Monroe doctrine, in its original and limited form, in the presidential message of December 2, 1823, alarmed him and revealed to him these suspicions. Henceforward he took up an attitude of opposition, or rather of armed neutrality, prepared to uphold what he conceived to be the claims of England against those of the United States. He was firm and yet cautious and reasonable, and his plan seems to have been to detach the South-American states from alliance with or dependence on the United States.

It will be best to discuss this later aspect of his policy under three heads: first to describe the exact amount of intercourse and diplomatic relation Canning felt England should observe with a South-American state; secondly to indicate, by a description of his influence on the congress of Panama, his policy toward Spanish America as a whole and its relations to the United States; thirdly to show in what light he regarded the question of Oregon, as affecting other parts of his American policy.

In his instructions given on February 28, 1826,[7] to Lord Ponsonby, appointed minister plenipotentiary to Buenos Ayres, Canning defines his view of the normal relations and attitude of England toward Spanish-American states. Ponsonby is to communicate the "Anxiety of H[is] M[ajesty's] Gov[ernment] to restore and preserve peace among the new states of America; or the deep interest, which in the opinion of this Government, those states have, in avoiding to give room, by their differences with each other, for the interference of foreigners in their political concerns." An em-

[6]See W. C. Ford, "John Quincy Adams and the Monroe Doctrine," *American Historical Review,* VIII. 38, on Adams' suspicions, and see Rush to Adams, November 26, 1823, in *Proceedings of the Massachusetts Historical Society,* second series, XV. 430–433. Both thought Canning did not really desire to separate from the Holy Alliance, whereas that was the main object of all his European policy. I cannot understand Mr. Paxson's contention in his *Independence of the South-American Republics,* 250, that England's policy was "legitimist in its real sympathies to the end." In view of the facts now known about Canning's attack upon the Holy Alliance, this seems to me untenable.

[7]Public Record Office, Foreign Office, Buenos Ayres 12.

bittered quarrel was in progress between Brazil and Buenos Ayres over the possession of Montevideo. In a supplementary despatch of March 18, 1826, Canning discusses the claims of the two governments. Ponsonby is to divert "the Brazilian Minister from any attempt to change the practical question at issue [the possession of Montevideo] into one of abstract legitimate right." The Emperor of Brazil had apparently thought of recognizing the "unextinguished rights of Spain" to Montevideo, and thus depriving Buenos Ayres of any claims. Canning therefore instructs Ponsonby as follows: "Important as the question of Monte Video may be to the Brazilian Gov[ernmen]t, it is scarcely less important that the discussion of that question should not be conducted on such principles, or supported on their side by such arguments, as to array against the monarchy of Brazil the common feeling and common interests of all the Republican States of Spanish America." Canning then warns the Brazilian government of trying "too high" the patience of Bolivar, who is being incited to undertake a war against Brazil, "for the express purpose of overturning a Monarchy, which stands alone on the vast continent of America, and which is considered by those enamoured of democratical forms of Government, as essentially inconsistent with the secure existence of the American Republicks." Canning suggests that Buenos Ayres has the strongest claim to Montevideo and has moreover force to back it. But if Montevideo were transferred to Buenos Ayres, it would still be reasonable "to secure to Brazil an uninterrupted enjoyment of the navigation of the river Plate." The British government would guarantee the observance of such stipulations. And though "on the general principle of avoiding as much as possible engagements of this character" the British government would prefer to stand aside, it would give this guaranty, "if it were desired by both parties . . . rather than that the treaty should not be concluded." Great Britain, "while scrupulously neutral in conduct" during the war, "cannot fail to be in favour of that Belligerent, who shall have shewn the readiest disposition to bring that dispute to a friendly termination." A secret instruction accompanies the despatch, informing Ponsonby that in case of "any essential change . . . in the form of government his functions will be suspended," and that he is "studiously to keep aloof from all political intrigues and all contentions of party in B[ucnos] A[yres]."

Ponsonby's efforts at mediation and his attempts to interpose the friendly office of Great Britain between Brazil and Buenos Ayres ended in failure, and war began. Canning at once wrote (November 27, 1826[8]): "As to taking part with either side in the Contest your Lordship cannot too peremptorily repress any expectation of that nature." He then proceeds to explain the failure of the negotiations. "There is much of the Spanish character in the inhabitants of the Colonial Establishment of Spain; and there is nothing in the Spanish character more striking than its impatience of foreign advice, and its suspicion of gratuitous service." His original instructions had foreseen that the suggestion respecting Montevideo "was not unlikely to excite a jealousy of some design favourable to British interests. Such a jealousy has been openly inculcated by the publick press of the United States of North America, and no doubt secretly by their diplomatic Agents." He advises Ponsonby therefore "to let that matter drop entirely," unless Buenos Ayres itself should raise it. The best chance to suggest their doing so would be by "some slight manifestation of resentment at any such misconstruction of our motives." The last instruction of Canning on this point was to Ponsonby on February 21, 1827[9]: "Mr. Gordon [the new ambassador] will press the many considerations which render peace essential to the interests and safety of Brazil . . . with all the means in his power short of that degree of importunity, which after the repeated refusal, would become derogatory to the dignity of Great Britain."

Cobbett called Canning "Aeolus,"[10] in contempt of the policy by which Canning sought to make England the arbiter of the world, by balancing parties and reconciling opinions in Europe. The policy is here seen, as applied to the New World. Non-intervention is strictly laid down as a principle, and is departed from only in the instance of offering a guaranty respecting Montevideo, and in that instance only in case both contracting parties agreed to and wished for it. Some suspicion of the United States is shown, and a clear desire expressed to maintain the monarchical principle in Brazil, not indeed by force of arms but by moral influence, and by dissuading its monarchical government from acts which might irritate the republics. This was to

[8]Public Record Office, F. O. Buenos Ayres 13.

[9]*Ibid.*

[10]In reference of course to Canning's famous application of the quotation "Celsa sedet Aeolus arce" to his own policy.

prevent the world's being split into two parts, one consisting entirely of effete monarchies, the other exclusively of vigorous republics. If a moderate constitutional monarchy, in the shape of Brazil, were to remain firmly established on the republican continent, England would thus be enabled to be arbiter between the New World and the Old, and hold the balance between the conflicting principles of despotism and democracy.

Canning's policy toward individual American states has thus been illustrated; it remains to describe it from the point of view of the American continent as a whole, and especially in its relation to the United States. This is best to be discerned in the negotiations relative to the congress of Panama, and in the various questions which there came up for discussion. The congress was announced with the most extravagant boasts and rodomontades, fully worthy of the swaggering Don Guzmans and Don Alvarados of Spanish romance. Bolivar and his friends frequently spoke of it as one of the most important events of the world's history. Vidiaurre, one of the Peruvian representatives at the congress, communicated his generous emotions to the press in the following fashion.[11] Other representatives disclaimed the responsibility for his communication, but it represented—more or less—the general feeling of the time:

> An entire world is about to witness our labours. . . . From the first sovereign, to the last inhabitant of the Southern hemisphere nobody is indifferent to our task. This will probably be the last attempt to ascertain whether Mankind can be happy. Companions! the field of glory—cleared by Bolivar, San Martin, O'Higgins, Guadalupe, and many others superior to Hercules and Theseus, is before us. Our names are about to be written either in immortal praise or in eternal opprobrium. Let us raise ourselves above a thousand millions of inhabitants, and may a noble pride inspire us, likening us to God himself on that day, when He gave the first laws to the Universe.

These aspirants after the fame of Moses, and even of God Himself, may not have had their names written "in eternal opprobrium," but they are hardly entitled to "immortal praise."

The gigantic pretensions of the congress were only equaled by its

[11]Translation sent by Dawkins to Canning.

eventual failure. But it is at least interesting, in so far as the decision of Canning to send a representative to the congress necessitated a clear definition of English policy, covering the whole field of American affairs. In 1822 Canning had broken up the congress of the despots at Verona, but in 1826 he showed no desire to break up or dissolve the congress of the republicans at Panama. That congress was summoned by Bolivar, and was intended primarily to induce the Spanish-American states to form a united league against Spain, and force her to grant them recognition. Incidentally the congress naturally tended to discuss other questions than those of war, such as free trade, international law, the Cuban question, and so forth. England and the United States[12] were invited to send representatives. Canning quietly assented, but the question formed a thorny subject of debate in the Congess and Senate of the United States. Canning selected a Mr. Dawkins as the British representative, and began his instructions on March 17, 1826,[13] by informing him that the sole object of despatching him was to "obtain the most regular and correct information of its proceedings, and to assure the American States collectively of the friendly sentiments and the lively interest in their welfare and tranquillity" felt and expressed by the British Government. He deduces the motive of summoning an English representative to have been "a due sense of the benefits which they [the American states] have derived and continue to derive from a friendly intercourse with Great Britain, and a very natural desire to increase the importance of that assembly in the estimation of the Old World."

Two subjects mentioned in these instructions may be speedily dismissed. Canning tells Dawkins to forward in every way the settlement of the dispute between Brazil and Buenos Ayes, if it should come before the congress. Secondly he tells him to represent, "not by direct official intimation but you should not disguise the sentiments of your Gov[ernmen]t,"[14] that Great Britain hopes the new states will adopt those principles of maritime law on which she has uniformly acted. "And you will take care to have it duly understood that our determination to act upon these principles, as it has not been shaken by

[12]The delegates from the United States never reached Panama at all. One of them died; the other did not go on his mission; and at Panama the congress was therefore without representation from the United States!

[13]Public Record Office, F. O., Colombia 50*.

[14]This method of representation was used by Dawkins throughout the congress.

European confederacies, so it will not be altered by any Resolution or combination of the States of the New World." The old contention of the United States that "free ships make free goods" was of course directly opposed to this. If the Spanish-Americans agreed with the United States, therefore, there might be serious trouble. Despite all his liberal and conciliatory ideas, Canning was immovable as adamant when he thought the honor or interest of England really concerned. He evidently did upon this occasion, and the words above quoted show that exclusively English policy which Adams described as the characteristic of Canning. Here then were the beginnings of a serious dispute, which the differences in the conference however rendered harmless.

Canning proceeds to define the general attitude of England toward the Spanish-American governments. He requests information

> about their feelings towards each other, and the degree of influence in their concerns, which they may appear inclined to allow to the United States of North America. You will understand that to a league among the States, lately colonies of Spain, limited to objects growing out of their common relations to Spain, H[is] M[ajesty']s Gov[ernmen]t would not object.
>
> But any project for putting the U[nited] S[tates] of North America at the head of an American Confederacy, as against Europe, would be highly displeasing to your Gov[ernmen]t. *It would be felt as an ill return for the service which has been rendered to those States, and the dangers which have been averted from them, by the countenance and friendship, and publick declarations of Great Britain; and it would too probably at no very distant period endanger the peace both of America and of Europe.*[15]

[15]The italics are my own. A passage of almost equal strength is to be found in further instructions of March 18, 1826, Canning to Dawkins (Public Record Office F. O., Colombia 50*). He has received a treaty between Colombia and Mexico (signed October 3, 1823) which serves to define the objects of the congress as: (1)"To confirm and establish intimate relations between the whole and each of the American States"; (2) "To serve as a council on great occasions; a point of union in common dangers; a *faithful interpreter of public treaties,* in cases of misunderstanding; and as an arbitrator and conciliator in disputes and differences." Canning comments: "If by the 'American States' in (1) are intended *only* the States heretofore Colonies of Spain; and if the functions, assigned to the Congress in (2), are to be discharged *only* between *those* States, there is no disposition in the British Govt. to question the propriety. . . . [You must] let it be known that an association in such mutual engagements of any State not partaking of the Spanish character, would be viewed by your government with great jealousy as approaching to that species of league of the Americas against Europe, which you are already apprized His Majesty could neither acknowledge nor approve." The italics here are Canning's.

It is hardly possible to overrate the importance of these words; they show the policy to the full, the attempt to detach the Spanish-Americans from the United States at all costs, by reminding them alike of the past services and the present power of England.

The two questions of real importance, which absorbed the attention of the congress, were the means of obtaining recognition from Spain for her revolted colonies, and the question of Cuba. In the first case the Spanish-American republics desired recognition from Spain, less because they feared her than because they feared complications or embroilments with France. Spain desired money, and therefore the question of a purchase scheme, of paying a sort of tribute in return for recognition, was discussed. It was eventually rejected. Canning had instructed Dawkins to offer the good offices of England for reopening negotiations with Spain, but refused to recommend or give an opinion on this purchase scheme. This plan was eventually thrown out by the congress.

Meanwhile Gual, the Colombian representative and the chief leader of the congress, read some published despatches of Everett, the United States minister in Spain. These had already been officially published, and were distinctly unfavorable in their criticism of the English attitude at Madrid. Among other things they stated, though quite inaccurately, that Mr. Lambe, the English ambassador at Madrid, had not been active in his exertions to persuade Spain to grant recognition. The astute Mr. Dawkins paid his almost daily visit to Gual on June 26,[16] and found him somewhat cold and incredulous as to the good wishes of England. Mr. Dawkins was surprised, went home and read the papers, and thereupon discovered the reason of this coldness in Mr. Everett's somewhat heated despatches. He promptly wrote to Gual and flatly contradicted Everett's statements; finally he supplied Gual with copies of various despatches from England, which proved the exertions and sincerity of English attempts to secure recognition. English ascendancy at the congress was soon and completely recovered. Gual talked "unreservedly" to Dawkins "of the imprudence of the United States, of the errors committed by Mr. Everett, and of the mischief which may be done by the indiscreet publication of his correspondance [*sic*]." Gual

[16]See the story in Dawkins to Canning, Public Record Office, F. O., Colombia 50*. Everett's chief despatch is dated October 20, 1825.

further promised to bring a project of English mediation between Spain and the colonies before the congress. Here was another source of irritation between the United States and England. It was increased by the signing of a general confederative treaty between the Spanish-Americans on July 15. That treaty was one arranging for a common army and mutual defense between Colombia, Mexico, Peru, and Guatemala. It contained the clause, "any American State may be admitted into the Confederation within a year after the signature of the treaty." Dawkins promptly inquired of Mr. Gual whether this principle extended to the United States. His answer was, "Certainly if they will declare war against Spain." This was disquieting, and it is to be presumed that Mr. Dawkins then clearly defined the attitude of England and her opposition to the United States' joining such a league. However, as the United States had no intention of declaring war and never joined the league, the question dropped.

It was on the question of Cuba that events really turned. Cuba has well been termed the "Turkey of transatlantic politics," for the destiny of Cuba was the problem which engaged the attention of all the diplomatists of the age, of Bolivar and Villèle, of Canning and Adams. As early as October, 1822,[17] Canning had feared that the United States desired to seize Cuba. He wrote to his cousin, the English ambassador at Washington,[18] mentioning evidence of various sorts from the press, and from the reports of the officers of the United States navy, etc., etc. He concluded that the "grounds of suspicion are not such as to warrant our imputing a Design [to the United States] that is not avowed: and a jealousy manifested without cause is apt to suggest the very Evil which it deprecates." He also details French fears of English designs on Cuba, and similar fears on the part of the United States about England. To quiet these fears he told Stratford to make an express disavowal to the United States of any English designs on Cuba. But suspicion was everywhere. Adams probably did not believe Stratford, and both England and the United States feared the French. Thus arose a strange kind of triangular duel, France suspecting England and the United States, the United States suspecting England and France, England suspecting France and the United States.

[17]George Canning to Stratford Canning, October 11, 1822, Public Record Office, F. O., America 165. Indorsed "Secret."

[18]George Canning to Stratford Canning, December 7, 1822, *ibid.*

The suspicions appear to have been well-founded only in the case of France, where aggressive designs on Cuba were maturing in the dreamy brain of Chateaubriand[19] (then foreign minister of France) and were transmitted by him to Villèle. They also had a modicum of truth with regard to the United States. Secretary Adams[20] did not indeed desire to annex Cuba, but he desired to make it possible for Cuba to join the Union and become incorporated with the United States. This was one of the reasons why Adams declined to join with Canning in a joint declaration against the Holy Alliance in September of 1823. Had Adams brought the United States into line with Great Britain, both countries would have been pledged by Canning's provision that neither contracting state should acquire fresh territory. Adams saw that Cuba might solicit a union with the United States, but would not with Great Britain. Hence Adams held off, refused the joint declaration, and enunciated the Monroe doctrine in the presidential message of December 2, 1823. Adams made it possible for Cuba voluntarily to incorporate herself with the United States, and hoped that she would do so. This was the extent of his design upon Cuba. It was not grasping or aggressive like that of France, but it was not disinterested like that of Canning. The latter's idea was as follows: he certainly never had any notion of annexing Cuba for England, but he desired to maintain the status quo. If that was impossible, he was resolved, whatever happened, not to allow either France or the United States to annex or secure it. In 1825 he made a definite offer of guaranteeing it to Spain, on condition of her recognizing her revolted colonies to be independent states. Spain supinely refused, and toward the end of 1825 Canning was therefore faced by a new phase of this disagreeable problem. Bolivar and his friends were openly announcing their design of

[19]*Œuvres Complètes* (ed. of -902), XII. 363 *et passim*.

[20]*Memoirs,* VI. 177–178; for his suspicions of English designs on Cuba see *ibid.,* 203. In 1823 Monroe amended a despatch of Adams to this effect: that the United States had "no intention of acquiring any portion of the Spanish possessions for ourselves, nor shall we ever do it by force." Adams brought on a debate in the Cabinet (November 21) and had the passage in question struck out! *Ibid.,* 193–196; AMERICAN HISTORICAL REVIEW, VIII. 36, 38–39. At one time, indeed, Canning had offered to guarantee Cuba to Spain as the price of her recognition of her revolted colonies, and of peace; but Spain had refused. This was not so great a departure from neutrality as was now planned by Adams. Canning had made this offer in order to insure peace; Adams uttered sentiments and resolutions which might prolong war.

"liberating" Cuba; and to "liberate" Cuba Canning saw was to give the United States a pretext for interference. France was not much to be feared. She had already been threatened with war by Canning, if she intervened in the New World. In any case the fleet of England and the opposition–moral or otherwise–of both North and South America made her attempts impossible. France was not dangerous as an enemy but might be useful as an ally to check the United States. The latter power was infinitely the more dangerous because of the silent moral influence it might exert, and because it might interfere in Cuba, after Bolivar and his liberating armies had driven out the Spaniards.

Matters were complicated in the autumn of 1825 by the appearance of a French squadron off the coast of Cuba, which came ostensibly to collect a debt from Hayti. The French army had prefaced its march into Spain in 1823 by declaring that it only massed on the frontier so as to form a quarantine to prevent yellow fever and constitutional principles from coming over the Pyrenees. The French might well preface a naval attack on Cuba by an announcement that they merely intended to collect a debt from Hayti. Adams was not the man patiently to suffer this, and he prepared vigorously to resist, in case of a French attack on Cuba. Negotiations were entered into between the English and American governments, with reference both to the designs of France and to the designs of Bolivar. Vaughan, the English minister at Washington, conversed with the new Secretary of State, Henry Clay, on the latter subject, and actually "suggested an interference by the United States of America to dissuade the Mexicans and Columbians from making any attack upon Cuba." Canning heard this with immense indignation, for it ruined all his plans. He promptly disavowed Vaughan, and wrote him fresh instructions on February 8, 1826:[21]

> If it had been intended that you should treat . . . in a matter so delicate, as the proposed interference of neutral Powers to controul the legitimate operations of belligerents against each other, You would not have been left without instructions, upon a point of as much novelty, as delicacy and importance. If [went on Canning] the United States think their interests likely to be affected by the continuance of the war between Spain and the

[21]Public Record Office, F. O., America 209.

new transatlantick States they are probably right, and perfectly at liberty to employ their good offices to bring about a pacification.

We have long endeavored to do so but in vain; and Spain has been uniformly the recusant party. If the United States think that particular interests of their own require that a certain operation of war should not be undertaken by one of the belligerents,–it is a question, and a very nice one for them, . . . but it is manifest that we have not the like interest either to induce or to justify us in so unusual an interposition. . . . If it be merely the interests of the United States that are concerned, that ground of interference can only belong to them, nor is there any obligation upon us, to share the odium of such an interposition.

Such then was the situation when the Panama congress met, Bolivar and his friends openly proclaiming their intention of attacking Cuba, France darkly pursuing her own designs, the United States openly proclaiming its intention of checking Bolivar in its own interests, Canning holding the balance aloof and neutral. He saw and took the opportunity of dividing the United States and the Spanish-American republics on this Cuban question, and of constrasting the moderation of England to the latter with the more aggressive attitude of the United States. In his instruction to Dawkins on March 18, 1826, he inclosed copies of despatches to and from France and the United States.

You will see how earnestly it is desired by the U[nited] S[tates], by France and by this country that Cuba should remain a Colony of Spain. The B[ritish] Gov[ernmen]t indeed, so far from denying the right of the new States of America to make a hostile attack upon Cuba, whether considered simply as a possession of a power with whom they are at war, or as an Arsenal from which expeditions are fitted out against them, that We have uniformly refused to join with the U[nited] S[tates] in remonstrating with Mexico and Columbia against the supposed intention, or intimating that we should feel displeasure at the execution of it. We should indeed regret it but we arrogate to ourselves no right to controul the operations of one belligerent against another. The Government of the U[nited] S[tates] however professes itself of a different opinion. It conceives that the interests of the U[nited] S[tates] would be so directly affected by either the occupation of Havannah by an invading force, or by the consequences which an attack upon Cuba, even if unsuccessful, might produce in the interior of the island, that the Cabinet of Washington hardly disguises Its intention to interfere directly, and by force, to prevent or repress such an operation. Neither England nor France could see with indifference the U[nited] S[tates] in occupation of Cuba. Observe, therefore, the complicated consequences to which an expedition to Cuba by Mexico or Columbia might lead, and let the States assembled at Panama consider whether it is worth while to continue a war, the only remaining operation of which, (that is likely to be sensibly felt by their adversary) is thus morally interdicted to them by the consequences to which it would lead.

As all know, the result of the congress was complete failure. It is probable that even the much-vaunted project of an attack upon Cuba by the Spanish-Americans was only a threat to dispose Spain toward recognition. The vast scheme of a united army of Spanish-American confederates was concluded upon paper but was never realized in fact. One result only followed, that the policy of Canning had certainly done something to make the United States an object of suspicion to the Spanish-Americans. This is shown by the despatch of Dawkins to Canning upon October 15, in which he summed up the general results of the congress. The United States, he says, had failed to get any commercial treaties in its favor, owing to the opposition of Mexico and Peru.

The general influence of the United States is not, in my opinion, to be feared. It certainly exists in Columbia, but it has been very much weakened even there by their protests against an attack on Cuba, and by the indiscretions they have committed at Madrid.[22]

In all this the general policy of Canning is clear. According to Adams the European and American continents were to be regarded as being in water-tight compartments; according to Canning there was to be a free intercourse between them, and American powers were, if necessary, to play their part in European politics. Canning sought to induce the United States into a joint declaration with him against the Holy Alliance in 1823, and failed. Circumstances drew him away from the United States in later years, but he did not scruple to introduce American influence into European affairs. On October 13, 1825,[23] he inserted

[22]Public Record Office, F. O., Colombia 36.
[23]Public Record Office, F. O., Turkey 133, quoted in my *Life of Canning,* 213.

the following most significant passage in his instructions to the English ambassador at Constantinople. The Sultan is to be warned of insulting too grossly, by his acts, the moral opinion of the world:

> The recent events in the Western hemisphere have approximated, as it were, the different divisions of the world to each other, and have brought new Powers to bear on every question of political struggle or change, in whatever part of the globe it may arise. The Porte cannot doubt that all the inhabitants of both Americas to a man, are in their hearts favourers of the Greek cause, and might at no distant period become active co-operators in it. This is not the language of intimidation, it is that of truth.

The contrast between the policy of Canning and that of Adams is very significant. Adams had, in the strongest manner, disclaimed any idea of anything but the merest expression of academic sympathy with the Greek struggle against the Turks, and had overruled Monroe with reference to this point in the autumn of 1823.

> The ground that I wish to take [writes he in his diary[24]] is that of earnest remonstrance against the interference of the European powers by force with South America, but to disclaim all interference on our part with Europe; to make an American cause, and adhere inflexibly to that.

England was desirous that America should mix in European politics, and for this reason: England had no entangling alliance either with monarchies in Europe or with republics in America; any interference or mingling of one with the other was bound to turn to the advantage of England. So much then for Canning's attempt to introduce America into Europe.

In attempting to break down that part of the Monroe doctrine which forbade America to be used for future European colonization, Canning used several means. As we have seen, the recognition of America was decided upon partly in order to teach the new states to lean upon England, not upon the United States. At the congress of Panama Canning played on the fears and jealousies excited between the Spanish-Americans and North-Americans over the question of Cuba.

[24]November 21, 1823. *Memoirs,* VI. 197–198, quoted by Reddaway, *Monroe Doctrine* (ed. of 1898), 64.

One further phase or aspect of his policy remains to be noticed, his attitude toward the Oregon question. The actual question of rights has never been definitely settled either way. What Canning felt on the subject is clear enough. Astoria had been made over to the United States in 1818. Canning commented upon this to Liverpool on July 7, 1826:

> . . . think what a task it will be to justify this transaction to Parl[iamen]t, if upon this transaction we rest our justification for abandoning the whole N. W. Coast of America to the Yankees. *I feel the shame of such a statement burning upon my face by anticipation.*[25]

Canning announced his intention of taking his stand immovably upon the forty-ninth parallel of latitude. The English boundary was to extend to that degree on the south, and no consideration would induce him to recede from this position. He was induced to this course by what he conceived to be the just claims, the honor, and the interest of England. He saw "that the ambitious and overbearing views of the [United] States are becoming daily more developed, and better understood in this country",[26] and he was resolved and determined to check them. Also he saw the advantages England would gain from an eventual "immense direct intercourse between China and what may be, if we resolve not to yield them up, her [England's] boundless establishments on the N. W. Coast of America."[27] For these reasons Canning decided to assert the claims of England and check the pretensions of England's great American rival.

> The avowed pretensions of the United States to put themselves at the head of the confederacy of all the Americans, and to sway that Confederacy against Europe (Great Britain included) is *not* a pretension identified with our interests, or one that we can countenance or tolerate. It is however a pretension which there is no use in contesting in the abstract, but we must not say anything that seems to admit the principle.[28]

[25]E. J. Stapleton, *Some Official Correspondence of George Canning,* II. 73; the italics are my own. On Astoria see Public Record Office, F. O., America 129, 165–168; on Oregon, America 191–192. There is not much in these two volumes on the Oregon question not indicated or described already in Stapleton.

[26]Stapleton, *op. cit.,* II. 73.

[27]*Ibid.,* 74.

[28]Canning to Vaughan, February 18, 1826, Public Record Office, F. O., America 209.

If Canning was not prepared to contest it in the abstract, he certainly was in the concrete. Hence his firm stand on the Oregon question was due to the advantages likely to accrue to British trade with China and British prestige in America. There was a further and unexpressed reason, and that is that Canning could not but have perceived the advantage of retaining this boundary, in order to bring England nearer to Mexico. For that state he had an especial care, both because of its resources and because of its proximity to the United States. He saw that it would be probable that any expansion of the United States would take place toward Mexico. Adams contemplated the eventual incorporation of Texas in the Union.[29] He also endeavored to advance the United States boundary to the River Bravo del Norte, but was overruled by his colleagues in the Cabinet. Here again would have been Canning's opportunity to use every fresh aggression from the United States to teach the Spanish-Americans that their true friend and ally was not the United States but England. Every such attempt of the United States would frighten Mexico and increase the bond between her and England.

Here then emerges a policy, definite, compact, and coherent, a resolute resolve not to admit the Monroe doctrine, a determination to bring the Spanish-American states into close relations with England. The Old World was to be revived with the vigorous life of the New, the New to be tempered with the moderation of the Old, England to hold the balance between them. It is impossible not to admire the boldness and extent of the design, the vastness or profundity of its conceptions. Great indeed was the insight which looked so far ahead as to see the

[29]Incorporation, not annexation. J. T. Morse, *John Quincy Adams* (ed. of 1898), 131, 135, 266–267; Adams, *Memoirs,* VI. 178. There is a most significant passage on Mexico in William Huskisson's *Speeches* (London, 1831, three vols.), III. 579–580, May 20, 1830: "If the United States have declared that they cannot allow the island of Cuba to belong to any maritime power in Europe, Spain excepted, neither can England, as the first of those maritime powers—I say it fearlessly, because I feel it strongly—*suffer the United States to bring under their dominion a greater portion of the shores of the Gulf of Mexico than that which they now possess.*" The italics are my own. This passage has a greatly added interest when we reflect that Huskisson was the devoted follower of George Canning, and had special knowledge of American affairs as joint-commissioner with Stratford Canning in the conference with Rush about Oregon in 1824. It may reasonably be deduced that, in the above-quoted passage, he is voicing the sentiments of his deceased master in foreign policy.

commercial advantages of a trade between China and northwest America, or to find in Mexico the most hopeful of Spanish-American states. On December 17, 1824, Canning wrote to Granville: "The deed is done, the nail is driven, Spanish America is free; and if we do not mismanage our affairs sadly, *she is English.*" In Canning's later policy may be found the explanation of this apparently cryptic sentence. England did "mismanage [her] affairs sadly"; for no English statesman after him realized, as Canning did, that the future lay as much in the New World as in the Old. The utter impotence of the Spanish-American republics could perhaps not have been foreseen, and was a cause of failure apart from the defects of British statesmen. But none the less the entire devotion of Palmerston and Aberdeen to affairs European explains much of the success of United States policy.

We are now in a position to understand what seem the strange comments of Adams and Rush upon Canning's policy. The first thought his policy entirely English, the second called Canning "a Briton, through and through;–British in his feelings, British in his aims, British in all his policy and projects."[30] This characterization is strange to Englishmen. The deliverer of Europe from the toils of the Holy Alliance acquired no territory but only influence for England. To Englishmen it seems that, though Canning may have loved England best, his heart yet beat high for the general interests of the world. Yet Canning's later attitude toward America explains this characterization, for during that time he was straining every nerve to foil the United States, and hence the judgment of its diplomatists upon him. Yet even toward America the policy of Canning was marked, in many respects, by a noble disinterestedness. At no time did he contemplate using disturbances in the New World as a pretext for seizing exclusive advantages for England. Annexation of territory is an object supposed by most other nations to be the key-note of England's foreign policy. At least it had no part in the plans of England's greatest foreign minister, during whose second period of office not a single inch of territory was annexed. All Canning ever aimed at was to exalt the influence of England and the principle of non-intervention. In only two cases did he

[30]Richard Rush, "Character of Mr. Canning," in *Occasional Productions* (Philadelphia, 1860), 190; Adam's view may be seen in W. C. Ford, "John Quincy Adams and the Monroe Doctrine," AMERICAN HISTORICAL REVIEW, VII. 680.

ever make any attempt to intervene in the internal affairs of states in the New World: in the one case when he offered to guarantee the stipulations of the treaty between Brazil and Buenos Ayres in 1826, in the other when he offered to guarantee Cuba to Spain in 1825. In both these cases his attitude was exceptional, and he stood to gain no exclusive advantage for England. He showed great disinterestedness by offering to Portugal and Spain most generous terms as the price of their recognition of Brazil and the Spanish-American colonies respectively. He agreed in each case that the mother-country should enjoy commercial advantages superior to those of any other nation, a concession of extraordinary generosity. He never claimed in commercial negotiations to get an exclusive or preferential treatment, but only an equality with other nations.

On the other hand, Adams aimed always at securing commercial treaties with Spanish America on the basis of exclusive treatment. And as with commercial, so with political advantages. In September, 1823, Canning offered to associate England with the United States in a joint declaration against the Holy Alliance, pledging neither to seize nor to occupy territory. Adams refused, because he desired (as Canning did not for England) to leave the door open for the incorporation, if not for the annexation, of such states as Texas or Cuba. Adams may have been right to refuse on the exclusive ground of the interests of the United States, and his declaration of the Monroe doctrine was certainly a most brilliant stroke of policy. But that Canning in his later policy was following the dictates of a larger and more tolerant doctrine seems also clear, though that the line which he adopted was likely to lead at length to conflict between the United States and England seems also unfortunately true.

The United States have now established beyond dispute their claims to forbid future European colonization in the American continent. But at least few can read without interest the views of the great English statesman, whose last years were spent in endeavoring, by every means of diplomatic skill and ingenuity, to check the pretensions of that Monroe doctrine which is inseparably associated with his own name and that of Adams. All must rejoice that, through whatever means, that conflict was avoided; and, since Americans have never refused a tribute to the genius of Canning, Englishmen should be the last to refuse to acknowledge that of Adams.

Selections from *The Voyage of the Beagle*

BY CHARLES DARWIN

Upon landing, I found to my great surprise, that I was to a certain degree a prisoner. A most violent revolution having broken out. . . .

Charles Darwin was only twenty-three years old when he served as a naturalist aboard H.M.S. *Beagle,* which was sent from England to complete a survey of the South American coast and to carry out a chain of longitude measurements around the world. The voyage lasted more than four and one-half years. The notes and diary Darwin kept during this trip formed the basis of his book titled *The Voyage of the Beagle,* which was first published in 1839 and revised in 1845. The book was an immediate success, and the research that Darwin conducted during his voyage and described in the book formed the basis for his subsequently developed theories of evolution.

Darwin's reactions to Latin America are helpful for an understanding of the area, as well as for a comprehension of European and North American attitudes toward it. Darwin, unlike Von Humboldt, who preceded him as a traveler in Latin America, held many of the typical British middle-class convictions of the nineteenth century. He deplored social and political violence and was anti-Catholic; he detested slavery and believed that thrift, industry, and sanctity of contract were important virtues. His failure to find these among the landholders whom he met in Latin America was to him a source of distress, never a source of intellectual curiosity. Perhaps, too, Darwin's social philosophy was aggravated by the fact that Captain Robert Fitz Roy who commanded the *Beagle,* combined in his own makeup many of the characteristics Darwin found among the Latin Americans. Fitz Roy was the grandson of a duke and the nephew of Lord Castlereagh. He was brilliant, erratic, emotional, and improvident, and when he died by suicide in 1865, a public subscription was needed to pay his debts. Since Darwin was confined in such close quarters for so long with such a man and was forced to avoid discussing subjects on which he and his captain disagreed, he perhaps felt an even greater need to express them in his diary. Thus, the Latin American's lack of middle-class virtues is noted in the book.

But Darwin has not been unique in this. Other European and American travelers, researchers, and residents since Darwin's time, even without a Captain Fitz Roy as a traveling companion, have made much of the same point—so much so that they have become the basis for the development of a U.S. policy that today seeks to encourage the emergence of a Latin American middle class.

Darwin's scientific observations, however, rise above class preoccupations and remain, to this day, as readable an account of the inherent violence of the area as has ever been written—a violence that at times seems so pervasive as to suggest that it in itself is a natural deterrent to the development of middle-class attitudes. As Darwin observed, in connection with the prevalence of earthquakes along the West Coast of Latin America, "if beneath England, the now inert subterranean forces should exert those powers . . . how completely would the entire condition of the country be changed! . . . England would at once be bankrupt . . . government being unable to collect the taxes, and failing to maintain its authority, the hand of violence and rapine would remain uncontrolled."

Charles Robert Darwin was born at Shrewsbury in England on February 12, 1809. His mother was the daughter of Josiah Wedgwood, the famous potter. After an unsuccessful start in the study of medicine at Edinburgh, he entered Christ's College, Cambridge, in 1828 with the idea of becoming a clergyman.

But this career, too, he gave up when he sailed on the *Beagle* in 1832, a voyage which was really the preparation for his life's work in science. Darwin's most important work, *On the Origin of the Species by Means of Natural Selection,* appeared in 1859. By this time he already had a considerable reputation in British scientific circles, and it is said that the entire first edition of 1,250 copies was sold out on the day of its issue.

Darwin had married his cousin, Emma Wedgwood, in 1839 and lived with her in London until 1842, when the family moved to Down, Beckenham, Kent, which was to be his home thereafter. His personal nature was one of great tenderness and kindness. After the voyage on the *Beagle* he was often in poor health; he suffered from fatigue and led the life of a semi-invalid and recluse under the constant care of his wife. When not well, he limited his work to four hours a day and spent the rest of his time resting, walking, and reading novels. He died in 1882 and was buried in Westminster Abbey. Four of his sons became distinguished scientists.

P. K.

BRAZIL: Leaving Socêgo, we rode to another estate on the Rio Macâe, which was the last patch of cultivated ground in that direction. The estate was two and a half miles long, and the owner had forgotten how many broad. Only a very small piece had been cleared, yet almost every acre was capable of yielding all the various rich productions of a tropical land. Considering the enormous area of Brazil, the proportion of cultivated ground can scarcely be considered as any thing, compared to that which is left in the state of nature: at some future age, how vast a population it will support! During the second day's journey we found the road so shut up, that it was necessary that a man should go ahead with a sword to cut away the creepers. The forest abounded with beautiful objects; among which the tree ferns, though not large, were, from their bright green foliage, and the elegant curvature of their fronds, most worthy of admiration. In the evening it rained very heavily, and although the thermometer stood at 65°, I felt very cold. As soon as the rain ceased, it was curious to observe the extraordinary evaporation which commenced over the whole extent of the forest. At the height of a hundred feet the hills were buried in a dense white vapour, which rose like columns of smoke from the most thickly-wooded parts, and especially from the valleys. I observed this phenomenon on several occasions: I suppose it is owing to the large surface of foliage, previously heated by the sun's rays.

In returning we spent two days at Socêgo, and I employed them in collecting insects in the forest. The greater number of trees, although so lofty, are not more than three or four feet in circumference. There are, of course, a few of much greater dimension. Senhor Manuel was then making a canoe 70 feet in length from a solid trunk, which had originally been 110 feet long, and of great thickness. The contrast of palm trees, growing amidst the common branching kinds, never fails to give the scene an intertropical character. Here the woods were ornamented by the Cabbage Palm – one of the most beautiful of its family. With a stem so narrow that it might be clasped with the two hands, it waves its elegant head at the height of forty or fifty feet above the ground. The woody creepers, themselves, covered by other creepers, were of great thickness: some which I measured were two feet in circumference. Many of the older trees presented a very curious appearance from the tresses of liana hanging from their boughs, and resembling bundles of hay. If the eye was turned from the world of foliage above, to the ground beneath, it was attracted by the extreme elegance of the leaves of the ferns and mimosae. The latter, in some parts, covered the surface with a brushwood only a few inches high. In walking across these thick beds of mimosae, a broad track was marked by the change of shade, produced by the drooping of their sensitive petioles. It is easy to specify the individual objects of admiration in these grand scenes; but it is not possible to give an adequate idea of the higher feelings of wonder, astonishment, and devotion, which fill and elevate the mind.

A person, on first entering a tropical forest, is astonished at the labours of the ants: well-beaten paths branch off in every direction, on which an army of never-failing foragers may be seen, some going forth, and others returning, burdened with pieces of green leaf, often larger than their own bodies.

A small dark-coloured ant sometimes migrates in countless numbers. One day, at Bahia, my attention was drawn by observing many spiders, cockroaches, and other insects, and some lizards, rushing in the greatest agitation across a bare piece of ground. A little way behind, every stalk and leaf was blackened by a small ant. The swarm having crossed the bare space, divided itself, and descended an old wall. By this means many insects were fairly enclosed; and the efforts which the poor little creatures made to extricate themselves from such a death were wonderful. When the ants came to the road they changed their course, and in narrow files re-ascended the wall. Having placed a small stone so as to intercept one of the lines, the whole body attacked it, and them immediately retired. Shortly afterwards another body came to the charge, and again having failed to make any impression, this line of march was entirely given up. By going an inch round, the file might have avoided the stone, and this doubless would have happened, if it had been originally there: but having been attacked, the lion-hearted warriors scorned the idea of yielding.

The number of spiders, in proportion to other insects, is here compared with England very much larger; perhaps more so than with any other division of the articulate animals. The variety of species among the jumping spiders appears almost infinite. The genus, or rather family of Epeira, is here characterized by many singular forms; some species have pointed coriaceous shells, other enlarged and spiny tibiae. Every path in the forest is barricaded with the strong yellow web of a species, belonging to the same division with the Epeira clavipes of Fabricius, which was formerly said by Sloane to make, in the West Indies, webs so strong as to catch birds.

URUGUAY: I staid [*sic*] ten weeks at Maldonado, in which time a nearly perfect collection of the animals, birds and reptiles, was procured. Before making any observations respecting them, I will give an account of a little excursion I made as far as the river Polanco, which is about seventy miles distant, in a northerly direction. I may mention, as a proof how cheap everything is in this country, that I paid only two dollars a day, or eight shillings, for two men, together with a troop of about a dozen riding-horses. My companions were well armed with pistols and sabres; a precaution which I thought rather unnecessary; but the first piece of news we heard was, that, the day before, a traveller from Monte Video had been found dead on the road, with his throat cut. This happened close to a cross, the record of a former murder.

On the first night we slept at a retired little country-house; and there I soon found out that I possessed two or three articles, especially a pocket compass, which created unbounded astonishment. In every house I was asked to show the compass, and by its aid, together with a map, to point out the direction of various places. It excited the liveliest admiration that I, a perfect stranger, should know the road (for direction and road are synonymous in this open country) to places where I had never been. At one house a young woman, who was ill in bed, sent to entreat me to come and show her the compass. If their surprise was great, mine was greater, to find such ignorance among people who possessed their thousands of cattle, and "estancias" of great extent. It can only be accounted for by the circumstance that this retired part of the country is seldom visited by foreigners. I was asked whether the earth or sun moved; whether it was hotter or colder to the north; where Spain was, and many other such questions. The greater number of the inhabitants had an indistinct idea that England, London, and North America, were different names for the same place; but the better informed well knew that London and North America were separate countries close together, and that England was a large town in London! I carried with me some promethean matches, which I ignited by biting; it was thought so wonderful that a man should strike fire with his teeth, that it was usual to collect the whole family to see it: I was once offered a dollar for a single one. Washing my face in the morning caused much speculation at the village of Las Minas; a superior tradesman closely cross-questioned me about so singular a practice; and likewise why on board we wore our beards; for he had heard from my guide that we did so. He eyed me with much suspicion; perhaps he had heard of ablutions in the Mohomedan religion, and knowing me to be a heretick, probably he came to the conclusion that all hereticks were Turks. It is the general custom in this country to ask for a night's lodging at the first convenient house. The astonishment at the compass, and my other feats in jugglery, was to a certain degree advantageous, as with that, and the long stories my guides told of my breaking stones, knowing venomous from harmless snakes, collecting insects, etc., I repaid them for their hospitality. I am writing as if I had been among the inhabitants of central Africa: Banda Oriental* would not be flattered by the comparison; but such were my feelings at the time.

The next day we rode to the village of Las Minas. The country was rather more hilly, but otherwise continued the same; an inhabitant of the Pampas no doubt would have considered it as truly Alpine. The country is so thinly inhabited, that during the whole day we scarcely met a single person. Las Minas is much smaller even than Maldonado. It is seated on a little plain, and is surrounded by low rocky mountains. Is is of the usual symmetrical form; and with its whitewashed church standing in the centre, had rather a pretty appearance. The outskirting houses rose out of the plain like isolated beings, without the accompaniment of gardens or court yards. This is generally the case in the country, and all the houses have, in consequence, an uncomfortable aspect. At night we stopped at a pulpería, or drinking shop. During the evening a great number of Gauchos came in to drink spirits and smoke cigars: their appearance is very striking; they are generally tall and handsome; but with a proud and dissolute expression of countenance. They frequently wear their moustaches, and long black

*An old name for Uruguay (Ed.).

hair curling down their backs. With their brightly-coloured garments, great spurs clanking about their heels, and knives stuck as daggers (and often so used) at their waists, they look a very different race of men from what might be expected from their name of Gauchos, or simple countrymen. Their politeness is excessive; they never drink their spirits without expecting you to taste it; but whilst making their exceedingly graceful bow, they seem quite as ready, if occasion offered, to cut your throat.

On the third day we pursued rather an irregular course, as I was employed in examining some beds of marble. On the fine plains of turf we saw many ostriches (Struthio rhea). Some of the flocks contained as many as twenty or thirty birds. These, when standing on any little eminence, and seen against the clear sky, presented a very noble appearance. I never met with such tame ostriches in any other part of the country: it was easy to gallop up within a short distance of them; but then, expanding their wings, they made all sail right before the wind, and soon left the horse astern.

At night we came to the house of Don Juan Fuentes, a rich landed proprietor, but not personally known to either of my companions. On approaching the house of a stranger, it is usual to follow several little points of etiquette: riding up slowly to the door, the salutation of Ave Maria is given, and until somebody comes out and asks you to alight, it is not customary even to get off your horse: the formal answer of the owner is, "sin pecado concebida," that is, "conceived without sin." Having entered the house, some general conversation is kept up for a few minutes, till permission is asked to pass the night there. This is granted as a matter of course. The stranger then takes his meals with the family, and a room is assigned him, where with the horsecloths belonging to his recado (or saddle of the Pampas) he makes his bed. It is curious how similar circumstances produce such similar results in manners. At the Cape of Good Hope the same hospitality, and very nearly the same points of etiquette, are universally observed. The difference, however, between the character of the Spaniard and that of the Dutch boer is shown, by the former never asking his guest a single question beyond the strictest rules of politeness, whilst the honest Dutchman demands where he has been, where he is going, what is his business, and even how many brothers, sisters, or children he may happen to have.

Shortly after our arrival at Don Juan's one of the large herds of cattle was driven in towards the house, and three beasts were picked out to be slaughtered for the supply of the establishment. These half-wild cattle are very active; and knowing full well the fatal lazo, they led the horses a long and laborious chase. After witnessing the rude wealth displayed in the number of cattle, men and horses, Don Juan's miserable house was quite curious. The floor consisted of hardened mud, and the windows were without glass; the sitting-room boasted only of a few of the roughest chairs and stools, with a couple of tables. The supper, although several strangers were present, consisted of two huge piles, one of roast beef, the other of boiled, with some pieces of pumpkin: besides this latter there was no other vegetable, and not even a morsel of bread. For drinking, a large earthenware jug of water served the whole party. Yet this man was the owner of several square miles of land, of which nearly every acre would produce corn, and, with a little trouble, all the common vegetables. The evening was spent in smoking, with a little impromptu singing, accompanied by the guitar. The signoritas all sat together in one corner of the room, and did not sup with the men.

So many works have been written about these countries, that it is almost superfluous to describe either the lazo or the bolas. The lazo consists of a very strong, but thin, well-plaited rope, made of raw hide. One end is attached to the broad surcingle, which fastens together the complicated gear of the recado, or saddle used in the Pampas; the other is terminated by a small ring of iron or brass, by which a noose can be formed. The Gaucho, when he is going to use the lazo, keeps a small coil in his bridle-hand, and in the other holds the running noose, which is made very large, generally having a diameter of about eight feet. This he whirls round his head, and by the dexterous movement of his wrist keeps the noose open; then, throwing it, he causes it to fall on any particular spot he chooses. The lazo, when not used, is tied up in a small coil to the after part of the recado. The bolas, or balls, are of two kinds: the simplest, which is chiefly used for catching ostriches, consists of two round stones, covered with leather, and united by a thin plaited thong, about eight feet long. The other kind differs only in having three balls united by the thongs to a common centre. The Gaucho holds the smallest of the three in his hand, and whirls the other two round and round his head; then, taking aim, sends them like chain shot revolving through the air. The balls no sooner strike any object, than, winding round it, they cross each other, and become firmly hitched. The size and weight of the balls varies, according to the purpose for which they are made: when of stone, although not larger than an apple, they are sent with such force as sometimes to break the leg even of a horse. I have seen the balls made of wood, and as large as a turnip, for the sake of catching these animals without injuring them. The balls are sometimes made of iron, and these can be hurled to the greatest distance. The main difficulty in using either lazo or bolas is to ride so well as to be able at full speed, and while suddenly turning about, to whirl them so steadily round the head, as to take aim: on foot any person would soon learn the art. One day, as I was amusing myself by galloping and whirling the balls round my head, by accident the free one struck a bush; and its revolving motion being thus destroyed, it immediately fell to the ground, and like magic caught one hind leg of my horse; the other ball was then jerked out of my hand, and the horse fairly secured. Luckily he was an old practised animal, and knew what it meant; otherwise he would probably have kicked till he had thrown himself down. The Guachos roared with laughter; they cried out that they had seen every sort of animal caught, but had never before seen a man caught by himself.

ARGENTINA: The encampment of General Rosas was close to the river. It consisted of a square formed by waggons, artillery, straw huts, &c. The soldiers were nearly all cavalry; and I should think such a villainous, banditti-like army was never before collected together. The greater number of men were of a mixed breed, between Negro, Indian, and Spaniard. I know not the reason, but men of such origin seldom have a good expression of countenance. I called on the Secretary to show my passport. He began to cross-question me in the most dignified and mysterious manner. By good luck I had a letter of recommendation from the government of Buenos Ayres to the Commandant of Patagones. This was taken to General Rosas, who sent me a very obliging message; and the Secretary returned all smiles and graciousness. We took up our residence in the *rancho,* or hovel, of a curious old Spaniard, who had served with Napoleon in the expedition against Russia.

We stayed two days at the Colorado; I had little to do, for the surrounding country was a swamp, which in summer (December), when the snow melts on the Cordillera, is overflowed by the river. My chief amusement was watching the Indian families as they came to buy little articles at the rancho where we stayed. It was supposed that General Rosas had about six hundred Indian allies. The men were a tall fine race, yet it was afterwards easy to see in the Fuegian savage the same countenance rendered hideous by cold, want of food, and less civilization. Some authors, in defining the primary races of mankind, have separated these Indians into two classes; but this is certainly incorrect. Among the young women or chinas, some deserve to be called beautiful. Their hair was coarse, but bright and black; and they wore it in two plaits hanging down to the waist. They had a high colour, and eyes that glistened with brilliancy; their legs, feet, and arms were small and elegantly formed; their ankles, and sometimes their waists, were ornamented by broad bracelets of blue beads. Nothing could be more interesting than some of the family groups. A mother with one or two daughters would often come to our rancho, mounted on the same horse. They ride like men, but with their knees tucked up much higher. This habit, perhaps, arises from their being accustomed, when travelling, to ride the loaded horses. The duty of the women is to load and unload the horses; to make the tents for the night; in short to be, like the wives of all savages, useful slaves. The men fight, hunt, take care of the horses, and make the riding gear. One of their chief indoor occupations is to knock two stones together till they become round, in order to make the bolas. With this important weapon the Indian catches his game, and also his horse, which roams free over the plain. In fighting, his first attempt is to throw down the horse of his adversary with the bolas, and when entangled by the fall to kill him with the chuzo. If the balls only catch the neck or body of an animal, they are often carried away and lost. As the making the stones round is the labour of two days, the manufacture of the balls is a very common employment. Several of the men and women had their faces painted red, but I never saw the horizontal bands which are so common among the Fuegians. Their chief pride consists in having everything made of silver; I have seen a cacique with his spurs, stirrups, handle of his knife, and bridle made of this metal: the head-stall and reins being of wire, were not thicker than whipcord; and to see a fiery steed wheeling about under the command of so light a chain, gave to the horsemanship a remarkable character of elegance.

General Rosas intimated a wish to see me; a circumstance which I was afterwards very glad of. He is a man of an extraordinary character, and has a most predominant influence in the country, which it seems probable he will use to its prosperity and advancement.* He is said to be the owner of seventy-four square leagues of land, and to have about three hundred thousand head of cattle. His estates are admirably managed, and are far more productive of corn than those of others. He first gained his celebrity by his laws for his own estancias, and by disciplining several hundred men, so as to resist with success the attacks of the Indians. There are many stories current about the rigid manner in which his laws were enforced. One of these was, that no man, on penalty of being put into the stocks, should carry his knife on a Sunday: this being the principal day for gambling and drinking, many quarrels arose, which from the general manner of fighting with the knife often proved fatal. One Sunday the Governor came in great form to pay the estancia a visit, and General Rosas, in his hurry, walked out to receive him with his knife, as usual, stuck in his belt. The steward touched his arm, and reminded him of the law; upon which turning to the Governor, he said he was extremely sorry, but that he must go into the stocks, and that till let out, he possessed no power even in his own house. After a little time the steward was persuaded to open the stocks, and to let him out, but no sooner was this done, than he turned to the steward and said, "You now have broken the laws, so you must take my place in the stocks." Such actions as these delighted the Gauchos, who all possess high notions of their own equality and dignity.

General Rosas is also a perfect horseman – an accomplishment of no small consequence in a country where an assembled army elected its general by the following trial: A troop of unbroken horses being driven into a corral, were let out through a gateway, above which was a cross-bar: it was agreed whoever should drop from the bar on one of these wild animals, as it rushed out, and should be able, without a saddle or bridle, not only to ride it, but also to bring it back to the door of the corral, should be their general. The person who succeeded was

*This prophecy has turned out entirely and miserably wrong. 1845.

accordingly elected; and doubtless made a fit general for such an army. This extraordinary feat has also been performed by Rosas.

By these means, and by conforming to the dress and habits of the Gauchos, he has obtained an unbounded popularity in the country, and in consequence a despotic power. I was assured by an English merchant, that a man who had murdered another, when arrested and questioned concerning his motive, answered, "He spoke disrespectfully of General Rosas, so I killed him." At the end of a week the murderer was at liberty. This doubtless was the act of the general's party, and not of the general himself.

In conversation he is enthusiastic, sensible, and very grave. His gravity is carried to a high pitch: I heard one of his mad buffoons (for he keeps two, like the barons of old) relate the following anecdote: "I wanted very much to hear a certain piece of music, so I went to the general two or three times to ask him; he said to me, 'Go about your business, for I am engaged.' I went a second time; he said, 'If you come again I will punish you.' A third time I asked, and he laughed. I rushed out of the tent, but it was too late; he ordered two soldiers to catch and stake me. I begged by all the Saints in heaven he would let me off; but it would not do;–when the general laughs he spares neither mad man nor sound." The poor flighty gentleman looked quite dolorous, at the very recollection of the staking. This is a very severe punishment; four posts are driven into the ground, and the man is extended by his arms and legs horizontally, and there left to stretch for several hours. The idea is evidently taken from the usual method of drying hides. My interview passed away without a smile, and I obtained a passport and order for the government post-horses, and this he gave me in the most obliging and ready manner.

During my stay at Bahía Blanca, while waiting for the *Beagle,* the place was in a constant state of excitement, from rumours of wars and victories, between the troops of Rosas and the wild Indians. One day an account came that a small party forming one of the postas on the line to Buenos Ayres, had been found all murdered. The next day three hundred men arrived from the Colorado, under the command of Commandant Miranda. A large portion of these men were Indians (*mansos,* or tame), belonging to the tribe of the Cacique Bernantio. They passed the night here; and it was impossible to conceive any thing more wild and savage than the scene of their bivouac. Some drank till they were intoxicated; others swallowed the steaming blood of the cattle slaughtered for their suppers, and then, being sick from drunkenness, they cast it up again, and were besmeared with filth and gore.

In the morning they started for the scene of the murder, with orders to follow the "rastro," or track, even if it led them to Chile. We subsequently heard that the wild Indians had escaped into the great Pampas, and from some cause the track had been missed. One glance at the rastro tells these people a whole history. Supposing they examine the track of a thousand horses, they will soon guess the number of mounted ones by seeing how many have cantered; by the depth of the other impressions, whether any horses were loaded with cargoes; by the irregularity of the footsteps, how far tired; by the manner in which the food has been cooked, whether the pursued travelled in haste; by the general appearance, how long it has been since they passed. They consider a rastro of ten days or a fortnight quite recent enough to be hunted out.

Being arrived at the mouth of the Paraná, and as I was very anxious to reach Buenos Ayres, I went on shore at Las Conchas, with the intention of riding there. Upon landing, I found to my great surprise that I was to a certain degree a prisoner. A violent revolution having broken out, all the ports were laid under an embargo. I could not return to my vessel, and as for going by land to the city, it was out of the question. After a long conversation with the commandant, I obtained permission to go the next day to General Rolor, who commanded a division of the rebels on this side the capital. In the morning I rode to the encampment. The general, officers, and soldiers, all appeared, and I believe really were, great villains. The general, the very evening before he left the city, voluntarily went to the Governor, and with his hand to his heart, pledged his word of honour, that he at least would remain faithful to the last. The general told me that the city was in a state of close blockade, and that all he could do was to give me a passport to the commander-in-chief of the rebels at Quilmes. We had therefore to make a great sweep around the city, and it was with much difficulty that we procured horses. My reception at the encampment was quite civil, but I was told it was impossible that I could be allowed to enter the city. I was very anxious about this, as I anticipated the *Beagle's* departure from the Río Plata earlier than it took place. Having mentioned, however, General Rosas's obliging kindness to me when at the Colorado, magic itself could not have altered circumstances quicker than did this conversation. I was instantly told that though they could not give me a passport, if I chose to leave my guide and horses, I might pass their sentinels. I was too glad to accept of this, and an officer was sent with me to give directions that I should not be stopped at the bridge. The road for the space of a league was quite deserted. I met one party of soldiers, who were satisfied by gravely looking at an old passport: and at length I was not a little pleased to find myself within the city.

This revolution was supported by scarcely any pretext of grievances: but in a state which, in the course of nine months (from February to October, 1820), underwent fifteen changes in its government – each governor, according to the constitution, being elected for three years– it would be very unreasonable to ask for pretexts. In this case, a party of men – who, being attached to Rosas, were disgusted with the governor Balcarce–the number of seventy left the city, and with the cry of Rosas the whole country took arms. The city was then blockaded, no provisions, cattle or horses, were allowed to enter; besides this, there was only a little skirmishing, and a few men daily killed. The outside party well knew that by stopping the supply of meat they would certainly be victorious. General Rosas could not have known of this rising; but it appears to be quite consonant with the plans of his party. A year ago he was elected governor, but he refused it, unless the Sala would also confer on him extraordinary powers. This was refused, and since then his party have shown that no other governor can keep his place. The warfare on both sides was avowedly protracted till it was possible to hear from Rosas. A note arrived a few days after I left Buenos Ayres, which stated that the General disapproved of peace having been broken, but that he thought the outside party had justice on their side. On the bare reception of this, the Governor, ministers, and part of the military, to the number of some hundreds, fled from the city. The rebels entered, elected a new governor, and were paid for their services to the number of 5500 men. From these proceedings, it was clear that Rosas ultimately would become the dictator: to the term king, the people in this, as in other republics, have a particular dislike. Since leaving South America, we have heard that Rosas has been elected, with powers and for a time altogether opposed to the constitutional principles of the republic.

During the last six months I have had an opportunity of seeing a little of the character of the inhabitants of these provinces. The Gauchos, or countrymen, are very superior to those who reside in the towns. The Gaucho is invariably most obliging, polite, and hospitable: I did not meet with even one instance of rudeness or inhospitality. He is modest, both respecting himself and country, but at the same time a spirited, bold fellow. On the other hand, many robberies are committed, and there is much bloodshed: the habit of constantly wearing the knife is the chief cause of the latter. It is lamentable to hear how many lives are lost in trifling quarrels. In fighting, each party tries to mark the face of his adversary by slashing his nose or eyes; as is often attested by deep and horrid-looking scars. Robberies are a natural consequence of universal gambling, much drinking, and extreme indolence. At Mercedes I asked two men why they did not work. One gravely said the days were too long; the other that he was too poor. The number of horses and the profusion of food are the destruction of all industry. Moreover, there are so many feast-days; and again, nothing can succeed without it be begun when the moon is on the increase; so that half the month is lost from these two causes.

Police and justice are quite inefficient. If a man who is poor commits murder and is taken, he will be imprisoned, and perhaps even shot; but if he is rich and has friends, he may rely on it no very severe consequence will ensue. It is curious that the most respectable inhabitants of the country invariably assist a murderer to escape: they seem to think that the individual sins against the government, and not against the people. A traveller has no protection besides his fire-arms; and the constant habit of carrying them is the main check to more frequent robberies.

The character of the higher and more educated classes who reside in the towns, partakes, but perhaps in a lesser degree, of the good parts of the Gaucho, but is, I fear, stained by many vices of which he is free. Sensuality, mockery of all religion, and the grossest corruption, are far from uncommon. Nearly every public officer can be bribed. The head man in the post-office sold forged government franks. The governor and prime minister openly combined to plunder the state. Justice, where gold came into play, was hardly expected by anyone. I knew an Englishman, who went to the Chief Justice (he told me that, not then understanding the ways of the place, he trembled as he entered the room), and said, "Sir, I have come to offer you two hundred (paper) dollars (value about five pounds sterling) if you will arrest before a certain time a man who has cheated me. I know it is against the law, but my lawyer (naming him) recommended me to take this step." The Chief Justice smiled acquiescence, thanked him, and the man before night was safe in prison. With this entire want of principle in many of the leading men, with the country full of ill-paid turbulent officers, the people yet hope that a democratic form of government can succeed!

On first entering society in these countries, two or three features strike one as particularly remarkable. The polite and dignified manners pervading every rank of life, the excellent taste displayed by the women in their dresses, and the equality amongst all ranks. At the Río Colorado some men who kept the humblest shops used to dine with General Rosas. A son of a major at Bahía Blanca gained his livelihood by making paper cigars, and he wished to accompany me, as guide or servant, to Buenos Ayres, but his father objected on the score of the danger alone. Many officers in the army can neither read nor write, yet all meet in society as equals. In Entre Ríos, the Sala consisted of only six representatives. One of them kept a common shop, and evidently was not degraded by the office. All this is what would be expected in a new country; nevertheless the absence of gentlemen by profession appears to an Englishman something strange.

When speaking of these countries, the manner in which they have been brought up by their unnatural parent, Spain, should always be borne in mind. On the whole, perhaps, more credit is due for what has been done, than blame for that which may be deficient. It is impossible to doubt but that the extreme liberalism of these countries must ultimately lead to good results. The very general toleration of foreign religions, the regard paid to the means of education, the freedom of the press, the facilities offered to all foreigners, and especially, as I am bound to add, to every one professing the humblest pretensions to science, should be recollected with gratitude by those who have visited Spanish South America.

While travelling through the country, I received several vivid descriptions of the effects of a late great drought; and the account of this may throw some light on the cases where vast numbers of animals of all kinds have been embedded together. The period included the years 1827 and 1830 is called the "gran seco," or the great drought. During this time so little rain fell, that the vegetation, even to the thistles, failed; the brooks were dried up, and the whole country assumed the appearance of a dusty high road. This was especially the case in the northern part of the province of Buenos Ayres and the southern part of St. Fe. Very great numbers of birds, wild animals, cattle, and horses perished from the want of food and water. A man told me that the deer used to come into his courtyard to the well, which he had been obliged to dig to supply his own family with water; and that the partridges had hardly strength to fly away when pursued. The lowest estimation of the loss of cattle in the province of Buenos Ayres alone, was taken at one million head.

I was informed by an eye-witness that the cattle in herds of thousands rushed into the Paraná, and being exhausted by hunger they were unable to crawl up the muddy banks, and thus were drowned. The arm of the river which runs by San Pedro was so full of putrid carcasses, that the master of a vessel told me that the smell rendered it quite impassable. Without doubt several hundred thousand animals thus perished in the river: their bodies when putrid were seen floating down the stream; and many in all probability were deposited in the estuary of the Plata. All the small rivers became highly saline, and this caused the death of vast numbers in particular spots; for when an animal drinks of such water it does not recover. Azara describes the fury of the wild horses on a similar occasion, rushing into the marshes, those which arrived first being overwhelmed and crushed by those which followed. He adds that more than once he has seen the carcasses of upwards of a thousand wild horses thus destroyed. I noticed that the smaller streams in the Pampas were paved with a breccia of bones, but this probably is the effect of a gradual increase, rather than of the destruction at any one period. Subsequently to the drought of 1827 to '32, a very rainy season followed, which caused great floods. Hence it is almost certain that some thousands of the skeletons were buried by the deposits of the very next year. What would be the opinion of a geologist, viewing such an enormous collection of bones, of all kinds of animals and of all ages, thus embedded in one thick earthy mass? Would he not attribute it to a flood having swept over the surface of the land, rather than to the common order of things?*

CHILE: The next day I landed at Talcahuano, and afterwards rode to Concepción. Both towns presented the most awful yet interesting spectacle I ever beheld. To a person who had formerly known them, it possibly might have been still more impressive; for the ruins were so mingled together, and the whole scene possessed so little the air of a habitable place, that it was scarcely possible to imagine its former condition. The earthquake commenced at half-past eleven o'clock in the forenoon. If it had happened in the middle of the night, the greater number of the inhabitants (which in this one province amount to many thousands) must have perished, instead of less than a hundred: as it was, the invariable practice of running out of doors at the first trembling of the ground, alone saved them. In Concepción each house, or row of houses, stood by itself, a heap or line of ruins; but in Talcahuano, owing to the great wave, little more than one layer of bricks, tiles, and timber, with here and there part of a wall left standing, could be distinguished. From this circumstance Concepción, although not so completely desolated, was a more terrible, and, if I may so call it, picturesque sight. The first shock was very sudden. The mayor-domo at Quiriquina told me, that the first notice he received of it, was finding both the horse he rode and himself, rolling together on the ground. Rising up, he was again thrown down. He also told me that some cows which were standing on the steep side of the island were rolled into the sea. The great wave caused the destruction of many cattle; on one low island near the head of the bay, seventy animals were washed off and drowned.

*These droughts to a certain degree seem to be almost periodical; I was told the dates of several others, and the intervals were about fifteen years.

It is generally thought that this has been the worst earthquake ever recorded in Chile; but as the very severe ones occur only after long intervals, this cannot easily be known; nor indeed would a much worse shock have made any great difference, for the ruin was now complete. Innumerable small tremblings followed the great earthquake, and within the first twelve days no less than three hundred were counted.

After viewing Concepción, I cannot understand how the greater number of inhabitants escaped unhurt. The houses in many parts fell outwards; thus forming in the middle of the streets little hillocks of brickwork and rubbish. Mr. Rouse, the English consul, told us that he was at breakfast when the first movement warned him to run out. He had scarcely reached the middle of the courtyard, when one side of his house came thundering down. He retained presence of mind to remember, that if he once got on the top of that part which had already fallen, he would be safe. Not being able from the motion of the ground to stand, he crawled up on his hands and knees; and no sooner had he ascended this little eminence, than the other side of the house fell in, the great beams sweeping close in front of his head. With his eyes blinded, and his mouth chocked with the cloud of dust which darkened the sky, at last he gained the street. As shock succeeded shock, at the interval of a few minutes, no one dared approach the shattered ruins; and no one knew whether his dearest friends and relations were not perishing from the want of help. Those who had saved any property were obliged to keep a constant watch, for thieves prowled about, and at each little trembling of the ground, with one hand they beat their breasts and cried "misericordia!" and then with the other filched what they could from the ruins. The thatched roofs fell over the fires, and flames burst forth in all parts. Hundreds knew themselves ruined, and few had the means of providing food for the day.

Shortly after the shock, a great wave was seen from the distance of three or four miles, approaching in the middle of the bay with a smooth outline; but along the shore it tore up cottages and trees, as it swept onwards with irresistible force. At the head of the bay it broke in a fearful line of white breakers, which rushed up to a height of 23 vertical feet above the highest spring-tides. Their force must have been prodigious; for at the Fort a cannon with its carriage, estimated at four tons in weight, was moved 15 feet inwards. A schooner was left in the midst of the ruins, 200 yards from the beach. The first wave was followed by two others, which in their retreat carried away a vast wreck of floating objects.

We reached Coquimbo, where we stayed a few days. The town is remarkable for nothing but its extreme quietness. It is said to contain from 6000 to 8000 inhabitants.

In the evening, Captain Fitz Roy and myself were dining with Mr. Edwards, an English resident well known for his hospitality by all who have visited Coquimbo, when a sharp earthquake happened. I heard the forecoming rumble, but from the screams of the ladies, the running of the servants, and the rush of several of the gentlemen to the doorway, I could not distinguish the motion. Some of the women afterwards were crying with terror, and one gentleman said he should not be able to sleep all night, or if he did, it would only be to dream of falling houses. The father of this person had lately lost all his property at Talcahuano, and he himself had only just escaped a falling roof at Valparaiso, in 1822. He mentioned a curious coincidence which then happened: he was playing at cards, when a German, one of the party, got up, and said he would never sit in a room in these countries with the door shut, as owing to his having done so, he had nearly lost his life at Copiapó. Accordingly he opened the door; and no sooner had he done this, than he cried out, "Here it comes again!" and the famous shock commenced. The whole party escaped. The danger in an earthquake is not from the time lost in opening a door, but from the chance of its becoming jammed by the movement of the walls.

It is impossible to be much surprised at the fear which natives and old residents, though some of them known to be men of great command of mind, so generally experience during earthquakes. I think, however, this excess of panic may be partly attributed to a want of habit in governing their fear, as it is not a feeling they are ashamed of. Indeed the natives do not like to see a person indifferent. I heard of two Englishmen who, sleeping in the open air during a smart shock, knowing that there was no danger, did not rise. The natives cried out indignantly, "Look at those heretics, they will not even get out of their beds!"

PERU: We anchored in the Bay of Callao, the seaport of Lima, the capital of Peru. We stayed here six weeks, but from the troubled state of public affairs, I saw very little of the country. During our whole visit the climate was far from being so delightful, as it is generally represented. A dull heavy bank of clouds constantly hung over the land, so that during the first sixteen days I had only one view of the Cordillera behind Lima. These mountains, seen in stages, one above the other, through openings in the clouds, had a very grand appearance. It is almost become a proverb, that rain never falls in the lower part of Peru. Yet this can hardly be considered correct; for during almost every day of our visit there was a thick drizzling mist, which was sufficient to make the streets muddy and one's clothes damp: this the people are pleased to call Peruvian dew. That much rain does not fall is very certain, for the houses are covered only with flat roofs made of hardened mud; and on the mole ship-loads of wheat were piled up, being thus left for weeks together without any shelter.

I cannot say I liked the very little I saw of Peru: in summer, however, it is said that the climate is much pleasanter. In all seasons, both inhabitants and foreigners suffer from severe attacks of ague. This disease is common on the whole coast of Peru, but is unknown in the interior.

No State in South America, since the declaration of independence, has suffered more from anarchy than Peru. At the time of our visit, there were four chiefs in arms contending for supremacy in the government: if one succeeded in becoming for a time very powerful, the others coalesced against him; but no sooner were they victorious, than they were again hostile to each other. The other day, at the Anniversary of the Independence, high mass was performed, the President partaking of the sacrament: during the *Te Deum laudamus,* instead of each regiment displaying the Peruvian flag, a black one with death's head was unfurled. Imagine a government under which such a scene could be ordered, on such an occasion, to be typical of their determination of fighting to death! This state of affairs happened at a time very unfortunately for me, as I was precluded from taking any excursions much beyond the limits of the town.

Lima stands on a plain in a valley, formed during the gradual retreat of the sea. It is seven miles from Callao, and is elevated 500 feet above it; but from the slope being very gradual, the road appears absolutely level; so that when at Lima it is difficult to believe one has ascended even one hundred feet: Humboldt has remarked on this singularly deceptive case. Steep, barren hills rise like islands from the plain, which is divided by straight mudwalls, into larger green fields. In these scarcely a tree grows excepting a few willows, and an occasional clump of bananas and of oranges. The city of Lima is now in a wretched state of decay: the streets are nearly unpaved; and heaps of filth are piled up in all directions, where the black gallinazos, tame as poultry, pick up bits of carrion. The houses have generally an upper story, built, on account of the earthquakes, of plastered woodwork; but some of the old ones, which are now used by several families, are immensely large, and would rival in suites of apartments the most magnificent in any place. Lima, the City of the Kings, must formerly have been a splendid town. The extraordinary number of churches gives it, even at the present day, a peculiar and striking character, especially when viewed from a short distance.

One day I went out with some merchants to hunt in the immediate vicinity of the city. Our sport was very poor; but I had an opportunity of seeing the ruins of one of the ancient Indian villages, with its mound like a natural hill in the centre. The remains of houses, enclosures, irrigating streams, and burial mounds, scattered over this plain, cannot fail to give one a high idea of the condition and number of the ancient population. When their earthenware, woollen clothes, utensils of elegant forms cut out of the hardest rocks, tools of copper, ornaments of precious stones, palaces and hydraulic works, are considered, it is impossible not to respect the considerable advance made by them in the arts of civilization. The burial mounds, called Huacas, are really stupendous; although in some places they appear to be natural hills incased and modelled.

There is another and very different class of ruins, which possesses some interest, namely, those of old Callao, overwhelmed by the great earthquake of 1746, and its accompanying wave. The destruction must have been more complete even than at Talcahuano. Quantities of shingle almost conceal the foundations of the walls, and vast masses of brickwork appear to have been whirled about like pebbles by the retiring waves. It has been stated that the land subsided during this memorable shock; I could not discover any proof of this; yet it seems far from improbable, for the form of the coast must certainly have undergone some change since the foundation of the old town; as no people in their senses would willingly have chosen for their building place, the narrow spit of shingle on which the ruins now stand.

CARRION-FEEDING HAWKS OF SOUTH AMERICA: The number, tameness, and disgusting habits of the carrion-feeding hawks of South America make them pre-eminently striking to any one accustomed only to the birds of Northern Europe. In this list may be included four species of the Caracara or Polyborus, the Turkey buzzard, the Gallinazo, and the Condor. The Caracaras are, from their structure, placed among the eagles: we shall soon see how ill they become so high a rank. In their habits they well supply the place of our carrion-crows, magpies, and ravens; a tribe of birds widely distributed over the rest of the world, but entirely absent in South America. To begin with the Polyborus Brasiliensis: this is a common bird, and has a wide geographical range; it is most numerous on the grassy savannahs of La Plata (where it goes by the name of Carrancha), and is far from unfrequent throughout the sterile plains of Patagonia. In the desert between the rivers Negro and Colorado, numbers constantly attend the line of road to devour the carcasses of the exhausted animals which chance to perish from fatigue and thirst. Although thus common in these dry and open countries, and likewise on the arid shores of the Pacific, it is nevertheless found inhabiting the damp impervious forests of West Patagonia and Tierra del Fuego. The Carranchas, together with the Chimango, constantly attend in numbers the estancias and slaughtering-houses. If an animal dies on the plain the Gallinazo commences the feast, and then the two species of Polyborus pick the bones clean. These birds, although thus commonly feeding together, are far from being friends. When the Carrancha is quietly seated on the branch of a tree or on the ground, the Chimango often continues for a long time flying backwards and forwards, up and down, in a semicircle, trying each time at the bottom of the curve to strike its larger relative. The Carrancha takes little notice, except by bobbing its head. Although the Carranchas frequently assemble in numbers, they are not gregarious; for in desert places they may be seen solitary, or more commonly by pairs.

The Carranchas are said to be very crafty, and to steal great numbers of eggs. They attempt, also, together with the Chimango, to pick off the scabs from the sore backs of horses and mules. The poor animal, on the other hand, with its ears down and its back arched; and, on the other, the hovering bird, eyeing at the distance of a yard, the disgusting morsel, form a picture, which has been described by Captain Head with his own peculiar spirit and accuracy. These false eagles most rarely kill any living bird or animal; and their vulture-like, necrophagous habits are very evident to any one, who has fallen asleep on the desolate plains of Patagonia, for when he wakes, he will see, on each surrounding hillock, one of these birds patiently watching him with an evil eye: it is a feature in the landscape of these countries, which will be recognized by every one who has wandered over them. If a party of men go out hunting with dogs and horses, they will be accompanied, during the day, by several of these attendants. After feeding, the uncovered craw protrudes; at such times, and indeed generally, the Carrancha is an inactive, tame, and cowardly bird. Its flight is heavy and slow, like that of an English rook. It seldom soars; but I have twice seen one at a great height gliding through the air with much ease.

The Polyborus Chimango is considerably smaller than the last species. It is truly omnivorous, and will eat even bread; and I was assured that it materially injures the potato-crops in Chiloé,* by stocking up the roots when first planted. Of all the carrion-feeders it is generally the last which leaves the skeleton of a dead animal; and may often be seen within the ribs of a cow or horse, like a bird in a cage.

The condors may oftentimes be seen at a great height, soaring over a certain spot in the most graceful circles. On some occasions I am sure that they do this only for pleasure, but on others, the Chileno countryman tells you that they are watching a dying animal, or the puma devouring its prey. If the condors glide down, and then suddenly all rise together, the Chileno knows that it is the puma which, watching the carcass, has sprung out to drive away the robbers. Besides feeding on carrion, the condors frequently attack young goats and lambs; and the shepherd dogs are trained, whenever they pass over, to run out, and looking upwards to bark violently.

*An island off the Chilean coast (Ed.).

When the condors are wheeling in a flock round and round any spot, their flight is beautiful. Except when rising from the ground, I do not recollect ever having seen one of these birds flap its wings. Near Lima, I watched several for nearly half an hour, without once taking off my eyes: they moved in large curves, sweeping in circles, descending and ascending without giving a single flap. As they glided close over my head, I intently watched from an oblique position, the outlines of the separate and great terminal feathers of each wing; and these separate feathers, if there had been the least vibratory movement, would have appeared as if blended together; but they were seen distinct against the blue sky. The head and neck were moved frequently, and apparently with force; and the extended wings seemed to form the fulcrum on which the movements of the neck, body, and tail acted. If the bird wished to descend, the wings were for a moment collapsed; and when again expanded with an altered inclination, the momentum gained by the rapid descent seemed to urge the bird upwards with the even and steady movement of a paper kite. In the case of any bird *soaring,* its motion must be sufficiently rapid, so that the action of the inclined surface of its body on the atmosphere may counterbalance its gravity. The force to keep up the momentum of a body moving in a horizontal plane in the air (in which there is so little friction) cannot be great, and this force is all that is wanted. The movement of the neck and body of the condor, we must suppose, is sufficient for this. However this may be, it is truly wonderful and beautiful to see so great a bird, hour after hour, without any apparent exertion, wheeling and gliding over mountain and river.

Selections from "Dr. Francia"

By THOMAS CARLYLE

For some thirty years he was all the government his native Paraguay may be said to have.

Thomas Carlyle's essay on Dr. Francia, the dictator of Paraguay, appeared six years after his *History of the French Revolution,* published in 1837, won him international fame. Although the Francia essay thus belongs to the earlier period of this irascible Scottish-Calvinist's historical writings, it reveals many of his later prejudices and tendencies.

Originally, Carlyle criticized the painting of historical portraits. He said of Scott's *History* and its author's preoccupation with Mary Queen of Scots, "strange that a man should think he was writing the history of a nation while he is chronicling the amours of a wanton young woman and a sulky booby blown up with gun powder." Yet it is in just this personalized area that Carlyle became such a master, so much so that, at his best, he is the greatest of English historical portrait painters. During the first half of the nineteenth century perhaps no British writer except Macaulay gave such an impetus to historical study.

It was Carlyle's habit to paste on a screen engraved portraits of the people about whom he was writing. A writer, according to Carlyle, must have a clear image of his subject in mind if he is to make it possible for the reader to see him. Unfortunately, however, Carlyle, who saw individuals with such incomparable clarity, was blind to the existence and fate of the masses. G. P. Gooch, the British historian, feels that Carlyle's conception of leadership assumes its most "repulsive aspect" in "Dr. Francia." It never occurred to Carlyle to investigate the effects of autocracy either on the ruler or the ruled. "The forerunner of Nietzsche forgot the golden truth expressed in Mill's dictum that where the schoolmaster does all the pupils' lessons, they never advance."

The importance of the Dr. Francia essay is derived both from its timing and philosophy. It is the first article by a recognized European scholar on Latin America's first republican dictator. Its inherent contempt for the poor and ignorant, its sympathy for the man of action as the backbone of nationality in Spanish America, and its argument that the common herd must be drilled and punished by their superiors in the interest of commerce, law, and progress have been repeated again and again by the advocates of other Latin American dictators both in Western Europe and the United States. Disciples of this school invariably claim originality for their thinking and fail to make attribution to Carlyle and his philosophy, even if they know of its existence. A reason, perhaps, is their reluctance to associate themselves publicly and intellectually, especially if they hold positions of power and influence in democratic countries, with a man who "sided with the South in the slavery struggle, and with Governor Eyre against 'quashee nigger.' "

Carlyle, born in Scotland in 1795, was the son of an uneducated stonemason. His mother was unable to write until she learned to do so in order to correspond with her son. He entered the University of Edinburgh in 1809, took a degree in mathematics, and taught until 1818 when he returned to the university. It was in 1820 that he decided that he had to write.

Originally interested in Germany, he published his *Life of Schiller* in 1824; this was soon followed by his translation of Goethe's *Wilhelm Meister*. Carlyle married in 1826 and shortly thereafter, in poor health, retired to his wife's farm, where he wrote *Sartor Resartus*.

In 1834, Carlyle and his wife moved to 5 Cheyne Row in London, and it was from there that he produced a stream of books, essays, and letters which was rarely interrupted, save for holidays in Scotland, two trips to Germany in 1852 and 1856, and the death of his wife in 1866. In later life, after fame and a certain amount of financial security had come to him, Carlyle characteristically refused most of the honors offered him, which included a title and a pension. He did, however, accept the Prussian Order of Merit in 1872 and an honorary degree from Harvard in 1875. Carlyle died in 1881.

P. K.

How is any picture of Francia to be fabricated. . . ? Certainly, first of all, by *omission* of the running shriek! This latter we shall totally omit. . . . We are to consider that, in all human likelihood, this Dionysius of

Paraguay did mean something; and then to ask in quietness, What? The running shriek once hushed, perhaps many things will compose themselves, and straggling fractions of information, almost infinitesimally small, may become unexpectedly luminous!

An unscientific Cattle-breeder and tiller of the earth, in some nameless *charca* not far from the City of Assumpcion, [*sic*] was the Father of this remarkable human individual; and seems to have evoked him into being sometime in the year 1757. The man's name is not known to us; his very nation is a point of controversy: Francia himself gave him out for an immigrant of French extraction; the popular belief was that he had wandered over from Brazil. Portuguese or French, or both in one, he produced this human individual, and had him christened by the name of José Gaspar Rodríguez Francia, in the year above mentioned. Rodríguez, no doubt, had a Mother too; but her name also, nowhere found mentioned, must be omitted in this delineation. Her name, and all her fond maternities, and workings and sufferings, good brown lady, are sunk in dumb forgetfulness; and buried there along with her, under the twenty-fifth parallel of Southern Latitude; and no British reader is required to interfere with them! José Rodríguez must have been a loose-made tawny creature, much given to taciturn reflection; probably to crying humours, with fits of vehement ill-nature. . . . There were other young Francias; at least one sister and one brother in addition; of whom the latter by-and-by went mad. The Francias, with their adust character, and vehement French-Portuguese blood, had perhaps all a kind of aptitude for madness. The Dictator himself was subject to the terriblest fits of hypochondria as your adust "men of genius" too frequently are! The lean Rodríguez, we fancy, may have a devotional turn withal; born half a century earlier, he had infallibly been so. Devotional or not, he shall be a Priest, and *do* the Divine Offices in Paraguay, perhaps in a very unexpected way.

Rodríguez having learned his hornbooks and elementary branches at Assumpcion, was accordingly despatched to the University of Córdova in Tucumán, to pursue his curriculum in that seminary. So far we know, but almost no farther. What kind of curriculum it was, what lessons spiritual-spoonmeat, the poor lank sallow boy was crammed with, in Córdova High Seminary; and how he took to it, and pined or throve on it, is entirely uncertain. . . .

Be that as it may, the lean Francia prosecutes his studies at

Córdova, waxes gradually taller towards new destinies. Rodríguez Francia, in some kind of Jesuit skullcap and black college serge gown, a lank rawboned creature, stalking with a downlook through the irregular public streets of Córdova in those years, with an infinitude of painful unspeakabilities in the interior of him, is an interesting object to the historical mind. So much is unspeakable, O Rodríguez; and it is a most strange Universe this thou hast been born into; and the theorem of Ignatius Loyola and Fatpauncho Usandwonto seems to me to hobble somewhat! Much is unspeakable; lying within one, like a dark lake of doubt, of Acherontic dread, leading down to Chaos itself. Much is unspeakable, answers Francia; but somewhat also is speakable–this for example: That I will not be a Priest in Tucumán in these circumstances; that I should like decidedly to be a secular person rather, were it even a Lawyer rather. Francia, arrived at man's years, changes from Divinity to Law. . . . Rodríguez quitted the Tucumán *Alma Mater* with some beard on his chin, and reappeared in Assumpcion to look-out for practice at the bar.

Assumpcion City, near three-hundred years old now, lies in free-and-easy fashion on the left bank of the Paraná River; embosomed among fruit-forests, rich tropical umbrage; thick wood round it everywhere – which serves for defence too against the Indians. Approach by which of the various roads you will, it is through miles of solitary shady avenue, shutting-out the sun's glare; overcanopying, as with grateful green awning, the loose sand-highway. . . .

The people of that profuse climate live in a careless abundance, troubling themselves about few things; build what wooden carts, hide-beds, mud-brick houses are indispensable; import what of ornamental lies handiest abroad; exchanging for it Paraguay tea in sewed goatskins. . . . In the damp flat country parts, where the mosquitoes abound, you sleep on high stages, mounted on four poles, forty feet above the ground, attained by ladders; so high, blessed be the Virgin, no mosquito can follow to sting–it is a blessing of the Virgin or some other. You sleep there, in an indiscriminate arrangement, each in his several *poncho* or blanket-cloak; with some saddle, deal-box, wooden log, or the like, under your head. For bed-tester is the canopy of everlasting blue; for night-lamp burns Canopus in his infinite spaces; mosquitoes cannot reach you, if it please the Powers. And rosy-fingered Morn, suffusing the east with sudden red and gold, and other flame-heraldry of swift-advancing Day, attenuates all dreams; and the Sun's first level light-volley sheers away sleep from living creatures everywhere; and living men do then awaken on their four-post stage there, in the Pampas – and might begin with prayer if they liked, one fancies! There is an altar decked on the horizon's edge yonder, is there not; and a cathedral wide enough? – How, overnight, you have defended yourself against vampires, is unknown to this Editor.

The Guacho [*sic*] population, it must be owned, is not yet fit for constitutional liberty. They are a rude people; lead a drowsy life, of ease and sluttish abundance–one shade, and but one, above a dog's life, which is defined as "ease and scarcity." The arts are in their infancy; and not less the virtues. For equipment, clothing, bedding, household furniture and general outfit of every kind, those simple populations depend much on the skin of the cow; making of it most things wanted, lasso bolas, ship-cordage, rimmings of cart-wheels, spatter-dashes, beds and house-doors. In country places they sit on the skull of the cow. . . .

One art they seem to have perfected, and one only–that of riding. Astley's and Ducrow's must hide their head, and all glories of Newmarket and Epsom dwindle to extinction, in comparison of Guacho horsemanship. Certainly if ever Centaurs lived upon earth, these are of them. They stick-on their horses as if both were one flesh; galloping where there seems hardly path for an ibex; leaping like kangaroos, and flourishing their nooses and bolases the while. They can whirl themselves round under the belly of the horse, in cases of war-stratagem, and stick fast, hanging-on by the mere great toe and heel. You think it is a drove of wild horses galloping up: on a sudden, with wild scream, it becomes a troop of Centaurs with pikes in their hands. . . . Their huts abound in beef, in reek also, and rubbish; excelling in dirt most places that human nature has anywhere inhabited. Poor Guachos! They drink Paraguay tea, sucking it up in succession, through the same tin pipe, from one common skillet. They are hospitable, sooty, leathery, lying, laughing fellows; of excellent talent in their sphere. They have stoicism, though ignorant of Zeno; nay stoicism coupled with real gaiety of heart. Amidst their reek and wreck, they laugh loud, in rough jolly banter; they twang, in a plaintive manner, rough love-melodies on a kind of guitar; smoke infinite tobacco; and delight in gambling and ardent-spirits, ordinary refuge of voracious empty souls. For the same reason, and a better, they delight also in Corpus-Christi ceremonies, mass-chantings, and devotional performances. These men are fit to be drilled into something! Their lives stand there like empty capacious bottles, calling to the heavens and the earth, and all Dr. Francias who may pass that way: "Is there nothing to put into us then? Nothing but nomadic idleness, Jesuit superstition, rubbish, reek and dry stripes of tough beef?" Ye unhappy Guachos–yes, there is something other, there are several things other, to put into you! But withal, you will observe, the seven devils have first to be put out of you: Idleness, lawless Brutalness, Darkness, Falseness–seven devils or more. And the way to put something into you is, alas, not so plain at present! Is it–alas, on the whole, is it not perhaps to lay good horsewhips lustily *upon* you, and cast out these seven devils as a preliminary?

How Francia passed his days in such a region, where philosophy, as is too clear, was at the lowest ebb? Francia, like Quintus Fixlein, had "perennial fire-proof joys, namely, employments." He had much Law-business, a great and ever-increasing reputation as a man at once skilful and faithful in the management of causes for men. Then, in his leisure hours, he had his Volneys, Raynals; he had secondhand scientific treatises in French; he loved to "interrogate Nature," as they say; to possess theodolites, telescopes, star-glasses–any kind of glass or book, or gazing implement whatever, through which he might try to catch a glimpse of Fact in this strange Universe: poor Francia! Nay, it is said, his hard heart was not without inflammability; was sensible to those Andalusian eyes still bright in the tenth or twelfth generation. In such case too, it may have burnt, one would think, like anthracite, in a somewhat ardent manner. Rumours to this effect are afloat; not at once incredible. Pity there had not been some Andalusian pair of eyes, with speculation, depth and soul enough in the rear of them to fetter Dr. Francia permanently, and make a house-father of him. It had been better; but it befell not. As for that light-headed, smart, brown girl whom, twenty years afterwards, you saw selling flowers on the streets of Assumpcion, and leading a light life, is there any certainty that she was Dr. Francia's daughter? Any certainty that, even if so, he could and should have done something considerable for her? Poor Francia, poor light-headed, smart, brown girl—this present Reviewer cannot say!

Francia is a somewhat lonesome, downlooking man, apt to be solitary even in the press of men; wears a face not unvisited by laughter, yet tending habitually towards the sorrowful, the stern. He passes everywhere for a man of veracity, punctuality, of iron methodic rigour; of iron rectitude, above all. "The skilful lawyer," "the learned lawyer," these are reputations; but the "honest lawyer"! This Law-case was reported by the Robertsons[1] before they thought of writing a *Francia's Reign of Terror,* with that running shriek, which so confuses us. We love to believe the anecdote, even in its present loose state, as significant of many things in Francia:

It has been already observed that Francia's reputation as a lawyer, was not only unsullied by venality, but conspicuous for rectitude.

He had a friend in Assumpcion of the name of Domingo Rodríguez. This man had cast a covetous eye upon a Naboth's vineyard, and this Naboth, of whom Francia was the open enemy, was called Estanislao Machain. Never doubting that the young Doctor, like other lawyers, would undertake his unrighteous cause, Rodríguez opened to him his case, and requested, with a handsome retainer, his advocacy of it. Francia saw at once that his friend's pretensions were founded in fraud and injustice; and he not only refused to act as his counsel, but plainly told him that much as he hated his antagonist Machain, yet if he (Rodríguez) persisted in his iniquitous suit, that antagonist should have his (Francia's) most zealous support. But covetousness, as Ahab's story shows us, is not so easily driven from its pretensions; and in spite of Francia's warning, Rodríguez persisted. As he was a potent man in point of fortune, all was going against Machain and his devoted vineyard.

At this stage of the question, Francia wrapped himself one night in his cloak, and walked to the house of his inveterate enemy, Machain. The slave who opened the door, knowing that his master and the Doctor, like the houses of Montagu and Capulet, were smoke in each other's eyes, refused the lawyer admittance, and ran to inform his master of the strange and unexpected visit. Machain, no less struck by the circumstance than his slave, for some time hesitated; but at length determined to admit Francia. In walked the silent Doctor to Machain's chamber. All the papers con-

[1]*Letters on Paraguay*. By J. P. & W. P. Robertson. 2 vols. Second Edition. London, 1839.

nected with the lawplea–voluminous enough I have been assured–were outspread upon the defendant's escritoire.

"Machain," said the Lawyer, addressing him, "you know I am your enemy. But I know that my friend Rodríguez meditates, and will certainly, unless I interfere, carry against you an act of gross and lawless aggression; I have come to offer my services in your defence."

The astonished Machain could scarcely credit his senses; but poured forth the ebullition of his gratitude in terms of thankful acquiescence.

The first "escrito," or writing, sent-in by Francia to the Juez de Alzada, or Judge of the Court of Appeal, confounded the adverse advocates, and staggered the judge, who was in their interest. "My friend," said the judge to the leading counsel, "I cannot go forward in this matter, unless you bribe Dr. Francia to be silent." "I will try," replied the advocate; and he went to Naboth's counsel with a hundred doubloons (about three hundred and fifty guineas), which he offered him as a bribe to let the cause take its iniquitous course. Considering too, that his best introduction would be a hint that his douceur was offered with the judge's concurrence, the knavish lawyer hinted to the upright one that such was the fact.

"Salga Usted," said Francia, *"con sus viles pensamientos y vilisimo oro de mi casa!* Out, with your vile insinuations, and dross of gold, from my house!"

Off marched the venal drudge of the unjust judge; and in a moment putting on his capote, the offended Advocate went to the residence of the Juez de Alzada. Shortly relating what had passed between himself and the myrmidon,–"Sir," continued Francia, "you are a disgrace to law, and a blot upon justice. You are, moreover, completely in my power; and unless tomorrow I have a decision of favour of my client, I will make your seat upon the bench too hot for you, and the insignia of your judicial office shall become the emblems of your shame."

The morrow *did* bring a decision in favour of Francia's client. Naboth retained his vineyard; the judge lost his reputation; and the young Doctor's fame extended far and wide.

On the other hand, it is admitted that he quarrelled with his Father, in those days; and, as is reported, never spoke to him more. The subject of the quarrel is vaguely supposed to have been "money matters." Francia is not accused of avarice; nay is expressly acquitted of loving money, even by Rengger.[2] But he did hate injustice;–and probably was

[2]*Essai Historique sur la Révolution de Paraguay, et le Gouvernement Dictatorial du Docteur Francia.* Par MM Rengger et Longchamp. Seconde édition. Paris, 1827.

not indisposed to allow *himself,* among others, "the height of fair play"! A rigorous, correct man, that will have a spade be a spade; a man of much learning in Creole Law, and occult French Sciences, of great talent, energy, fidelity:—a man of some temper withal; unhappily subject to private "hypochondria"; black private thunder-clouds, whence probably the origin of these *lightnings,* when you poke into him! He leads a lonesome self-secluded life; "interrogating Nature" through mere star-glasses, and Abbé-Raynal philosophies—who in that way will yield no very exuberant response. Mere law-papers, advocate-fees, civic officialities, renowns, and the wonder of Assumpcion Guachos;—not so much as a pair of Andalusian eyes that can *lasso* him, except in a temporary way: this man seems to have got but a lean lease of Nature, and may end in a shrunk condition! A century ago, with this atrabiliar earnestness of his, and such a reverberatory furnace of passions, inquiries, unspeakabilities burning in him, deep under cover, he might have made an excellent Monk of St. Dominic, fit almost for canonisation; nay, an excellent Superior of the Jesuits, Grand Inquisitor, or the like, had you developed him in that way. But, for all this, he is now a day too late. Monks of St. Dominic that might have been, do now, instead of devotional raptures and miraculous suspensions in prayer, produce—brown accidental female infants, to sell flowers, in an indigent state, on the streets of Assumpcion! It is grown really a most barren time; and this Francia with his grim unspeakabilities, with his fiery splenetic humours, kept close under lock-and-key, what has he to look for in it? A post on the Bench, in the municipal *Cabildo*—nay he has already a post in the Cabildo; he has already been Alcalde, Lord-Mayor of Assumpcion, and ridden in such gilt-coach as they had. He can look for little, one would say, but barren moneys, barren Guacho world-celebrities; Abbé-Raynal philosophisms also very barren; wholly a barren life-voyage of it, ending—in *zero,* thinks the Abbé-Raynal?

But no; the world wags not that way in those days. Far over the waters there have been Federations of the Champ-de-Mars; guillotines, portable-guillotines, and a French People risen against Tyrants; there has been a *Sansculottism,* speaking at last in cannon-volleys and the crash of towns and nations over half the world. Sleek Fatpauncho Usandwonto, sleek aristocratic Donothingism, sunk as in death-sleep in its well-stuffed easy-chair, or staggering in somnambulism on the housetops, seemed to itself to hear a voice say, Sleep no more,

Donothingism; Donothingism doth murder sleep! It was indeed a terrible explosion, that of Sansculottism; commingling very Tartarus with the old-established stars;–fit, such a tumult was it, to awaken all but the dead. And out of it there had come Napoleonisms, Tamerlanisms; and then as a branch of these, "Conventions of Aranjuez," soon followed by "Spanish Juntas," "Spanish Cortes"; and, on the whole, a smiting broad awake of poor old Spain itself, much to its amazement. And naturally, of New Spain next–to *its* double amazement, seeing itself awake! And so, in the new Hemisphere too, arise wild projects, angry arguings; arise armed gatherings in Santa Marguerita Island, with Bolívars and invasions of Cumaná; revolts of La Plata, revolts of this and then of that; the subterranean electric element, shock on shock, shaking and exploding, in the new Hemisphere too, from sea to sea. Very astonishing to witness, from the year 1810 onwards. Had Rodríguez Francia three ears, he would hear; as many eyes as Argus, he would gaze! He is all eye, he is all ear. A new, entirely different figure of existence is cut-out for Doctor Rodríguez.

The Paraguay People as a body, lying far inland, with little speculation in their heads, were in no haste to adopt the new republican gospel; but looked first how it would succeed in shaping itself into facts. Buenos-Ayres, Tucumán, most of the La Plata Provinces had made their revolutions, brought in the reign of liberty, and unluckily driven out the reign of law and regularity; before the Paraguenos could resolve on such an enterprise. Perhaps they are afraid? General Belgrano, with a force of a thousand men, missioned by Buenos-Ayres, came up the river to countenance them, in the end of 1810; but was met on their frontier in array of war; was attacked, or at least was terrified, in the night-watches, so that his men all fled;–and on the morrow, poor General Belgrano found himself not a countenancer, but one needing countenance; and was in a polite way sent down the river again![3] Not till a year after did the Paraguenos, by spontaneous movement, resolve on a career of freedom;–resolve on getting some kind of Congress assembled, and the old Government sent its ways. Francia, it is presumable, was active at once in exciting and restraining them: the fruit was now drop-ripe, we may say, and fell by a shake. Our old royal

[3]Rengger.

Governor went aside, worthy man, with some slight grimace, when ordered to do so; National Congress introduced itself; secretaries read papers, "compiled chiefly out of Rollin's *Ancient History*"; and we became a Republic: with Don Fulgencio Yegros, one of the richest Guachos and best horseman of the province, for *President,* and two Assessors with him, called also *Vocales,* or Vowels, whose names escape us; Francia as *Secretary,* being naturally the Consonant, or motive soul of the combination. This, as we grope out the date, was in 1811. The Paraguay Congress, having completed this constitution, went home again to its field-labours, hoping a good issue.

. . . Francia withdrew to his *charca,* a pleasant country-house in the woods of Ytapúa not far off; there to interrogate Nature, and live in a private manner. . . . Here is the figure of his library:

He introduced me to his library, in a confined room, with a very small window, and that so shaded by the roof of the corridor, as to admit the least portion of light necessary for study. The library was arranged on three rows of shelves extending across the room, and might have consisted of three hundred volumes. There were many ponderous books on law; a few on the inductive sciences; some in French and some in Latin upon subjects of general literature, with Euclid's Elements, and some schoolboy treatises on algebra. On a large table were heaps of law-papers and processes. Several folios bound in vellum were outspread upon it; a lighted candle (though placed there solely with a view to light cigars) lent its feeble aid to illumine the room; while a maté-cup and inkstand, both of silver, stood on another part of the table. There was neither carpet, nor mat on the brick floor; and the chairs were of such ancient fashion, size and weight, that it required a considerable effort to move them from one spot to another.[4]

Peculation, malversation, the various forms of imbecility and voracious dishonesty went their due course in the Government-offices of Assumpcion, unrestrained by Francia, and unrestrainable:—till, as we may say, it reached a height; and, like other suppurations and diseased concretions in the living system, had to burst, and take itself away. To the eyes of Paraguay in general, it had become clear that such a reign of liberty was unendurable; that some new revolution, or change of ministry was indispensable.

[4]Robertson.

In 1813 a second Congress is got together: we fancy it was Francia's last advice to the Government suppuration, when it flattered him back, for the last time, to ask his advice, That such suppuration do now dissolve itself, and a new Congress be summoned! In the new Congress, the *Vocales* are voted out; Francia and Fulgencio are named joint *Consuls:* with Francia for Consul, and Don Fulgencio Yegros for Consul's *cloak,* it may be better. Don Fulgencio rides about in gorgeous sash and epaulettes, a rich man and horse-subduer; good as Consul's cloak;–but why should the real Consul have a *cloak*? Next year in the third Congress, Francia, "by insidious manoeuvring," by "favour of the military," and indeed, also, in some sort, we may say, by law of Nature,–gets himself declared *Dictator:* "for three years," or for life, may in these circumstances mean much the same. This was in 1814. Francia never assembled any Congress more; having stolen the constitutional palladiums, and insidiously got his wicked will! Of a Congress that compiled constitutions out of *Rollin,* who would not lament such destiny? This Congress should have met again! It was indeed. . . a Congress which knew not its right hand from its left; which drank infinite rum in the taverns; and had one wish, that of getting on horseback again, home to its field-husbandry and partridge-shooting again. The military mostly favoured Francia; being gained-over by him,–the thief of constitutional palladiums.

With Francia's entrance on the Government as Consul, still more as Dictator, a great improvement . . . did in all quarters forthwith show itself. The finances were husbanded, were accurately gathered; every official person in Paraguay had to bethink him, and begin doing his work, instead of merely seeming to do it. The soldiers Francia took care to see paid and drilled; to see march, with real death-shot and service, when the Indians or other enemies showed themselves. *Guardias,* Guard-houses, at short distances, were established along the River's bank and all round the dangerous Frontiers: wherever the Indian centaur-troop showed face, an alarm-cannon went off, and soldiers, quickly assembling, with actual death-shot and service, were upon them. These wolf-hordes had to vanish into the heart of their deserts again. The land had peace. Neither Artigas, nor any of the firebrands and war-plagues which were distracting South America from side to side, could get across the border. All negotiation or intercommuning with Buenos-Ayres, or with any of these war-distracted countries, was peremptorily waived. To no "Congress of Lima," "General Congress of Panama," or other general or particular Congress, would Francia, by deputy or message, offer the smallest recognition. All South America raging and ravening like one huge dog-kennel gone rabid, we here in Paraguay have peace, and cultivate our tea-trees; why should not we let well alone? By degrees, one thing acting on another, and this ring of Frontier "Guard-houses," being already erected there, a rigorous *sanitary line,* impregnable as brass, was drawn round all Paraguay; no communication, import or export trade allowed, except by the Dictator's license–given on payment of the due moneys, when the political horizon seemed innocuous; refused when otherwise. The Dictator's trade-licenses were a considerable branch of his revenues; his entrance-dues, somewhat onerous to the foreign merchant, . . . were another. Paraguay stood isolated; the rabid dog-kennel raging round it, wide as South America, but kept out as by lock-and-key.

These were vigorous measures, gradually coming on the somnolent Guacho population! It seems, meanwhile, that, even after the Perpetual Dictatorship, and onwards to the fifth or the sixth year of Francia's government, there was, though the constitutional palladiums were stolen, nothing very special to complain of. Paraguay had peace; sat under its tea-tree; the rabid dog-kennel, Indians, Artiguenos and other war firebrands, all shut-out from it. But in that year 1819, the second year of the Perpetual Dictatorship, there arose, not for the first time, dim indications of "Plots," even dangerous Plots! In that year the firebrand Artigas was finally quenched; obliged to beg a lodging even of Francia, his enemy;–and got it, hospitably, though contemptuously. And now straightway there advanced, from Artigas's lost wasted country, a certain General Ramírez, his rival and conqueror, and fellow-bandit and firebrand. This General Ramírez advanced up to our very frontier; first with offers of alliance; failing that, with offers of war; on which latter offer he was closed with, was cut to pieces; and–a Letter was found about him, addressed to Don Fulgencio Yegros, the rich Guacho horseman and Ex-Consul; which arrested all the faculties of Dr. Francia's most intense intelligence, there and then! A Conspiracy, with Don Fulgencio at the head of it; Conspiracy which seems the wider-spread the farther one investigates it; which has been brewing itself these "two years," and now "on Good-Friday next" is to be burst out; starting with the massacre of Dr. Francia and others, whatever it may close with![5]

Francia was not a man to be trifled with in Plots! He looked, watched, investigated, till he got the exact extent, position, nature and structure of this Plot fully in his eye; and then—why, then he pounced on it like a glede-falcon, like a fierce condor, suddenly from the invisible blue; stuck beak and claws into the very heart of it, tore it into small fragments, and consumed it on the spot. It is Francia's way! This was the last plot, though not the first plot, Francia ever heard of during his Perpetual Dictatorship.

It is, as we find, over these three or these two years, while the Fulgencio Plot is getting itself pounced upon and torn in pieces, that the "reign of terror," properly so called, extends. Over these three or these two years only—though the "running shriek" of it confuses all things to the end of the chapter. It was in this stern period that Francia executed above forty persons. Not entirely inexplicable! "*Por Dios,* ye shall not conspire against me; I will not allow it! The Career of Freedom, be it known to all men and Guachos, is not yet begun in this country; I am still only casting out the Seven Devils. . . . By Heaven, if you aim at my life, I will bid you have a care of your own!" He executed upwards of forty persons. How many he arrested, flogged, cross-questioned—for he is an inexorable man! If you are guilty, or suspected of guilt, it will go ill with you here. Francia's arrest, carried by a grenadier, arrives; you are in strait prison; you are in Francia's bodily presence; those sharp St. Dominic eyes, that diabolic intellect, prying into you, probing, cross-questioning you, till the secret cannot be hid; till the "three ball-cartridges," are handed to a sentry;—and your doom is Rhadamanthine!

But the Plots, as we say, having ceased by this rough surgery, it would appear that there was, for the next twenty years, little or no more of it, little or no use for more. The "reign of terror," one begins to find, was properly a reign of rigour; which would become "terrible" enough if you infringed the rules of it, but which was peaceable otherwise, regular otherwise. Let this, amid the "running shriek," which will and should run its full length in such circumstances, be well kept in mind.

It happened too . . . that a visitation of locusts, as sometimes occurs,

[5]Rengger.

destroyed all the crops of Paraguay; and there was no prospect but of universal death or famine. The crops are done; eaten by locusts; the summer at an end! We have no foreign trade, or next to none, and never had almost any; what will become of Paraguay and its Guachos? In Guachos is no hope, no help: but in a Dionysius of the Guachos? Dictator Francia, led by occult French Sciences and natural sagacity, nay driven by necessity itself, peremptorily commands the farmers, throughout all Paraguay, to sow a certain portion of their lands anew; with or without hope—under penalties! The result was a moderately good harvest still: the result was a discovery that Two harvests were, every year, possible in Paraguay; that Agriculture, a rigorous Dictator presiding over it, could be infinitely improved there.[6] . . . Thus, one thing acting on another—domestic Plot, hanging on Artigas's country from without; and Locust swarms with Improvement of Husbandry in the interior; and those Guard-houses all already there, along the frontier—Paraguay came more and more to be hermetically closed; and Francia reigned over it, for the rest of his life, as a rigorous Dionysius of Paraguay, without foreign intercourse, or with such only as seemed good to Francia.

Of Francia's improvements there might as much be said as of his cruelties or rigours; for indeed, at bottom, the one was in proportion to the other. He improved agriculture:—not two ears of corn where one only grew, but two harvests of corn, as we have seen! He introduced schools, "boarding-schools," "elementary schools," and others . . . everywhere he promoted education, as he could; repressed superstition as he could. Strict justice between man and man was enforced in his Law-courts; he himself would accept no gift, not even a trifle, in any case whatever. . . .

That he had to maintain himself *alive* all the while, and would suffer no man to glance contradiction at him, but instantaneously repressed all such: this too we need no ghost to tell us; this lay in the very nature of the case. His lease of Paraguay was a *life-lease*. He had his "three ball-cartridges" ready for whatever man he found aiming at *his* life. He had frightful prisons. He had *Tevego* far up among the wastes, a kind of

[6]Rengger, pp. 67.

Paraguay-Siberia to which unruly persons, not yet got the length of shooting, were relegated. . . .

But let us listen for a moment to the Reverend Manuel Pérez as he preaches, "in the Church of the Incarnation at Assumpcion, on the 20th of October 1840," in a tone somewhat nasal, yet trustworthy withal.

"Amid the convulsions of revolution," says the Reverend Manuel, "the Lord, looking down with pity on Paraguay, raised up Don José Gaspar Francia for its deliverance. . . .

"What measures did not his Excellency devise, what labors undergo, to preserve peace in the Republic at home, and place it in an attitude to command respect from abroad! His first care was directed to obtain supplies of Arms, and to discipline Soldiers. To all that would import arms he held out the inducement of exemption from duty, and the permission to export in return whatever produce they preferred. An abundant supply of excellent arms was, by these means, obtained. I am lost in wonder to think how this great man could attend to such a multiplicity of things! He applied himself to the study of the military art; and, in a short time, taught the exercise, and directed military evolutions like the skilfullest veteran. Often have I seen his Excellency go up to a recruit, and show him by example how to take aim at the target. Could any Paragueno think it other than honourable to carry a musket, when his Dictator taught him how to manage it? The cavalry-exercise too, though it seems to require a man at once robust and experienced in horsemanship, his Excellency as you know, did himself superintend; at the head of his squadrons he charged and manoeuvred as if bred to it; and directed them with an energy and vigour which infused his own martial spirit into these troops.

"What evils do not the people suffer from Highwaymen!" exclaims his Reverence, a little farther on; "violence, plunder, murder, are crimes familiar to these malefactors. The inaccessible mountains and wide deserts in this Republic seemed to offer impunity to such men. Our Dictator succeeded in striking such a terror into them that they entirely disappeared, seeking safety in a change of life. His Excellency saw that the manner of inflicting the punishment was more efficacious than even the punishment itself; and on this principle he acted. Whenever a robber could be seized, he was led to the nearest Guard-house (*Guardia*); a summary trial took place; and straightway, so soon as he had made confession, he was shot. These means proved effectual. Erelong the Republic was in such security, that, we may say, a child might have travelled from the Uruguay to the

Paraná without other protection than the dread which the Supreme Dictator had inspired. . . ." [7]

But enough, O Pérez; for it becomes too nasal! Pérez with a confident face, asks in fine, Whether all these things do not clearly prove to men and Guachos of sense, that Dictator Francia *was* "the deliverer whom the Lord raised up to deliver Paraguay from its enemies?"–Truly, O Pérez, the benefits of him seem to have been considerable. Undoubtedly a man "sent by Heaven,"–as all of us are! Nay, it may be, the benefit of him is not even yet exhausted, even yet entirely become visible. Who knows but, in unborn centuries, Paragueno men will look back to their lean iron Francia, as men do in such cases to the one veracious person, and institute considerations! . . .

The City of Assumpcion, full of tropical vegetation and "permanent hedges, the deposits of nuisance and vermin,"[8] has no pavement, no straightness of streets; the sandy thoroughfare in some quarters is torn by the rain into gullies, impassable with convenience to any animal but a kangaroo. Francia, after meditation, decides on having it remodelled, paved, straightened–irradiated with the image of the one regular man. Robertson[9] laughs to see a Dictator, sovereign ruler, straddling about, "taking observations with his theodolite," and so forth: O Robertson, if there was no other man that *could* observe with a theodolite? Nay, it seems further, the improvement of Assumpcion was attended, once more, with the dreadfullest tyrannies: peaceable citizens dreaming no harm, no active harm to any soul, but mere peaceable passive dirt and irregularity to all souls, were ordered to pull-down their houses which happened to stand in the middle of streets; forced (under rustle of the gallows) to draw their purses, and rebuild them elsewhere! It is

[7]Foreign Quarterly Review, No. 62—Funeral Discourse delivered on occasion of celebrating the Obsequies of his late Excellency the Perpetual Dictator of the Republic of Paraguay, the Citizen Dr. José Gaspar Francia: by Citizen the Rev. Manuel Antonio Pérez, of the Church of the Incarnation, on the 20th of October 1840. (In the British Packet and Argentine News, No. 813. Buenos-Ayres, March 19, 1842.)

[8]Pérez.

[9]Letters on Paraguay. By J. P. & W. P. Robertson. 2 vols. Second edition. London, 1839.

Francia's Reign of Terror. By the same. London, 1839.

Letters on South America. By the same. 3 vols. London, 1843.

horrible. Nay, they said, Francia's true aim in these improvements, in this cutting-down of the luxuriant "cross-hedges" and architectural monstrosities, was merely to save himself from being shot, from under cover, as he rode through the place. It may be so; but Assumpcion is now an improved paved City, much squarer in the corners (and with the planned capacity, it seems, of growing even squarer[10]); passable with convenience . . . to wooden bullock-carts and all vehicles and animals.

Francia was a man that liked performance: and sham-performance, in Paraguay as elsewhere, was a thing too universal. What a time of it had this strict man with *un*real performers, imaginary workmen, public and private, cleric and laic! Ye Guachos—it is no child's play, casting-out those Seven Devils from you!

Monastic or other entirely slumberous church-establishments could expect no great favour from Francia. Such of them as seemed incurable, entirely slumberous, he somewhat roughly shook awake, somewhat sternly ordered to begone. *Debout, canaille fainéante,* as his prophet Raynal says; *Debout: aux champs, aux ateliers!* Can I have you sit here, droning old metre through your nose; your heart asleep in mere gluttony, the while; and all Paraguay a wilderness or nearly so—the Heaven's blessed sunshine growing mere tangles, lianas, yellow-fevers, rattlesnakes, and jaguars on it? Up, swift, to work;—or mark this governmental horsewhip, what the crack of it is, what the cut of it is like to be!—Incurable, for one class, seemed archbishops, bishops, and such like; given merely to a sham-warfare against extinct devils. At the crack of Francia's terrible whip they went, dreading what the cut of it might be. A cheap worship in Paraguay, according to the humour of the people, Francia left; on condition that it did no mischief. Wooden saints and the like ware, he also left sitting in their niches: no new ones, even on solicitation, would he give a doit to buy. Being petitioned to provide a new patron-saint for one of his new Fortifications once, he made this answer: "O People of Paraguay, how long will you continue idiots? While I was a Catholic, I thought as you do: but I now see there are no saints but good cannons that will guard our frontiers!"[11]

[10]Pérez.
[11]Rengger.

Equal trouble had Francia with his laic workers, and indeed with all manner of workers; for it is in Paraguay as elsewhere, like priest like people. Francia had extensive barrack-buildings, nay city-buildings (as we have seen), arm-furnishings; immensities of work going on; and his workmen had in general a tendency to be imaginary. He could get no work out of them; only a more or less deceptive similitude of work! Masons so-called, builders of houses, did not build, but merely seem to build; their walls would not bear weather, stand on their bases in high winds. Hodge-razors, in all conceivable kinds, were openly marketed, "which were never meant to shave, but only to be sold!" For a length of time Francia's righteous soul struggled sore, yet unexplosively, with the propensities of these unfortunate men. By rebuke, by remonstrance, encouragement, offers of reward, and every vigilance and effort, he strove to convince them that it was unfortunate for a Son of Adam to be an imaginary workman; that every Son of Adam had better make razors which *were* meant to shave. In vain, all in vain! At length, Francia lost patience with them. "Thou wretched Fraction, wilt thou be the ninth part even of a tailor? Does it beseem thee to weave cloth of devil's-dust instead of true wool; and cut and sew it as if thou wert not a tailor, but the fraction of a very tailor! I cannot endure everything!" Francia, in despair, erected his "Workman's Gallows." Yes, that institution of the country did actually exist in Paraguay; men and workmen saw it with eyes. A most remarkable, and, on the whole, not unbeneficial institution of society there. . . .

Such an institution of society would evidently not be introducible, under that simple form, in our old-constituted European countries. Yet it may be asked of constitutional persons in these times, By what succeedaneum they mean to supply the want of it, then? In a community of imaginary workmen, how can you pretend to have any government, or social thing whatever, that were real? Certain Tenpound Franchisers, with their "tremendous cheers," are invited to reflect on this. With a community of quack workmen, it is by the law of Nature impossible that other than a quack government can be got to exist. Constitutional or other, with ballot-boxes or with none, your society in all its phases, administration, legislation, teaching, preaching, praying, and writing periodicals per sheet, will be a quack society; terrible to live in, disastrous to look upon. Such an institution of society, adapted to our European ways, seems pressingly desirable. O Guachos, South-American and European, what a business is it, casting out your Seven Devils!—

But perhaps the reader would like to take a view of Dr. Francia in the concrete, there as he looks and lives; managing that thousand-sided business for his Paraguenos. . . ? It is our last extract, or last view of the Dictator, who must hang no longer on our horizon here:

I have already said, that Doctor Francia, so soon as he found himself at the head of affairs, took-up his residence in the habitation of the former Governors of Paraguay. This Edifice, which is one of the largest in Assumpcion, was erected by the Jesuits, a short time before their expulsion, as a house of retreat for laymen, who devoted themselves to certain spiritual exercises instituted by Saint Ignatius. This Structure the Dictator repaired and embellished; he has detached it from the other houses in the City, by interposing wide streets. Here he lives, with four slaves, a little negro, one male and two female mulattoes, whom he treats with great mildness. The two males perform the functions of valet-de-chambre and groom. One of the two mulatto women is his cook, and the other takes care of his wardrobe.

He leads a very regular life. The first rays of the sun very rarely find him in bed. So soon as he rises, the negro brings a chafing-dish, a kettle and a pitcher of water; the water is made to boil there. The Dictator then prepares, with the greatest possible care, his *maté,* or Paraguay tea. Having taken this, he walks under the Interior Colonnade that looks upon the court; and smokes a cigar, which he first takes care to unroll, in order to ascertain that there is nothing dangerous in it, though it is his own sister who makes-up his cigars for him. At six o-clock comes the barber, an ill-washed, ill-clad mulatto, given to drink too; but the only member of the faculty whom he trusts in. If the Dictator is in good-humour, he chats with the barber; and often in this manner makes use of him to prepare the public for his projects: this barber may be said to be his *official gazette.* He then steps out, in his dressing-gown of printed calico, to the Outer Colonnade, an open space with pillars, which ranges all round the building: here he walks about, receiving at the same time such persons as are admitted to an audience. Towards seven, he withdraws to his room, where he remains till nine; the officers and other functionaries then come to make their reports, and receive his orders. At eleven o-clock, the *fiel de fecho* (principal secretary) brings the papers which are to be inspected by him, and writes from his dictation till noon. At noon all the officers retire, and Doctor

Francia sits down to table. His dinner, which is extremely frugal, he always himself orders. When the cook returns from market, she deposits her provisions at the door of her master's room; the Doctor then comes out, and selects what he wishes for himself.

After dinner he takes his *siesta.* On awakening, he drinks his *maté,* and smokes a cigar, with the same precautions as in the morning. From this, till four or five, he occupies himself with business, when the escort to attend him in his promenade arrives. The barber then enters and dresses his hair, while his horse is getting ready. During his ride, the Doctor inspects the public works, and the barracks, particularly those of the cavalry, where he has had a set of apartments prepared for his own use. While riding, though surrounded by his escort, he is armed with a sabre, and a pair of double-barrelled pocket-pistols. He returns home about nightfall, and sits down to study till nine; then he goes to supper, which consists of a roast pigeon and a glass of wine. If the weather be fine, he again walks in the Outer Colonnade, where he often remains till a very late hour. At ten o-clock he gives the watchword. On returning into the house, he fastens all the doors himself.[12]

Francia's brother was already mad. Francia banished his sister by and by, because she had employed one of his grenadiers, one of the public government's soldiers, on some errand of her own.[13] Thou lonely Francia! . . .

It remains still that we say a word, not in excuse, which might be difficult, but in explanation, which is possible enough, of Francia's unforgivable insult to human Science in the person of M. Aimé Bonpland. M. Aimé Bonpland, friend of Humboldt, after much botanical wandering, did, as all men know, settle himself in Entre Ríos, an Indian or Jesuit country close on Francia, now burnt to ashes by Artigas; and there set-up a considerable establishment for the improved culture of Paraguay tea. With an eye to Botany? Botany? Why, yes–and perhaps to commerce still more. "Botany!" exclaims Francia: "It is shopkeeping agriculture, and tends to prove fatal to my shop! Who is this extraneous French individual? Artigas could not give him right to Entre Ríos; Entre Ríos is at least as much mine as Artigas's! Bring him to me!" Next night, or next, Paraguay soldiers surround M.

[12]Rengger.
[13]Rengger.

Bonpland's tea-establishment; gallop M. Bonpland over the frontiers, to his appointed village in the interior; root out his tea-plants; scatter his four-hundred Indians, and—we know the rest! Hard-hearted Monopoly refusing to listen to the charmings of Public Opinion or Royal-Society presidents, charm they never so wisely! M. Bonpland, at full liberty some time since, resides still in South America. . . .

Francia's treatment of Artigas, his old enemy, the bandit and firebrand, reduced now to beg shelter of him, was good; humane, even dignified. Francia refused to see or treat with such a person, as he had ever done; but readily granted him a place of residence in the interior, and "thirty piasters a month till he died." The bandit cultivated fields, did charitable deeds, and passed a life of penitence, for his few remaining years. His bandit followers, such of them as took to plundering again, says M. Rengger, "were instantly seized and shot."

On the other hand, that anecdote of Francia's dying Father—requires to be confirmed! It seems, the old man, who, as we saw, had long since quarrelled with his son, was dying, and wished to be reconciled. Francia "was busy;—what use was it?—could not come." A second still more pressing message arrives: "The old father dare not die unless he see his son; fears he shall never enter Heaven, if they be not reconciled." "Then let him enter—!" said Francia, "I will not come!"[14] If this anecdote be true, it is certainly of all that are in circulation about Dr. Francia, by far the worst. If Francia, in that death-hour, could not forgive his poor old Father, whatsoever he had, or could in the murkiest sultriest imagnination be conceived to have done against him, then let no man forgive Dr. Francia! But the accuracy of public rumour, in regard to a Dictator who has executed forty persons, is also a thing that can be guessed at. To whom was it, by name and surname, that Francia delivered this extraordinary response? Did the man make, or can he now be got to make, affidavit of it, to credible articulate-speaking persons resident on this earth? If so let him do it—for the sake of the Psychological Sciences.

One last fact more. Our lonesome Dictator, living among Guachos, had the greatest pleasure, it would seem, in rational conversation—with Robertson, with Rengger, with any kind of intelligent human creature, when such could be fallen-in with, which was rarely. He would question

[14]Robertson.

you with eagerness about the ways of men in foreign places, the properties of things unknown to him; all human interest and insight was interesting to him. Only persons of no understanding being near him for most part, he had to content himself with silence, a meditative cigar and cup of *maté*. O Francia, though thou hadst to execute forty persons, I am not without some pity for thee!

In this manner, all being yet dark and void for European eyes, have we to imagine that the man Rodríguez Francia passed, in a remote, but highly remarkable, not unquestionable or unquestioned manner, across the confused theatre of this world. For some thirty years, he was all the government his native Paraguay could be said to have. For some six-and-twenty years he was express Sovereign of it; for some three, or some two years, a Sovereign with bared sword, stern as Rhadamanthus: through all his years, and through all his days, since the beginning of him, a Man or Sovereign of iron energy and industry, of great and severe labour. So lived Dictator Francia, and had no rest; and only in Eternity any prospect of rest. A Life of terrible labour;–but for the last twenty years, the Fulgencio Plot being once torn in pieces, and all now quiet under him, it was a more equable labour: severe but equable, as that of a hardy draught-steed fitted in his harness; no longer plunging and champing; but pulling steadily–till he do all his rough miles, and get to his still *home*.

. . . He is dead, this remarkable Francia; there is no doubt about it: have not we and our readers heard pieces of his Funeral Sermon! He died on the 20th of September 1840, as the Rev. Pérez informs us; the people crowding round his Government House with much emotion, nay "with tears," as Pérez will have it. Three Excellencies succeeded him; as some "Directorate," "*Junta Gubernativa*," or whatever the name of it is, before whom this reverend Pérez preaches. God preserve them many years.

The Rise and Fall of the Mexican Empire

By LORD ACTON

The Indians were not satisfied and the land owners were alienated.

The struggle between Juárez, the Indian, and Maximilian Hapsburg, the European prince, for control of Mexico has today an aura of unreality. It tends to be dismissed as a historic aberration occasioned by the U.S. Civil War. A scheming Napoleon III of France, so this interpretation goes, took advantage of the U.S. Civil War to impose on Mexico an alien European type of government that was bound to crash as soon as the United States was reunited and again able to assume its rightful position among nations. In this lecture on the Mexican Empire, delivered in 1868, less than a year after the execution of Maximilian at Querétaro in Mexico, Lord Acton suggests that there were other aspects as well and that one of these was the Indian–his poverty and servitude.

It is Acton's argument that the Indians greeted the arrival of Maximilian as the "dawn of their deliverance" and "he might have made of them a prop of the imperial throne" had he distributed land to them. Instead, Maximilian was satisfied with compromise. Rather than meet their demands, he was content to abolish their debts, thus alienating their landlords but not satisfying their aspirations.

A curious aspect of the essay, which remains to this day perhaps the best account of the events in Mexico during the U.S. Civil War, is the suggestion that Maximilian's execution might presage the conquest of Mexico by the United States. Acton's basic prejudices surface here. In the Civil War, Acton sympathized with the South. He felt that absolute power was more intolerable and more criminal than slavery, and since he feared that a Northern victory would impair the federal aspects of the U.S. Constitution, which he felt were liberty's most important safeguard, he was apprehensive about the future. It is this concern for liberty as a result of the Northern victory that made him speculate about the future of Mexican nationality, a fear which a moment later he extinguishes with the more accurate prediction that "the Americans will bind their neighbors by treaties, which will throw open the whole continent to their own influence and enterprise, without destroying their separate existence."

Acton's sentiment in favor of Maximilian as well-nigh "the noblest of his race" and as someone "who devoted his life to the good of Mexico and died for a guilt which was not his own" is characteristic of him. Acton essentially believed in constitutional monarchy. He was especially conscious of the difference in the races and the classes of the Mexicans. He felt that "where society is constituted without equality of condition or unity of race, where there are different classes and national varieties, they require a protector in a form of government which shall be distinct from, and superior to, every class, and not the instrument of one of them. . . . The tyranny of republics is greatest when differences of races are combined with distinctions of class. Hence South America was a prosperous and flourishing country so long as the Spanish Crown served as a moderator between the various races."

P. K.

The scene of the tragedy which I will attempt to describe is a country on which Nature's fairest gifts have been lavished with an unsparing hand, but where man has done his utmost to thwart the designs of Providence. Its social condition is so far removed from our experience that I must ask you to forget this evening the maxims and even the political terms we use nearer home.

Mexico possesses a territory more than thrice as large as France, with the fertility of the tropics, and the climate of the temperate zone, seated between two oceans, in the future centre of the commerce of the world. Its wealth in precious metals is so enormous that the time will come when the market will be flooded with silver, and its price will not allow the mines to be worked with profit. The only drawbacks on its prosperity are the badness of the harbours, the excessive dryness of the plains, and the disappearance of the forest timber, a curse which almost always follows the footstep of the Spaniard.

When England recognised the independence of the Spanish colonies,

Mr. Canning declared that he had called a new world into existence to redress the balance of the old. But it was long before the new States justified the boast, and it is still generally believed that in point of political and material success they contrast much to their disadvantage with the North American Republic. In the greater part of South America this is no longer true, for in several of those vast communities population and trade are growing at a rate that exceeds that of the Union.

Mexico is the saddest and most conspicuous exception in the midst of the general improvement. It is the pride of the colonial system of Spain, and the one merit in which it was superior to our own, that it succeeded in preserving and partially civilising the native race. The English settled in a region where the natives were hunters and wanderers, unskilled in the cultivation of the soil, who roamed into the West to elude the grasp of civilisation, or perished by its contact. The colonists retained their own congenial laws, the purity of European blood was maintained, and the portentous problem of race was happily averted. But in Mexico Cortez found a numerous and settled population, dwelling in cities, tilling the land, and brilliantly though superficially civilised. It was part of the Spanish system to protect, to preserve, and to convert the conquered heathens, whose number vastly exceeded that of their masters; a people of mixed blood sprang up between them, and thus there were three races separated by a very broad line, and isolated by the pride and the jealousy of colour. The Indian nobles were mostly exterminated, and the land was distributed among the families of a small group of conquerors. This arrangement of property remains unchanged. The natives are still without any interest in the land, and the immense estates have not been subdivided. In one of the richest districts on the Atlantic, the coast, for one hundred and fifty miles, is owned by one proprietor.

A society so constituted could not make a nation. There was no middle class, no impulse to industry, no common civilisation, no public spirit, no sense of patriotism. The Indians were not suffered to acquire wealth or knowledge, and every class was kept in ignorance and in rigorous seclusion; when, therefore, the Mexicans made themselves independent, the difficulty was to throw off, not the bondage, but the nonage in which they had been held, and to overcome the mental incapacity, the want of enterprise, the want of combination among themselves, and the want of the enlightenment which comes from intercourse with other nations. They formed a republic after the model of their more fortunate neighbours, and accepted those principles which are so inflexible in their consequences, and so unrelenting in their consistency. It soon appeared that there was not propelling power in the State equal to the heavy burden of a half-barbarous population. The intelligent minority was too undisciplined and too demoralised to elevate and to sway the degraded millions of the Indian race. The habits of authority and subordination departed with the Spaniards, and the faculty of organisation could not exist in a people that had never learned to help themselves. No man of very superior character and understanding arose. The leading men in the various provinces sought to maintain their own power by the continuance of anarchy; they combined against the central authority as fast as it changed hands, and overthrew thirty Presidents in thirty years. The requisite conditions of a Republican government did not exist. There was the greatest social inequality that can be conceived between the wealthy landowners and the Indian masses, who possessed neither the mental independence conferred by education nor the material independence which belongs to property. There was Democracy in the State, while society was intensely aristocratic.

The largest landowner in Mexico was the Church; and as there was no religious toleration, it was the Church of the whole nation, the only teacher of the moral law to the natives, the sole channel through which the majority of the people had access to the civilisation of Christendom. Therefore the clergy enjoyed an influence of which there has been no example in Europe for the last five hundred years, and formed a strong basis of aristocracy and the most serious barrier to the realisation of the Democratic principle that nominally prevailed. To establish a real Democracy the first thing to be done was to reduce this immense and artificial influence. For the last twelve years this has been the one constant object of the Democratic party. It was a war of principles, a struggle for existence, on either side, in which conciliation was impossible, and which could only terminate by the ruin of one of the contending forces.

Now, as long as the conflict was confined to America, the Republicans could not be utterly defeated, for they could fall back on the unfailing sympathy and resources of the United States. Sooner or later the end would be the confiscation of the lands in mortmain, and the downfall of the Conservatives. Their only hope was in the assistance of Europe, and the establishment of a monarchy under foreign protection. Long before the antagonism became so definite and so extreme, the idea had begun to gain ground that a monarchy was the only form of government adapted to the character of Mexican society, and capable of arresting its decay; and the monarch, if he was not to be a party chief, must be a European prince. Negotiations for this object were opened as early as 1846; Mexican emissaries, acting in concert with the then president, addressed themselves to Prince Metternich, who received them coldly, to Bavaria, and then to France, where the plan was favourably entertained, when it was interrupted by the revolution of 1848. It was revived twelve years later by the progress of events in Mexico. In 1857 the Democratic party carried a new Constitution, abridging the privileges of the clergy, and including a law of mortmain which obliged them to convert their estates into money.

This was the signal for civil war. The Conservatives, led by a young man who, at the age of twenty-seven, had shown a remarkable capacity for war, Miguel Miramon, gained possession of the captial, and their President was recognised by Europe. The Constitutional President held the important seaport of Vera Cruz, and was recognised by the United States. His name, destined like that of his rival to a wide and melancholy celebrity, was Benito Juarez. He was an Indian of pure blood, nearly sixty years old. He had ascended to power by means of his eminence as a lawyer, and because, in the midst of almost universal corruption, he was deemed incorruptible. Unlike the intriguers and the soldiers of fortune who were his rivals, he had risen slowly, without perfidy and without violence,–a patient, steadfast man, and, as we should say, a man of extreme opinions. It would seem that in this educated, ambitious, successful Indian, the pent-up hatred of the oppressed race for the oppressor had broken forth, and formed his strongest political motive; and that he was striving for the social and political emancipation of his people when he tore down the privileges and annihilated the power of the class that lorded over them. He professed the principles of 1789, principles which had triumphed in France by a civil war, a reign of terror, ten years of military despotism, and sixty years of intermittent revolution. There was no reason to think they would succeed more easily in a country so backward as Mexico, but Juarez was ready to abide the issue. As there was no system of regular taxation, and all manufactured articles were imported by sea, the customs were the chief source of revenue. It was an advantage to Juarez to possess the chief seaport of the country, and as he dwelt under the cannon of European men-of-war, he was careful not to make enemies by plundering the foreigners.

Miramon, up in the interior, had neither the same resources nor the same restraint. There was no money to be had but that of foreign residents, or of the Church. He could not rob his own party, so he determined to turn to the other source of supply. He had so used his power, and his lieutenant, Marquez, had acted so ferociously, that the English Minister had left Mexico, when Miramon seized a sum of £130,000 belonging to British landholders, which was deposited at the Legation. He also contracted a loan with the Swiss banker, Jecker, on terms so exorbitant that it seems to have been a stratagem to embarrass those who were to come after him. These two measures were eventually fatal to Miramon, for they were the cause of the European intervention.

Juarez immediately obtained his recognition by England by promising to restore the stolen money, and to satisfy other British claims. He made the same promise to France. With this moral support, and by undertaking to grant away to his partisans the property of the Church, he obtained the means of expelling Miramon from Mexico, and in 1861 he was elected President for a term of four years. He at once dismissed the Spanish and the Papal envoys, decreed the absolute confiscation of the Church lands, and carried out with ruthless energy the triumph of his opinions. But he proved incapable as a ruler, and utterly unequal to the desperate task of restoring order in a country distracted by passion and ruined by anarchy.

The condition of affairs in the summer of 1861 is described by the English Minister in the following passages, which are important because they determined the policy of England: "As long as the present dishonest and incapable administration remains in power, things will go from bad to worse; but with a government formed of respectable men, could such be found, the resources of the country are so great that it might easily fulfil its engagements, and increase threefold the amount of its exportations, not only of the precious metals, but of those productions for which they receive British manufactured goods in exchange. Mexico furnishes two-thirds of the silver now in circulation, and might be made one of the richest and most prosperous countries of the world; so that it becomes the interest of Great Britian to put a stop by force, if necessary, to its present state of anarchy, and insist on its government paying what it owes to British subjects. All the respectable classes look forward with hope to a foreign intervention as the sole means of saving them from ruin, and preventing a dissolution of the Confederation, as well as a general rising of the Indians against the white population. Every day's experience duly tends to prove the utter absurdity of attempting to govern the country with the limited powers granted to the Executive by the present ultra-liberal Constitution, and I see no hope of improvement unless it comes from a foreign intervention, or the formation of a rational government, composed of the leading men of the moderate party, who, at present, are void of moral courage and afraid to move, unless with some material support from abroad. If the question was, what form of government would most conduce to the welfare of Mexico, by the establishment of order and a permanent state of things, there can be no doubt that a Constitutional monarchy is the one most likely to have central power sufficient to enable it to consolidate the nation, perhaps the only form of government that would give much hope of such a result; but as the question is not what is best for Mexico, but what are the wishes of the Mexican people, I fear that the answer must be that the great mass of the intelligent population are in favour of Republican institutions. Many well-educated and intelligent individuals who stand well in society form a well-grounded desire for a strong government, but these people are unfortunately timid, and passive in action, ready to accept what is done for them, but incapable of doing anything to bring about what they desire."

As it turned out, these were prophetic words. The sale of the Church property was carried on in a very disorderly way, and the money was squandered. A scheme to satisfy the urgent European claims with money lent by the United States, though entertained by the American Government, was rejected by the Senate, and in July 1861 the Mexican Congress resolved that all payments on European agreements should be suspended for two years.

The Powers most concerned in this act of repudiation–France, Spain, and Great Britian–now determined to intervene jointly, and to obtain by force of arms some real security for the property of their subjects, and for the establishment, if necessary, of a more trustworthy government. The conjuncture was favourable, for the Civil War had just broken out in the United States, and from that quarter there was no immediate danger of interruption. Spain took the lead, her military establishment at Cuba enabling her to act promptly, with some suspicion of a desire to recover her ancient dominion. England followed warily, with an eye only to mercantile interests. France did not yet reveal her intentions, and probably had not yet matured them.

The allied forces, amounting to about 6000 men, without means of transport or materials for a campaign in the interior, were placed under the command of the Spanish general Prim, a clever, showy, and ambitious officer, but a capricious and unstable politician. On their arrival, the town and fort of Vera Cruz were evacuated by the Mexican troops. In this extremity Juarez strengthened himself by putting at the head of the Ministry General Doblado, the leader of the moderate party, a man whose reputation for caution and ability stood high, and whose acts in office prove that it was well-deserved. In January 1862, he issued a decree directing all those who should be taken in arms against the Republic to be tried by court-martial and put to death as traitors. This is the law by which the Emperor was to die, and which gave a legal character to his execution. Doblado had an interview with Prim, expatiated on the deplorable condition of the country, and undertook that the legitimate demands of the allies should be faithfully complied with, provided only they would recognise the existing government. These terms seemed acceptable to the allies, who were not equipped for a campaign, and they took Doblado at his word. But the agreement had to be sent to Europe for approval, and in the meantime it was arranged that the allies should move up from the pestilential swamp of Vera Cruz to healthier quarters on the first range of hills. This placed them within the outer line of the Mexican defences, and it was stipulated that if the preliminaries were not ratified, before commencing hostilities they should first withdraw to the plain below.

The claims of the three Powers had now to be specified. Those of Spain and England were clear, and easily ascertained. The French commissioners demanded, in addition to other large sums, three millions sterling for the banker Jecker. Their colleagues protested against this excessive demand. They affirmed that the sum advanced by the banker to Miramon was only £160,000, and they pointed out that he was not a Frenchman but a Swiss, and that the guardianship of Swiss interests in Mexico pertained to the American Legation. Jecker was immediately naturalised a Frenchman, and the French Government bought up his bonds. Agents were sent for this purpose with sealed instructions to America, two of whom, when they discovered the errand upon which they were employed, indignantly threw up the commission. Whilst this transaction was sowing discord in the allied camp, several Mexican exiles of the Conservative party made their appearance at Vera Cruz. One of these was Miramon. He was arrested and sent away by the British Commodore, on the ground that the expedition could not connect itself with one party while acknowledging the government of the other.

Miramon was speedily followed by General Almonte, for many years the chief agent of the Conservative party in Europe, and the secret councillor of the French Government, a man of high character and great influence. He stated that he came with a mission from France to establish a provisional government, to introduce a monarchy, and to procure the election of the Archduke Maximilian. The English and Spanish Commissioners demanded his expulsion, when General Lorencez arrived with French reinforcements, and announced that Napoleon had rejected the convention with Doblado, that he had sent Almonte to Mexico, and meant war. The alliance of the three Powers was at once dissolved; the Spaniards sailed for Cuba in English ships, and France was left alone, to accomplish the avowed design of erecting a throne beyond the Atlantic.

In the intention of the Emperor Napoleon, the Mexican expedition was the first step towards the execution of a bold and magnificent scheme, to which he gave the name of the regeneration of the Latin world. The ancient rivalry between France and England was expanded into the rivalry of the Latin with the Anglo-Saxon race. If we carry back our thoughts for a century, it will not be difficult to find in the history of the two nations the motives which suggested the idea. Scarcely one hundred years ago vast territories in Canada, on the Mississippi, and in the West Indies belonged to the Crown of France, and French adventurers of great daring and ability were laying the foundation of an Empire in Hindostan. One by one these possessions have gone, and France, watched by jealous neighbours, has nearly lost the power of expansion in Europe.

What has been, in the meantime, the progress of England? The colonies which France has lost have almost all been won by her. England, not France, wields the sceptre of the Great Mogul. Her people have encircled the globe with a girdle of British settlements. New continents, I may almost say, have arisen out of the Southern ocean to receive the incessant overflow of her population. Her colonial empire is a nursery of mighty nations, that carries to the distant places of the earth the language and the laws of home. George III. inherited dominions peopled perhaps by ten million human beings. His grand-daughter reigns over two hundred millions. In America the children of our race are waiting the time when the whole continent shall be theirs.

But on that continent there are thirty millions of men, not of French descent, but of a stock allied with the French, who derive their literary culture and intellectual impulse from Paris, whose traffic is carried on with French ports, who look up to France as their head, and turn to her to protect them from being absorbed by an alien race. The trade of France with South America is nearly equal to her trade with the United States, and is more profitable because it is carried in French ships. In the ten years before the expedition, it had grown from £6,000,000 to £20,000,000 a year. South America is the largest and safest opening that remains for the development of French commerce, the most increasing market for French industry. It was manifestly the interest of France to prevent it from falling under the control of the narrow mercantile policy of the United States, and to secure her own influence over nations with such a future. In the words of the Emperor: "It is not our interest that the United States should grasp the whole Gulf of Mexico, the Antilles, and South America, and become the sole dispensers of the produce of the New World. We have seen by sad experience how precarious is the fate of an industry which is forced to seek its raw material in a single market, under all the vicissitudes to which that market is liable." The establishment of a French dependency in Mexico would have checked the southward progress of the Union, and have cut the continent in two.

When Juarez repudiated his engagements with European creditors the Confederates had won their first victories, and the North was not able to repel the intervention upon its frontier. Shortly after, the Southern Commissioners were seized on board the *Trent,* and England began to arm. The French Emperor calculated that he would be able to do his work without interruption, and that England, in case of need, would help him to support the South. Therefore, from the end of 1861 he lent a willing ear to the Mexican exiles, who displayed the sufferings and the capabilities of their country, and allured him with the splendid vision of a nation to be regenerated by France. They persuaded him that the presence of his troops would be welcomed, that there would be no serious resistance, and that a powerful party would rally to his standard. In this belief, and with Almonte in their camp, the French advanced against Mexico, 6000 strong. On the 5th of May 1862, they appeared before Puebla, the second city in the land, on the road from Vera Cruz to the capital. They were received with so vigorous a cannonade that they were forced to retire to a position where they could await reinforcements without danger of being dislodged. After this military repulse, public opinion in France supported the Emperor in despatching an army of 30,000 men, provided with all the appliances of war. They landed in the autumn, and the winter was spent in preparations.

A whole year had been lost before Puebla fell, after an obstinate defence, and in June 1863 the French entered the city of Mexico. The early reverses and the long delays of the French greatly strengthened the position of Juarez. The invasion exalted the Indian leader of an extreme party into a champion of the dignity and the independence of the country, and his tenacity in upholding the cause did not allow this halo to depart from him even in the worst times. The capital was not fortified, and when the French appeared, Juarez carried the seat of his government to one of the Northern towns.

A new provisional government was instituted, in which Almonte was associated with the Archbishop of Mexico, and an assembly of notables, selected and convened by the French, met to decide on the future of the country. Many of the principal men in the capital who had been invited, refused to attend, and the assembly was composed of Conservatives who took their orders from Almonte and the French. The orders were to proclaim a monarchy, and to offer the Crown to the Archduke. They were obeyed on the 8th July 1863. The long-deferred hopes of the Mexican royalists seemed to be fulfilled, when a deputation proceeded to Europe to invite the Archduke to ascend the throne of Montezuma. Ferdinand Maximilian, the next brother of the Emperor of Austria, had long occupied a peculiar and exceptional position in his native country.

There were circumstances which made him appear a possible rival to his brother, and the many errors of Francis Joseph, the waning confidence in his fortune and his judgment, kept alive the habit of looking to the Archduke, who was altogether excluded from the conduct of affairs, as a refuge in extremity. He possessed some of the best qualities of a ruler, honesty and firmness of purpose, a kind and true heart, and a mind fixed on high designs. In spite of much and various experience of mankind, he retained an unpractical imaginativeness, which is often connected with extreme cultivation, and a certain impetuous generosity frequently marred the effect of his sagacity. Though undoubtedly very intelligent, he was so often deceived that he must have lacked the faculty of judging men and choosing friends, without which there is no success in government. His ardent, lofty spirit, perpetually curbed and chafed by the prevailing dulness, selfishness, and incapacity in Austria, imparted something that was cold and sarcastic to his manner. His outspoken censure of his brother's unstable policy caused an estrangement between them, which was increased by his marriage with the daughter of the wise Leopold, a clever and accomplished woman, whose family has grown great by renouncing those principles of strict legitimacy which Austria specially represents. The Archduke was the last Austrian Governor of Lombardy. In that thankless office it was impossible to conciliate the Italians, and he could not permanently serve the interests of his country. But he made many friends, and men believed that he would willingly have been the Minister of a less unpopular system. It was even whispered that he had wished to set up a throne for himself in Lombardy and Venice, separate from the Austrian monarchy. At least he had so far deserted the ancient ways of his family as to fall under the ban of distrust and suspicion at Vienna. About the time of the marriage of the Princess Royal he visited the British Court, and made so favourable an impression that there were some who regretted that he could not have been a candidate for her hand. For who could then have dreamed that the reserved and unpretending Prussian was to be the spoilt darling of victory, while the genial, frank, and brilliant Austrian was destined to a traitor's death? He devoted his care to the navy, a department always neglected in Austria, and the virtue of his administration became apparent when the fleet which he had created won the greatest sea-fight of our time. The war of 1859 deprived him of his high position, and reproaches and recriminations followed, which separated him yet more from the Emperor. He dwelt in his castle of Miramar at the head of the Adriatic, mourning over wasted talents, a ruined career, and an unsatisfied ambition.

Very soon the prospect of a new adventure opened before him. By a strange fatality his wife, the daughter of a Princess of the House of Orleans, was an enthusiastic Bonapartist, and not only admired, but trusted the Emperor Napoleon. When, therefore, he proposed to hand over his conquest to the Archduke, hoping thereby to conciliate Austria, the Archduchess Charlotte urged her husband to accept it. Their unsettled position must have become very irksome to her, for when they left their home Maximilian wept bitterly, and she showed no emotions but hope and joy. His brother's government employed strong measures to dissuade him from accepting, and it was decided that he must renounce his place in the succession, and be counted last after all the princes of the line.

When the vote of the Assembly of Notables was made known to him, he replied that he could not accept the crown unless he was assured of the support of the great Powers, or until it was offered to him by the free choice of the whole Mexican people. The French are skilled in managing the machinery of a spontaneous election; and in April 1864, a second deputation carried to Miramar a sceptre of Mexican gold, with the assurance that the whole nation had elected Maximilian Emperor. In reality the French were masters of a very small portion of the country, and the vast majority were not polled at all. Where the French were present there was no serious difficulty, though in some places the chief inhabitants were thrown into prison before they gave in their adhesion. Maximilian was fully informed that the pretended election was nothing but a ceremonious farce. A Mexican Republican made his way to Miramar, and warned him that the real feeling of the country was adverse to the invaders, and that the expedition would end in disaster.

But the promises of France were excessively enticing. The French army was to complete the pacification of the country, and a powerful corps was to be left for several years in the service of Maximilian. France negotiated a loan in his behalf, and seventeen chests filled with gold pieces found their way to Miramar. The Archduke was not in a position to disregard such inducements, for his private fortune was in disorder, and the first £300,000 of the Mexican loan went to clear his debts. Other points were raised which have been kept secret, and the friends of Maximilian still look for important revelations.

At his trial he instructed his counsel to say that Napoleon had required the cession of a portion of Mexican territory as large as Great Britain, and that he had indignantly refused to dismember the country which had given him a crown. He accepted it at a time when the tide of success had turned in the American War, and the prospects of the Confederacy were no longer hopeful. The Archduke demanded a pledge that he should be supported by a French alliance in case of war with the United States; and it is positively asserted that Napoleon gave the required pledge. He gave it believing that England would join him in recognising the South, if it was found that its resistance would be crushed without aid from Europe, and the time came when he made the proposal of a joint recognition to Lord Palmerston. It happened that the two foremost statemen in the Ministry had made speeches in the provinces which appeared to show a disposition favourable to the Confederates; and the Emperor believed that they would carry their colleagues with them. This was the gravest miscalculation he made in the whole Mexican affair. The Cabinet, taking one of the most momentous resolutions ever adopted by a Ministry, rejected the proposal, and the Emperor shrank from a war single-handed with the United States.

Maximilian, on his part, undertook to pay a million a year while the French remained, and to liquidate all those accumulated claims which Juarez had rejected. In fact, he submitted to conditions impossible to meet, and commenced an undertaking predestined to financial ruin. He reached Mexico in June 1864, and was favourably if not warmly received. The French had ruled the country through the provisional government for a whole year, with almost uninterrupted military success. But they had encountered a difficulty of a formidable and unexpected kind. Juarez had had more than two years to accomplish the overthrow of the clergy, and their property had passed into the hands of speculators, chiefly foreigners, who, it was thought, would not easily be compelled to restore it. The Church party had called for intervention in the hope of recovering these losses, and when the French placed the leaders of the party at the head of the State, they preferred their claims with a sure expectation of success.

The Church in France is supported by the State, and owns no independent property. The French supposed that the practice of their own country could not be unsuitable to Mexico, where a revolution would be required to restore the ancient order, and where the clergy would not bear a comparison with the salaried priesthood of France. The demand was summarily refused. The Episcopate united to denounce the sacrilegious invaders, and the Archbishop ceased to be a member of the provisional government. The breach, for the moment, was complete; and the only hope of the clergy was in Maximilian. He knew that, for a Sovereign to be strong, he must be identified with no party. It was his mission to conciliate and blend together interests severed by years of antagonism. In declining the crown for the first time, he had signified that he would consent to receive it only as the gift of the entire nation. In accepting it afterwards, he made known that he looked upon himself as the elect of the nation, not as the nominee of a powerful interest. From the moment of his arrival he held out the olive branch to the Republicans, and sought their confidence by offering them place and power. Many accepted his offers, and he was surrounded by men who were hateful to those who had seated him on the throne. In adopting this policy it was impossible to draw a line, to examine antecedents, or to reject utterly any candidate for favour. The Emperor was often deceived, and lost on one side without gaining on the other.

After a long delay, which exasperated the trembling holders of Church property, as well as those whom they had despoiled, he decided that all legal purchases should be confirmed, and those which were fraudulent revised, but that nothing should be restored to the clergy, who were to be paid by the State. The Nuncio quarrelled with him upon this, and left the country. Maximilian, irritated by the hostile attitude of the clergy, went further, and restored what was called the *Exequatur,* a law forbidding any document to be published in ecclesiastical affairs without the consent of the civil power. This right has been abandoned by his brother, in Austria; by the Italian Government, last year; and even in Mexico, by Juarez, who adopted the voluntary principle. It could not be defended as a liberal law, and its revival seemed to be simply a blow at the independence of religion. The clergy protested that they had not borne the burden of civil war and brought foreign armies into the country, in order that a prince of their choosing should confirm decrees which had made their property the spoil of their enemies.

They declared that their position was worse under their friend than it had been under their persecutor Juarez. Thenceforth they withdrew their support, and observed a hostile neutrality, watching the time when the Emperor, driven to extremities, would be ready to purchase their assistance at any sacrifice they might demand. In some instances they even fomented the Republican opposition.

This was the first great and visible disaster that the Empire incurred. Another was soon known to be imminent. Financial capacity, rare in every country, was not to be found in Mexico; and Napoleon, who wished his creation to succeed, sent out a Chancellor of the Exchequer from France, with a staff of clerks. But the imported Minister died, and could not be replaced. The finances broke down so completely that Maximilian was obliged to ask for money from the military chest of the French army, and thus fell into the power of its commander. As he could not fulfil his engagements with the Emperor Napoleon, he was guilty of a breach of the treaty signed between them, and gave France an excuse, when her turn came, to justify her own breach of faith.

The year 1865 passed prosperously, on the whole. Maximilian visited many of the towns, saw what he could with his own eyes, and devoted his time to the fabrication of decrees by which he hoped to regenerate the country. These decrees are generally sensible and just; they incline in a good direction, but not always by the right road, and ornamental superfluities sometimes usurp the place of more difficult but more essential things. Maximilian was an anxious and determined educator, and his zeal was praiseworthy, for ninety per cent of the people could neither read or write. But it shows a want of practical capacity when in a community wanting the first necessaries of popular instruction the Sovereign founds an Academy of Sciences, and gravely inculcates on his Ministers the importance of encouraging the study of metaphysics. He found himself in the rare position of a lawgiver called to legislate in a country for which everything remained to be done, and he enjoyed the luxury of carrying out, at least on paper, systems nurtured in days of visionary retirement. He had not time or vigour to execute much of what he had projected.

There was one question that called for an act of high and generous statesmanship. The Indians had been reduced by their poverty and want of energy to the position of serfs. They were in debt to their landlords, and the whole hopeless labour of their lives, without the chance of profit or release, was due to their creditors. They had greeted the coming of Maximilian as the dawn of their deliverance, and he might have made them the willing prop of the imperial throne. In the 800,000 square miles of Mexico, peopled by 8,000,000 of men, but capable of sustaining 100,000,000, it would have been easy, without any spoliation, to distribute land among the countrymen of its ancient owners. Maximilian adopted a half measure. He abolished the debts of the Indians, and thus made them free; but he did no more, and left them to relapse, under pressure of the old causes, into the old degradation. The Indians were not satisfied, and the landowners were alienated.

Something, but not enough, was done for the creation of a native army to defend the crown and country when the French should depart. An Austrian and a Belgian corps were formed, but did not answer expectation. Next to the French, the most efficient body was the division of the Indian general Mejia, a man of a very pure fame. But the French were successful in all they undertook during the whole of 1865. The Republican bands were scattered, many of their generals made their submission, and Juarez, driven from place to place, disappeared at last at a point in the extreme north of Mexico, on the American frontier, more than a thousand miles from the capital. It was reported that he had escaped into the United States. At this time also the four years for which he had been elected expired, and it was impossible to convene a Congress for a new election. Many of his followers now held that he had ceased to govern, and the Vice-President Ortega, the defender of Puebla, claimed the vacant post. The strict legality which had been the strength of the position of Juarez was seriously impaired, and his authority was unquestionably shaken. The country was in a wretched state of insecurity and misery. Plunderers and assassins plied their trade under pretence of being real combatants. Mexican warfare is often scarcely distinguishable from armed robbery, and, as it was the plan of the Republicans to fight in small guerilla bands, the line separating the soldier from the brigand was often indistinct. The Government thought the time had come to exterminate these bands, and to protect the inhabitants against their incursions. The victory over the regular army was complete, and it seemed that men who infested the roads, when organised resistance was over, did not deserve the treatment of prisoners of war.

On the 2nd of October Maximilian drew up a decree ordering all who should be taken with arms in their hands to be shot, and when he signed it he signed his own death-warrant. Immediately after its publication a Republican force, commanded by Arteaga, was defeated, and the leaders were captured. In obedience to the new order the Imperial General Mendez put them to death. But the Republicans, though dispersed and dispirited, were not destroyed. A report made to the Emperor in November 1865 estimates their force at 24,000 men, and Juarez had not abandoned the struggle. He remained on Mexican territory, in a town on the Rio del Norte, from which a boat could take him in a few minutes to the American bank, and he remained in communication with the generals of his party. There he waited for the deliverance which he knew was coming. For at that moment, near the close of 1865, his cause was taken up by an ally so powerful and so much feared as to be able, without firing a shot or wasting a single life, to expel the French from Mexico, and to lay the Empire in the dust.

The United States had watched the intervention and the erection of the Empire with anger and alarm. They knew that it had sprung from a desire to cripple their influence, and they could not be indifferent to the presence of an European army on their frontier while they were embarrassed by a civil war. They denied that the Empire was the free choice of the Mexicans, and they highly disapproved of an Emperor that was absolute, for he retained in his own hands all the powers of the State. They refused to recognise him, but they remained neutral, determined not to act until they could act decisively. They rejected various schemes for assisting Juarez with money in return for land, and they declined not only the overtures of Napoleon and of Juarez, but one which was still more tempting. During the seige of Richmond the Confederates proposed that they should unite their armies for the conquest of Mexico and of Canada, but the North refused.

When the war of Secession was over, the Government of Washington had to apply a little diplomatic pressure to the Emperor Napoleon to hasten the recall of his troops. The pressure quickly took the form of threats, and Napoleon very speedily gave way. Events were passing in Europe which made him impatient that Maximilian should restore his legions. In June 1866 war broke out in Italy and in Germany, and in the first week of July Prussia had struck a blow that made half Europe tremble, and menaced the military supremacy and the pride of France. In these circumstances it was certain that the offensive language of America could not be resented, and Mr. Seward used his advantage with cruel complacency. Napoleon informed Maximilian that he must provide for himself, and he informed the American Government that he would retire from Mexico in March 1867.

Rumours of this strange correspondence, and of its probable result, reached Mexico and gave new spirit to the Republicans. Maximilian had refused permission to 25,000 confederates to settle in his dominions; but stragglers found their way to the armies of Juarez, and in June 1866 the important town of Matamoros was surrendered to Escobedo by Mejia. From the moment of that reverse fortune began rapidly to change; and as the French retired from more distant posts, swarms of Republicans appeared in every direction.

When Maximilian learnt the altered intention of Napoleon, he foresaw the end, and spoke of abdication. The Empress persuaded him to remain, while she undertook a journey to Europe. She would compel the French Emperor to fulfil his promises. She would induce the Pope to reconcile the clergy with the Empire. She failed utterly in both endeavours, and in her last interview with Pius IX., perceiving that all hope was ended, she went out of her mind. Early in October the news reached her husband, and then his courage gave way. He had lately exchanged what was called a Liberal for a Conservative Ministry, and had offered the principal departments to two French generals. But they were forbidden by Napoleon to accept, and still no substantial help came from the clergy. Worn out with illness and sorrow, deserted on all sides, and knowing that his Empire was crumbling, Maximilian started for the coast with an undefined intention of sailing for Europe. His most trusted adviser, a Belgian, who had accompanied the Empress, attempted at this conjuncture to draw him away by an appeal to his ambition. He described the discontent of the humbled Austrians and assured him that they wished his brother to abdicate, while sympathy for himself was increasing throughout the country.

Francis Joseph was aware of this intrigue, but he made a last effort to save his brother by restoring to him, if he would return, his position at the head of the princes of the blood. An aide-de-camp of Napoleon arrived in Mexico to hasten the departure of the troops, and instructed to use everything but force to induce Maximilian to abdicate. The French did not like the dishonour of leaving him to his fate, and they hoped, if he ceased to reign, to make their own terms with the Mexicans, and to leave behind them a government not utterly hostile to themselves. That the expedition was a gigantic failure, injurious to the reputation of the army and the stability of the throne, could not be disguised. But the blow would be more keenly felt if the man on whom they had made war for four years, and with whom they had refused to treat, remained unshaken in his office, victorious over the arms and arts of Napoleon III. So great was their urgency that Maximilian felt insulted, and at last believed himself betrayed.

Whilst he was wavering and lingering near the coast, an American frigate appeared at Vera Cruz, conveying General Sherman and Mr. Campbell, accredited as envoys to Juarez. They had sailed from New York on the 11th of November, when it was supposed that Maximilian had abdicated, leaving the French in the country. The Government at Washington were determined that in that case their candidate, and not that of Napoleon, should prevail. Mr. Campbell was charged to offer support and aid to the Republic, and the presence of the ablest soldier of the Union indicated ostentatiously of what nature that aid was to be. When these envoys found that Maximilian had not departed, they understood that their mission was a blunder and withdrew. The Emperor did not believe that an American Minister, escorted by such a personage as Sherman, had come all the way to Vera Cruz and had gone away without doing anything. He persuaded himself that France and America had come to an understanding, and had made a bargain of which his crown was to be the price. The pressing invitations to depart with the French appeared to him perfidious, and he thought it would be disgraceful that his life should be rescued by those who had bartered his throne.

Meantime the Church party, which had so long coldly stood aloof, thought that the moment had arrived when it could impose its own conditions. It was represented to the Emperor that the disappearance of the invaders would remove the cause of his unpopularity, and that good patriots would support him now, who had refused to acknowledge the nominee of a foreign Power. Miramon arrived from Europe at the critical moment and offered his sword to Maximilian. The Prussian Minister also advised him to remain. The clergy promised their powerful aid, and he yielded. There was nothing for him to look forward to in Europe. No public career was open to the man who had failed so signally in an enterprise of his own seeking. His position in Austria, which was distressing before, would be intolerable now. He had quarrelled with his family, with his church, with the protector to whose temptations he had hearkened. And for him there was to be no more the happiness of the domestic hearth.

In Mexico there were no hopes to live for, but there was still a cause in which it would be glorious to die. There were friends whom he could not leave to perish in expiation of measures which had been his work. He knew what the vengeance of the victors would be. He knew that those who had been most faithful to him would be most surely slaughtered; and he deemed that he, who had never yet been seen on a field of battle, had no right to fly without fighting. Probably he felt that when a monarch cannot preserve his throne, nothing becomes him better than to make his grave beneath its ruins. He yielded, and returned, sullenly and slowly, to the capital. What concessions had been wrung from the party in whose hands he was, I do not know. But he addressed a letter to the Pope, expressing regret for the policy which had failed, and at Rome, where he was once regarded as a persecutor and almost an apostate, the letter was hailed as a solemn and complete retraction.

From that moment Maximilian was no longer the chief of a national government, but a partisan leader, who had not even the control of his party. He laid aside the pomp of Majesty, and lived in private houses, especially as the guest of the clergy. He declared that he was only provisionally the chief of the State, and held office only until a national assembly had decided what should be the future of Mexico. He invited Juarez to submit his claim to the same peaceful arbitration, and proposed that there should be a general amnesty, to stop the shedding of blood. The Republicans saw nothing in all this but the signs of weakness, and of their own approaching triumph. They opposed no obstacles in the way of the departing French, but they closed in overwhelming numbers upon the feeble army of the Empire.

The defeat of Miramon on the great North road in February compelled Maximilian to take the field. He put himself for the first time at the head of his troops, and joined Miramon at Queretaro. On this day last year he was surrounded and besieged by Escobedo with an army which rose speedily to more than 40,000 men. Marquez was sent to Mexico for reinforcements, but he never returned, and spent the short time that remained in wringing money from the inhabitants. The siege proceeded slowly, and on the 24th of April Miramon made a successful sally, and opened for a moment the road to the capital. But the men were worn out with fighting, and the Emperor refused to leave them. He declared he had not come to Queretaro to fly from danger. To those who saw him during those anxious days, haggard and aged, with a long beard flowing over his breast, and the fever of despair in his eyes, conducting the defence and constantly under fire, it seemed that he was longing for the glory of a soldier's death. At length the supplies were nearly exhausted, the certainty of the treason of Marquez removed all hope of relief, and it was resolved that the garrison should make an attempt to cut its way through the enemy on the 15th of May. It was too late. For four days Lopez, the second in command, had been in communication with Escobedo, and had accepted a bribe of £1400. Late in the night of the 14th he saw the Emperor; and then, at two in the morning, he introduced a Republican general into the fort. This general was disguised, and carried concealed arms. He remained two hours, and examined the interior of the works. Then Lopez withdrew the Imperial sentries, and their posts were silently occupied by the soldiers of Riva Palacio, the only officer who had been excepted, by name, from the decree of October.

At daybreak the bells of the churches of Queretaro announced to the Republican camp that the place was won. The traitor went up to the Emperor's room, and told him that the enemy was in the town. Maximilian rushed forth, and was stopped by Republican soldiers, who did not recognise him. Lopez whispered to the officer who it was. Then the generous Mexican allowed the Emperor to pass, pretending to take him for a civilian; and he escaped to a fortified position at some distance. Here he was joined by the faithful Mejia, and as many officers and men as could hew their way through the columns of Republicans that were now pouring into the town. Miramon alone attempted a forlorn resistance. A shot struck him in the face, and he fell, blinded with blood, into the hands of his enemies.

The position occupied by the Imperialists was swept by artillery and could not be defended, and at eight o'clock they surrendered. Among the prisoners was Mendez, who had caused the decree of October to be executed on Arteaga and his companions. He was shot the same day. The Emperor was shut up, with Miramon and Mejia, in a cell of the Capuchin convent, and it was announced to them that they would be tried by court-martial, under the decree of January. From that moment Maximilian retained no hope of life. He presented his war-horse to Riva Palacio, the most chivalrous of his enemies, and telegraphed to Mexico for the Prussian Minister, and for legal advice in preparing his defence.

Mexico was already besieged by a Republican army, and hollow shells were thrown into the town, stuffed with telegrams proclaiming the fall of Queretaro. But Marquez, the most detested of the Imperial generals, wished to gain time, and he suppressed the news. Maximilian had deposited his abdication in the hands of the President of Council, to be produced if he died or fell a prisoner; but Marquez compelled him to keep it secret, and prevented for several days the departure of the defenders who had been summoned. The most eminent of these was the advocate Riva Palacio, the father of the general, a leading Republican, who had refused all solicitations to serve the Emperor in the days of his power. The others seem to have been less distinguished, but they were all chosen among the Republicans. The Prussian Minister, Baron Magnus, had lived on intimate terms with the Emperor, and had been one of the advisers of the expedition which had ended so fatally. No European Power was less compromised in Mexican affairs, or less obnoxious to the dominant party than Prussia, and it was thought that Baron Magnus would be the best mediator.

The seat of Government was at San Luis, 200 miles beyond Queretaro, but connected with it by telegraph. Two lawyers remained with the Emperor, while Riva Palacio and the Prussian Minister repaired to San Luis to intercede with Juarez. The court-martial which was to try the prisoners met on the stage of the theatre of Queretaro on the morning of Friday, the 14th of June. The house was lighted up and full of spectators. Maximilian had been ill in bed for several days, and self-respect forbad him to appear on such a scene. The two generals were present. Their case was manifestly desperate; yet the defender of Mejia caused a deep impression when he claimed for his client the same mercy, which, in spite of stern decrees, he had always shown to his captives, and appealed to Escobedo to say how he had fared when he was Mejia's prisoner. The defence of Miramon was less dignified and less loyal. He pleaded that he had had no command while the French were in the country, that he had been hostile to the Empire which had sent him on an idle mission to Europe, and that he had offered his services to the chief of the Republic. These facts were true; and at Paris Miramon had said openly that the end of the intervention would be to make him President again. Maximilian knew all this, and he knew the manner of his defence. This must not be forgotten when we come to the last scene of all, and see how the Emperor bore himself towards the brave but ambitious soldier, who had been ready to desert the cause in which he was to die.

The strongest points of the indictment against Maximilian were, that he had known the decree of January, which had been published long before he came; that the necessity of foreign support must have proved to him that he was not the legitimate, national Sovereign, and that he could not therefore justify the October decree, by which it was pretended, with great exaggeration, that 40,000 Mexicans had suffered death; that he was responsible for the continuance of civil war after the departure of the French, and for the introduction of Belgian and Austrian soldiers, whose Governments were not at war with the Republic, and who came therefore in the character of filibusters and assassins. The reply to these charges was narrow and technical, and not worthy of the occasion. It amounted in substance to that which the Emperor had said himself: "You may dispute the original probability of my success, but not the sincerity of my motives." As to the decree of October, his advocates defied the prosecution to name a single instance in which he had refused a pardon.

A little before midnight on the 15th the prisoners were found guilty, and their sentence having been confirmed by Escobedo on the Sunday morning, they were informed that they would be shot at three o'clock on the same day. Meanwhile the issue of the trial had been foreseen, and the friends of the Emperor were pleading with Juarez for his pardon. On the ground of political expediency their position was undoubtedly more favourable than that of men restricted to legal arguments. During the war in Mexico a yet deadlier struggle had raged beyond the American border. The author of Secession was not a foreigner, like Maximilian, but a citizen of the country in which he had conspired. He too had been defeated and captured, and then, while European monarchies suppressed revolution with atrocious cruelty,

Jefferson Davies [*sic*] had been released by the great Republic. Therefore, they said, the honour of Republican institutions was in the keeping of Juarez, and required that Mexico should follow that example of triumphant clemency, and should betray neither hatred for the past nor alarm for the future.

The President and his minister, Lerdo, listened patiently but coldly. They said that Europe could give no guarantee that it would not renew the same attempt, that Maximilian would continue, even in spite of himself, to be a pretext and a rallying cry for faction, and an instrument by which foreign Powers, when complications arose, might gain a party in the country. The decree of October cried for expiation, and the death of its author would enable them to spare the rest. Many Mexicans had been put to death under the decree of January, and the punishment of inferiors could not be justified if that of the leader was remitted. They seem to have believed that if the doorposts of the Republic were marked with the blood of a prince, the angel of destruction would pass them by. They showed no inclination to cast on others the responsibility of their act, but it is difficult to believe that it was determined by reason of state dispassionately weighed.

Juarez possessed but a precarious authority over the army; and the army was infuriated by strife, and thirsted to avenge the comrades who had been executed like murderers. We can imagine what their feelings would be towards the foreigner whose title was a vote extracted by the bayonets of invaders, who had ordered their countrymen and themselves to be slaughtered, and who was now convicted of having been a pretender and a usurper, as he was the champion of the weaker party. It is probable that the real author of the Emperor's execution is Escobedo, and that Juarez was powerless to save him. When the news that he was to die in three hours reached San Luis at noon on the Sunday, the Prussian Minister prayed for a short delay. He knew that Maximilian had matters to settle before death, and there was some hope that foreign intercession would be in time to save his life. But the American Government, at the request of the Emperor of Austria, had already interceded for his brother, and had interceded in vain. A delay of three days was granted, but the order did not reach Queretaro till the last moment, when the prisoners had made themselves ready for immediate death. For himself, indeed, Maximilian had no hope, and was perfectly resigned. A report that his wife was dead made him meet his fate with joy. On the eve of his execution he telegraphed to Juarez requesting that he might be the only victim.

At six in the morning of Wednesday, the 19th of last June, he was led forth to the doom he had not deserved. His last act before going to the place of execution had been to write the following letter to his implacable conqueror: "I give up my life willingly, if the sacrifice can promote the welfare of my new country. But nothing healthy can grow upon a soil saturated with blood, and therefore, I entreat you, let mine be the last you shed. The fortitude with which you upheld the cause that triumphs now won my admiration in happier days, and I pray that it may not fail you in the peaceful work of conciliation that is to come." When they came to the appointed place, he gave money to the soldiers by whose hands he was to fall, asking them to aim at his heart, for he wished that his mother might look upon his face again. The officer who was to give the word assured him that he detested the duty, and implored him not to die with a feeling of resentment against him. Maximilian thanked him, and said that he must obey orders. Mejia was in great trouble and dejection. His wife had just borne him a son, and as he left his prison he had seen her rushing through the streets, raving mad, with the child in her arms. The Emperor bade him farewell affectionately, saying: "There is a reward in the next world for that which is not requited here." He was standing between the Mexicans, but out of humility, or magnanimity, or because a solemn and sacred memory was present to his mind at that last awful moment, he turned to Miramon and said that out of esteem for his courage he would yield to him the place of honour. His last words were: "I die for a just cause—the independence and the liberty of Mexico. May my death close the era of the misfortunes of my adopted country: God save Mexico!" Then he crossed his hands upon his breast and fell, pierced by nine balls.

He fell, and carried with him in this fall the independence of the people he had come to save. Nothing henceforth remains that can permanently arrest the United States in the annexation of Spanish America. If they have prudence to avoid European war, and wisdom to compose their own dissensions, they may grasp the most glorious inheritance the earth affords. The conquest of Spanish America would be easy and certain, but beset with dangers. A confederacy loses its true character when it rules over dependencies; and a Democracy lives a threatened life that admits millions of a strange and inferior race which it can neither assimilate nor absorb. It is more likely that the Americans will bind their neighbours by treaties, which will throw open the whole continent to their own influence and enterprise, without destroying their separate existence.

The memory of the fair-haired stranger, who devoted his life to the good of Mexico, and died for guilt which was not his own, will live in sorrow rather than in anger among the people for whom he strove in vain. Already we may pronounce the verdict of history upon his sad career—his worst crime was in accepting the treacherous gift of Empire, but his misfortune was greater than his fault. I think he was well-nigh the noblest of his race, and fulfilled the promise of his words: "The fame of my ancestors will not degenerate in me."

The Relation of the Races in South America

By LORD BRYCE

... the existence of this aboriginal population ... still is a factor of the first magnitude.

Because North Americans have ever been preoccupied with their problems of race, they have tended to overlook such problems in the other American republics. An example is their insistence on calling the land area to the south Latin America, despite the fact that a large percentage of its inhabitants are neither "Latin" nor American, but black African; another large percentage is not Latin, but Indian; and an additional large percentage is a mixture of Indian, Negro, and Latin in varying proportions.

Racial considerations are of the utmost importance in Latin America, and in some countries an understanding of this is vital to a comprehension of national behavior. Thus, for example, during the U.S. Civil War, the mestizos and mulattoes of the Dominican Republic preferred to revert to colonial status under Spain rather than risk independence and possible reconquest by neighboring Haiti, which, it was felt, might become a dangerous aggressor if encouraged by the pro-Negro U.S. North. A political career in Mexico today is almost impossible for the Mexican who cannot claim some Indian blood, and the economic interests of the Negro, Protestant, English-speaking Panamanian of West Indian origin have always been subordinated to the interests of the Spanish-speaking mestizo.

Racial considerations in Latin America are different, however, from those in the United States, and this is another reason why North Americans have tended to overlook their importance and influence. In Latin America there was always a body of laws regarding the treatment of the Negro slave. He was never chattel, as in the United States, but a legal personality with duties and rights. These duties and rights were enforced by the crown, just as the duties and rights of the Indians under Spanish law were protected and enforced.

This does not mean that there were no atrocities committed by the ruling classes on the subject races; there *were,* just as there were atrocities committed by the subject peoples on their masters. It does mean, however, that the whole question of race in Latin America has had a different evolution from that in the United States.

Lord Bryce, British ambassador to the United States from 1907 to 1913, was one of the first, in fairly recent times, to point to this great difference. Bryce had established his reputation as a scholar as early as 1864 with his publication of *The Holy Roman Empire. The American Commonwealth,* published in 1888 and revised after he had taken up residence as ambassador in Washington, was the first book in which the institutions of the United States were thoroughly discussed from the point of view of both a historian and a constitutional lawyer, and it at once became a classic.

As a consequence, no British ambassador in Washington, either before or since, has ever achieved the position of Lord Bryce. In those days the British ambassador was allowed two months' leave each year. Bryce, who took no leave in 1909, applied for a double leave in 1910 to permit him time to visit South America. The request was granted, and Lord Bryce and his wife sailed from New York on September 1, 1910; they returned on January 1, 1911. The Bryces arrived in Panama on September 9 and stayed with Colonel Gorgas, chief medical officer of the Canal Commission, to observe the construction of the Panama Canal. It was characteristic of Bryce's position at the time that upon observing the enormity of the Culebra cut and noting the absence of geologists on the Isthmus to observe what could be learned of the earth's structure from this deepest of open excavations, he wrote to President Taft to suggest a special geological mission. Taft read the letter to his Cabinet and at once proceeded to act on Bryce's suggestion.

From Panama, the Bryces traveled to Peru, Bolivia, Chile, Argentina, Uruguay, and Brazil, and the book that he based on this trip, titled *South America: Observations and Impressions,* was first published in 1912, while he was still ambassador in Washington.

The book was not profound. It was not intended to be, but because of Bryce's enormous prestige in academic, as well as political, circles, it had great influence. The chapter, "The Relation of the Races in South America," reprinted here, introduced an entire generation to some of the racial aspects of South America. Although it ignored the existence of Negro minorities in South America save in Brazil, and it tended to observe the problem of race from the standpoint of genetics rather than from that of cultural, social, and political considerations, it did represent a significant first step in the examination of the nature of Latin America. Also, it tended to suggest the need for further scholarship and examination by stressing the importance of race and the difference between North and South America from the standpoint of racial evolution. A generation of diplomats, subsequent to Lord Bryce, read his book while proceeding to their posts in the other American republics.

James Bryce, born in 1838, was the son of Dr. James Bryce, who had a school in Belfast, Ireland. He went to Trinity College, Oxford, and in 1862 became a fellow of Oriel College. Subsequently, he practiced law in London, but he was called back to Oxford to be regius professor of civil law from 1870 to 1893. An ardent member of the Liberal Party, he first entered Parliament in 1880, and in 1886 he entered the Cabinet. In 1907 he left party politics to become the British ambassador in Washington, a post he held until 1913. In January, 1914, he went to the House of Lords. Lord Bryce died in 1922.

P. K.

ALTHOUGH races, unlike in character and differing in the scale of upward progress, must have come into contact from earliest times, it is only in recent years that the phenomena attending that contact have been carefully observed and studied. From the end of the 15th century European nations have been conquering the backward races. In some countries they enslaved, in others they extirpated these races. They have now portioned out the whole world of savagery, barbarism and semi-civilization among themselves, so that, as the result of discoveries, wars and treaties, six great and three smaller powers[1] have now appropriated all the extra-European world, except three or four ancient Asiatic states. In our own day the questions connected with race contact have obtained both a new moral interest, because the old methods of killing off the so-called lower branches of mankind by the sword or by slavery have fallen into discredit, and also a new scientific interest, because we have become curious to know what are the effects

[1]Britain, France, Germany, Italy, Russia, the United States, Belgium, Holland and Portugal.

of a mixture of markedly dissimilar racial stocks. Such mixture raises some of the most obscure problems in the doctrine of heredity. Does the blending of one race with another tend to weaken or to improve the breed, and how far are any marked qualities of one parent stock transmissible by blood to a mixed progeny which is placed and powerfully affected by a different environment? Spanish America offers a large and fertile field for the study of these and other similar questions, and a field which has been, so far, little examined. My own knowledge does not go far enough to enable me to do more than state a few broad facts and suggest to those who have better opportunities for enquiry some of the problems which the subject presents.

When the Spanish and Portuguese conquerors began to occupy the New World they found it peopled everywhere by native tribes whose physical characteristics, and to some extent their languages also, indicated that although they had inhabited America during countless ages, they probably all had the same, and that an east Asiatic origin. No part of the two continents from Behring's Straits [*sic*] to Cape Horn (except a few hopelessly barren deserts) was quite untenanted, but some regions were far more populous than others. These regions were the high plateaus of Anahuac (Mexico) with the adjoining lower regions of Yucatán and Guatemala, the plateau of Bogotá and the plateau of Peru. It was in these that the greatest progress had been made toward civilization and a settled agricultural life; while the lower woodlands and the more or less arid prairies, such as those of the Missouri and of southern Argentina, were more thinly inhabited. There may well have been in Anahuac and Yucatán as many people as in the rest of North America, and in the Peruvian realm of the Incas as many people as in all the rest of South America.

Now the existence of this aboriginal population has been and still is a factor of the first magnitude in all parts of the continent (except Argentina and Uruguay, where it hardly exists) and in this fact lies one of the most striking contrasts between the northern and southern halves of the Western Hemisphere. The importance of the native Indian element in South America—and the same thing holds true of Mexico and Central America—resides partly in the fact that it furnishes the bulk of the laboring people and a large part of the army, partly in the influence which it has exerted, and still exerts, on the whites, comingling its blood with theirs and affecting their habits and life in many ways.

When the Spaniards came to the New World, they came mainly for the sake of gold. Neither the extension of trade, the hope of which prompted the Dutch, nor the acquisition of lands to be settled and cultivated, thereby extending the dominion of their crowns, which moved most of the English and French, nor yet the desire of freedom to worship God in their own way, which sent out the Pilgrims and Puritans of New England–none of these things were uppermost in the minds of the companions of Columbus and Ponce de León, of Vasco Nuñez and Cortés and Pizarro. No doubt they also desired to propagate the faith, but their spiritual aims were never suffered to interfere with their secular enterprises. Few settlers came from Spain to till the land. The first object was to seize all that could be found of the precious metals, much to the astonishment of the natives who thought that gold must be to them a sort of fetich [*sic*]. The next was to discover mines and make the Indians work them. The third was to divide up the more fertile districts into large estates, allotting to each adventurer his share of labouring natives along with his share of the lands. No settlers came out to clear the ground from wood and build homes upon it as did the colonists of New England, and those also who sought to create a New France on the St. Lawrence. No Spaniard thought of tilling the soil himself. Why should he, when he could make others till it for him? Where it was already under cultivation by the native peasants, they were turned into serfs attached to the *encomienda.* Where there was forest, the conquerors seldom troubled themselves to fell it, and that which they found a wilderness remained a wilderness in the hands of the savage tribes. Where it was open prairie, there was little reason for disturbing the nomads who wandered over it. Accordingly, the invaders became a ruling caste, living on the labour of their Indian serfs, and for a long time they confined themselves to the lands on which the latter were already established. So it befell that the aborigines, who in the northern parts of North America were either destroyed or driven out to the West, continued to be in Spanish America one half or more of the population, those who were already semicivilized being kept as labourers, those who were savages being left to themselves in the forests or half-desert prairies. No agricultural European population grew up in the settled districts. As there were aborigines on the spot to cultivate the land already improved, comparatively few negroes were transported from Africa, and these chiefly to the shores of the Caribbean and to

Peru. It was only in the tropical regions of the Antilles and (somewhat later) of Brazil that negro slavery grew up on a large scale; and even there, mining rather than agriculture was the first cause of their being brought from Africa. The need for negroes was not great in Mexico or Peru, because the native Indians were of a hardier stock than the feeble Arawaks of the Antilles, and lived on under their European masters, though ground down and reduced in numbers by ill treatment. Thus when at last the Spanish colonies asserted their independence, they started without that incubus of a mass of negro slaves which brought so much trouble upon the southern states of the North American union.

Between the numerous aboriginal tribes there were the greatest differences not only in their degree of advancement toward civilization, but in intelligence, in virility, in fighting quality, and in that kind of resisting power which enables people to survive under oppression. The best fighters seem to have been–I am not now including the tribes of eastern North America–the Aztecs of Mexico and the Mapoche or Araucanians of Chile. The Caribs in some of the Lesser Antilles and in Venezuela were fierce and tenacious, while their neighbours, the Arawaks of the other Antilles, seem to have become extinct under Spanish severities in one half a century. We have no material, for even the vaguest guess at the number of these tribes, but it is evident that some disappeared altogether, and that others were greatly reduced. The Chibchas of Bogotá, who were estimated at a million when first reached by the Conquerors, are said by a Spanish annalist to have been almost exterminated in twenty years. Of the Mochicas or Yuncas on the Pacific coast, still numerous at the coming of Pizarro, though many had perished during their conquest by the Incas, few were left after one half a century, and their cities have long been heaps of ruins, perhaps partly because the irrigation works which brought water to them were allowed to perish. A census taken in Peru by the Viceroy Toledo in A.D. 1575 is said to have shown eight millions of Indians in what is new Peru and Bolivia. Two centuries later there were less than one half that number. So it is stated that the Indians round Panama rapidly declined in number when the Spanish established themselves there. The natives of northeastern Brazil were killed off in the end of the 16th century, though the tale that two million were destroyed in about twenty years is scarcely credible, and the less numerous tribes of central Argentina and Uruguay have entirely vanished. The process still goes on, though today the means are usually less violent. It is intoxicating liquors and European diseases, not any ill treatment by the Chileans that have been reducing the stalwart Araucanians to a quarter or a fifth part of what they were eighty years ago, and the Tehuelches and other Patagonian tribes, including the wretched Fuegians, are dying out largely from natural causes. But in the Amazonian forests along the Putumayo river–and within the last few years–the cruelties and oppressions practiced by the rubber gatherers upon the helpless Indians have destroyed many thousands of lives and apparently altogether blotted out some tribes.

How many aborigines now remain in Latin America it is impossible to ascertain. Even in such advanced countries as Mexico and Peru, there are no trustworthy figures, not only because it is impossible to find means of counting the wild nomads of northwestern Mexico and the still wilder savages of eastern Peru, but also because, even in the civilized districts, it is hard to determine who is to be deemed an Indian and who a mestizo, or half-breed. However, any estimate, if clearly understood to be merely conjectural, is better than none at all, so I may say that in Mexico there are probably, out of fifteen millions of people, about eight millions of Indians, with at least six millions of mixed blood, and the rest Spaniards; while in Peru and Bolivia, out of a total of about six millions, three and a half millions are Indians, one and a half millions mestizos, and the rest more or less pure Spaniards. The one state which is almost wholly Indian, so that the Guarani language is the prevailing tongue, is the inland country of Paraguay, and the one which has no Indians at all is Uruguay, lying on the coast, not far from Paraguay. Of the total population of South America, estimated at forty-five millions, probably eight to nine millions may be pure Indians. Besides these there are possibly, thirteen millions of mestizos or half-breeds, and fifteen of persons who deem themselves white, even if a good many have some infusion of aboriginal blood. But if we omit Argentina, almost entirely, and Uruguay entirely white, as well as Brazil, and confine our view to the other eight republics in which the Indian element is larger, a probable estimate would put the number of pure Indians at more than double that of the whites, and a little less than of the mestizos. Upon such a computation the total quantity of native blood would much exceed the European. Such an estimate, however, can make no claim to accuracy. I give it only because it seems, from all I could gather, to represent, in a rough sort of way, the proportions of the races. Anyone who chooses to consider all the more educated mestizos as whites, and all Indians with any touch of white blood as mestizos, would, of course, bring out different figures. The tendency of official statistics is in that direction, for everybody wishes to be reckoned as a white man, but such a method does not truly represent the racial facts.

Of the total of about nine million of Indians, two or three may be wild, *Indios bravos,* as the South Americans call them, and in little contact with civilized whites or mestizos. To this class belong many of the aborigines in Brazil, Colombia, Ecuador, and Venezuela, as well as most of the far smaller number still left in Argentina. Of the more or less civilized and settled Indians, more than one half, about three and one half millions, are in Peru and Bolivia; and it is of these that I shall now proceed to speak, as I had opportunities in these countries of ascertaining their position, and as they are themselves more interesting, because they are the descendants of what was, before the Spanish Conquest, a comparatively advanced people. What is true of them is, moreover, true in a general sense, as regards the settled aborigines of the northern republics. In those states, however, there is no such solid mass of sedentary agricultural Indians as dwell on the plateaux and inter-Andean valleys of Peru and Bolivia.

Though at the time of the Conquest there were probably in the Inca empire many different tribes speaking different languages, all have now been fused into two, the Quichuas to the north of Lake Titicaca, and the Aymaras, both around its shores and to the south of it in Bolivia. . . . [The] two languages are generally spoken all over the central Andes from the frontiers of Ecuador on the north to those of Chile and Argentina on the south. Comparatively few of these Indians, probably less than a fifth, are able to talk Spanish. Some few live in the towns and practice handicrafts. Three fourths of the population of La Paz is Aymara, while in Cuzco at least one third is Quichua. The vast majority, however, are country folk cultivating the soil as tenants or labourers or tending sheep and cattle as herdsmen for the landowners, who are, of course, either of Spanish or of mixed blood. Comparatively few Indians own small plots of their own. The landlords, who in the colonial times oppressed the peasants so atrociously as from time to time to provoke even this naturally submissive people to rebellion, no longer venture to practise the exactions and cruelties of those days. Authority is not feared as it was then, and could not be used to support such flagrant injustice. Neither do the clergy wring money from their flocks, as in those bad old days, though even now the fees charged for marriages are so high that the rite is commonly neglected. The ancient tribal system has melted away and the *cacique,* as the Spaniards called him, who was the head of a local community down till the end of the 18th century, is now gone, but the old organization of the dwellers in a village by brotherhoods, and resting, or supposed to rest, upon blood relationship, still exists, and local affairs are managed by the local officials mentioned in an earlier chapter. Thus the Indian is left very much to himself, except that he pays rent to the landlord and is often bound to render him personal service at his residence during part of the year. This is called the *Mita.* His food is not very nutritious, consisting largely of *chuno,* i.e. frozen potatoes, usually ground into flour. His clothing is scanty, his mode of life hard and wretched, especially on the bleak plateaux. Yet he is not in that abject poverty which fears starvation; perhaps, indeed, not so near the minimum level of subsistence as are millions of the people in China and India. He does not contrast his own evil case with the luxury of the rich, as do the slum dwellers of European cities, nor does he feel his case to be evil, for it is no worse than his forefathers have borne for ten generations, and he knows no other.

Not only the Quichuas and Aymaras, but the Indians of the northern republics of southern Chile are quite illiterate, and, as respects education, just where they were under the Incas, perhaps rather farther back, because there was then a sort of national life which has been long since quenched. There seems to be among them little or no desire for instruction. Even should any seek to rise in life, he would find no means of doing so, unless perchance some kindly priest should give the rudiments of knowledge to a boy brighter than the rest. Religion does nothing to stir their minds. They are nominally Christians, but of many of them that may be said today which was said in 1746 by the humane and orthodox Spaniards, Antonio de Ulloa and Jorge Juan, whose secret report upon things in South America, and among others upon the condition of the Indians in Peru and Ecuador, made to the King of Spain, was published in England eighty years later. They say:—

"The religion of the Indians is no more like the Christian religion than it is to that which they had while they were pagans, for if the matter be well examined it will be found that notwithstanding the nominal conversion of these tribes, so small is the progress they have made in knowledge that it will be hard to discover any difference between the state in which they now find themselves, and that in which they were at the time of the Conquest."[2]

That the influence of the priesthood did not commend religion to the people to relieve their misery may be gathered from this further extract from the same secret report:—

"The miserable state of the Indians is to be ascribed to the vices of the parish priests (*curas*), the extortions of the corregidores, and the bad treatment which they generally receive from all Spaniards. Unable to endure their sufferings, and longing to escape from slavery, many of them have risen up and moved off to unconquered districts, there to continue in the barbarous practices of heathenism. . . . In the community of Pimampiro in the province of Quito, which consisted of more than 5000 Indians, and was prosperous, the conduct of the parish priest drove the Indians to despair. Uniting in one body, they rose in rebellion and in one night passed to the Cordillera, where they joined themselves to the wild heathen Indians, with whom they have continued until now."[3]

It ought to be remembered that the avarice and moral faults charged upon the clergy in these reports, as well as in other accounts belonging to the 18th century are brought against parish priests rather than the religious orders, although Ulloa describes the level of conduct as having sadly declined among these also. To some of the orders, most of all to the Jesuits, and in a less degree to the early Dominicans, much credit is due for their efforts not only to spread the gospel, often at the risk of their lives, but also to secure justice for the unfortunate Indians. The great Las Casas was only the most conspicuous among many admirable Spanish churchmen who threw their hearts into this campaign of humanity, though they seldom prevailed against the hard-hearted rapacity of the land owners and mine owners who wished to keep the Indians in serfdom and did not care how many perished under their hands. These worthy ecclesiastics sometimes secured good ordinances from the Council of the Indies in Spain, but the colonial governors

[2]*Noticias Secretas de America,* p. 353, David Barry, London 1826.
[3]*Noticias Secretas, ut supra,* p. 343.

found that the path of least resistance was to proclaim the ordinance and wink at its neglect. On many a law was the note made, "It is obeyed, but not executed" (*Se obedece pero no se ejecuta*). In Paraguay, where the population was almost wholly Indian, the reign of the Jesuits was generally beneficent. They could not do much for the education of the mass of their subjects, but while they trained some few of the promising youth, they impressed habits of industry and good conduct upon the rest. Perhaps it is to the excessive inculcation of obedience that the blind submissiveness of the later Paraguayans to such despots as Francia and López may be partly attributed.

The oppressions, both civil and ecclesiastical, referred to in the extracts given above, have long since ceased, but their consequences remain in the abject state of the aborigines and their ignorance of the truths and precepts of Christianity. As a learned student of Indian life observes, it is to them a kind of magic, more powerful for some purposes than their own ancient magic which was based on nature worship. . . . They worship evil spirits and make offerings to the mountain *Achachilas* and to the Earth. Even in Mexico, where the Indians are, as a rule, much more subject to enlightening influences, I was told in 1901 that an archbishop, visiting the parishes of his diocese not long before, had found the ancient idols hidden away behind the altars and occasionally brought out at night to receive marks of reverence. The Peruvians had at the conquest hardly advanced to the state of a regular mythology with images of the deities, so idols were less common and prominent, while the worship of the spirits immanent in natural objects was universal.

Where the church fails to stir the currents of intellectual life among the masses of such a people as this, what other influence is there to make for progress?

These Peruvian races were specially unfortunate because their natural leaders, the *caciques* or local chieftains who had formed a sort of aristocracy before the Conquest, were either slaughtered or, in some few cases, incorporated into the colonial upper class, so that they were lost, as protectors, to the subject class, who, having little force of character, sank unresistingly into serfdom. Once, in 1781–1783, under the leadership of Tupac Amaru . . . they rose in a revolt which lasted for three years. Being unwarlike and untrained, ill-armed and ill-led, they were defeated with great slaughter, after atrocious cruelties had been perpetrated on both sides. But they accomplished one feat rare in the annals of war in destroying, along with its Spanish garrison, the city of Sorata, which they had long besieged in vain, by damming up the course of a mountain torrent and turning its full stream on the place. Since those days, even the few chiefs that then remained have vanished, and the aboriginal race consists wholly of the poorest and most neglected part of the population. That which to them makes life tolerable is the incessant chewing of coca, a very old habit, but now less costly than in Inca days, because the leaf can be more easily imported from the hot country east of the Andes.

Their enjoyments are two. One is intoxication, mostly with chicha, the old native beverage, but now also with fiery alcohol, made from the sugar-cane. The other is dancing at their festivals. The priests, when they were converting the natives, thought it better not to disturb the ancient heathen dances, but to transfer them to the days which the church sets apart for its feasts, expunging, so far as they could, the more offensive features of the dance, though what remains is sufficiently repulsive. Such ceremonial performances are common among the Indians of North America, also, and used often to be kept up for days together before a declaration of war. The dances of the Hopi and other Indians which the visitor sees today in Arizona are dull and decorous affairs. A striking description of the dances which he saw at Tiahuanaco on Corpus Christi Day is given by Mr. Squier[4] and the much more recent account given by Mr. Bandelier of those he witnessed on another festival at Copacavana shew that things are much the same today. The music, of a drum-and-fyfe type, is loud, harsh, and discordant, but this does not imply that a taste for sweet sound is wanting, for the Indian often carries his simple flute or pipe with him on his journeys and enjoys the monotonous ditties which he makes it discourse.

Three other facts may be adduced to illustrate the condition of the aborigines. There is no recent literature in their languages, not even a newspaper or magazine. They seem to be very rarely ordained as priests, though I was told in Mexico that there are a good many Indian priests there; and it seldom happens that any Indian rises into the learned or even into the educated class. I heard of one such at Lima,

[4]*Travels in Peru,* p. 305 sqq.

who had a remarkable knowledge of natural history. There may have been others.

Whether owing to the character of the Indians, or to their fear of the white man, robberies and assaults are rare not only among the more gentle Quichuas, but also in Bolivia, where the Aymaras, a more dour and sullen race, frequently break the peace among themselves, village attacking village with sticks and slings, while the women carry bags of stones to supply ammunition for the men's slings. In fact the safety of the solitary European traveller in most parts of South America is almost as remarkable as the like circumstance in India.

In respect of civil rights, there is no legal distinction between the Indian and the white. Both enjoy the same citizenship for all private and public purposes, to both is granted the equal protection of the laws, equal suffrage, equal eligibility to office. This is to some extent a guarantee to the Indian against ill treatment, but it does not raise him in the social scale. He seldom casts a vote; not, indeed, that it makes much difference in these countries whether the citizen votes or not, for a paternal government takes charge of the elections. He is never–so far as I could learn–a candidate for any national office. The laws of the two republics interfere very little with his life, which is regulated by ancestral custom. Even in revolutions, he does not seem to come to the front. He is, however, willing to fight, and a good fighter both in foreign and in civil wars, however little interest he may take in the cause. But for this fact there would have been fewer and shorter revolutions. Thus the Indian is a member of the nation for military, if not for political purposes. The former are at least nearer to his comprehension than the latter, for he cares, and thinks of caring, about politics no more than did the needy knife-grinder in Canning's verses. No one has yet preached to him the gospel of democracy; no one has told him that he has anything to gain from action as a citizen. The whole thing is as completely out of his sphere as if he were still living under the Spanish viceroys, or, indeed, under the rule of the Inca Huayna Capac. There is therefore, not yet any "Indian question" in South America. There ought to be an Indian question: that is to say, there ought to be an effort to raise the Indians economically and educationally. But they have not yet begun to ask to be raised.

So much for the Indian as he is in Peru and Bolivia; and, apparently, also in those settled parts of northwestern Argentina where Indians still remain. In Paraguay the position is so far different that the Indians form not the lowest class, but the bulk of the nation. In the forest-covered regions of the Amazon and its tributaries, the *Indios bravos* are outside civilization altogether.

To understand the social relations of the white and Indian races one must begin by remembering that there is in Spanish and Portuguese countries no such sharp colour line as exists where men of Teutonic stock are settled in countries outside Europe. As this is true of the negro, it is even more true of the Indian. He may be despised as a weakling, he may be ignored as a citizen, he may be, as he was at one time, abominably oppressed and ill treated, but he excites no personal repulsion. It is not his race that is against him, but his debased condition. Whatever he suffers, is suffered because he is ignorant or timid or helpless, not because he is of a different blood and color. Accordingly the Spanish Americans do not strive to keep off and keep down the Indian in such wise as the North Americans and the Dutch and the English–I do not mean the governments, but the individuals–treat their black subjects. There is not even such aversion to him as is shewn in California and in Australia to the Chinese, Japanese, and Hindus. The distinction between the races in Spanish America is a distinction of rank or class rather than of colour. Against intermarriage there is therefore, no more feeling than that which exists against any union palpably below a man's or woman's own rank in life. If it is rare for a pure white to espouse a pure Indian, that is because they are of different ranks, just as it is rare for a well-born Englishman to marry a peasant girl. There is nothing in the law to oppose such a union, and though whites seldom marry pure Indians, because the classes come little into contact, the presence of an unmistakable Indian strain in a suitor makes no difference to his acceptability to a white woman of the same rank. Whether this contrast between the Spanish attitude towards the Indian and the Anglo-American attitude to the negro is due to differences between Roman Catholicism and Protestantism, or to the fact that the Indian was never legally a slave, or to the fact that the aboriginal American races shew a less marked divergence of colour and features from the white than does the negro, is a question which need not be here discussed. Possibly all three causes may contribute to the result; and probably the circumstance that most of the early Spaniards, having brought no wives with them, treated their numerous children by

Indian women as being legitimate and belonging to their own race, was also a factor. Such a usage, established in the days of the Conquest, would naturally continue to affect men's attitude. The result is anyhow one of great significance, and makes the racial problem here quite different from what it is in the southern states of North America.

The most salient point of difference lies in the position of the half-breed or mestizo. In North America a mulatto, a quadroon, even an octoroon who is only one-eighth black, counts as a negro. Here, except perhaps in a few of the oldest cities, a mestizo counts as a white. His half-Indian blood is no disparagement to his social standing, no obstacle to his reaching any public position. One may remark of such and such a person that he has evidently a strong infusion of Indian blood, or such another that he looks a Spaniard through and through, and the latter doubtless cherishes a secret satisfaction in his pure Iberian stock. But for the practical purposes of business and politics, the two, supposing them to belong to the same educated class, stand upon the same level. The families which value their lineage so highly that they would deem the marriage of a child to a person of mixed blood, otherwise desirable, to be a *mésalliance,* must be now few, and hardly exist outside five or six cities–such as Bogotá, Lima, Arequipa, and Santiago.

Thus one may say that there is no "colour question" in South America. Its republics have political and economic problems enough, but they are spared a source of embarrassment and danger constantly present to the minds of thoughtful North Americans, and present also (though less painfully) to the minds of South Africans. Although, therefore, both in Spanish America and in the United States there are social distinctions which coincide with race distinctions, the character of those distinctions is different. In both countries there are two sections. But in the United States everyone who is not white is classed as coloured, however, slight the trace. In Spanish America everyone who is not wholly Indian is classed as white, however marked the Indian tinge. Thus the mixed population, which in the United States swells the negro element, is in Spanish America a part of the white nation, and helps to give that element its preponderance. And a further difference appears in the fact that whereas in the United States the man of colour is discriminated against for social purposes, irrespective of his wealth, education or personal qualities, in Spanish countries race counts for so little that when he emerges out of the poverty and ignorance which mark the Indian, his equality with the white man is admitted. So rarely, however, does he emerge that one may broadly say that the Nation consists in these republics of white men and mestizos only, the Indian constituting, if not another nation, yet a separate nationality, marked off not merely by poverty, but by its language and the adherence of its members to ancient superstitions. They have nothing, except the worship of the saints and a fondness for liquor, in common with the class above them, for they speak a different language, think differently, feel differently, have their own amusements, and cherish in a dim way, faint memories of a time when their forefathers were masters of the land. They are not actively hostile to the white people, and, indeed, get on better with their landlords than some European peasantries have done with theirs. But they live apart, inside the nation, but not of it. The Aymaras are silent, suspicious, sullen. The Quichuas are more kindly, but hardly less reserved. This reserve and suspicion characterize the Mexican Indian also, who is generally more intelligent than the Peruvian. Both Aymaras and Quichuas are tenacious of their customs, and do not seek to assimilate any of that modern life and lore which has found its slow way even into the recesses of the Andes. No one from without tries to give it to them, no one rises from among themselves stirred by a desire to acquire it and then impart it to his fellows.

This want of leading, and want not only of light but of a wish for light, is the feature of the Indian population which most surprises the traveller, because he knows of no parallel to it among the subject races of Europe in the past or those of western Asia today. The Greek and Armenian in Turkey have at times suffered from his conquerors the Turk as the Quichua has suffered from his conquerors in Peru, but in intelligence and capacity for progress they have been the superiors of the Turk; and had there been more of them, they would before now have shaken off his control.

If it is asked how the presence of this solid Indian mass, unassimilated by the white nation, has affected that nation and the progress of the country as a whole, the answer is that in the first place it prevented all chance of a growth of a free European agricultural population, even in those high valleys where Europeans could work and thrive. Had the hardy and laborious peasantry of Galicia, Asturias, and Aragón settled in these regions, how much more robust, mentally and physically, might the nation have been! How much might agriculture have been improved had there been intelligent labour! But besides this want, and besides the weakening of the state by the lack of national spirit in half its population, the presence of a large mass of ignorance and superstition has operated to reduce the general intellectual level. There have been countries where a small rich and ruling class, living on the toil of inferiors, has cultivated art and letters with brilliant success, but we find nothing of the sort here. The ignorant mass has depressed the whole, as a glacier chills the air of its valley.

Whether the Spanish stock has deteriorated through the mixture of Indian blood is a more difficult matter to determine. The Peruvians and Bolivians of today, both whites and mestizos–and the same thing is true of Venezuelans and Ecuadoreans–differ much from the Spaniards of the 16th century and from the European Spaniards of today. They are probably more excitable; they are naturally less industrious because they live in hot countries and have Indians to work for them. But in Spain itself there are great differences between the peoples of the north and the south and the east. The Catalans are more energetic than the Andalusians, the Gallegos more industrious than the Valencians. The conditions of colonial life in the presence of a large aboriginal population, coupled with long misgovernment and intellectual stagnation, account for a good deal of the variation from the Spanish type. It is a sound maxim never to lay weight upon uncertain causes when certain causes are available as explanations. Moreover our knowledge of heredity in its influence on race development is still imperfect. The Argentines, who are of an almost pure white stock, also differ much from the modern Spaniard.

It might seem natural to assume *a priori* that men of pure European race would continue to hold the foremost place in these countries, and would shew both greater talents and a more humane temper than those in whose veins Indian blood flows. But I doubt if the facts support such a view. Some of the most forceful leaders who have figured in the politics of these republics have been mestizos. I remember one, as capable and energetic and upright a man as I met anywhere in the continent, who looked at least half an Indian, and very little of a Spaniard. Nor have there been any more sinister figures in the history of South America since the days of Pedro de Arias the infamous governor of Darien who put to death Vasco Nuñez de Balboa, than some who were pure Spaniards. No half-breeds have shewn more ruthlessness than the Spanish Carbajal in the days of Pizarro, or than Rosas, the Argentine dictator of 70 years ago. And in this connection it deserves to be noticed that the ancient Peruvian Indians, though they thought nothing of indiscriminate slaughter and occasionally tortured captive enemies, did not generally shew the same taste for blood as the Aztecs shewed in their sacrifices nor the same propensity to methods of elaborate and long-drawn-out cruelty as did the Red men of North America.

As I have so far been speaking chiefly of Peru and Bolivia, where the Indian population is larger and more civilized than elsewhere, a few observations ought to be added regarding the other republics in which a considerable aboriginal population remains. I omit Uruguay, because it has none at all. In Argentina there are some civilized Indians in the northwestern districts round the cities of Jujuy and Tucumán, and to these the remarks made regarding their neighbours, the Bolivian Indians, apply. There are also wild Indians, perhaps 100,000, perhaps more, on the Gran Chaco of the far north, and the scattered remnants of nomad Patagonians in the far south, and in Tierra del Fuego. They seem to be disappearing. The Onas in that island have been freely killed off by the ranchmen on whose flocks they preyed, and tubercular disease is destroying the rest. In Chile, besides the Araucanians, there are a few small tribes, in a low state of barbarism, left in the archipelago of wet and woody isles along the Pacific coast. The rural population of the republic—indeed, nearly all of the poorer and less educated part of it—is mestizo, a bold and vigorous race, good workers and fine fighters. Paraguay is an almost purely Indian country.

Of the four northern republics, Panama, Colombia, Venezuela, and Ecuador, I have seen only the first. In each of these the number of purely Spanish families is small. It is probably largest in Columbia. In Venezuela the Indians have been more largely absorbed into the general population than has happened in Colombia and Ecuador. In all four states such of the Indians as remain wild forest dwellers are passive, and practically outside the nation, which is, as a social and political entity, predominantly mestizo. What has been said of Peru and Bolivia is true of these states also: there is no colour line; the mestizos are treated as white and are not, as a class, intellectually inferior to the white. The Indian forms the lowest stratum, and seldom rises out of it.

There remains Brazil, distinguished from the other republics by the fact that in addition to her small mestizo population and her pure Indian population, most of it wild, she has a great mass of negroes and a still larger mass of mulattoes and quadroons. It is hardly too much to say that along the coast from Rio to Bahia and Pernambuco, as well as in parts of the interior behind these two cities, the black population predominates. In character and habits it somewhat resembles the negroes of the British West Indies and Santo Domingo, being superior to the Haytians, but inferior in education and enterprise to the coloured people of the southern states of North America. High as is its fecundity, its death-rate is also so high, owing to the general neglect of sanitary precautions, that it does not appear to be increasing relatively to the general population. It is well treated–slavery was seldom harsh among the kindly natured, easy-going Portuguese–and bears no ill-will to its former masters. Neither do they feel toward it that repulsion which marks the attitude of the whites to negroes in North America and South Africa. The Brazilian middle class intermarries with mulattoes and quadroons. Brazil is the one country in the world, besides the Portuguese colonies on the east and west coasts of Africa, in which a fusion of the European and African races is proceeding unchecked by law or custom. The doctrines of human equality and human solidarity have here their perfect work. The result is so far satisfactory that there is little or no class friction. The white man does not lynch or maltreat the negro: indeed, I have never heard of a lynching anywhere in South America except occasionally as part of a political convulsion. The negro is not accused of insolence and does not seem to develop any more criminality than naturally belongs to any ignorant population with loose notions of morality and property.

What ultimate effect the intermixture of blood will have on the European element in Brazil I will not venture to predict. If one may judge from a few remarkable cases, it will not necessarily reduce the intellectual standard. One of the ablest and most refined Brazilians I have known had some colour; and other such cases have been mentioned to me. Assumptions and preconceptions must be eschewed, however, plausible they may seem.

The chief conclusions which the history of the relations of races in the South American continent suggests are the three following. The first may be thought doubtful. It is negative rather than positive, and though it seems worth stating, I state it with diffidence.

The fusion of two parent stocks, one more advanced, the other more backward, does not necessarily result in producing a race inferior to the stronger parent or superior to the weaker. The mestizo in Peru is not palpably inferior in intellect to the Spanish colonial of unmixed blood, but seems to be substantially his equal. The mestizo in Mexico is not palpably superior—some doubt if he is at all superior either physically, morally, or intellectually—to the pure Tarascan or Zapotec Indian, who is, no doubt, a stronger human being than the South American Quichua or Aymara.

The second conclusion is this: Conquest and control by a race of greater strength have upon some races a depressing and almost ruinous effect. The Peruvian subjects of the Incas had reached a state of advancement which, though much below that of the ancient Egyptians and Babylonians, was remarkable when one considers that their isolation deprived them of the enormous benefit of contact with other progressive peoples, and when one considers also the disadvantage of living at a greater altitude, the absence of milk-yielding animals, and the paucity both of animals capable of domestication and of cereal plants. The impact of Spanish invasion not only shattered their own rudimentary civilization to pieces, but so took all the heart and spirit out of them that they have made practically no advances during four centuries, and have profited hardly at all by the western civilization of their masters. The aborigines of Mexico, having more stamina of intellect and will, have suffered less by the shock, but have done almost as little to assimilate the arts and ideas of Europe.

Thirdly, the ease with which the Spaniards have intermingled by marriage with the Indian tribes—and the Portuguese have done the like, not only with the Indians, but with the more physically dissimilar negroes—shews that race repugnance is no such constant and permanent factor in human affairs as members of the Teutonic peoples are apt to assume. Instead of being, as we Teutons suppose, the rule in this matter, we are rather the exception, for in the ancient world there seems to have been little race repulsion; there is very little today among Mohammedans; there is none among Chinese. This seems to suggest that since the phenomenon is not of the essence of human nature, it may not be always as strong among the Teutonic peoples as it is to-day. Religion has been in the past almost as powerful a dissevering force as has racial antagonism. In the case of Spaniards and Portuguese, religion, as soon as the Indians had been baptized, made race differences seem insignificant. Islam has always done this in the East and in Africa.

As touching the future, it seems as certain as anything in human affairs can be that the races now inhabiting South America, aboriginal, European, and African, will be all ultimately fused. The Spanish republics (except the purely white Argentina and Uruguay) will be Ibero-American, Brazil will be Ibero-American-African. All present facts point that way, and that any hitherto unfelt repulsion will arise seems most improbable. When, however, will the process be complete? In the Spanish republics, hardly before two centuries, probably not even then. It seems not much nearer now than it was in 1810, when the revolutionary struggles began, though anything which stirred up the Andean population, such as the discovery of a large number of new rich mines, bringing in foreign labour and increasing the demand for domestic labour, or anything that raised a spirit of economic and political change, might accelerate the consumation.

Still less predictable is the quality of the mixed race that will emerge. One cannot but fear that the Portuguese of tropical Brazil may suffer from the further infusion of an element the moral fibre of which is conspicuously weak, though there are those who argue that the blood of the superior race must ultimately transmute the whole. But we need not assume that the peoples of the Spanish republics will necessarily decline, for the present degredation of the Indians may be due as much to their melancholy history as to inherent defects. It is still too soon to be despondent. There may be in the Indian stock a reserve of strength, dormant, but not extinct, ready to respond to a new stimulus and to shoot upwards under more inspiriting conditions.

Whose Hemisphere?

By ARTHUR PRESTON WHITAKER

The Progressives . . . were interventionists abroad because they wanted to be interventionists at home.

From 1900 to World War I, Britain's position as the prime world empire was threatened by the rise of Germany, particularly by its growing navy. "The rivalry of these two powers canceled them both out so far as sea power in America was concerned . . . to the great benefit and relief of the United States." In this deadlock, U.S. hegemony in the Western Hemisphere took great leaps forward. Meanwhile, U.S. foreign investments in Latin America rapidly increased to make the United States, for the first time in its history, the chief creditor of the other American republics. This continued after World War I and added additional force to Latin American charges of "imperialism," which had originated in the prewar period of Anglo-German naval rivalry when U.S. marines were first landed in Caribbean countries.

It is the merit of Dr. Whitaker's work that he keeps in mind the worldwide forces at work on the hemisphere, as well as the details of purely inter-American situations. Furthermore, his examination of the intellectual ferment within liberal and conservative U.S. circles and the impulse that ideas ultimately gave to U.S. action in the Western Hemisphere is a distinct contribution to understanding. Dr. Whitaker is ever alive to the importance of ideas which he feels are not the effect but the cause of public events.

"Whose Hemisphere?" is reprinted from the book *The Western Hemisphere Idea,* first published in 1954. A difficulty in the study of U.S.–Latin American relations from 1900 to 1940 is that much of the research of the authoritative books on the subject has not always "taken shape in the tranquil regions of the air above the tumult and tempest of life," but as part of domestic U.S. political debate either for or against the concept of a U.S.-dominated Western Hemisphere isolationism. J. Fred Rippy in his *America and the Strife of Europe* (Chicago, University of Chicago Press, 1938), for example, used the same background facts as Dr. Whitaker to come to the conclusion that the United States should remain aloof from Europe and continue to use Europe's strife to make itself supreme in the Western Hemisphere. The opposing views of these two scholars thus emphasize a point suggested in the Introduction: in dealing with inter-American problems that have become embroiled in the conflicting arguments of domestic political debate, the editors of a selection of essays are forced, by space alone, to avoid controversy and make their choice on the basis of what they feel is significant and contributory to the forward movement of ideas. With this in mind, Dr. Whitaker must appear on anyone's list of outstanding living scholars who know Latin America.

R. E. M.

IN THE quarter century from the first pronouncement of the Roosevelt corollary in 1904 to the beginning of the Great Depression in 1929, two major trends in inter-American relations raised the question of Western Hemisphere unity in a way that suggests a comparison with the Babylonian captivity and the Great Schism of the late Middle Ages.

The first was a trend toward the hegemony of the United States in Western Hemisphere affairs, a hegemony based upon an increasing proponderance of power—naval, economic, and political—deliberately exercised in accordance with the new concept of the civilizing mission of the United States in the New World. As many Latin Americans saw it, the result was to place the Pan American movement in a dependent relation to Washington rather like that in which the papacy had stood with regard to the French monarchy when certain fourteenth-century popes lived in "Babylonian captivity" at Avignon.

The second trend was stimulated by a reaction against the first. In twentieth-century America, as in fourteenth-century Europe, the subordination of an international institution to a single nation provoked mounting resentment and schismatic tendencies among the rest. In America these reached their climax at the Fifth Pan American Conference, held at Havana in 1928, and turned that meeting into a fiasco which gave warning that the loose-knit Pan American family might disintegrate completely if grievances were not redressed.

Colossus of the Western Hemisphere

First let us look at the Babylonian captivity–the growth of the power of the United States in the Western Hemisphere in this quarter-century, the use that was made of it, and the conception of hemispheric relations that underlay this.

An examination of the unfolding power situation properly begins with sea power, for in the communications of the United States with Latin America in the preair age, sea power was decisive. This fact was vividly illustrated by a chain of events that began, on the very eve of the period we are considering, with the secession of Panama from Colombia (in 1903).[1] Though it was impossible for troops from the loyal Colombian mainland to reach the infected Isthmian area by land, they could have reached it by sea; but the United States Navy prevented all but one battalion from doing so, and as a result the Panamanians won their independence in the twinkling of an eye. The United States recognized their independence no less quickly and then went on to negotiate with the new Republic of Panama a treaty which made it a satellite of the Union and opened the way for the construction of a fortified Panama Canal. The way for its fortification had already been cleared by the Hay Pauncefote Treaty of 1901 with an obliging British government. Completed and opened to traffic in 1914, the fortified Panama Canal was at once the chief prop and the clearest symbol of the revolution in sea power that had taken place in the Caribbean in the previous two decades–the replacement of British control by the unchallenged and unchallengeable domination of the United States.[2] What is more, by 1914 the preponderance thus firmly established in the Caribbean area had made it possible for the United States to exercise effective control of the high seas throughout the Western Hemisphere.

The year 1914 may therefore be taken as marking the completion

[1]Dwight C. Miner, *The Fight for the Panama Route* (New York, 1940), ch. x, "Revolution in Panama."

[2]Harold and Margaret Sprout, *Toward a New Order of Sea Power, 1918–1922* (New York, 1940), p. 26.

of the first stage in the rise of the United States to hemispheric sea power, but an examination of the four major factors that had produced this rise shows that south of the Caribbean it did not yet rest on a firm foundation. Two of these factors might be presumed to be constant, as in fact they proved to be. One was the will of the people and government of the United States to build and maintain an ever-increasing navy. This they did, with some fluctuations but no major interruptions, from the 1890's until, in the 1920's, the world situation seemed to justify a relaxation. The other was the advantage which the United States enjoyed over Europe in naval operations in American waters as a result of the late nineteenth-century development of the iron-clad, steam-propelled warship. This change greatly increased the fighting strength of warships within their radius of action, but it also greatly reduced this radius by the rigid requirements of fuel and service which it imposed.[3] No major variation in this factor seemed likely in 1914, and in fact none occurred until a quarter-century later, in World War II.

But a scrutiny of the other two major factors gave no cause for complacency in the Washington of 1914. These factors were interlocking: one was the friendly diplomatic and naval retirement of Great Britain in favor of the United States which began in 1896 . . . , and the other was the increasingly tense balance-of-power situation in Europe, which was partly responsible for Britian's more conciliatory attitude toward the United States. After 1900, we are told, this tension repeatedly frustrated her imperial ambitions in America as well as other parts of the world and led to a greater and greater concentration of the British fleet in European waters. The same was true of her chief rival, Germany, and the big new German navy. As a result, after about 1900 the rivalry of these two powers canceled both of them out so far as sea power in America was concerned—to the great benefit and relief of the United States. The eminent American naval strategist and historian Alfred Thayer Mahan took note of this European balance-of-power situation frequently, and always with solid satisfaction; and in 1910 he stressed the fact that the mutual antagonism between Britain and Germany chained the two strongest fleets in the world to European waters "in peace as well as war."[4]

[3]*Ibid.*, p. 25.
[4]*Ibid.*, p. 24.

This situation, so happy from Washington's point of view, was rendered almost ideal in 1914 by the opening of the fortified Panama Canal; but one of its essential conditions was destroyed by World War I, which broke out just as the canal was opened. The war ended in the annihilation of the German navy and a reduction in the relative strength of the French navy, so that by 1919 Britain was once more, for the first time since 1900, without a serious European rival for sea power. In the meantime, however, the United States had undertaken and was rapidly carrying out a gigantic naval construction program. It thereby in effect provided from its own resources a substitute for that prewar balance-of-power rivalry in Europe which had for a time given it national protection and Hemisphere preponderance at a bargain price. The British Admiralty was, understandably, reluctant to accept the logic of a situation which seemed in some of its major outlines so painfully like the one that Britain had just fought a successful war to liquidate.

How this potentially dangerous problem in Anglo-American relations resisted successful settlement at the Paris Peace Conference of 1919 and was finally solved only after an interval of more than two years, at the Washington Conference of 1921–1922,[5] are questions we cannot enter into here. Suffice it to say that one of the major agreements reached by this latter conference crystallized the new order of sea power based upon regional distribution, which since 1900 had gradually supplanted the old nineteenth-century order of world sea power concentrated in Britannia's hands. She was still mistress of the seas in the eastern Atlantic, the North Sea, and other areas; but Japan was now accorded this role in the western Pacific, and the United States in the Western Hemisphere. As a result, so far as sea power was concerned, the position of the United States in the Western Hemisphere had never been stronger—nor, conversely, had the rest of the Western Hemisphere ever been in a weaker position vis-à-vis the United States—than in the last seven years of the period with which we are concerned in this essay, namely, the seven years from the end of the Washington Conference to the beginning of the Great Depression in 1929.

By an interesting coincidence—perhaps it was nothing more than

[5]*Ibid., passim,* especially pp. 61–66, on "the naval battle of Paris."

that–these years also saw the greatest outburst of United States investment in South America that had ever taken place, and one of the greatest that has ever occurred in a comparable period anywhere in the world. In 1924 United States investments in South America already amounted to the tidy sum of $1,411,000,000; by 1929 they had more than doubled, amounting at the end of that year to $3,014,000,000. Though the volume of American investments was larger in Canada and Europe than in Latin America, the rate of increase in the former areas in the same five years was considerably lower–about 35 per cent in the case of Canada and 75 per cent in that of Europe.[6]

The rapid penetration of South America by United States capital was particularly important because, before 1924, the Latin American investments of the United States had been concentrated mainly in Middle America. Even there they had been built up almost entirely in the past quarter-century. In 1897 the total for all Latin America was only $308,000,000; of this Mexico alone accounted for $200,000,000, or nearly two thirds, and Cuba and the other West Indies came next, with $49,000,000, leaving only $69,000,000, or less than 25 per cent, for all Central and South America. By 1929 the Latin American total had increased nearly eighteenfold, to $5,430,000,000; and South America alone accounted for over half of this huge investment. Only Great Britian still led the United States in the field of Latin American investments. No other competitor remotely approached these two; and not only was Britain's lead narrow, but most of her investments were concentrated in southern South America, and above all in a single country, Argentina.

In the foreign trade of Latin America, the progress made by the United States after 1914 was still more impressive, for in this respect it drew far ahead of Britain as well as all other competitors. Though it was aided in doing so by the wartime dislocation of European trade from 1914 to 1918, the process was already manifestly under way before the war began. One factor was the growth of investments, which had increased fivefold between 1897 and 1914. Another was the

[6]Data on investments in this paragraph and the next were drawn from Cleona Lewis, *America's Stake in International Investments* (Washington, D.C., 1938), p. 606. See also Max Winkler, *Investments of United States Capital in Latin America* (Boston, 1928).

establishment of Latin American branches of United States national banks, which was first made possible by the Federal Reserve Act of 1913. There had also been by 1914 a considerable improvement in shipping facilities and cable communications.

Nevertheless, it was only after 1914 that most of these factors came into full play. Thus, in the next ten years United States-owned cable mileage in Latin American waters increased from 14,000 to 38,000 while European-owned mileage declined slightly from its prewar figure of 25,000. Partly as a result of this, United States news services, which had played a minor role in Latin America before 1914, were by 1924 supplying its newspapers with most of their foreign news, and a larger part of this than ever before related to the United States.[7] All this was gratifying to the latter's national pride, but by 1925 one of its writers who took a sympathetic view of this wave of expansion was warning: "As the stronger state–as the creditor state–we must be prepared to be suspected and hated in many South American circles even if we behave well."[8]

The civilizing mission

And how was the United States behaving? While its government and people were building up its naval and economic preponderance in the New World in the manner just described, they were also developing a new concept of the role their country ought to play in relation to its southern neighbors. Until about 1920 this can be summed up in the term "civilizing mission," which connoted unilateral action, both political and economic, supported by missionary zeal and, if necessary, by armed force as well. After 1920, while there was no abrupt break, there was a sharp decline both of missionary zeal and of confidence in any unilateral approach to hemispheric problems.

With one brief exception, however, the Western Hemisphere idea in

[7]Julius Klein, "Economic Rivalries in Latin America," *Foreign Affairs,* III (1924), 242–243. Topically arranged information on many aspects of the early stage of this multiplication of the United States' contacts with Latin America will be found in William Spence Robertson, *Hispanic American Relations with the United States* (New York, 1923).

[8]Herbert Feis, "The Export of American Capital," *Foreign Affairs,* III (1925), 681.

one form or another dominated both public opinion and government action in the field of United States foreign policy throughout this quarter-century. The exception consisted in the frustrated experiment with universalism and the League of Nations from 1916 to 1920 under the leadership of Woodrow Wilson, but the net result of that episode was to provoke a reaction in favor of the Hemisphere idea.

The concept of the civilizing mission of the United States took shape in the first decade of the century and received its classic formulation in Herbert Croly's widely read book, *The Promise of American Life,* published in 1919.[9] Croly's book has a special interest for us because it was produced by the fusion of the Western Hemisphere idea with the idea of Manifest Destiny. This was a development which could hardly have been foreseen in the mid-nineteenth century, when . . . the two ideas were mutually antagonistic, if not mutually exclusive. Thus, during the first grand climacteric of Manifest Destiny in the 1840's, that term meant continental expansion to the Pacific, largely at the expense of one of the sister republics of America. By 1900, however, the process of continental expansion had long since been completed and the great majority of the people of the United States of all shades of opinion were agreed that their country did not need and should not take any more territory in the Western Hemisphere, except a few feet here and there for a Panama Canal or a Guantánamo naval base.

But new forces were now at work in the United States which produced a new form of expansionism. Added to the determination, which grew so rapidly in the 1890's, to take a more active part in world affairs was the conviction that the United States had a unique contribution to make to the betterment of the world. It could not only do as much for backward peoples as any other civilized nation and do it better; it was also uniquely qualified to confer upon those who should in time become worthy of it the ultimate boon of democracy. This was a new kind of Manifest Destiny. It obviously had global implications, but it was oriented mainly toward Latin America by the ingrained hemispheric habit of thought. Thus the civilizing mission was first and foremost a mission to be performed in Latin America.

[9]On this subject I am much indebted to the excellent article by William E. Leuchtenburg, "Progressivism and Imperialism: The Progressive Movement and American Foreign Policy, 1898–1916," in *Mississippi Valley Historical Review,* XXXIX (1952), 483–504.

Obviously, there was a close connection between this notion of a civilizing mission and the protective imperialism represented by the Roosevelt corollary. Indeed, the former was an outgrowth of the latter–Croly's book, published five years after the corollary, makes that unmistakably clear. But the point to be stressed is that the outgrowth was in fact a growth, an extension; for while the civilizing mission subsumed and strongly reaffirmed protective imperialism, including specifically armed intervention in Latin America, it contemplated an intervention of a much broader, deeper, and more lasting kind. Protective imperialism would intervene to correct situations of chronic wrongdoing and chaos only to the extent necessary to prevent European intervention and would then withdraw. The civilizing mission, on the other hand, had no such *ad hoc* character or limited objective. The missionary's work is not done when the devils have been cast out; it has hardly begun. He must stay on until he has taught his charges how to lead the good life, and that may take quite a long time.

All this had highly important implications for hemispheric relations, and these were brought out clearly in Croly's book of 1909. The first task of a truly national policy, he wrote, was to develop hemispheric solidarity within a "stable American international system." He then went on to describe how this was to be achieved:

> In all probability no American international system will ever be established without the forcible pacification of one or more centers of disorder. . . . Any international American system might have to undertake a task in states like Venezuela, similar to that which the United States is performing in Cuba [where the United States intervened under the Platt Amendment for three years, 1906–1909]. . . . The United States has already made an effective beginning in this great work, both by the pacification of Cuba and by the attempt to introduce a little order into the affairs of the turbulent Central American republics.[10]

[10]*Ibid.*, pp. 501–502. For earlier and broader discussions of the background, see Ralph H. Gabriel, *The Course of American Democratic Thought* (New York, 1940), ch. xxvi, "The 'Mission of America' in the Progressive Era"; Merle Curti, *The Growth of American Thought* (New York, 1943), ch. xxvi, "America Recrosses the Oceans," especially pp. 659–675; and Richard Hofstadter, *Social Darwinism in American Thought,* 1860–1915 (Philadelphia, 1945), ch. ix, "Racism and Imperialism." See also the words cited in Essay V, note 9. Cf. Dexter Perkins, *The American Approach to Foreign Policy* (Uppsala and Stockholm, 1949), ch. ii, "Is There an American Imperialism?"

To be sure, Croly proposed that the United States carry forward this "great work" on the basis of inter-American co-operation. But given the great disparity of strength between the United States and the other American republics, there could be no doubt as to which of them would have the guiding hand in an enterprise admittedly based upon the use of force.

Croly and his fellow Progressives were in fact strong supporters of imperialism during their most flourishing period, from about 1905 to 1915. That was paradoxical, for it seemed in headlong conflict with their domestic policy, which was one of reform in the interest of social welfare and justice and at the expense of predatory capitalism. Actually, as they saw it, there was no such conflict; on the contrary, an imperialist foreign policy would give positive support to their domestic reforms by breaking down the prevalent Jeffersonian, laissez-faire tradition. This would facilitate the revival of the Hamiltonian tradition and that extension of the area of government control over the economic and social life of the nation which the Progressives' domestic program required. In other words, they were interventionists abroad because they wanted to be interventionists at home. Note the satisfaction with which Herbert Croly described this process:

> Not until the end of the Spanish War [of 1898] was a condition of public feeling created, which made it possible to revive Hamiltonianism. That war and its resulting policy of extra-territorial expansion, so far from hindering the process of domestic amelioration, availed, from the sheer force of the national aspirations it aroused, to give a tremendous impulse to the work of national reform . . . and it indirectly helped to place in the Presidential chair the man who . . . represented both the national idea and the spirit of reform.[11]

That man was, of course, Theodore Roosevelt. First and foremost a nationalist, Roosevelt stepped into the leadership of Progressivism after it had developed from a movement into a national party (in 1912). He was able to do this the more easily because he shared many other assumptions of the Progressives besides their Hamiltonian creed. Among the most important of these for the development of the

[11]Leuchtenburg, *op. cit.*, p. 502.

Progressives' Western Hemisphere imperialism was a belief in the supremacy of the white race, more specifically the Anglo-Saxon race, and in the duty of the United States to help carry the "white man's burden."

Clearly, the Anglo-Saxon white man had a heavy burden to carry in Latin America, where the only whites were "decadent" Latins, and the majority of the population were Indians, Negroes, or (worst of all, according to racist doctrine) mixed races. And, of course, under the Monroe Doctrine, the white man's burden in that part of the world would have to be carried by the United States. The temper of the Progressives in this matter was foreshadowed as early as 1898 by one of their first and most influential leaders, Albert J. Beveridge, the eloquent young senator from Indiana. Advocating the annexation of Cuba and Puerto Rico, Beveridge brushed aside impatiently the objections that to rule those peoples without their consent would be contrary to the principles of the United States' own Declaration of Independence and that in any case they could never form a natural part of the United States since they were not contiguous:

> The proposition of the opposition [snorted Beveridge] makes the Declaration of Independence preposterous, like the reading of Job's lamentations would be at a wedding. . . . I answer, the rule of liberty, that all just governments derive their authority from the consent of the governed, applies only to those who are capable of self-government. Cuba not contiguous? Porto Rico not contiguous? . . . Our navy will make them contiguous![12]

So far, we have been speaking only of the Progressives; but by 1910 the idea of the civilizing mission which underlay their imperialism had permeated the other two major political groups as well—the "Old Guard" conservatives who now controlled the Republican party and also the Democratic party which was soon to come to power under the leadership of Woodrow Wilson through the presidential election of 1912. About 1900 the conservative Republicans had opposed imperialism, in America as elsewhere. Now they supported it—not so much the booted-and-spurred imperialism of a Beveridge or a Roosevelt, but rather the milder variety known as Dollar Diplomacy.

[12]Claude G. Bowers, *Beveridge and the Progressive Era* (Boston, 1932), pp. 73–76.

First fully developed and given this name during the administration of President Taft and his Secretary of State Philander C. Knox, a Pennsylvania corporation lawyer, this device for the financial and economic penetration and control of backward countries was applied on a considerable scale only in Latin America. It was pictured as not a selfish but a noble policy, which would help the Latin Americans to raise their standard of living and their standard of political behavior and ultimately to achieve internal order and democracy à la Uncle Sam, substituting ballots for bullets in the settlement of their political disputes.[13] This may have been mere rationalization, but it was rationalization in terms of the civilizing mission and the Hemisphere idea.

Wilson: From regionalism to universalism

As for Woodrow Wilson, who occupied the White House for the next eight years (1913–1921), the civilizing mission is one of the chief clues to a mystery which has puzzled many students of his Latin American policy—the contradiction between his liberal principles and his imperialistic practices.[14] What has not been so often noticed is the fact that Wilson also made two striking and mutually contradictory contributions to the history of the Western Hemisphere idea, which he first exalted as never before and then abased to the point of extinction. Interesting in themselves, these contradictory developments are deserving of attention here because of their bearing upon the Hemisphere idea, and because . . . they were repeated in the same order after 1933.

Wilson came into office in 1913 promising a new deal in foreign as

[13]Arthur P. Whitaker, "From Dollar Diplomacy to the Good Neighbor Policy," *Inter-American Economic Affairs,* IV (1951), 13–15.

[14]After the foregoing was written, I was happy to find confirmation of this view in Arthur S. Link, *Woodrow Wilson and the Progressive Era,* 1910–1917 (New York, 1954), in which the first chapter on Wilson's foreign policy bears the title "Missionary Diplomacy." The reader is referred particularly to the paragraph on p. 82 beginning "The missionary impulse helps to explain much that is baffling about Wilson's foreign policy. . . ." Important information about William Jennings Bryan's role in 1913–1915 is contained in Selig Adler, "Bryan and Wilsonian Caribbean Penetration," *Hispanic American Historical Review,* XX (1940), 198–226.

well as domestic policy. He began by denouncing imperialism and by repudiating Dollar Diplomacy and intervention; he applied these principles specifically to Latin America in his notable Mobile Address of October 1913, in which he assured the southern neighbors that the United States would henceforth treat them as equals. Yet in the end he carried out more armed interventions in Latin America than Roosevelt and Taft combined, revived and extended Dollar Diplomacy, and developed still another form of intervention by changing the United States' recognition policy from *de facto* to constitutional.

In Wilson's own mind, however, there was no inconsistency between his principles and his practice, for with him the overriding principle was the responsibility of power. The United States had now acquired so great a preponderance of power in the Western Hemisphere that it had not only the right but the duty to intervene in other American states in the performance of its civilizing mission.

Intervention, however, was not the only alternative considered, for the whole question of Western Hemisphere relations was re-examined during his first term. The climate of opinion favored the inquiry. Outside government circles, a sign of the times was the publication in 1913 of Hiram Bingham's *The Monroe Doctrine: An Obsolete Shibboleth,* which argued that that unilateral doctrine had outlived its usefulness and become an incitement to Yankeephobia and that the establishment of a new relationship of inter-American reciprocity was overdue. A member of Wilson's official family, Robert Lansing, then counselor for the Department of State, wrote to somewhat the same effect, though in much more measured terms, in a memorandum of June 11, 1914.[15] Lansing distinguished sharply between the unilateral Monroe Doctrine, with its claim to primacy, and multilateral Pan Americanism, with its basic principle of juridical equality. Pointing out, as Drago had done (though without mentioning him or his proposal), that foreign economic penetration of Latin America had created a danger against which the Monroe Doctrine provided no defense, he urged a redefinition of the latter to meet the new danger and to serve the interests not only of the United States but of all the American states. The new policy, he concluded, should be based on

[15]Department of State, *The Lansing Papers, 1914–1920* (Washington, 1940), II, 460–465.

"more altruistic and humanitarian principles, which will be in harmony with the sense of fraternal responsibility, which is increasingly dominant in all our international relations."

By November 1915 Lansing had swung around to the support of widespread unilateral intervention in the Caribbean danger zone and had abandoned humanitarianism as an argument, though not as a purpose. "The argument based on humanitarian purpose," he explained, "does not appeal to me, even though it might be justly urged, because too many international crimes have been committed in the name of humanity."[16] For the Hemisphere as a whole, he nevertheless continued to urge a Pan American policy based on principles of equality and reciprocity, as in his address to the Pan American Scientific Congress on December 27, 1915. A week later his young relative John Foster Dulles followed this with an address in the same vein, though with even stronger multilateral implications. . . .

While World War I led to further interventions, it also for a time promoted Pan Americanism. Combined with the other factors just noted, it produced the first of Wilson's two innovations in the political application of the Western Hemisphere idea. This was the Pan American Pact which he drafted in conference with his close adviser, Colonel E. M. House, in December 1914, and then took up with various Latin American governments in January 1915.[17] The most important of the Pact's four articles was the first, which provided that "the high contracting parties . . . hereby join one another in a common and mutual guarantee of territorial integrity and of political independence under republican forms of government." This, together with the other articles (on the settlement of boundary disputes, control of the export of arms, and suppression of revolutionary expeditions

[16]*Ibid.,* 466–467, Secretary of State Lansing to President Wilson, November 24, 1915.

[17]Bemis, *Latin American Policy,* pp. 194–197. As Bemis points out, the idea of the pact originated not with House but with another Texan, Representative James L. Slayden. A more detailed analysis of the genesis of this pact and its epilogue is contained in Malbone W. Graham, *American Diplomacy in the International Community* (Baltimore, 1948), Appendix IV, pp. 162–174. Link, *op. cit.,* p. 106, believes that "the historian must be allowed a few doubts as to the administration's sincerity in proposing it [the Pan American Pact]." See also Harley Notter, *The Origins of the Foreign Policy of Woodrow Wilson* (Baltimore, 1937).

from one country against the government of another), envisaged the creation of a true regional security system in America.

The general idea of the pact was as old as Bolívar, and its revival at this time was due to a familiar motivation—that combined fear of European aggression and the desire to widen the gap between the "hemisphere of peace" and the broils of Europe which had from the outset been a chief component of the Western Hemisphere idea. What was novel was that now for the first time the United States sponsored the idea and that in some respects Wilson carried it even further than Bolívar had done. From the point of view of the United States, Wilson's Pan American Pact was a startling innovation, for it was intended to multilateralize the hitherto jealously guarded Monroe Doctrine.

Though six of the smaller Latin American states signified their approval of the pact, it was not adopted. Chile opposed it because of a territorial dispute with Peru; Brazil held back out of deference to Chile; and Argentina's attitude, originally favorable, was reversed by a change of administration in 1916. The United States' own interventions in Mexico and the Caribbean countries were a further obstacle.[18]

After two years of futile effort on behalf of his pact, Wilson executed one of those changes of front which have so often made the foreign policy of the United States puzzling to its own people as well as to foreigners. In May 1916, little more than a year after first taking up the Pan American Pact with the Latin American neighbors, he came out strongly for a global association of nations, and after the middle of 1917 he dropped the Pan American Pact completely.[19] In Western Hemisphere affairs he reverted to a unilateralism as pronounced as Theodore Roosevelt's. Wilson was still the internationalist, more than ever the internationalist; but he seemed to pride himself on having graduated from regionalism to universalism.

As many writers have pointed out, there is no necessary contradiction between these two types of international co-operation, but apparently

[18]Link, *op. cit.*, p. 197.

[19]Graham, *op. cit.*, p. 134, dates the beginning of the shift earlier (January 1916), and states (p. 173) that "the final transit from a regional to a world-wide Covenant was made in Wilson's mind some time between June 9 . . . and July 29 [1918]." But evidence in *Lansing Papers*, II, 500 indicates that for all practical purposes the pact was discarded in May 1917.

Wilson thought there was. At any rate, the League of Nations Covenant of 1919, which represents his fully matured thought on the subject, made no reference whatever to the thirty-year-old Pan American system. It did make a reference to the Monroe Doctrine, thereby according a measure of recognition to the Western Hemisphere idea, but this was only because irresistible political pressure from home forced Wilson to get the Doctrine written into the Covenant. So distasteful did he find the task that he left the drafting of the passage to others. Many tried their hands at it. Midway in the months-long peace conference at the Hotel Crillon in Paris, one of the participants noted in his diary: "I am probably the only person in the Crillon who is not working on a draft of the [Monroe Doctrine] reservation. . . . And scores of people outside the Crillon are also working on drafts."[20] It was another case of too many cooks, for the reservation finally adopted inaccurately described the Monroe Doctrine as a "regional understanding." That was something it had never been; it had been only a unilateral policy of the United States. It is true that, according to Wilson, the Covenant was "but a confirmation and an extension of the Monroe Doctrine,"[21] but to give the Doctrine world-wide extension was to negate the Western Hemisphere idea underlying it.

"Pan Americanism is a living force"

After the defeat of Wilson and the League, the Hemisphere idea, unilaterally interpreted, resumed its sway in the United States and maintained it throughout the Republican Restoration of 1921–1933. Even Archibald Cary Coolidge (the historian, not the President), who was primarily interested in relations with Europe, recorded in 1927 that "Pan Americanism . . . is a living force today . . . [and] is popular with public opinion."[22] The Republican Restoration gave the

[20]Stephen Bonsal, *Unfinished Business* (New York, 1944), p. 150; Thomas A. Bailey, *Woodrow Wilson and the Lost Peace* (New York, 1945), pp. 214–218.

[21]Bonsal, *op. cit.,* p. 158, Bonsal's entry for March 25, 1919. On April 12, 1919, Wilson further assured the delegates that the Monroe Doctrine was "the real forerunner of the League of Nations," and asked rhetorically, "Indeed are we not assembled here to consecrate and extend the horizon of this document as a perpetual charter for all the world?" (*ibid.,* pp. 184–185).

[22]Archibald Cary Coolidge, "The Grouping of Nations," *Foreign Affairs,* V (1927), 182–183.

Hemisphere idea a tone which was less minatory than that of the Big Stick era. Indeed, the first Secretary of State during this period, Charles Evans Hughes, aided for a time by Sumner Welles, began to liquidate imperialism and the interventions in the Caribbean area which constituted its most obvious expression. He also interpreted the Monroe Doctrine in such a way as to restore to it its earlier character as "solely a policy of self-defense" and made it what his latest biographer calls the foundation for a hemispheric policy of positive helpfulness.[23] He thus anticipated the Clark Memorandum of 1930 and, to a limited degree, the Good Neighbor Policy of the following decade.

Hughes also explicitly stated his belief in the existence of a special relationship among the American states:

> There can be no doubt that there are Pan American interests and that there is a Pan American sentiment which demands the special cooperation of the American states. . . . Pan Americanism rests upon the solid fact of our neighborhood and intercourse. It is not simply for our generation, but for all time.[24]

But his idea of hemispheric co-operation did not extend into the field of security. Wilson's Pan American Pact found no echo in his policy. The other American states were encouraged to adopt "Monroe Doctrines" of their own, but the Monroe Doctrine would be interpreted and applied by the United States in its own way.[25] In short, while Hughes thought in hemispheric terms, and while he acted benevolently in the special relationship implied by those terms, his policy was one of the lone hand; and so were the policies of his successors during the remainder of the Republican Restoration.

By this time enthusiasm for the militant civilizing mission had withered away, partly under the wintry blasts of general disillusionment that swept over the United States as well as many other countries after the war and partly from distaste for the fruits of such missionary activity. Haiti illustrated the latter point. It was the scene of one of those police actions so much admired by Herbert Croly. In 1916 the United States Navy took over this little country and gave it the benefits

[23]Merlo J. Pusey, *Charles Evans Hughes* (New York, 1951), II, 531, 536–537.
[24]Charles Evans Hughes, *Our Relations to the Nations of the Western Hemisphere* (Princeton, 1928), pp. 117–118.
[25]Pusey, *op. cit.*, II, 535–536.

of civilization under a constitution drawn up by no less a person than Franklin Delano Roosevelt, then Assistant Secretary of Navy; but the Haitian people did not co-operate fully, and an uprising was suppressed only after nearly 2,000 of them had been killed by the Marines. The Haitian affair was apparently the starting point of a complete reversal of the remnant of the Progressive party's attitude toward imperialism; henceforth the party was its sharpest critic.[26]

In the 1920's, however, the Progressives were a small and badly organized remnant, and the Republicans were in firm control. The latter, too, abandoned the idea of the civilizing mission in the old form, but they produced a new edition of it bearing the imprint of the business ethos, which could be summarized in the proposition that business brings uplift, and uplift pays dividends. Yet business alone did not bear the whole burden; soldier, sailor, and diplomat were there to help—and they did. That they would do so more and more seemed to be indicated by President Coolidge's public assertion in 1927, apropos of a situation in Central America, that an American citizen and his property in a foreign country are a part of the national domain of the United States.[27] What this view had already meant for Latin America was shown by the fact that, according to a survey made in 1924, only six of the twenty Latin American republics were free from interference by the United States in one form or another, including official direction of financial policy, and in six interference was backed by the presence of armed forces.[28]

"We could not be Pan Americanists"

In these circumstances, Yankeephobia flourished in Latin America. At the very beginning of the century, it had been given a literary vogue by leading men of letters such as the Nicaraguan poet Rubén Darío

[26]E.g., Robert Morse Lovett, "American Foreign Policy: A Progressive View," *Foreign Affairs,* III (1924), 49–60, especially p. 52: "The difference between the Third Party movement of 1912 and that of today is at no point more striking than in the attitudes respectively taken toward the question of imperialism. The Progressives of 1912 blindly followed Roosevelt in his defense of a predatory policy of which he was one of the conspicuous exponents. But during the next four years the Progressives awoke."

[27]Bemis, *Latin American Policy,* p. 419, n. 15.

[28]Lovett, *op. cit.,* p. 51, citing a recent article by S. G. Inman.

and the Uruguayan essayist José Enrique Rodó. This vogue was kept alive by others such as the Mexican Carlos Pereyra and the Argentine Manuel Ugarte, whose book *The Destiny of a Continent* won continent-wide renown as the classic indictment of Yankee imperialism. As the economic penetration by the Yankees proceeded apace, Wall Street came to be as cordially detested by the generality of Latin Americans as it was by the farmers of the United States itself in William Jennings Bryan's day; but in Latin America, detestation was aggravated by growing nationalism. In 1922, at a banquet given in Buenos Aires for the distinguished Mexican Minister of Public Education, José Vasconcelos, the then even more distinguished Argentine sociologist José Ingenieros said:

> We are not, we do not want to be any longer, we could not be Pan Americanists. The United States is to be feared because it is great, rich, and enterprising. What concerns us is to find out whether there is a possibility of balancing its power to the extent necessary to save our political independence and the sovereignty of our countries.

Moreover, the process of economic penetration had cost the United States much of the support it had formerly had among Latin American liberals. The latter were alienated by the unholy alliance, as they regarded it, between expanding Yankee business enterprise and the reactionary oligarchies in their own countries. Anti-imperialism flourished, and the United States was its principal target, as in the program of the APRA (American Popular Revolutionary Alliance), first formulated by the Peruvian Víctor Raúl Haya de la Torre in Mexico in 1924.[29] "Yankee imperialism" had become in effect a single word, like "damn Yankee" in the post-Civil-War South.

For our purpose, the significance of this rising tide of Yankeephobia lies in the fact that it choked the hemispheric spirit south of the Rio Grande. Other forms of association were sought; this was one reason for the popularity of the League of Nations in Latin America.[30] At one time or another, all of its twenty republics were members of the League.

[29] Luis-Alberto Sánchez, "A New Interpretation of the History of America," *Hispanic American Historical Review,* XXIII (1943), 444. See also Robert E. McNicoll, "Intellectual Origins of Aprismo," *ibid.,* 424–440.

[30] Warren H. Kelchner, *Latin American Relations with the League of Nations* (Boston, 1929), pp. 13–14.

Discontent boiled over at the Sixth Pan American Conference, held at Havana in 1928.[31] The instructions to the United States delegates informed them that "among the Foreign Relations of the United States as they fall into categories, the Pan American policy takes first place in our diplomacy."[32] None but the United States' satellite states spoke of Hemisphere relations in like terms at Havana. Many of the delegates had come there determined to break the unwritten Pan American rule against the discussion of controversial questions and to pillory Uncle Sam. They did so. Intervention took first place in the wrangle, and Latin Americans were not appeased by chief delegate Charles Evans Hughes' assurance that the United States would never practice intervention but only "interposition." In the end, the best that could be obtained was an agreement to disagree and to discuss this and other matters on a later occasion. The economic policy of the United States also came in for sharp criticism, and when this was not answered to his satisfaction, the head of the influential Argentine delegation walked out of the meeting.

When the Conference adjourned, Pan Americanism was at ebb tide.[33] The authorities at Washington saw that the time had come when they would either have to change their ways radically or be left alone with their Hemisphere idea. Accordingly, in November President-elect Hoover set out on a South American good-will tour on a battleship;[34] and as soon as he took office in March 1929, the change began. Before the year was out, the first shock of the Great Depression had accelerated the rate of change. This change continued through the next two decades, but there was no continuity in the direction of development. After 1930 Wilson's fellow countrymen duplicated his tergiversation regarding the Western Hemisphere idea by repeating, in the same order, first one and then the other of his two opposite excursions, so that while the 1930's saw the apotheosis of this idea, the 1940's witnessed its euthanasia.

[31]John P. Humphrey, *The Inter-American System: A Canadian View* (Toronto, 1942), pp. 92–93.

[32]Department of State, *Papers Relating to the Foreign Relations of the United States, 1928* (Washington, D.C., 1942), I, 534.

[33]Laurence Duggan, *The Americas: The Search for Hemisphere Security* (New York, 1949), p. 52.

[34]Alexander DeConde, *Herbert Hoover's Latin American Policy* (Stanford, 1951), p. 16.

Chile: The Economic Crisis

BY ANDRÉ SIEGFRIED

It is difficult to build up a sound public economy on a private economy which is unsound.

The Great Depression of the 1930's had an enormous impact on the political and economic structure of the Latin American countries. The prices that Latin America received for its exports of food and raw materials declined more rapidly than the prices that it paid for its manufactured imports, with the consequence that the majority of the Latin American governments went bankrupt. They found that they could not meet the principal and interest payments on their foreign debts. A period of political instability resulted during which there was much soul-searching into the basic economic scheme.

Being small powers which had long looked to Europe for intellectual inspiration, Latin American countries tended to accept the opinion of Europeans on the reasons for their predicament. At this time, André Siegfried, the political scientist, was regarded as the leading French authority on the political, economic, and religious life of other countries, especially those outside Europe. His *America Comes of Age* had been a best seller in the United States. This had added to his stature among Latin American intellectuals since he had been critical of the United States and called it "a theocracy of exploitation," a comforting description of a creditor for a defaulted debtor.

In the early 1930's Siegfried traveled in South America, and in 1933 he published his *Impressions of South America*. The chapter on the economic plight of Chile is reprinted here. It was widely read at the time and accepted in Latin America as authoritative, so that its importance far exceeded its depth or penetration into the details of Chile's economic predicament. After Siegfried's visit, Chile, as well as other South American countries in similar economic straits, began to take economic matters far more seriously than it had in the past. Thus, today one hears far more about "economic growth," "capital accumulation," and "development" than one used to do. Young men who in the 1920's would have become poets now seek careers "in trade," have graduate degrees in economics, and work for organizations like the World Bank.

The preponderance of debt owed a single creditor, the United States, has, as Siegfried suggested, become a political problem and is today a political issue in many Latin American countries. Furthermore, since this selection was written, many of the governments of Latin America have recognized their role in the field of economics and have sought to improve the Latin American terms of trade by entering into agreements to withhold their particular exports from the world market.

Specifically, as regards Chile, Siegfried's concern in 1931 over the fact that its principal sources of wealth were controlled by foreigners (U.S. citizens) and that the country thus had no reserves of wealth was finally resolved in 1966 after three decades of local debate and political discussion. As the New York *Times* observed on October 12, 1966:

> The Chileanization of that country's vast copper industry has now reached a point where success is simply a matter of ironing out some final details. Between $400 and $450 million of new investments are involved in an industry that provides 80 per cent of Chile's foreign exchange earnings.
>
> The unique feature of the program that President Frei conceived and patiently nursed through a sometimes recalcitrant Congress is that it gives the Government a majority interest in one private American company and a quarter interest in new mines of the other two large American companies, all negotiated on a voluntary basis.
>
> The political importance of the Chileanization plan is that it provides a new method for meeting and perhaps overcoming one of the most vexing problems in United States–Latin American relations. This is the invariably disturbing effect of American ownership of a nation's natural resources.

What the Frenchman Siegfried said about the Chilean economy in 1931, was eventually adopted by the Chileans as political doctrine, implemented by an elected government thirty-five years later, and accepted as a solution for overcoming difficult problems in U.S.–Latin American relations by a leading U.S. newspaper. The incident is an illuminating example of the origin, spread, adoption, and implementation of economic ideas among the

American republics and suggests that the solution of Latin American economic problems is essentially political.

André Siegfried was born at Le Havre, France, on April 21, 1875. He was from birth surrounded by a political atmosphere. His father had been a minister of commerce of France and a member of the Chamber of Deputies. Siegfried himself ran for the chamber in his youth but was defeated. His wife's father had been a deputy and had also served as president general of Madagascar.

Siegfried was educated at the Lycée Condorcet and at the Sorbonne and became professor of economic geography at the Ecole Libre de Science Politique in Paris in 1911. From 1920 to 1922 he served as the chief of the Economic Section of the League of Nations. In 1919 he became an officer of the Legion of Honor and in 1927 a fellow of All Souls College, Oxford. In the same year he received the Montoyon Prize of the Académie Française for his book *America Comes of Age.*

Siegfried stayed in Paris during the Nazi occupation and was accused of making anti-American statements, which he has since denied, claiming that he was always a friend of the United States and that he did not hesitate to say so, even during the occupation. In 1944 he was elected to the French Academy. He remained in Paris after the war and became an honorary professor at the College de France. In 1955, a generation after his *America Comes of Age,* he published *America at Mid-Century*. It is a reflection of contemporary European attitudes toward America.

P. K.

Santiago-de-Chile
31 August 1931

CHILE is in the throes of the world economic crisis like every other country, but here it is exceptionally severe, as it arises from three distinct causes, all equally serious.

In the first place we have the great fall in the price of raw materials. In 1928, the last year of prosperity, raw materials accounted for 90 per cent of the Chilian exports. Saltpetre made up 47 per cent of the total, and copper 31 per cent, i.e., 78 per cent for these two alone. When we realize the heavy decline that has taken place in the price of these commodities, we can picture the effect on a country which exports the greater part, if not all, of the saltpetre and copper it produces.

Superimposed on this general crisis in the raw material markets is a special crisis in the nitrate industry (of which saltpetre is the raw material). Synthetic fertilizers are tending to supplant the natural nitrates very rapidly. In 1894 natural fertilizers obtained from saltpetre accounted for 73 per cent of the world's production, as against the remaining 27 per cent of synthetic fertilizers. In 1926 the proportions were almost reversed: 26 per cent as against 74. It looks as if this decline will remain permanent, and if so it strikes a devastating blow at the wealth of Chile.

The third crisis lies directly at the door of the foolhardy borrowing of the late dictator, Ibanez, who in four years more than tripled the national debt. During this period the United States was lending without stint, in fact the American banks were urging borrowers to take the money. Today after the fall in the price of raw materials Chile has had to default on the interest on her foreign loans.

Such a situation would be disquieting in any country, but here it is doubly so since the principal sources of national wealth are controlled by foreigners, and the Chilians themselves have no reserves. Hence the question of the balance of international payments assumes a pressing and terrible gravity. The nitrate industry is almost entirely in the hands of the Americans–the Guggenheim group alone owns over half of it. The copper also belongs to America, at any rate most of it does. Thus the profits from this wealth, when there are any, leave the country in the form of dividends. It is easy to realize how foreign payments under such conditions can only be compared to a hemorrhage.

Let us now study Chile's balance of international payments. The chief item on the credit side is exports, but as soon as a crisis occurs with a fall in prices, this item is immediately deflated. From 1928 to 1930, exports fell from 1,964 million pesos to 1,328 million. (The gold peso is worth 12 cents.) Now a country with no reserves abroad must depend entirely on its exports to meet its foreign payments. The debit items in the balance of payments are positively crushing. In the first place there is the interest on foreign loans, both public and private. The country naturally could not be developed without foreign capital, but it was tempted to go ahead too quickly and borrow too heavily, beyond the limits of prudence. Now it has to pay outside of its frontiers interest and dividends on capital so borrowed. Then there is the question of the importation of goods into a country which cannot exist without a whole series of manufactured articles. Even the most ultra-protectionism could only create certain types of industry.

I have, however, left the worst feature to the last. The Chilians themselves have always had an incurable habit of taking their money out of the country. Absenteeism is the trouble everywhere in South America. Ever so many Chilian families live for years in France or elsewhere abroad, in fact anywhere except at home. Some never come back at all, although their wealth is still invested in their own country. In order to meet the expense, often very considerable, of so much travelling, very large sums are continually being withdrawn. I have not even mentioned the flights of capital which take place when a ruler persecutes certain elements of the population, or when doubt is cast upon the stability of the currency.

Under these conditions–and such is the case at present–Chile finds it practically impossible to pay the foreigner what it owes him. It can only do so by borrowing afresh, and this is not easy so long as the coupons of earlier bonds are in default. The policy of the present government is to suspend the service of the debt and practise drastic economy, to reduce imports by increasing tariffs, and to control rigidly the sending of even the smallest sum of money out of the country. It was hoped that in this way they would succeed in maintaining the internal value of the peso. Danger lurks, however, in the fact that in order to raise funds to pay the civil servants, to support the unemployed, and so forth, the government may be tempted to resort to currency inflation.

Let us try to get at the source of the trouble, for obviously the position of the country is not healthy. It has borrowed too much, that is evident, but the trouble would not be so serious if the borrowed money had been spent on something productive instead of being squandered on display. From my hotel window in Santiago I look out on unfinished buildings fifteen storeys high, for which there was no need, and which bring in no income. The capital thus dissipated had at any rate been useful to maintain the support of the partisans of the government, but this government has since fallen.

It is natural that a new country should go abroad in search of the capital needed for its development, and Chile in this respect will have to be considered at the colonial stage for a long time to come. But what is so striking when one studies the details, is the way in which individuals as well as the State are living on borrowed money. Private budgets do not balance. People spend more than they receive, and consider it perfectly natural too. A certain land owner decides that he would like to travel, so he mortgages his property–almost all property is mortgaged, and often to its full value. These people it seems will borrow even when they do not need money, for they feel that they consolidate their credit by showing that they can borrow. Therefore, with the exception of the great wealth amassed in certain enterprises, the old fortunes of the Chilian governing classes are gradually dwindling. Many of the aristocratic homes in Santiago are for sale. This is of course quite apart from the public auctions of household effects which seem to be an everyday affair.

It is difficult to build up a sound public economy on a private economy which is unsound. Individually the Chilians are charming, cultivated, generous, and kind, but in this country, as in many others on this continent, one feels that they do not take economic matters seriously enough. During the years of plenty they spend recklessly, and then when the lean years come there is nothing left, and they are at the mercy of their creditors. How will Chile ever attain to real political independence when almost its entire debt is in the hands of a single creditor, the United States? This is a difficult problem, which belongs less to the sphere of economics properly speaking, than to politics. Perhaps it is simply a question of everyday utilitarian morality.

Selections from "The Rich Culture of Mexico"

BY F. S. C. NORTHROP

One feels the beauty of the sunset, before one learns the internal constitution of the stars.

Proponents of the Monroe Doctrine, hemispheric solidarity, the Good Neighbor Policy, etc. have often preferred, in the interest of the unity they advocate, to overlook the differences between Latin America and the United States and to stress the similarities. Professor Northrop's contribution has been to stress the differences—spiritual, cultural, philosophical—and, at the same time, to maintain a positive attitude toward them, insisting that they are neither incomprehensible nor irreconcilable.

Professor Northrop in his book *The Meeting of East and West,* which was published in 1946, devotes one chapter to the culture of Mexico and stresses the importance of understanding that culture as a key to the formulation of a synthesis of the philosophies of the Occident and the Orient. An abridgment of this chapter is reproduced here.*

Mexico, according to Professor Northrop, started with a multicultured precolonial civilization, whose values of art and religion were oriented and defined with respect to geometrical and astronomical science. This civilization was conquered by Cortez and destroyed by Christianity. Enough of it survived, however, to cause the intrusion into Spanish colonial values of the worship of the Indian Madonna, the Virgin of Guadalupe, alone and in her own right, representing the female *erōs,* or the emotional, passionate, metaphysical principle in the nature of things.

*Extracts from *The Meeting of East and West.* Copyright 1946 by the Macmillan Co.

This culture, in turn, yielded in the nineteenth century to French intellectual domination. The Positivism of Comte and the theories of Voltaire, Rousseau, and others combined with John Locke and scientific skepticism to destroy devotion to inherited institutions and led to the dictatorship of Porfirio Díaz, "which took positivism as its model, extended science, secularized education and felt it necessary to move away from and curb not merely the Christian religion but also democracy." All this, in turn, yielded to revolution, rejection, and ultimate reformulation of new esthetic, cultural, religious, and political values, the uniquely rich and rewarding culture that is Mexico today. It is this new culture, Professor Northrop believes, which offers, in part, the key to the meeting of East and West.

Filmer S. C. Northrop, Sterling professor emeritus of philosophy and law at Yale, is one of the nation's leading philosophers. He was born on November 27, 1893, in Janesville, Wisconsin. He received an A.B. degree from Beloit College in 1915. After doing graduate work at Yale, he served with the Y.M.C.A. in Hong Kong and Canton.

Upon returning to the United States, he did further graduate work at Harvard and received a Ph.D. degree in 1924. Subsequently, he studied at the University of Freiburg in Germany, the Institute of Technology in London, and Trinity College, Cambridge. Dr. Northrop then returned to the United States, joined the faculty at Yale, and became a professor of philosophy in 1932. For his writing on Mexican culture, he was decorated with the Order of the Aztec Eagle by the Mexican government in 1949.

Dr. Northrop's other books include *The Taming of the Nations, The Complexity of Legal and Ethical Experience,* and *Man, Nation and God.* Recently he was selected as one of ten leading American scholars to receive the prize stipend of the American Council of Learned Societies in recognition of his distinguished accomplishments in humanistic scholarship.

P. K.

The Mexico of the Indians

THE purely Indian pre-colonial civilization of Mexico is not one culture but many; differing as much among themselves as the British, German, French, Italian, and Spanish diversify Europe. Among the more important are the Mayan in Yucatán, the Tarascan in Michoacán, the Mexteco-Zapotecan in Veracruz and Oaxaca, the

Aztec in and around Mexico City, and the Toltec to be seen now at Teotihuacán, which existed even before the coming of the Aztecs.

Let us concentrate upon the Ancient Toltec in its original setting at one important place, Teotihuacán, some forty-five kilometers north and east of Mexico City.

One approaches this Place of the Gods across a flat, dusty plain, broken at occasional spots by village dwellings and green trees. Of a sudden the geometrically regular Pyramid of the Sun stands directly before one. Larger at its base than the Great Pyramid of Egypt, it is not quite so tall. . . . Only from its top can one immediately experience and come to understand that unique and remarkable achievement of the Indian's aesthetic intuition which we shall find reappearing in quite different forms throughout every historical stage of Mexican civilization.

There it is everywhere below and around one: the sense of the aesthetic form of the whole carried architecturally and geometrically literally over square miles, no one yet knows how far. It appears not merely in the perfect yet terraced geometrical form of this Pyramid of the Sun, and in the smaller Pyramid of the Moon to the right at the end of the Avenue of the Dead which one faces directly below, but also in the equally perfect yet varied sense of form, geometrical and conscious in pattern, extending block after block, perhaps mile after mile, binding all together and including the orientation to the rounded hill behind, the contrast of straight and curved lines enhancing each—embracing even the heavens above and the stars in their courses.

. . . The official publication of the Instituto Nacional de Antropología e Historia informs us:

> The City is not laid out according to the cardinal points; that is, the "Avenue of the Dead" does not extend exactly from south to north, nor does the Pyramid of the Sun face exactly to the west, but its center deviates from the west to the north, at an angle of approximately 17°. For a long time the cause of this was not known, but recent investigations have shown that it is due to the fact that the monuments on the ground are oriented, not toward the true west but toward the point where the sun sets on the days when it passes through the zenith, a fact that proves that this pyramid was dedicated to that celestial body.

Consider the significance of this. It means that the scientific, aesthetic, and religious values of the Toltecs functioned together harmoniously, the one reinforcing the other, and that the values of art and religion were oriented and defined with respect to those of geometrical and astronomical science.

The art, sociology, and religion of the Indians were not independent subjects, artificially robbed of their proper vitality by being cut off from each other and their sources in nature; instead, they were defined as to their values and aims as well as to their instruments, by a science which was geometrical and astronomical in its emphasis. Because of the central place of the sun in the entire scientific conception, their art and their religion expressed themselves not merely through the edifices and ground plan of the metropolis as a whole, but also in its relation to the heavens above. For such an art, the cultivation of the aesthetic intuition of the whole was inescapable.

Alfonso Caso, in his *Religion of the Aztecs,* writes of Quetzalcoatl that "most important of all, he taught men science, giving them the means to measure time and to study the movements of the planets; taught them the calendar, invented ceremonies, and fixed the days for prayer and sacrifice." It is significant also for religion as well as art that they regarded Quetzalcoatl as "god of life." In short, human values and scientific values coincided.

We are now prepared to pick our dizzy way down the steps of the Pyramid of the Sun in order to proceed along the Avenue of the Dead to the Citadel, which contains the Temple of Quetzalcoatl. . . .

Climbing the steps up the outer wall of the rectangular Citadel and descending again onto the flat plain of its interior one finds its rigid geometrical lines and proportions as emotive and moving in their effect as they are unified and simple in themselves. . . .

Large enough to enclose the stadium of a university in the United States, with its flat playing ground, this Citadel, when experienced from the center of its paved field within, with the triangular form of the Pyramid of the Sun rising above its north wall, never loses its integrity or its essential geometrical and aesthetic connection with the larger design and intuition beyond. Instead, one feels oneself emotionally taken hold of from without by the vast pattern of the entire geometrically conceived, communal and cosmological system, rather than merely in the role of an isolated spectator looking at a local architectural unit from within.

Even more important is the Temple of Quetzalcoatl hidden behind a smaller pyramid on the far side of the Citadel's inner expanse. Between the persisting horizontal levels and straight lines which enter into the Temple's composition there run the naturalistic curves of the serpents and the petals of flowers surrounding the serpents' protruding heads. Most important of all, the whole was originally in vivid colors. Only fragments of the blues and reds and greens remain, but that everything here and elsewhere throughout the city was ablaze with color seems probable. . . . It reminds us again that the Aztecs did not separate the geometrical forms or the religious meaning of things from the moving, vivid, aesthetic qualities in which they exhibit themselves to us with immediacy. Evidently the purely aesthetic was a value in and for itself, and not a mere appearance to be dropped as if it did not matter, or added merely as an afterthought.

This second distinctive trait we shall find recurring again and again throughout the entire history of Mexican art and culture. . . . Geometrical form and naturalistic, human and aesthetic values were inseparably merged by the Mexican Indians.

The Spanish Colonial Period

Aztec legend had prepared the way for the coming of the Spaniards. Quetzalcoatl, before departing this earth by descending into the West, had promised to come back to earth again by the East. "That is why," Alfonso Caso writes, "when the Spanish conquerors landed at Veracruz in the year 1519 . . . the Emperor Moctezuma never had a doubt that Quetzalcoatl was returning to take possession of his Toltec Kingdom." This accounts for the quickness of the triumph of Cortés. It also enables us to understand why the Spaniards won the souls as well as commanded the bodies of the Indians, even to the extent of enticing them to make the language, art, and religion of Spain their own. But it does not explain why the coming of Cortés resulted in the complete destruction of the very high Aztec culture rather than merely its enrichment and fulfillment.

The rigidity of the Aztec aesthetic and religious forms has been advanced by many as the cause of their decline. . . . Even if the rigidity . . . be admitted, it is hardly sufficient to account for the reduction of their remarkable achievements to pulverized, buried fragments. Only an enemy of the Aztec culture could produce such terrible effects. This enemy appeared in two forms: the conquistador's sword and the Christian religion. Of the two the latter was the more devastating. . . . For, whereas Cortés and his soldiers merely defeated the Indians to place them under the weak political domination of a distant Spain, the Christian priests and their religion remained to bury and well-nigh destroy Aztec culture.

Fortunately, . . . certain fragments of the native insight, especially in the aesthetic sphere, persisted. To these were added certain superior, more humane religious practices of worship and the ecclesiastical, architectural forms which the Christian Spaniards brought. The product was a second culture in Mexico, termed the Spanish colonial, which, in copying Europe, added Indian elements that make it something precious and unique. It must be emphasized also that even when the Indians copied the Spaniards, by following them in their language, architecture, and religion, they did this at most points with a spontaneous and free movement of their own spirits, as the care and devotion which they gave to the building of the Catholic churches in Mexico unequivocally indicate.

This shows itself clearly in the Jesuit monastery constructed over the years between 1582 and 1767 at Tepotzotlán, some thirty miles north and a little west of Mexico City. . . . The monastery as a whole, with its surrounding wall, its inner courts, its several chapels, and its principal church of baroque style, is typical of monasteries and churches of this Spanish Catholic type anywhere. In its interior, also, apart from the tremendous amount of Mexican gold that surfaces the extremely rich and complicated interior decoration of its principal church, the same impression prevails.

It is only after one has remained for a time in certain of the smaller chapels to the Virgin and in some of the minor reception rooms and has permitted the general impression of the baroque to wear off, so that the broader spaces within the main lines of the architecture impress one, that something unique and important appears. One finds this novel element first and in its most remarkable form in a little octagonal chapel, the Camarín, located immediately behind the Loretto Chapel dedicated to the worship of the Virgin. It was in the octagonal Camarín, Alexander von Wuthenau tells us, that "the Indians used to clothe the Virgin and delight in the costly vestments she wore for her various feast days of the liturgical calendar of the Roman Catholic Church." He adds that "the style and feeling of the designs of this room are distinctly Indian," and that it is not "to be wondered at that they should decorate it with special care and love." Its dome is broken at the top with an opening which reveals an octagonal cupola extending upward to culminate in a silver dove representing the Holy Ghost, whose reflected light fills the whole room with a cheerful brightness. Everywhere–in the cupola, surrounding its opening, and filling in the open spaces of the dome, even standing out in three dimensions from its surface–are the bright faces and warm, soft bodies of very human angels with their vividly colored wings and their brightly decorated robes. Over all the main supporting and dividing lines of the dome there runs also a slightly formalized but purely decorative naturalistic pattern. Also, as one's eyes move gradually from the dome down the main supporting lines and columns to the floor, one's gaze comes upon partly nude, brown, human figures with naturalistic grass or floral skirts hanging from their waists. It is clear that the aesthetic appreciation of naturalistic color and form for their own sake, which we found . . . on the Temple of Quetzalcoatl . . . are here also.

It would be a mistake to suppose that the Spanish Catholic influence in Mexico is merely a thing of the past. On the north-eastern edge of Mexico City but three miles from its Zócalo, at Villa Gustavo Madero, formerly Guadalupe, is the nation's religious shrine. On a Sunday afternoon, the public square and large church are filled with people of all stations in life but predominantly Indian. Clearly, here is something which has captured the emotions and the souls of the people. Entering the great church one realizes immediately that something more than its colors or its architecture inspires the worshippers. A continuing mass of penitents, dropping to the floor at the first vision of the high altar, moves forward step by step on its knees to the altar railing, where those in the front rank bow and pray, before breaking into two groups slipping out to either side to release the prized position for those behind them. Nothing to be seen in Canada or Europe equals it in the volume or the vitality of its moving quality or in the depth of its spirit of religious devotion.

Wonder arises about the object of this quest. . . . This is the shrine of the beloved Patron Saint of Mexico, the Dark Madonna, Our Lady of Guadalupe. On the windshield of taxicab after taxicab in Mexico City and in the front interior of almost every bus, often with a miniature electric bulb illuminating her presence, one sees her image. Here, in the vast Catholic edifice, . . . is the original image from which all the others are copied. . . . In some way, the Virgin of Guadalupe and the story of her revelation, directed especially to the Indians, call forth from the Mexican spirit a devotion and sweeping response not equaled by any other influence in Mexico even today.

There is something unique about this Madonna, something typical of Mexican Catholicism, and of far-reaching consequences. She is dark of skin and an Indian. . . . That the Virgin Mary in Mexico should be an Indian is significant. It means that the Virgin has won the Indians' spirit. . . . Our Lady of Guadalupe is to the Indians not divine mediately, by virtue of being the purely earthly mother of Christ, but is, like the Aztec goddess of the spot in which her spirit first appeared, divine in her own right. Her image in the shrine supports this conclusion. For the churchmen in their artistry did not dare to tamper with the spontaneous movement of the Indians' spirit by even attempting to insure the orthodoxy of the Virgin by placing a Christ-child in her arms. She appears in the shrine of the basilica of Guadalupe alone and in her own right.

That this is what she means to the Mexicans is evidenced again and again throughout the churches of Mexico. To be sure, there are pilgrimages in the church calendar over great distances where the object of the quest is the Christ. Undoubtedly the priests, if pressed on the point, would maintain that her virtue is only mediate through Christ and not immediate in her own nature. But that this is not what she means to the vast majority of Mexicans there can be little doubt. The truth is that it is the Virgin representing what Plato termed the female *erós* (the emotional, passionate, metaphysical principle in the nature of things) and not the Christ representing the male *logos* (the rational, doctrinal principle, formalized explicitly for orthodox Catholicism by St. Thomas Aquinas) who has for the most part caught the imagination and the devotion of the Mexicans.

These considerations make it evident that the Spanish Colonial component of the culture of Mexico is something truly original and unique and by no means typical, orthodox Roman Catholicism.

French Nineteenth Century

THE nineteenth century . . . was a century partially influenced by the United States but dominated by France. The influence from the north appears in the incorporation of the presidency into the legal democracy of Mexico. The French predominance shows itself in the building of the rest of the democracy upon the French model. The talented Mexican scholar and diplomat Alfonso Reyes, in *Ultima Tule*, has summarized the relative contributions to the Latin-American republics in the following manner: "Our constitutional utopias combine the political philosophy of France with the federalist presidency of the United States." In the volatility and frequency of its shifts of personnel and even in its departures from democracy itself with France's Maximilian and the dictatorship of Porfirio Días, Latin-American democracy more closely follows its French model in practice as well as in theory.

The adjective "Latin" is the key to this preference. "Between our country and France," Samuel Ramos adds "exists the affinity of the Latin spirit. Mexico became Latinized by the double influence of the Catholic Church and Roman legislation." . . . Alfonso Reyes agrees that "in general," without denying affinities "with the other America (i.e. the United States), the intelligence of our America encounters in Europe a vision of the human more universal, more basic, more in conformity with its proper feeling."

This is not difficult to understand. The people of the United States . . . are not essentially aesthetic in their interests. For them art tends to be merely a utilitarian instrument or an unnecessary luxury brought in as an afterthought. It is not the substance of human life. On the other hand, the native Indians in Mexico possess a natural and ineradicable aesthetic sense. The Spanish Colonial Period enabled them to express it in their own unique way. The French exhibit a similar appreciation of art, as do the Spaniards. Thus the feeling of the Mexicans for the culture of Paris or Madrid rather than for that of nineteenth-century Chicago or New York is natural.

France is also predominantly a Catholic country. Even though her political forms are modern, the architecture in which they are housed and the religious institutions with which they were associated are medieval or classical. Similarly, her literature extends continuously into the medieval and ancient past. Even as advanced a writer as Anatole France has no sense of leaving his modern cultural homeland in entering into the mind of Abélard or into the thoughts of Cicero or Plato. Mexico also, because of the Spanish colonial influence, is Catholic and medieval in religious orientation and architectural forms. Her contemporary poet Alfonso Reyes, as his *Crítica en la Edad Ateniense* shows, moves as easily amid the *Dialogues* of Plato and the literary criticism of Aristotle as he does within the embassies of the modern nationalistic states.

. . . It was precisely because of this that Mexico in the nineteenth century found democratic French culture, with its roots in the medieval and ancient past, rather more to its liking than the purely modern culture of the United States, even when the Mexicans were in quest of purely modern political and educational values. This French influence led them first to sixty years of democracy, broken by interruptions, some of which also had a French source, and finally to approximately thirty-five years of the dictatorship of Porfirio Díaz in which the idea of the good for the Mexican state was defined by the positivistic philosophy of the Frenchman Comte, supplemented, as Leopoldo Zea has shown, under the leadership of Justo Sierra with the British positivism of Mill and Spencer.

The appeal of the modern democratic political and secular educational ideals introduced by the French influence is easy for us in the Anglo-American tradition to appreciate. To understand, however, why in a country predominantly Catholic these ideals led to the nationalization and confiscation of church property and a secularization of all education, going beyond anything experienced by Catholics in the United States, requires attention upon factors in the Mexican situation differing from those in the English-speaking democracies.

. . . The English-speaking world . . . received its democratic theory directly from its major original English source in John Locke. It might be thought, since French democracy is largely merely a systematic working out of the Newtonian and Lockean ideas which Voltaire brought to France following his visit in England, that this difference would be minor. But Locke in all his writings gave expression to the conventional religious sentiments carried over by habit from the medieval past, not realizing, as tended to become clear later, that on his own premises they were without meaning. Consequently, except for Thomas Paine, democratic ideas came to the English-speaking people directly from their main source with no disturbing, anti-religious associations.

In the hands of the acute Voltaire, however, Locke's ideas were a different thing. With Voltaire words about God and religion could not pass without having their meanings challenged. Before being admitted as anything more than noises they had quite rightly to be defined in terms of the modern assumptions to which Newton's physics and Locke's philosophy entitled one, just as Catholic, medieval religious concepts were defined, as the sequel will show, in terms of Aristotle's physics and St. Thomas's philosophy. Otherwise, one's religion would be presupposing still the medieval assumptions and Locke's, and the modern democratic contention that the medieval political doctrine of the divine right of kings had to go would be quite unjustified. In this manner the semanticist Voltaire was led to see that the relation between the basic assumptions of modern democracy and of religion was not the simple, congenial one which Locke's language suggested. Quite the contrary. Consequently, for Voltaire, the acceptance of the scientific, philosophical, and democratic political doctrines of the modern world carried with it skepticism if not atheism, or at best deism with respect to religion.

The Mexicans' association of democracy with Rousseau did not help matters. For this Frenchman, the good life was to be found in "the state of nature." Evil was to be downed not merely by setting man free by means of democratic processes but also by removing the traditional "artificial" institutions which civilization had created. From this standpoint the Catholic religious and the monarchical political institutions and doctrines of the colonial period were on exactly the same footing. If democracy calls for the removal of the one, then it also calls for the removal of the other.

Comte gave to the Mexicans, in the name of modern social science, his law of the three stages of cultural development, according to which the first, theological or fictitious stage, as he termed it, passes over into the second, metaphysical or abstract stage, which in turn culminates in the scientific or positive stage. One has then but to identify the Spanish colonial period of Mexican history with the theological stage, and the democratic period from 1810 to 1876 with the metaphysical stage, to appreciate why the dictatorship of Porfirio Díaz, which took positivism as its model, extended science, secularized education, and felt it necessary to move away from, and curb, not merely the Christian religion but also democracy.

An even more surprising paradox remains. It arises when one asks how the Mexicans learned of the French ideas which produced their anti-religious, anti-Catholic reaction. The answer is that they were taught these French ideas, every one of which is on the Index, by the Roman Catholic Church itself.

The evidence for this is clear. The French came into Mexico, to be sure, in 1862, but the Frenchmen who came were soldiers, not teachers or skeptical democratic philosophers. They entered, moreover, because of the appeal to Europe to remove the Reform Laws which had nationalized the church property. Hence, the French soldiers did not bring the French philosophical ideas which had produced the supposed evil they came to remove. The Reform Laws were passed in 1857, several years before the French came. Moreover, the democratic revolution occurred much earlier, in 1810. It was led by Miguel Hidalgo. Hidalgo was a Catholic priest. He had read and taught his followers the unorthodox French philosophical doctrines. Because of this, in 1811, he was, as Anita Brenner has written, "unfrocked, excommunicated, and executed." Nevertheless, it is important to remember that he had the support of the Madonna of Guadalupe. Immediately, he was succeeded by José María Morelos. The new leader also was a priest, and as Samuel Ramos indicates, "was prosecuted in the Inquisition for his devotion to the French Encyclopaedists." Nevertheless, he obtained a great following. One of the present states of Mexico bears his name.

That one or two individual priests should do this is perhaps not too surprising, but upon further investigation one finds that they did not read these forbidden books surreptitiously; instead, they taught them openly in official Jesuit Roman Catholic colleges. . . . In fact, Samuel

Ramos tells us that "the Royal and Pontifical Seminary of Mexico was a focus of the insurrection."

Contemporary Mexico

While preserving and extending the secular development of education, the pursuit of science as a human value, and the principles of French political democracy, contemporary Mexico has modified or departed from its French culture of the nineteenth century in four major ways: (1) the philosophical and political rejection of positivism with the development of a new and creative humanism; (2) the extension of French legal democracy to include Anglo-American economic and cultural values; (3) the suggested combination of Anglo-American democracy with certain Russian economic values; and (4) a reaction against all these secular trends to the Spanish individualistic, or the orthodox Catholic, hierarchical, religious and philosophical values of the colonial period. How these four developments, each one of which is vital, are to be reconciled is the fundamental present problem of Mexico's culture and politics.

The rejection of positivism in the political sphere dates from the second democratic revolution in 1910 which overthrew the dictatorship of Porfirio Díaz. Samuel Ramos informs us that a "revolutionary intellectual movement" with the support of the Minister of Public Education, "antedates by two years the political revolution which broke out in 1910." The intellectual revolution was important. This is shown by the fact that it has persisted, growing in strength and influence up to the present moment, and that the victory of democracy over the dictatorship and positivism was not consolidated in the political sphere until the new constitution of 1917 under Venustiano Carranza and the regime of Alvaro Obregón in the twenties.

The new intellectual movement supported by Justo Sierra, which nursed and sustained the reborn and reconstructed democracy, took two main forms: First, positivism was shorn of its appeal to the imagination by a critique pursued by the philosophers Antonio Caso and José Vasconcelos which revealed its inadequacy in the face of the facts of cultural history and the inescapable, intuitive aesthetic and emotional components of the Indian and the Spanish spirit. Second, a large and distinguished group of philosophically minded creative poets, essayists, and statesmen, including Alfonso Reyes, Pedro Henríquez Ureña, Eduardo Colin and González Martínez, created a richer and more historically enlightened humanism in its place. The two movements were fostered in their earlier period by the intuitive philosophy of the Frenchman Henri Bergson. Recently the defeat of positivism has been made triply secure by the advent throughout Mexico and the whole of South America of the phenomenological and axiological philosophy of Edmund Husserl, Max Scheler, and Nicolai Hartmann.

Introduced by the popular and brilliant writings of the Spaniard Ortega y Gasset, the latter doctrine represents the most vital philosophical movement in the Latin-American world at the present time. Its appeal is by no means restricted to professional philosophers. Legal thinkers, psychologists, essayists, and students of art such as Justino Fernández, have been profoundly and permanently influenced. This phenomenological philosophy of Husserl and his followers is doing for the Latin-American world in the twentieth century what the ethics of Bishop Butler and of Kant did for the English-speaking world in the nineteenth century. One need have no fear of the return of a positivistically oriented dictatorship in Mexico.

The philosophical and political defeat of positivism was a rejection not merely of Díaz and dictatorship but also of the last and culminating French influence. This made it natural for the Mexicans upon their return to democracy to be guided for the first time predominantly by the United States and by Anglo-American rather than French thought in their politics.

It might be supposed that Mexico's long and difficult struggle during the second decade of this century to re-establish democracy, taking the United States rather than France as her model, would receive the wholehearted support of her neighbor to the north. The facts were, however, quite to the contrary. In 1914, during Mexico's struggling democratic revolution, Woodrow Wilson and his country, which a few years later were to fight a "war to save democracy," sent an army into Mexico. To be sure, the situation was trying, but revolutions, even when led by democrats in the United States, England, or France, are rough, upsetting, and erratic things. Also, the disturbances of the revolution were not the sole cause of the military invasion. The truth, as

Anita Brenner has shown, is that the regime which all too many in the United States and Great Britain then or since really liked was the dictatorship of Díaz.

. . . For under Porfirio Díaz North American and British capitalists and their engineers went into Mexico. The Díaz dictatorship is called by them, not untruthfully, "The Golden Age." From the standpoint of the efficiency of the railways, the production of petroleum, the development of the mines, and the pursuit of science and secular education along restrictedly practical lines, they are right. But unfortunately neither the industries nor the government belonged to the people of Mexico. Everything was undoubtedly more efficient and orderly, but the last thing one could say of it was that it was democratic or Mexican.

It happened, therefore, following the second democratic revolution, in 1910, when the Mexican people attempted to take the political democracy of the United States as their model and attempted to reap, in a higher standard of living for their people, what the more universal, secular, scientific, public education of the previous century had sown, that they found their similarity with the United States, notwithstanding all their efforts, remaining more nominal than real. Thus it became increasingly clear to them during the second decade of this century that they could only reap the fruits of their education, scientific training and labor by at least a partial return of the economic natural resources of their country to Mexican ownership.

The Mexicans encountered a second difficulty. When they attempted to regain a reasonable portion of their own national economic resources they found themselves confronted not merely by an international law which had been formulated by Great Britain, the United States, and others during an imperialistic era but also, as examination of the Anglo-American culture of the United States will show, by a political idealism grounded in the Lockean philosophy of the state, which underlies the Declaration of Independence and the Constitution of the United States. . . . According to this Lockean theory the justification for the existence of government is the preservation of private property. Under these circumstances even the most elementary attempt upon the part of the Mexican Government to establish economic justice within its own country by regaining some of its natural resources would appear to the United States and Great Britain, as it did to Woodrow Wilson in 1916, as a breach not merely of traditional international law but also of the elementary principles of political morality. This international impasse, which is philosophical in its origin and basis, constitutes not merely the fundamental problem of Mexican foreign policy but also one of the inescapable problems in international relations throughout the entire world in the twentieth century.

The exchange of correspondence between Secretary Hull and the Mexican Foreign Minister of the Cárdenas regime with respect to the attempt of the Mexican Government to get certain natural resources back into Mexican hands is illuminating. It shows that our foreign relations bring us face to face with a conflict of ideological values, fundamentally philosophical in character, which needs to be made explicit and brought out into the open instead of covered up with verbal ambiguities which seem to place the United States on a lofty, noble, and generous plane, but which to the Latin Americans, if taken seriously, can only produce false hopes, followed by later disillusionment and bitterness and which, if not taken seriously, add another fact to support the traditional Latin-American belief that the people of the north "talk big" in terms of the most high and humane principles but do not mean what they seem to say.

. . . The time has come when one must either stop talking about the priority of human rights over property rights, and of economic as well as political democracy for every people everywhere, regardless of whether they possess titles to the resources within their national borders or not; or else define the terms carefully and develop a set of principles from which new laws both national and international can be derived which can be used to resolve on a basis of principle the disputes to which the hopes raised by such words give rise. More specifically, we had better stop making general statements in the Fourteen Points, in the Atlantic Charter, at Monterrey, and elsewhere about economic as well as political democratic justice, until we have thought through what, under democratic processes such as those bringing into power the democratic governments of Mexico since 1910, our words may reasonably be supposed to mean, and we are prepared in practice to accept the consequences.

It must be pointed out that no policy of the United States with respect to Mexico could have been more effectively designed than was the literal insistence upon the property rights interpretation of the minimum standard international law to persuade the Mexicans that it is impossible to extend democracy in their country from the political to the economic sphere without replacing the Lockean with the Marxian philosophy. This in fact is the point of the frescoes of Diego Rivera and David Siqueiros and their tremendous influence. . . .

The basic human value which Diego Rivera is portraying is that of the imaginations of men freed and fascinated by scientific knowledge, and of their social and economic well-being raised by the application of its principles to agriculture, mining, the harnessing of the waterfalls, and industry.

. . . Diego Rivera and his colleague David Siqueiros have . . . provided the world with a new political and economic philosophy in which French and Anglo-American political democracy is combined with certain elements in Russian economic communism. Considering the background of Mexican experience we hardly need wonder at their influence. But unless one recalls the tremendous part which art and particularly painting have played continuously in the culture of Mexico from even its earliest Indian beginnings, one can hardly grasp the magnitude of this influence. Moreover, the frescoes of these two creative and arresting Mexican painters have, since 1920, covered the walls not merely of the patios of the Secretariat of Public Education but also of the National Preparatory School and the National University, even entering into the National Palace and the Palace of Fine Arts and extending to the Cortés Palace at Cuernavaca and to other major Mexican cities. Over the past twenty-five years each Mexican student has had this idea of the good put movingly and arrestingly before him as he walked through corridor after corridor of the higher institutions of learning. In the light of all this the wonder is not that Mexican policy has come at points into conflict with the legal and political doctrines of the United States, but that in her internal and international behavior she has been as restrained and conventional as has been the case.

Two factors have contributed to this state of affairs. One is the unequivocal democracy of the Cárdenas Government between 1934 and 1940 which, coming after fifteen years of influence by Diego Rivera and David Siqueiros, caught the full brunt of their influence. Clearly something had to be done to bring the natural resources of Mexico under Mexican ownership and control. No government could have remained in power which sidestepped this issue any longer. The Cárdenas regime had no alternative, therefore, but to raise the issue in unequivocal terms with the State Department of the United States and the Foreign Office of the British Government. Its hand was strengthened by the fact that it went into office in 1934 and it went out of office in 1940 by thoroughly democratic processes; also, by the fact that during and since its administration the cultural forms of the United States have been more and more incorporated into Mexican life. This is shown unequivocally in the automobiles and buses from Detroit, the moving pictures from Hollywood, the skyscrapers and business practices from New York, the baseball games and horse-racing which are now competing with bull-fighting, and even in the increasingly significant interest in the literature, science, and philosophy of the neighbor to the north.

The other factor is that, thanks to the foundations for understanding between Mexico and the United States constructed by Dwight Morrow and to the Good Neighbor Policy initiated by President Roosevelt and Secretary Hull, the latter–very wisely, in the final stages of the negotiations–did not insist upon the letter of the minimum standard law, as he had previously interpreted it, but instead accepted a compromise. . . .

With the advent of the Camacho Government in 1940 one other factor entered into the contemporary Mexican scene. This is the relaxing of the repression of religion which had accompanied the traditional Mexican democracy since 1810, and an attendant revival of humanistic as opposed to merely positivistic, and Spanish colonial in addition to merely French nineteenth century, values.

This vital contemporary development in Mexican culture has many sources. One is the emphasis upon the aesthetic intuition and the individual, mystical, religious passion by the philosopher José

Vasconcelos in his critique of positivism. Another is the influence throughout Mexico and the whole of Latin America of the very popular individualistic and socially anarchistic writings of the Spaniard Miguel de Unamuno. A third is the recently growing interest in the works of the German philosopher Heidegger, with their somewhat similar emphasis upon human experience as being laden with care. A fourth is the revival of neo-Scholasticism, as evidenced by the fact that in 1943 both the Rector of the National University and the Chairman of its Department of Philosophy were orthodox Thomists. Even more important, since it is led by humanists with an appreciation of the riches of the whole history of Western civilization rather than by neo-Thomists, with their restriction to the merely Aristotelian and Thomistic Western values, is the rebirth of intense scholarly study of the culture of the colonial period and its historical roots in the European philosophical and literary tradition as evidenced (a) by the Institute for Aesthetic Investigation directed by the scholarly expert in colonial art, Manuel Toussaint, and (b) by the Colegio de Mexico, presided over by the distinguished humanist Alfonso Reyes.

An additional evidence is the moving devotion at Guadalupe and the frank showing of its image of the Virgin everywhere, even on the banners of the democratic reformers as well as in the permanent construction of the most modernistic of contemporary apartment houses. Perhaps most important of all, certainly, the most striking in their appeal to "the passion of the Spanish soul" and to the aesthetic intuition of the Indians' spirit, are the frescoes of José Clemente Orozco, especially in the light of the brilliant and profound exposition of them, commending them to contemporary intellectuals, given by Justino Fernández. In fact, José Orozco's art conveys analogically in vivid, emotionally moving, aesthetic materials the philosophical doctrine of this fourth vital movement in contemporary Mexican culture just as Diego Rivera's frescoes function for its third movement.

José Orozco's most striking, important, and universal symbol is fire. Justino Fernández informs us that for Orozco it always symbolizes the human spirit. Its two most notable uses are in the cupola of El Hospicio Cabañas at Guadalajara, and facing the stairway in the House of Tiles in Mexico City. At the former place the fire is seen completely enflaming a human body straining and immersed with it. . . . As Justino Fernández has shown, this expresses the essence of the human consciousness as a tragic yet glorious commitment–tragic because for all man's voluntary, free struggle for specific ideals he is thwarted, even punished, because of the conflict with other, equally human values and impulses, both good and bad; glorious because, notwithstanding the inevitable defeat and failure, man, exercising the freedom of his own spirit, makes his choice and accepts the consequences. Clearly this is no pragmatic philosophy; nor is it a utilitarian hedonism.

At no point do the values of the Indian and the Spanish spirit stand in greater contrast to those of the Anglo-American people to their north than in these frescoes of Orozco: Spanish America with its conviction that tragedy, brutality, chaos, failure, and death, as well as triumph and compassion, aim at order, and earthly life are an essential part of the glory of man; Anglo America with its pollyannic tendency, its Christian Science, its life under the elms as if there were no desire there also, its worship of the successful businessman, its formal Kantian idealism empty of empirical content, and its pragmatism making even truth itself dependent upon a successful reward at the end. This opposition must be understood and reconciled if Pan-Americanism is ever to become a spontaneous movement of the spirit.

José Orozco's second typical use of the flame appears in the symbolism of the hands above the upper left-hand portion of the fresco "Omniscience," which faces the stairway in the House of Tiles in Mexico City. The symbolism exhibits two larger hands cupped to contain the flame, extending down from above toward a smaller hand open to receive it immediately below. . . . Justino Fernández informs us that the larger hands represent God presenting the flame to the smaller hand of man beneath. Thus when the theoretical meaning of the immediately sensed aesthetic materials is correctly read, one finds that this painting saying that man does not create his own spirit but that it is a gift of Divine Grace. This is the Christian Catholic doctrine requiring the science and philosophy of the medieval period (or its equivalent) to give it meaning.

The return to the values of the Spanish colonial period is evident. Man is not merely a vibrant frenzy, possessed of free will, living dangerously, and realistically facing death as well as life, and his evil passion as well as his sublime movements; but he is also not his own creator or explanation but a gift of Divine Grace. The irreducible humanism and individualism deriving from the *cogito* or primacy of the human self of Descartes and Locke upon which the Modern World was reared, and the evolutionary optimism and pragmatic instrumentalism in which the Modern World found itself with Hegel and Darwin, have been rejected.

One understands also why José Orozco and Diego Rivera, notwithstanding their opposition on all other points–Orozco's Spanish and Catholic values being Rivera's evils, Rivera's economic and scientific values being Orozco's evils–agree upon one point: namely, the inadequacy of the traditional modern Lockean Anglo-American values. This agreement, to be sure, arises for different reasons–for Rivera, because the Anglo-American Lockean doctrine of the primacy of property rights, like the colonial society which Orozco's Spanish Christian values nourished, has the consequence of drawing off the fruits of the humanistically good science and technology applied to the nation's resources from the people's pockets to the coffers of Rome or the banks of Wall Street; for Orozco because (a) the physical science essentially connected with Lockean Anglo-American democracy leads to scientific technology which, by mechanizing man's life, destroys his soul, and (b) its political and Protestant emphasis, through standardized universal education, starting from the conception of man as an emotionless blank tablet, and aiming at the uniform majority opinion necessary to make democracy function, places the free imagination and the rich warm bodily feelings of men in a straitjacket, so that the individualism, the spontaneity and the freedom of the emotions, necessary for a vital, fresh, aesthetic sense and a deep, personal, religious passion tend to be destroyed.

Put positively, what José Orozco is doing for us is the revealing of a new freedom–the freedom of the aesthetic intuition, the individualistic emotions, and the sentiments. To political freedom and economic freedom, psychological freedom is being added.

. . . There is no incompatibility whatever between the intuitive, passionate, immediately apprehended aesthetic values which José Orozco conveys and the postulated, theoretical, and attendant technological, scientific values which Diego Rivera portrays with equal artistic and human appeal. The ancient Indian culture showed the Mexicans, as it now shows us, how a geometrically informed, aesthetically vivid, astronomically oriented art, religion, and agriculture can function together harmoniously and with human appeal.

It is significant that the medieval culture of Spain was created as much by an Arabian invasion from the East as by indigenous influences within the West. Also, men everywhere, as the Orientals and the ancient Aztecs indicate, begin with the aesthetic emotional principle in the nature of things and come to the rational principle, which is the great discovery of Western science and philosophy and its religion of God the Father, only later, if at all. One feels the beauty of the sunset before one learns of the internal constitution of the stars. The most typical representative in the Orient of this purely intuitive, compassionate, aesthetic view of life is the Buddha.

The true relation between intuitive, aesthetic, and religious feeling and scientific doctrine is one of mutual supplementation. For we have a conception of the meaning of man and the universe which it is trustworthy for art and religion to convey, only by the aid of scientific knowledge pursued to its basic theoretical assumptions, and then developed with respect to its philosophical and theological consequences. And conversely, we can attain verified scientific knowledge only by observing what is immediately apprehended, and this is always aesthetically vivid and emotionally moving. Furthermore, the whole of mankind, as opposed to a few artists and saints, can obtain the leisure to pursue the aesthetically immediate and the intuitive religion of compassion of the Virgin and the Buddha for its own sake, only if scientific knowledge is applied to the world's resources under legal principles defined by an economic theory which permits the fruits of man's knowledge to redound to the benefit of all men. This is the reason why Orozco's psychological and religious values and Rivera's scientific and economic values are all bound together and equally essential.

Intellectual Origins of Aprismo

By ROBERT E. McNICOLL

My judgments are nourished from my ideals, my sentiments, my passions.—MARIÁTEGUI

The development of a political group in Peru called the *Alianza Popular Revolucionaria Americana* (Aprismo) by Víctor Raúl Haya de la Torre in 1924 provided an ideological bridge between the country's brilliant non-Communist nineteenth-century reformers and those who sought to apply Marxist solutions to the problems of an underdeveloped nation and an underdeveloped continent. Essentially, Aprismo sought to incorporate the Indians and the disenfranchised lower classes into Peru's political structure and thus to destroy the power of the oligarchy. The degree of Communist philosophic orientation of Aprismo has thus been the subject of continuing controversy. Present-day Apristas and present-day Communists dispute whether José Carlos Mariátegui (1894–1930), the intellectual predecessor of Haya de la Torre, was in fact the founding philosopher of Aprismo or of Peruvian Communism, a bitter enemy of Aprismo. Writers in the Soviet Union claim Mariátegui was a Communist and dispute the contention of the Apristas that he was not. The truth is that the intellectual origins of Aprismo, which has influenced not only Peru but also other Latin American countries, are so diverse that no single political party or group can claim all of them as its own.

The following article, which deals with Aprismo only to World War II, has been discussed by Moscow academicians, who reject its thesis that Mariátegui was a predecessor of Aprismo rather than the founder of Peruvian Communism, while they admit that the same point of view was erroneously held by many early Marxist writers.

Although intellectual disputes of this nature seem to have little practical value in present-day power politics, an understanding of them is of importance. As Latin America accomplishes its history, its poets, writers, and historians are continually reexamining its past with a view to the discovery, creation, and rejection of earlier leaders. Just as the great Whig historians of nineteenth-century England, for reasons of domestic political debate, portrayed earlier British leaders as knaves, charlatans, or heroes, depending on the political orientation of the writer, so the history of Latin America is presently being rewritten. Politics is the lifeblood of Latin America, and few of its writers can remain aloof from it and afford to continue their researches.

The author of this essay is presently professor of history at the University of Miami, an institution with which he was first associated in 1933. After a number of governmental and academic positions, which led to residence in three Latin American countries—Cuba, Chile, and Peru—he is now director of the Institute of Inter-American Studies at the University of Miami. He was founding editor of the *Journal of Inter-American Studies* from 1958 to 1964.

McNicoll was born in St. Louis, Missouri, and attended the University of Miami and Duke University, from which he obtained his Ph.D. in Latin American history in 1938. His articles on Peru and other Latin American countries have appeared in a number of academic journals.

THE term *Aprismo* is one which has acquired a varied ideological content during the past ten years. It refers not only to the political tenets and programs of the *Alianza Popular Revolucionaria Americana*, headed by Víctor Raúl Haya de la Torre (1895), but also to the philosophies, theories, and ideals set forth by a very able group of writers who look to Haya de la Torre as party chief and intellectual guide. While many of their viewpoints might be traced back to sources among Peruvian and other liberals of the epoch of the Wars of Independence, more immediate and direct connections are found in the period following Peru's disastrous war with Chile (1879–1883).

The War of the Pacific meant a rude awakening for many Peruvians who had felt their country to be one of the leading nations of Hispanic America. Its effect on the intellectual life of the country was quite similar to that of the Spanish-American War on Spain. Just as Spain's defeat produced the famous "Generation of 1898," able, iconoclastic writers who sought to reform and modernize Spanish institutions, so Peru's humiliating defeat brought about a new and critical study of Peruvian social organization. This "literature of disillusionment," as Jorge Basadre calls it,[1] was produced by a few mature writers, but also by a group of younger men who developed in the years following the war. This group has sometimes been called the "Generation of 1910" because many of them completed their education around that date. Four main themes of recurrent emphasis are found in their writings. First was concern for the Indian population, beginning with a mere humanitarian interest in hardships suffered in the native villages of the *sierra,* continuing with a study of the social and economic institutions surviving under Spanish and Peruvian rule, to culminate in a cult of everything native as is found in the modern "Indo-America" movement. Luis-Alberto Sánchez considers the first Peruvian novel to be the book *Aves sin nido,* written by Clorinda Matto de Turner in 1889.[2] This may be taken as the first great *Indianista* book and is an impassioned plea for the Indian. It contains several other elements which make it an epoch-marking book. One is the use of realism which is a break with the romantic style of its time. The other is the criticism of the clergy which is entertwined with its humanitarian concern for the Indian.

A second theme which ran through much of this literature of protest was the criticism of the wealthy, aristocratic, creole ruling class of Lima which drew its livelihood from Peru but which was spiritually and intellectually foreign in its own country. Paris and Europe formed the cult of the educated who sought to be adept in European culture but who scorned the possibilities and ignored the importance of the Peruvian back-country with its silent native population. Lima was criticized as being a little European colony set down on the coast, turning its back to the awe and wonder of the brooding majesty of the Andes and the challenge of its oppressed and misunderstood Indian population.

The third theme of the reformers, allied with the preceding, is the problem of the *latifundia* and the Indian-exploiting *gamonales.* The land-owners not only held the Indians in subjection but they made difficult the development of a land-owning middle class, the proper basis

[1]Jorge Basadre, *Perú: problema y posibilidad* (Lima, 1931), p. 156.
[2]Luis-Alberto Sánchez, "Notas sobre la novela peruana contemporánea," *Revista Universidad de la Habana,* No. 19 (October, 1938), p. 66.

for the liberal democratic government desired by many of the reformers. The fourth consideration of the reformers was the Church. The traditional clericalism of Peru was attacked because of its alliance with the ruling class, its alleged lack of concern over the temporal fate of the Indians, and because of its own economic situation as a large land-owner and a recipient of government taxes under the state patronage of the Church.

The greatest figure among these reformers, the founder of a school of younger writers, and one who might be called the precursor of later criticism is Manuel González-Prada (1846–1918).[3] One critic says of him, "Fué el escritor más lapidario y el espíritu más diamantino que ha dado el Peru."[4] González-Prada began his studies in a traditional Hispanic manner, writing verses and making a profound study of the mystic Fray Luis de León.[5] During the War with Chile he enlisted in the army and served in the Battle of Miraflores in which the Chileans besieged the outskirts of Lima. During the occupation of the capital he retired to his home and refused to leave it as long as the Chileans remained in the city. Patriotic as most Peruvians, but with the further sensitivity of a zealot, he felt his nation's disgrace and subjection most keenly. When peace came the former romantic poet appeared in the role of a fiery reformer, excoriating the institutions which he held responsible for his country's defeat. He even went so far as to preach the *revanche*. "His words, striking sparks and terrible . . . are those of a Jeremiah accuser," says Carleton Beals.[6]

Something of a Peruvian Voltaire, his first and principal animus was directed against the Church. Starting as a critic of corrupt clericalism, he ended by becoming atheistic and in opposition to religion *per se*. The

[3]Federico de Onís says, "Manuel González-Prada is without doubt one of the first precursors of the present epoch in America, because his spirit, since his youth, was characterized by its noncomformity and its lack of satisfaction." "Contemporaneidad de González-Prada," p. 6, *González-Prada,* Instituto de las Españas (New York, 1938).

[4]Luis-Alberto Sánchez, *Historia de la literatura americana* (Santiago de Chile, 1937), p. 363.

[5]There is an excellent novelized biography of González-Prada in *Don Manuel* by Luis-Alberto Sánchez (Santiago de Chile, 1937). A critical study of González-Prada has been made by John H. Cutler, *Manuel González-Prada, Precursor of a Modern Peru,* MS. Ph.D. Thesis. Pp. 315. Harvard, 1936. A bibliography on the subject is given in the Instituto de las Españas publication cited above.

[6]Carleton Beals, *Fire on the Andes* (Philadelphia, 1934), p. 442.

economic absurdity of a vast number of priests and nuns living on the bounty of the country seemed to him as reprehensible as the effect of the superstitions they maintained. In 1903 he wrote an article denouncing the immigration of more and more foreigners to enter the religious communities of Peru:

> Immigrants who come to exercise a trade or a profession have to overcome great obstacles and often are not able to establish themselves. Those who bring in only a tonsure and a little Latin do not fail to find a spacious nest in which to lodge nor fertile soil in which to grow . . . the cleric or friar, no matter where he comes from, finds no rivalries nor resistance, his shaven head is his passport and recommendation, proof of honesty and sign of omniscience.
>
> What has Lima become? A Dead Sea in which the churches and monasteries stand out like islands without water or vegetation. . . . Thus a city which includes more than a hundred edifices devoted to worship and religious education has not a single municipal school worthy of a civilized nation.[7]

In his antipathy to the Church González-Prada went beyond the bounds of reason, gratuitously blaming it for many things not in its control. His arguments and his language suffered from his extreme fanaticism in this regard. This tendency is behind such appraisals as the following: "He was not only anti-Catholic, but anti-clerical; not only anti-clerical, but anti-Christian; not only anti-Christian, but anti-religious."[8] In this respect he is sometimes considered less a champion of religious liberty in Peru, for which a long and difficult campaign had to be waged, than a bitter free-thinker. The liberal writer Dora Mayer de Zulen points this out in her pamphlet, *El desarrollo de las ideas avanzadas en el Perú* (Callao, 1934). The breaches in the walls of uncompromising Catholicism, she says, had already been made by the slow-working acids of modern thought before Francisco de Paula Vigil, Peru's famous atheist, and González-Prada made their spectacular attacks upon them. The "anti-friarism" which motivated ninety per cent of these writers merely led them to a fanaticism which cut down their potentially constructive influence on the nation.[9]

[7]Manuel González-Prada, *Horas de lucha* (Lima, 1908), pp. 230–231.
[8]J. H. Cutler, *González-Prada,* p. 227.
[9]Dora Mayer de Zulen, *El desarrollo de las ideas avanzadas en el Perú,* p. 10.

Besides the economic effect of the Church, González-Prada found most harmful its control of education. In one place he attacks the Church as being anti-educational[10] while in another he attacks the educational methods of the Jesuits as being designed "not to teach one to be wise, but to seem to be."[11]

In the course of his many speeches and essays González-Prada reviewed the entire history of the nation and put a very pessimistic interpretation upon it. The political parties, he said, were no more than syndicates of ambitious individuals; the leaders nothing more than agents of the great business houses (referring mainly to the companies competing for the handling of the guano trade) or soldiers who saw in the presidency the last step in a military career.[12] All of the many domestic struggles had worked no healthful change. In other countries "revolutions come as a painful but fruitful step in the evolution of the people." "They shed blood but they create light."[13] In Peru this was not the case. After the poor Indians had killed one another fighting on both sides of a civil struggle, the same groups of leaders would gather around a festal board with fraternal embraces to divide the spoils of office. He scorned the vaunted aristocracy of Lima. It had become one of profiteers and plantation owners. The first should have emblazoned on its coat of arms a hand reaching into a money sack, and the second, a hand brandishing a whip over the back of an unfortunate plantation serf. Those of proud lineage which they traced back to Pizarro's immortal "Thirteen of Gallo," were also linked by innumerable unofficial matings to the humble natives of the *sierra* or the Negroes of the coast.[14] He ended this particular philippic by the blasting assertion that the religious fervor of a Liman matron could serve as a measure for the percentage of African blood in her veins. The pure Negro displayed

[10]"La secular y magna labor de la Iglesia Romana se resume en tres vocablos: fomentar la ignorancia." González-Prada, *Propaganda y ataque* (Buenos Aires, 1939), p. 39.

[11]*Ibid.*, "La educación de los jesuitas," p. 88. Published first in *El libre pensamiento,* June 16, 1900. This and many unpublished works have been gathered together and published by the son of the author, Sr. Alfredo González-Prada, resident in the United States until his recent death.

[12]Manuel González-Prada, *Horas de lucha,* p. 2.

[13]*Ibid.,* pp. 112–113.

[14]Manuel González-Prada, *Horas de lucha,* p. 192.

greater religiosity than the quadroon; the quadroon, more than the octaroon, and so in decreasing intensity up to the pure white.[15]

The impact of such statements on a proud and religious society can easily be imagined. Later writers have pointed out that he was only a "rebellious bourgeois." While he gave lectures on "The Intellectual and the Worker," he was merely bringing to Peru the middle-class positivism which had ruled Europe for several decades.[16] The intellectual, but conservative Catholic, Víctor Andrés Belaunde, who is himself one of the greater minds of the post-war generation, admires González-Prada as a literary artist but denounces him as a philosopher in political and religious matters. He admits that he gave "stimulus and new vigor to the fallen and humiliated national spirit," but Belaunde thinks his "anti-clerical complex" had disastrous consequences in "artificially creating the religious problem in Peru." Apparently Belaunde's most valuable criticism of him is to point out that he was purely Spanish in type. With all his new radicalism, there was still present the individualism, the spirit of affirmation, the fanaticism of the Hispanic temperament. A new age and the "Science" of Europe had merely cast into a new mold the old Spanish nature.[17] An excellent summation of his role in Peruvian letters is given by Carleton Beals who reflects the opinion of the modern Aprista group: "He was a sort of purifying flame, but could not create in accordance with his critical understanding, perhaps because, as D'Ors has stated, he galloped in two centuries."[18] The anti-clerical trend taken by González-Prada was less imitated by his followers than his criticisms of other conditions. Perhaps Luis-Alberto Sánchez expresses a partisan view, since he is one of the Aprista group, when he says of González-Prada, "He molded the mind of Peruvian youth."[19] His place as leader of the modern reformers is unquestioned.

In the thinking of Peruvian writers in the years between González-Prada and Aprismo, other influences were working besides that of the "Precursor." Some of these reinforced the course already charted and

[15]*Ibid.*, p. 198.
[16]Jorge Basadre, *op. cit.*, p. 165.
[17]Víctor Andrés Belaunde, *La realidad nacional* (Paris, 1931), pp. 163–168.
[18]Carleton Beals, *op. cit.*, pp. 442–443.
[19]Luis-Alberto Sánchez, *Historia de la literatura americana*, p. 365.

added new preoccupations. The most powerful literary force in all Spanish America was *Modernismo*. *Modernismo* was the name given to a new literary movement which swept from Spanish America to dominate Spain itself. It had French beginnings in the Parnassians and the *symbolistes.* According to Northrup,[20] "It is the synthesis of the two, aiming to achieve form, color, and music, and appealing both to the eye and to the ear." Spanish America was very close to France intellectually and found in Rubén Darío (1867–1916) of Nicaragua a writer whose influence molded these currents into a more Hispanic pattern and established *Modernismo* as a literary school on both sides of the Atlantic. Besides its technical effects it contained a philosophy of its own which emphasized a number of themes. One of these was opposition to the so-called imperialism of the United States which had reached new highs in the years beginning with the Spanish-American War and the Panama episode of 1903. Rubén Darío, one of the founders of the movement, fired a heavy broadside in his "Ode to Roosevelt."[21] José Enrique Rodó in his *Ariel* established as a fixed idea in the Hispanic mind the concept that practical Anglo-America bore a Caliban-like relationship to the poetic Ariel of Hispanic America. This in a world where, unfortunately, the Calibans seemed to be in control. Writers less important as literary artists but more engrossed with the anti-American campaign, such as Manuel Ugarte, kept up the agitation. Alberto Ghiraldo wrote *Yanquilandia bárbara,* obviously continuing the thought of Rodó. Thus a new element was added to the *impedimenta* carried by the González-Prada school. Peruvian writers also were influenced by the anti-American campaign.

The anti-Yankee bent is well mingled with the Indianist strivings already typical of the Peruvian liberal writers in the work of the Mexican José Vasconcelos. He must be accounted an important influence on Peru. His *Bolivarismo y monroísmo* illustrates the anti-American trend while *Raza cósmica* (1925) and *Indología* (1927) provide views of the Indian problem. His idea of fusing races and

[20]George Tyler Northup, *An Introduction to Spanish Literature* (Chicago, 1925), p. 410.

[21]E. C. Lefort, "Anti-imperialism," *University of Miami Hispanic-American Studies,* No. 2 (Coral Gables, 1941), pp. 189–219.

organizing truly American social and educational systems really provide a more imaginative approach than much of the strictly *Indianista* literature. The powerful prose of Vasconcelos must be included as one of the important non-Peruvian factors in the background of Aprismo.

Peruvian writers influenced by *Modernismo,* like the poet José Santos Chocano (1875-1934), showed the other dominant interest of the modernists, that in everything native. Santos Chocano's *Alma América* combined the author's singing of "native America, savage and wild," with praise of the descendants of the *conquistadores* and occasional blows at the Colossus of the North. The Indianism was continued in Peru by a young writer who was a great short-story writer who might in time have become a great novelist. This was Abraham Valdelomar (1897–1919) who in his *Hijos del sol* recounted the glories of the Incas. While he "vindicated the native,"[22] it is well to remember that this interest may take either of two forms, as one author points out; either it is an impassioned protest against existing conditions with the hope of causing them to be remedied, in the style of González-Prada and Matto de Turner; or it is merely a romantic utilization of the Indian as local color, in the style of Ricardo Palma.[23] Valdelomar is much nearer the second form. Yet his work gave additional strength to the Indianist preoccupation. In a similar vein is the work of Enrique López Albujar, *Cuentos andinos* (1920). The most famous of recent exploiters of this novelistic interest in the Indian is Ciro Alegría, whose prize-winning novel is well known under its English title, *Broad and Alien Is the World* (1941).

More important than the writings of Valdelomar, in connection with the background of Aprismo, was his leadership of a group of writers who formed what was called the *Colónida.* This may be regarded as a link between the González-Prada group and the present Apristas. Valdelomar and the poet José María Eguren led the writers who showed their discontent with existing conditions and gave new volume and tone to the Peruvian literature of protest. Julio de la Paz (Julio Baudoin) wrote a play, *El cóndor pasa* (1916), which set forth the problems of the Indian. The same author collaborated with José

[22]Luis-Alberto Sánchez, *op. cit.,* p. 516.

[23]Arturo Torres-Ríoseco, *Epic of Latin-American Literature* (New York, 1942), p. 188.

Carlos Mariátegui, another of the same group, in a play recalling the atmosphere of colonial Lima (*Las tapadas*). The Incan vien, mined deeper by studious writers of similar sympathies, produced *Del ayllu al imperio, De la vida incaica,* and *Tempestad en los Andes* by Luis E. Valcárcel and the sociological *Nuestra comunidad indígena* by Hildebrando Castro Pozo.[24]

So far, most of this interest was purely literary or scholarly. Not only was it non-political in nature but the writers failed to present any definite program to remedy conditions. The first writer to cast his ideas into a definite political mold, and thereby prepare the way for Aprismo, was José Carlos Mariátegui, mentioned above as one of the *Colónida*. The personality of Mariátegui is fully as interesting as his works. Unlike González-Prada, who after all was personally connected with the Peruvian aristocracy, Mariátegui was a member of the small Peruvian middle class which finds itself separated by a gulf from the aristocrats, but only a step away from the Indian masses.

He was a self-taught man and began his career working in the daily newspapers of Lima. He was crippled and continually in danger of death from the tuberculosis which sapped his vitality and ultimately brought about his demise. Yet, though imprisoned and exiled, through the force of his flaming intelligence he exerted an influence on his country which is strong even today. The years during which he developed as a revolutionary writer ended when Augusto B. Leguía came to power in Peru. He closed up Mariátegui's paper and, at the same time, gave the young man a scholarship to go to Europe where he remained during the post-war period of 1919–1923. There he came into contact with the socialistic movement and its leaders, acquiring a vast and abiding faith in the justice and expediency of the socialist cause. When he returned to Peru, he is supposed to have called on the dictator whose largesse had sent him to Europe. Waldo Frank gives an apocryphal account of this visit which is valuable in that it typifies the spirit of the man:

[24]Most of the background for these statements is found in Luis-Alberto Sánchez' work already cited. The dates for the publication of the works mentioned are as follows:
. . *Las tapadas,* 1916; *Del ayllu al imperio,* 1925; *De la vida incaica,* 1925; *Tempestad en los Andes,* 1927; *Nuestra comunidad indígena,* 1924. A valuable work on the same line, deriving from Aprismo, is Moisés Sáenz, *Sobre el indio peruano y su incorporación al medio nacional,* Mexico, 1933.

In a small republic ruled by a single will, there are many favors to be meted out to a brilliant young writer who knows the ways of the world. Dictators need talent; a man like Leguía can always find a lucrative and serviceable post for a man like Mariátegui–provided Mariátegui is willing. He can make him editor of a paper, have him elected to Congress, place him in the Ministry of Education or, if he still hankers to go abroad, he can turn him with the flourish of a pen into a diplomat or a consul.

Mariátegui sitting with President Leguía needed patronage more than ever. He was still penniless; he had found a wife in Italy and they had returned with a child, and his obscure tubercular disease was still gnawing at his limbs. He had been too busy to spend his little purse on European doctors; he had gone to Europe to meet ideas and men, not to trouble with his body. But his body was going its own way, and the youth now sitting beside the President was more than half a cripple.

Leguía smiled on Mariátegui. He saw the fleshless figure clad in black, the exquisite hands; he saw the head, narrow at the chin, magnificently broadened at the brow, the firm mouth, the eagle nose, the eyes black, brooding, hard as metal. Leguía saw the message of the eyes and stopped smiling.

"Mr. President," said Mariátegui, "I should have come, even if you had not sent for me. Since you sent me to Europe, I owe it to you, Sir, to have you know at once the state in which I return. I am your enemy, Mr. President. I am going to devote my life to fighting you and what you stand for."[25]

Mariátegui proceeded at once to publish a book, *La escena contemporánea* (Lima, 1925), which revealed the power and appeal of his new viewpoint. Three years later he brought out his masterpiece, *7 ensayos de interpretación de la realidad peruana.* In this work he applied the economic interpretation to the whole course of Peruvian history and pointed out the manifest weaknesses of the existing organization. He had none of the virulence of the school of González-Prada. His statements were careful, documented, restrained, scientific. As Basadre says, "His style is precise as an engineer's, aseptic as a physician's."[26] A relatively small number of problems receive the major part of his attention. The economic evolution of the country, the problem of the Indian, of the land system, of education, religion, and of

[25]Waldo Frank, "America Hispana," *Scribners* (New York, 1930), p. 166.
[26]Jorge Basadre, *op. cit.,* p. 197.

regionalism constitute his major themes. While his method of approach was new and valid, he suffered somewhat from the myopia caused by a rigid application of his previously conceived theories. As Basadre says, "One always knows whither his arguments are going to lead, just as one always knows the end of a Yankee moving-picture."[27]

In beginning his book, Mariátegui warns his readers, "I am no impartial and objective critic. My judgments are nourished from my ideals, my sentiments, my passions. I have a strong and declared aim: to contribute to the creation of a Peruvian socialism.[28] This is, perhaps, a higher form of academic honesty than the often iterated "objectivity" of many American writers and reveals a sincerity and earnestness matching the ability of the author. His principal innovation, in fact, was not merely the application of Marxist theories to Peruvian conditions but the thesis that Peru needed its own type of socialism based on native American institutions. He points out that the Spanish conquest of the Incan empire implanted a foreign and unbalanced economic system on a people which had previously enjoyed a collective society admirably adapted to the region and the needs of the inhabitants. The European system, unsupported by a numerous and dense immigration as in Anglo-America, failed to reach a state of equilibrium during the whole colonial epoch. The republic began with the same difficulties. The period of the guano and nitrate booms formed a new monied class, "confused and interlaced in its origin with the earlier aristocracy formed principally of the descendants of the *encomenderos* and large land owners."[29] The physical revival of Peru after the loss of these assets in the War of the Pacific did not result in the development of a unified modern state. The feudalism of the vast estates with their Indian *enganchados* or serfs persisted at the same time that the Lima businessmen were active in capitalistic enterprises of a more modern type.

Mariátegui set forth for the first time the real tragedy and problem of the Indian population in its sociological aspects. For him the problem of the Indian was merely part of the problem of the system of land tenure. The large land-owners kept the natives in a feudal condition

[27]*Ibid.*, pp. 197–198.

[28]José Carlos Mariátegui, *7 ensayos de interpretación de la realidad peruana* (Lima, 1928), p. 6.

[29]Mariátegui, *op. cit.*, p. 15.

which prevented either a return to the communal system of the Incas or an advance to the existence of large numbers of small, privately-owned farms. Even education, while the same economic conditions were maintained, could do little to advance the status of the Indian. Mariágetui favored a return to a modified form of the old Incan system of communal use of the soil–a system which in fact persisted in many parts of the *sierra* although unrecognized by law and discouraged under four centuries of European domination. This Incan communism, he pointed out, was something quite different from the modern communism advocated by the Marxists. The first was an agrarian system which grew out of the needs of the country and the times. The second postulates modern industrialism as its basis.[30] The plan of the Peruvian state should be to regain the advantages of the pre-colonial economic system with whatever alterations a new time and new conditions should make necessary. The middle-class reformers who looked to Europe and the United States for models were disregarding the character of the population and the heritage of both the Incan and the Spanish economic systems which had determined the lines of national development. Such statements as those of Francisco García Calderón to the effect that Peru would advance as European immigration increased revealed that a foreign model was being followed which could not possibly function until the foreign population was imported and, possibly, the native Indian removed. Mariátegui did not believe that every native institution represented a backwardness which would have to be eliminated before Peru could take its place among modern nations.

One of Mariátegui's essays attacked another problem which was fairly general in Hispanic America at this time and since. The university, he said, had never been either a popular or a national institution and was in no way ministering to the regeneration he felt to be needed. "Spain left us an aristocratic, ecclesiastical, and literary concept of education."[31] The revolution introduced a temporary cult of egalitarianism which was held to apply to the creoles rather than to the Indians. Unfortunately, even this cult was of only temporary vogue. The Spanish idea of a classical and literary education for the few continued. As Dr. Manuel Vicente Villarán said, the Peruvians were a

[30]*Ibid.*, p. 63.
[31]Mariátegui, *op. cit.*, p. 89.

nation infected with the mania of old and decadent nations, the illness of talking and writing but not working. The educated Peruvian wished the calm, the peace, the security of a bureaucratic position in Lima—not the risks, the hardships, and the possible profits of pioneering in the jungle or the *sierra,* or the tumult and uncertainty of an active trade or business. Mariátegui called for a reform of the university to throw it open to the entire population of the country, Indian as well as white, to remove the exclusionist and aristocratic concept of education. The government of the university was to be divided between the state government and the students, instead of being left in the hands of the politico-professional group which was merely another segment of the ruling oligarchy.

The move for university reform gained a large popular following. In connection with this activity among the students themselves, Víctor Raúl Haya de la Torre first came to prominence. Many intellectuals agreed at least in part with the contentions made by Mariátegui. Even conservatives like Víctor Andrés Belaunde commented on the fact that the life of the university was divorced from that of the nation in general. He set it down to a "sad destiny which has caused our University to fill a professional purpose, and perhaps one of scientific snobbism, but not an educative purpose, much less to become an expression of the national consciousness."[32] The "sad destiny" mentioned by Belaunde was, in Mariátegui's opinion, the fact that the political and economic structure of the nation had remained that of the colony before it. Economic and political reorganization was necessary.

Mariátegui lacked the animus of his predecessor, González-Prada, in his study of the religious question. The epoch of the free-thinkers was past, he said. They had made a violent attack on the Church only to uphold another set of dogmas, those of orthodox atheism or rationalism.[33] The time had come to study religion calmly, merely as a social phenomenon. With his usual thoroughness he went back to the Incan religion which served him as a clue to the psychology of the people who still made up the bulk of the nation. In tracing the history of religion in Peru, he showed that the liberal revolt, resulting in separation of Church and State in most countries, had never come to Peru. The Church maintained its ancient privileges just as the lay

[32]Víctor Andrés Belaunde, *La vida universitaria* (Lima, 1919).
[33]Mariátegui, *op. cit.,* p. 141.

aristocrats had managed to keep their feudal rights during a century of republican life. Mariátegui showed no particular interest in religion as such, but felt that the Church as the largest of the land owners and as a recipient of taxation should be reduced to its proper sphere, a concern of its communicants only, playing no part in the economic or political scene.

The last problem discussed by Mariátegui was the apparent conflict of interests between the various regions of Peru under the centralized system of government which tied the whole nation to the wheels of the Lima chariot. He expressed his own views as a new interpretation of the resurgent federalism which plagued so many South American countries. Manuel Pardo, the founder of the Civilist party, had been the first since Revolutionary times to advance regionalism as a basic principle of government. Nicolás de Piérola, founder of the Democratic party, had accepted this same viewpoint: "Our diversity of races, languages, and climate, no less than the distances between our centers of population . . . call for the establishment of a federative form of government."[34] But as the Civilists enlarged their control over the government, they became more and more the partisans of centralism, as shown in the writings of Francisco García Calderón. The support of federalism was left to the several radical groups which developed in Peru after the revolution of 1895. Mariátegui, while sympathizing with the needs of the back country, did not consider strong local governments a solution, because they would merely increase the power of the local *gamonales* or local *caudillos*. Again, Mariátegui insisted that the liquidation of the whole feudal-capitalistic system was necessary for real reform.

The attack of Mariátegui on the state of the "reality" in Peru, bulwarked as it was by the economic and sociological thought of modern Europe, was a real challenge for the defenders of the *status quo*. As such, it had the effect of defining the lines and the grouping for intellectual and party conflict. It was not without its answer. One of the principal books accepting the challenge was *La realidad nacional* published in 1931 by Víctor Andrés Belaunde. This was a revised version of a book published by him in 1917. The new edition, directed at Mariátegui, was made as a reply to the "evident injustice" with which

[34] *Declaración de principios del Partido Demócrata* (Lima, 1897), p. 14.

Mariátegui had treated the generation to which Belaunde belonged. Belaunde felt that the work of Mariátegui represented mere emendations to the great masterpiece of Peruvian sociology, García Calderón's *Le Pérou Contemporain,* published in Paris in 1907. That work posed all the basic questions which would require generations to answer. To these, according to Belaunde, Mariátegui gave dogmatic answers of limited value. Belaunde denied the legitimacy of the exclusive application of the principles of the economic interpretation of history. He also denied the justice of Mariátegui's charges against Spain as a colonizing power. This amounted to little less than a restatement of the "Black Legend" which the more able students were far from accepting. He also defended Piérola's work in its historical setting and charged Mariátegui with "inexplicable silences" in regard to Leguía's activity. Belaunde himself had been exiled for his criticism of Leguía.[35]

This work represents a viewpoint less conservative than that of García Calderón, but one which defended the Church, Spanish institutions, and liberal-democratic institutions while accepting much of the other criticisms of Mariátegui. A work nearer to the viewpoint of Mariátegui himself, but failing to accept his extreme socialistic thesis, is the volume of interpretation by Jorge Basadre, *Peru: problema y posibilidad* (Lima, 1931) Basadre in his many writings represents what would seem to be a reasonable middle ground between Mariátegui's views and those of the defenders of the *status quo.*

It still remained for someone to use these ideas for the building of a political party. The link between the writers and thinkers and the vast illiterate mass of the underprivileged was constituted by Haya de la Torre and his associates. The phrase, "and his associates," is made because the lines of conflict and the grouping on the basis of common sympathies were already made among the leaders by the effect of the work of Mariátegui. The succession from the intermediate group of the *Colónida* is direct. As mentioned above Haya de la Torre first came to prominence in the move for university reform. Only four years younger than Mariátegui, Haya took the control of the student group in 1919 and 1920, thereby developing into a popular leader. In 1923 when Mariátegui returned from Europe he seconded Haya's protest against Leguía's purpose to dedicate the republic to the Sacred Heart of Jesus.

[35]Belaunde, *La realidad peruana,* p. 27 *et seq.*

In the disturbances taking place at this time a student and a workman were killed by the armed forces of the government. The funeral of the deceased student gave Haya the opportunity to make a glowing speech which did much to consolidate the group and to make himself the undisputed leader. When Leguía exiled him in consequence, he named Mariátegui his successor as director of the periodical *Claridad*. Mariátegui then directed the fight on the journalistic front until his death in 1930. Thus intimate was the connection between the two leaders.[36]

Haya de la Torre, while a man of action more than a writer and thinker, is not to be ignored in the second classification.[37] His major works: *Por la emancipacion de la América Latina* (1927), *El anti-imperialismo y el Apra* (1936), *¿Adónde va Indoamérica?* (1935), and others have the advantage of definiteness of program over earlier works, but together show more of the nature of a politician than that of a profound long-range thinker. The theme he emphasizes more than the preceding writers considered here is that of anti-imperialism which leads him also to consider the possibilities of international coöperation in behalf of the downtrodden in "Indo-America."

The spread of the catch-words of Aprismo and its basic ideas among a great mass of the Peruvian population between 1930, the fall of Leguía, and 1936 when it no doubt represented the desires of a majority of the population, has focused great attention on the moment. As a political movement it may have passed its peak. As a group of ideas and viewpoints, it represents the latest segment of a continuing development which dates back to the War of the Pacific at least. It is not the purpose of this paper to study the effects of Aprismo itself, but it may be noted in closing that the international effects of the movement may be nearly as important as the effects within Peru. There, while Aprismo has been generally defeated at the polls, it has caused all groups to pay attention to its basic viewpoints and to the aroused power of the Indian masses. By so doing, it may have served its historic purpose and prepared the way for a new generation of dissatisfied intellectuals whose political and economic panaceas may bear only slight resemblance to Aprismo.

[36]Samuel Guy Inman, *El destino de América latina* (Santiago de Chile, 1940), pp. 249 *et seq.* and Luis-Alberto Sánchez, *op. cit.*, p. 600.

[37]Luis-Alberto Sánchez has a biography of Haya, *Haya de la Torre o el político* (Santiago de Chile, 1934).

Some Effects of Population Growth on Latin America's Economy

BY ALFONSO GONZALEZ

The pressure of a rapidly expanding population is being exerted with increasing effect on the resource base of Latin America.

It is generally recognized that the major current problem of Latin America–transcending the purely political or social–is the need to increase production and average income at a faster rate than the unprecedented increase in the population itself. The difficulties inherent in accomplishing this task have been heightened by the impact of the so-called revolution of rising expectations, which has had the result that each individual of Latin America's exploding population demands more and more of both necessities and luxuries than he used to. The subsequent pressures derived from the interaction of these factors constitute a force that no Latin American government and no Latin American leader can ignore–especially since the patience of the Latin American masses now appears to be coming to an end. The foregoing is a possible source of revolution. No survey of Latin America's past, looking to its future, can omit some statement of this problem.

Dr. Alfonso Gonzalez, a geographer, formerly of the University of South Florida and now of the University of Calgary, Alberta, has written a succinct and quantitative statement of this situation. This unimpassioned, factual survey is useful for an assessment of the basic problem of Latin America today–how to feed and support Latin Americans whose rate of population growth continues to exceed the rate of economic growth, despite the efforts of local governments, the Alliance for Progress, and interested scientists and engineers.

R. E. M.

The stability of Latin America rests essentially on the solution of two interrelated problems—population growth and economic development. A further corollary, and an extremely significant one, will be the social distribution of the benefits accruing from economic betterment. Latin America is both the fastest growing world region in population and also the most advanced (in terms of the death rate, literacy, and per capita income) of the underdeveloped regions of the world. It is also the only region of the underdeveloped world that had evolved from political colonial status prior to World War II. This region, therefore, has had the longest history of endeavoring to solve directly many of the problems that plague the 70 per cent of mankind that lives in the underdeveloped countries. Since mortality is lower in Latin America than in the other underdeveloped regions, undoubtedly due to the earlier and more widespread application of modern medical technology, the rate of natural increase is higher in this region than elsewhere since birth rates vary less than death rates among underdeveloped regions. Latin America serves as a harbinger of conditions that will soon prevail in the other underdeveloped regions as the latter's mortality rates continue to decline. The pressure of population on resources will increase in all the underdeveloped regions because even in Latin America mortality continues to decline resulting in an ever-widening gap between births and deaths in the absence of significant fertility control.[1]

Population Growth

In mid-1965 the population estimate of Latin America was 248 million with a forecast for 1970 ranging from a low of 278 to a high (based on continuing demographic trends) of 284 million.[2] By 1980 the estimates range from 352 to 387 million and by the end of the century the population of Latin America may be between 514 and 756 million. The range of population estimates varies with the assumptions regarding the timing of declines in fertility because a

[1]The discussion on population in this paper is based on the assumption that there will be no nuclear war, general political disintegration, or spectacular fertility control technique.

[2]Population Reference Bureau, *Population Bulletin*, Vol. XXI, No. 4, October 1965.

continued trend in the decline of mortality is highly likely. The fundamental reason for this rapid increase in population is the same factor that has accounted for the rapid increase in the world's population since the advent of the industrial revolution, *viz.*, control of mortality. In the 1945-50 period the crude death rate (number of deaths per 1000 population) for Latin America was 17-19 and by 1955-60 it had declined to 13-15 and about 1962-63 the average of 17 Latin American countries was 10-11.[3] This represents an overall decline of approximately 40 per cent in the post-World War II period. Since the crude birth rate (number of births per 1000 population) has remained consistently high (41–43) the rate of population growth has increased from 2.5 per cent annually in the late 1940's to about 3 per cent in the 1960's (Table 1). At present growth rates the population of Latin America will double in less than a quarter century. The fastest growing world sub-region is undoubtedly mainland Middle America (with the Levant probably second) where every country in the 1958-64 period increased at least 3 per cent annually with a maximum (and the world leader) of 4.3 per cent in Costa Rica.

Improved health conditions have increased life expectancy over much of tropical Latin America to about 58 years and present-day trends, if projected to the end of the century, would increase this to 73 years (or approximately present-day levels in the advanced regions of the world). The Latin American infant mortality rate (number of deaths of infants less than one year of age per 1000 live births), which along with life expectancy at birth comprise the best indexes of health conditions, has improved from about 103 in the late 1940's to about 75 in the early 1960's.[4] The latter figure is still about three times greater than that prevailing in the United States and other advanced countries.

The differences in natality between Latin America and the other underdeveloped regions are rather insignificant, especially if the low fertility countries of Latin America (*viz.*, Argentina and Uruguay) are discounted. However, the mortality rate of Latin America overall is

[3]*Economic Bulletin for Latin America,* United Nations, Vol. VIII, No. 1 (October 1962). Statistical Bulletin.
Demographic Yearbook: 1963, United Nations, Table 19.

[4]Based on the average of 16 countries for both periods from the *Demographic Yearbook: 1963,* Table 22.

from one-third to perhaps one-half less than in the Afro-Asian regions. This differential accounts for Latin America's greater rate of population growth. The Afro-Asian underdeveloped regions are increasing at about 2 per cent annually or slightly less, but Latin America is increasing at about 3 per cent. Current Afro-Asian mortality rates prevailed in Latin America during the 1940's. Mortality in Latin America began to decline slowly about 1920, with the post-World War I health programs, but declined precipitously with World War II programs and the decrease was especially marked during the 1950's. The decline in mortality was most significant among the younger age groups due to the application of programs combating infectious diseases and malnutrition (especially among children).

The factors lying behind the high fertility of Latin America are readily apparent: (a) the large family is an ingrained trait of the national ethos, (b) women in reproductive ages represent a relatively high proportion of the total population, (c) women enter consensual union at an early age, (d) a large percentage of women are married (either legally or by common-law) (Latin America has the highest illegitimacy rate in the world), and (e) (most importantly) the general absence of family planning—even among the urban and better educated sectors of the population.

The rate of population growth in the near future will be at least as great as at present because of the presumed continued decline in mortality over practically all of Latin America. Fertility, on the other hand, is only under effective control in Argentina and Uruguay, with incipient decline discernible in Chile and Cuba.

Demographic Consequences

There are a number of demographic consequences of considerable importance to economic development resulting from past and present population characteristics. These features are also to be found in the other underdeveloped world regions. One of these consequences is the youthful age composition of the population resulting from high natality. Slightly more than two-fifths of the population is younger than 15 years of age but due to relatively high mortality only about 3 per cent of the population is older than 65. The net result is that only about 55 per cent of the population of Latin America is in the economically productive ages, *i.e.,* 15-64, in contrast to about 60-65 per cent in the developed countries. Only in Argentina and Uruguay, where birth rates have been less than 30 since the 1940's, are about two-thirds of the

TABLE 1

LATIN AMERICA: POPULATION CHARACTERISTICS[1]

	Pop 1964 (*m*)	*Annual Inc* 1958-64 (%)	*Birth Rate* (*cis*-1960)	*Death Rate* (*cis*-1960)	*Inf Mort*[2] *Rate* (*cis*-1960)	*Est Pop* 1980 (*m*)
Mexico	39.6	3.1	45.0	10.4	67.7	70.6
Guatemala	4.1	3.2	47.7	17.3	92.8	6.99
El Salvador	2.8	3.6	48.6	10.8	65.5	4.6
Honduras	2.1	3.0	45-50	15-20	47.0	3.7
Nicaragua	1.6	3.5	45-52	12-17	53.9	2.8
Costa Rica	1.4	4.3	49.9	8.5	77.6	2.4
Panama	1.2	3.3	40.1	8.0[2]	42.9	2.0
Cuba	7.3	2.0	30-34	9-13	41.8	10.0
Dominican Republic	3.5	3.6	48-54	16-20	79.5	6.2
Haiti	4.5	2.2	45-52[2]	21.6[2]	171.6	6.9
Venezuela	8.4	3.4	45-50	10-15	47.9	14.9
Colombia	15.4	2.2	43-46	14-17	88.2	27.7
Ecuador	4.8	3.2	45-50	15-20	95.6	8.0
Peru	11.9	3.0	42-48	13-18	94.8	17.5
Bolivia	3.7	1.5	41-45	20-25	86.0[a]	6.0
Paraguay	1.9	2.4	45-50	12-16	98.0[b]	3.0
Chile	8.4	2.4	34.2	11.8	111.0	12.4
Argentina	21.7	1.6	21.8	7.9	60.7	29.0
Uruguay	2.6	1.4[2c]	21-25	7-9	47.4	3.1
Brazil	79.8	3.0	43-47	11-16	170[d]	123.7
LATIN AMERICA	226.8	2.9[3]	41-43[2]	13-14[2]		361.4

[1]*World Population Data Sheet.* Population Reference Bureau. December 1964.
[2]*Demographic Yearbook, 1964* and *1963.*
[3]*Statistical Bulletin for Latin America.* United Nations. Vol. II, No. 2 (August 1965). Table 1.

[a]1959.
[b]1945–49.
[c]1958–62.
[d]1940–50.

population in the productive ages. In Cuba and Chile, where fertility is intermediate between the typical high levels prevailing in Latin America and the low levels of Argentina and Uruguay, slightly less than three-fifths of the population is in the productive ages. In the remaining countries the proportion is 55 per cent or less. The result is that in most Latin American countries only about one-third of the population is economically active whereas in the developed countries of the world the proportion is 40–45 per cent. Thereby, the dependency ratio (number of persons dependent upon each thousand of the economically productive age population) is higher in Latin America (and underdeveloped countries generally) than it is in the developed regions. Even more critical is that the dependency ratio in Latin America will actually increase from a 1960 level of 815 (compared with about 500-650 in developed countries) to 890-940 by 1975.[5]

A further demographic handicap that Latin America is facing, and it will become increasingly even more severe in the near future, is that increasingly larger groups of males will enter the labor force and that employment opportunities must be provided. In the period 1965–70 the proportion of males in the Latin American population will increase by 15-20 per cent since more than three times as many males will be entering the labor force as leaving it. At present more than 1.6 million males are entering the labor force every year and unless the economy can absorb them they constitute a potential for political instability.

The youthful structure of the population virtually ensures a continued high rate of population increase in the near future. By 1975 there will be 50-60 per cent more women in the child-bearing ages than in 1960 so that unless social patterns change significantly by that time the absolute population growth (as well as the rate of growth) will be prodigious.

Population Pressure on Resources

The pressure of a rapidly expanding population is being exerted with increasing effect on the resource base of Latin America. This pressure of absolute numerical increase is being compounded by the revolution

[5]Irene B. Taeuber, "Population Growth in Latin America: Paradox of Development," *Population Bulletin,* Vol. XVIII, No. 6 (October 1962).

in rising expectations that is sweeping Latin America. The demand for a better livelihood now is augmenting the rising demand due to demographic increase and the combination of these two elements is severely straining the limited resources, in view of the technological level applied, of an already politically unstable region.

The rate of economic expansion in Latin America overall varies significantly according to sectors and Latin America does not compare favorably with the rate of economic development in the underdeveloped world generally (Table 2). The one major category in which Latin America clearly excels is in the rate of population growth and this, obviously, has a detrimental effect in terms of production increments on a per capita basis.

TABLE 2

POPULATION AND ECONOMIC INDEXES: 1963[1]
(1958=100)

	Latin America	*Underdeveloped Regions*	*Developed Regions*	*World*
Population	114	110	106	109
Agriculture[2]	116	117[a]	110[a]	111
Industry	128	149	136	137
Manufacturing	129	141	137	138
Mining	124	172	112	127
Energy: Production	133	151	120	126
Consumption	134	147	124	127
Foreign Trade	111	122	148	142

[1]*Statistical Yearbook: 1964,* United Nations, Table 12 and computations from Tables 3, 160, 130.

[2]*The World Agricultural Situation: Review of 1965 and Outlook for 1966,* Foreign Agricultural Economic Report No. 28, U.S. Dept. of Agriculture, Table 1.

[a]Approximate (computed); "underdeveloped regions" excludes Communist Asia.

Agriculture. Population pressure on available resources in Latin America is most critically apparent in agriculture. Although the density of population based on cultivated land for Latin America is comparable to that for the world (332 inhabitants per square kilometer of cultivated land in 1962 compared with the world average of 340), this relatively low figure for Latin America is due essentially to low densities prevailing in the three leading agricultural countries of the region (Brazil, Mexico, and Argentina). The median density for Latin America (479-500) is between one-third and one-half greater than the world average and this density is exceeded by few of the major agricultural countries of the world (*viz.*, Japan, United Kingdom, West Germany, United Arab Republic, China, Indonesia, East Germany, and the Philippines).[6]

The actual pressure of population on the cultivated land in Latin America becomes even clearer if consideration is given to the yields obtained from the land under cultivation. Although the yields obtained in Latin America are fairly high by the standards of the underdeveloped world (only the Orient, of the latter, exceeds Latin America in yields), Latin American yields are below the world average and are only about 50–60 per cent of those obtained in the more advanced world regions. The net result is that the number of inhabitants per unit of arable land (and giving weight to yields) in Latin America is about comparable to that of the Middle East and these two regions are exceeded only by the Orient among the world's regions.

The cropland-yield densities (Table 3) prevailing in virtually all the Latin American countries (the notable exceptions are Argentina and Brazil) are considerably above the average. In four Latin American countries (Haiti, Bolivia, Nicaragua, and Peru) the cropland-yield density exceeds that of the most dense of the major agricultural countries of the world (Sudan: 791). An additional eight Latin American countries have a density exceeding that of the tenth leading major world country (Pakistan: 521). It therefore seems clear that at present, population pressure on agricultural productivity in Latin America already is formidable.

Agricultural development is being given considerable attention widely in Latin America and one very fundamental reason why this must be so is in order to cope with the rapidly expanding population. In

[6]Major agricultural countries are here defined as those having more than 5 million hectares of arable land according to the *Production Yearbook: 1963*, Food and Agriculture Organization of the United Nations, Table 1. The countries of sub-Saharan Africa (except South Africa) are excluded because of the incompleteness of data regarding cultivated land.

TABLE 3
WORLD REGIONS: COMPARATIVE POPULATION & AGRICULTURE DATA (1962)*

	Population (m)	*Arable Land (m ha)*	*Arable Land Density*[a]	*Cereal Yields (100 kg/ha)*[b]	*Arable Yield Density*[c]
Latin America	224.1	103	218	12.67	251
Middle East	190.5	113	169	9.74	253
Orient	1,645.5	383	429	13.82	451
Africa (Sub-Saharan)	178.1	207	86	7.93	158
Europe	432.5	153	283	20.84	198
USSR	221.5	230	96	10.99	127
Anglo-America	205.3	227	90	24.43	54
Oceania	16.5	34	49	12.25	58
WORLD	3,114.0	1,449	215	14.60	215

*Based on data from *FAO Production Yearbook: 1963.*
[a]Number of inhabitants per square kilometer of arable land.
[b]Average for 1961–63, except for U.S.S.R. and Orient which are for 1961–62.
[c]Figure for "Arable Land Density" is divided by ratio of the region's cereal yields to the world cereal yields.

addition, the rising expectations of greater food consumption and the necessities for greater export surplus in order to secure foreign exchange to further economic development also give rise to serious pressures on agriculture for increased productivity. Broadly speaking, increased productivity is being achieved in Latin America by increasing both cultivated land and yields, with the former more significant.

The area devoted to the major crops in Latin America increased overall between the 1948-52 period and 1962-63 by one-third (32.3 per cent, which was somewhat less than the overall population increment (38.3 per cent) for the same period.[7] The improvement in agricultural yields overall in Latin America was relatively small during

[7]Cultivated area is based on summation of area cultivated for all crops given in the *FAO Production Yearbook: 1963*. Some significant crops are excluded from the totals (because areas are not given), *viz.*, the deciduous mid-latitude fruits, citrus, the palms, and some tropical fruits. The population estimates are also those provided by the same FAO source (Table 3).

TABLE 4
LATIN AMERICA: ECONOMIC CHARACTERISTICS

	% of econ. act. pop. in agric. (c1950-60)	Cropland-Yield Density[2]	Calories per capita[3] (1959-61)	Income per capita[4] (1961, $)	GDP Growth Rate[5] (c1960-63)	Agric. Prod. 1964[3] 1958 = 100 Total	Per Capita	Mfg. Prod.[6] 1963-64 1958 = 100
Mexico	54	428	2,580	415	4.9	183	131	162
Guatemala	68	629	1,970	258	4.8	196	142	123
El Salvador	60	614	2,000	268		203	150	152
Honduras	66	448	2,330	252	5.4	162	117	
Nicaragua	68	868	2,190	288	10.8	226	166	134
Costa Rica	55	583	2,520	362		119	78	
Panama	46	753	2,370	371	8.1	144	104	
Cuba	42	445	2,730	516	9.0[7]	86	68	
Dominican Repbulic	56	582	2,020	313		144	99	
Haiti	83	2,684	1,780	149		104	83	
Venezuela	32	768	2,330	645	4.0	176	117	175
Colombia	54	630	2,280	373	5.0	135	99	141
Ecuador	53	626	2,100	223	3.7	195	138	
Peru	46[8]	827	2,060	269	6.7	136	105	154
Bolivia	72	992	2,010	122		160	125	
Paraguay	54	564	2,400	193	3.6	117	92	92[a]
Chile	28	488	2,610	453	5.8	122	95	146
Argentina	19	179	3.220	799	Œ0.1	122	101	107
Uruguay		430	3,030	561		110	92	98
Brazil	58	303	2,710	375	4.7	131	94	147
LATIN AMERICAz	47[4]	382	2,570	421	3.6[7]	133	98	129

[1] *FAO Production Yearbook*, 1963, Table 5a.

[a] 1961.

[2] Number of inhabitants per square kilometer of cropland divided by the ratio of cereal yields obtained to the average world cereal yields. Cropland computed from the summation of crop data available in *FAO Production Yearbook*, 1963.

[3] *The* 1965 *Western Hemisphere Agricultural Situation*, ERS-Foreign 113, U.S. Dept. of Agriculture, Tables 5, 1, 2.

[4] *The Economic Development of Latin America in the Post-War Period*, United Nations, 1964. Tables 51, 26.

[5] *Yearbook of National Accounts Statistics:* 1964. United Nations, Part D, Table 4B.

[6] *Statistical Bulletin for Latin America*, Vol. II, No. 2, Table 19.

[7] *Economic Survey of Latin America:* 1963, Economic Commission for Latin America (UN), Tables 257, 6.

[8] Approximate; based on *Statistical Bulletin for Latin America*, Vol. II, No. 1, Table 3.

the 1950's. The yield for maize only increased by about one-eighth between the periods 1948-52 and 1960-62 with only a slightly greater relative increase for wheat, the second crop in cultivated area in Latin America. In contrast, in the same period the yields for both crops in the United States increased by one-half and in Europe maize yields increased by more than two-thirds and wheat by one-third. Generally, the greatest improvements in agricultural yields in the post-World War II period have occurred in the more advanced regions of the world. The net result is that Latin America's maize yields have declined relatively from 67 per cent of the world's average in the 1948-52 period to 58 per cent in 1960-62.

The endeavor to increase yields can be measured by the notable increase in commercial fertilizer consumption in Latin America. The use of nitrate, phosphate, and potash fertilizers more than doubled during the 1950's in Latin America. The production, however, of commercial fertilizer in Latin America remains insignificant (by world standards) and occurs only in Chile, Peru, Mexico, and Brazil. The use of commercial fertilizers is still abysmally low in Latin America compared with the more advanced regions, especially since the increase in fertilizer consumption in the latter regions is almost as great as in Latin America. So that West Germany, with only about one-twelfth the cultivated area of Latin America, uses about one and one-half the nitrates, more than double the phosphates, and about five times the potash that Latin America does. The same holds true for the mechanization of agriculture. The number of tractors in Latin America nearly tripled during the 1950's (a slower rate than Europe) yet Canada with only about a quarter of Latin America's cultivated area has appreciably more tractors.

The combined increase in cultivated area and improvement in yields has resulted in a notable increase in crop production during the 1950's in Latin America. Between the 1948-52 and 1960-62 periods maize production overall increased by three-fifths and comparable or greater relative increments in production occurred for bananas, coffee, cotton, rice, the oilseeds, and the palms. With regard to livestock numbers in Latin America, only swine have increased faster than the human population and meat production overall has fallen drastically behind in per capita output.

The net result is that overall net agricultural production between the early 1950's and the 1960's increased in Latin America by one-third.[8] This exceeds the increment for Anglo-America, both Western and Eastern Europe, and the Middle East. In this period there were nine Latin American countries in which the overall increment was one-half or greater. This prodigious increase would represent an average annual increment of 3.7 per cent or greater in agricultural production (the average for the 20 republics was 2.6 per cent).[9] Of the major Latin American countries Mexico exhibited the greatest average annual increment (6.4 per cent) and would rank among the world's leaders in the rate of agricultural expansion. In comparison, the average annual increment in the United States during the war periods when governmental policies encouraged augmented production was less than 3 per cent.[10] In only one country (Cuba) did agricultural production actually decline during the period and Haiti and Uruguay increased production by only 5 per cent overall.

Despite the overall rapid expansion of agricultural production during the 1950's and early 1960's, the agricultural sector has only been able to maintain parity with population growth during the period. Therefore, in 1964 food production per capita in Latin America overall was little different from that of the 1952-54 period.[11] No underdeveloped region is performing so poorly in agricultural output with reference to population growth as is Latin America. The fundamental reason is that population growth is more rapid in Latin America than elsewhere so that agricultural output improvements are instantaneously eroded away by further population increases.

Several Latin American countries have sustained a significant

[8]*The 1965 World Agricultural Situation,* Foreign Agriculture Economic Report No. 22, U.S. Department of Agriculture.

The 1965 Western Hemisphere Agricultural Situation.

[9]The overall figure of 2.6 per cent annual increment for Latin America is undoubtedly too low because 1964 was a poor crop year (especially in South America) so that if either 1963 or the preliminary figures for 1965 (*The World Agricultural Situation:* Review of 1965 and Outlook for 1966, Table 1) is used instead of 1964 then the overall rate of agricultural production increased from 1952–54 to the 1960's by about 3.1 per cent annually.

[10]*Foreign Agriculture,* Foreign Agricultural Service, U.S. Dept. of Agriculture, III, No. 50 (December 13, 1965), 4.

[11]However, if either 1963 or the preliminary 1965 production figures are used, per capita output would have been 3 per cent greater than in the early 1950's (an insignificant increase).

reduction in per capita food production during this period and the situation is most acute in Cuba, Costa Rica, El Salvador, Haiti, and Paraguay, and only somewhat better in Chile, Peru, and Uruguay. The greatest relative improvements (despite large population increments) have occurred in Mexico, Ecuador, Venezuela, and Bolivia.

The pressure of population can be seen in the more rapid increments accruing to crop and livestock production in Latin America destined for domestic consumption rather than for the export market.[12] This has necessitated a curtailment of the expansion of the export trade and constitutes a serious problem for Latin America's further economic development.[13] This lagging sector restricts the accumulation of necessary foreign exchange and presents serious balance-of-payments problems to a number of countries (especially Argentina, Colombia, and Uruguay).

In comparing the periods 1956-58 and 1959-61, eleven Latin American nations had a reduced caloric content in food availability per capita and one evidenced no change. Seven of the above countries (Haiti, Guatemala, El Salvador, Dominican Republic, Nicaragua, Colombia, and Panama) were below the level regarded by the U.S. Department of Agriculture as calorie-deficient (*i.e.,* 2400 calories daily).[14] In addition to these seven there were an additional five countries that had less than 2400 calories per capita in the 1959–61 period (Table 4). Undoubtedly, Cuba must now be added to the food-deficit countries of Latin America. Only in Uruguay and Argentina is the food consumption level comparable to that of the more advanced regions of the world. Overall for Latin America the daily caloric consumption is probably slightly in excess of 2500 calories which would represent a deficiency of about 500–600 calories daily per capita compared to Anglo-America or Western Europe. With the existing socio-political instability of the region it is questionable how long Latin America will be able to endure such food consumption levels (especial-

[12]*Economic Survey of Latin America: 1963,* Chapter III.

[13]"Latin America at Mid-Decade," *Latin American Business Highlights.* XV, No. 3 (Third Quarter, 1965), 8–9.

[14]*The 1965 Western Hemisphere Agricultural Situation,* pp. 3, 57. A daily caloric consumption of only 2400 calories would appear insufficient in view of the 3000 calories or more consumed in Anglo-America, Western Europe, European Oceania, and even in Argentina and Uruguay.

ly in view of the rate of population growth) without serious political upheavals.

Industry. The pressure of population growth on industrial output (mining, manufacturing, and utilities) is both less critical and less urgent in Latin America. This sector is growing appreciably faster than the population and, since large segments of the peoples of Latin America are in basically subsistence or local economies, the necessities of food are of more overriding immediate importance than the access to very high rate of expansion in order to ensure employment for the manufactured goods. However, the industrial sector must maintain a rapidly increasing population. Traditionally, Latin America (like other underdeveloped regions) has been basically agricultural, with about three-fifths of the economically active population in the pre-World War II period engaged in agriculture. However, the proportion had declined to 56 per cent overall for Latin America by 1945 and 1955 agriculture was exceeded by the non-agricultural sectors.[15] In 1960 the non-agricultural sectors accounted for 53 per cent of the economically active population. Since World War II the agricultural labor force has only been increasing at one-half the overall rate for the total economically active population. With the agricultural sector, therefore, declining relatively and with the labor force increasing annually by nearly two million (about one-fifth being females) in the early 1960's, the burden of employment falls increasingly on the industrial sectors of the economy, especially manufacturing. It is questionable how long the Latin American economies can sustain a relatively high proportion engaged in the services with a relatively small industrial base.

As is the case with the economically active population, so the sector origins of the gross domestic product (GDP) reflect a decreasing share being contributed by agriculture and the opposite trend for manufacturing and (to a much smaller degree) mining. In fact, the latter two activities (along with perhaps services) are the only sectors that have rather steadily increased significantly their share of the GDP in Latin America overall from 1950 to 1963.[16] In Latin America over-

[15]*The Economic Development of Latin America in the Post-War Period,* Table 23.

[16]*Economic Survey of Latin America: 1963,* Table 17.

all the manufacturing sector exceeded the agricultural beginning in the late 1950's. Manufacturing already contributes a greater share of the GDP than agriculture in Chile, Argentina, Venezuela, Cuba, and Mexico (and almost surely Uruguay). In both Brazil and Peru manufacturing had almost reached parity with agriculture by 1963.

The industrial sector has been expanding faster in Latin America than the agricultural. Whereas the agricultural sector of the GDP increased overall in Latin America by slightly more than 3 per cent annually during the 1950's and 1960–63, the manufacturing sector expanded by 6.4 per cent annually during the 1950's and 3.8 per cent in the early 1960's–even slightly higher rates prevailed for mining. Of the 13 Latin American countries for which data are available, all countries had a more rapid rate of industrial expansion than agricultural growth during both the 1950's and early 1960's except Paraguay in the 1950's and Panama, Ecuador, Guatemala, and Venezuela for the early 1960's, with Peru exhibiting equal growth rates in the latter period.[17] Due to the appreciably greater growth rate, the industrial sector in Latin America has been in a much more favorable circumstance with regard to population than is true of agriculture. During the 1950's only Paraguay (of the 13 countries for which data was available) did not attain at least parity between industrial expansion and population growth and in the 1960–63 period only Argentina failed to expand industrially at a rate comparable to demographic increase.

Social Services. Improvement in social services has been an important cornerstone of the Alliance for Progress and a change in U.S. policy about 1958 has resulted in considerably expanding social services in Latin America. The betterment of social services can help ameliorate existing conditions should some sector of the economy falter in its developmental plans.

The pressure of population growth, however, aggravates existing pressures on the already meager social services in Latin America. Notable material progress has been made in recent years in education, housing, and public health. Education now accounts for 18 per cent of national budgets overall and public health between 10–15 per cent.

[17] *Yearbook of National Accounts Statistics: 1964,* Part D, Table 4B.

Also many new housing units have been constructed in Latin America due to public, private, and Alliance efforts. The infant mortality rate (probably the best gauge for determining existing medical and health conditions) may have declined by one-quarter between the late 1940's and early 1960's but still remains three or perhaps four times greater than that prevailing in the advanced countries of the world. It may take another decade and a half (or more) for most Latin American countries to attain the level prevailing now in Puerto Rico (40-45 infant deaths per 1000 live births), which is quite comparable to the non-white population of the United States. Few Latin American countries are in that category now (Table 1) but in the 1930's Puerto Rico's infant mortality rate (132 in 1932) was typical of Latin America. Improvements in sanitation and potable water supplies, the anti-malarial campaigns, health clinics, and other public health measures are undoubtedly having their effect on reducing mortality and, thereby, increasing population totals. But nutritional problems are of a different nature because a fundamental improvement in agriculture is necessary, despite the Food for Peace programs. The latter must increase considerably in the future to keep pace with population growth (not to mention improvement in the per capita food consumption), but U.S. domestic policy and foreign assistance have notably decreased the available surplus food stocks in the United States.

Considerable expansion of the educational facilities in Latin America has also occurred in recent years. In a recent OAS survey of 15 Latin American countries the elementary school enrollment increased from 18.5 million in 1960 to 22.7 million in 1964.[18] However, the elementary school age population of those 15 republics in that four-year period increased by approximately 4 million so that most of the expansion represents population increments. In 1964 about 42 per cent of elementary school children in Latin America were not attending classes. The deficit in higher education is also critical. Latin America has a population one-fifth larger than that of the United States but has less than a fourth of the students attending universities and advanced technical teaching centers.

[18]*Alliance for Progress Weekly Newsletter,* Pan American Union, January 31, 1966. The five Latin American nations not included in the study were Mexico, Cuba, the Dominican Republic, El Salvador, and Uruguay.

A substantial housing deficit also exists in Latin America–probably about 15.5 million units and the housing shortage has been increasing since 1950 although during the early 1960's the rate of deterioration was slowed.[19] The annual rate of new housing construction (for the few countries for which data are available) represents only about one-half of 1 per cent of existing housing units and far below the 2-3 per cent construction rate that characterizes the advanced countries (the latter also have far slower rates of population growth). The net result is that the combining of poor existing housing conditions with the rapidly expanding population (especially in urban centers) creates a virtually insurmountable gap between the needs of attaining adequate housing facilities and actual accomplishments. Approximately 3.3 million units must be constructed annually during the balance of this decade and probably only a small fraction of this is actually being constructed (there is insufficient data on building activity).

Alternative Policies and Outlook

During 1964 and 1965 the Alliance for Progress recorded more significant material advances than in the earlier years of its operations. In both those years the Alliance objective of an annual increment of per capita product of 2.5 per cent was achieved for Latin America overall despite an annual population growth of 2.9 per cent.[20] Two major Latin American countries, Argentina and Brazil, that have had recent difficulties maintaining an adequate growth rate improved very significantly in 1965. Most of the remaining major countries of Latin America (Mexico, Peru, Venezuela, and Chile) are expanding economically at a satisfactory rate according to Alliance standards. Apparently the only countries encountering serious problems in the Alliance (resulting from both internal and external causes) in 1965 were Colombia, Costa Rica, Ecuador, Paraguay, and Uruguay. Under the stimulus of the Alliance, central planning agencies have now been established in all Latin American countries with the Inter-American Committee on the Alliance (CIAP) as a multilateral supervisory

[19]*Economic Survey of Latin America: 1963,* Chapter VII.
Alliance for Progress Weekly Newsletter, November 15 and December 6, 1965.
[20]*Alliance for Progress Weekly Newsletter,* August 16, 1965 and January 24, 1966.

organization. Industrial growth overall appears to continue at a very satisfactory rate of expansion with Mexico achieving a 12.9 per cent increment in 1965, one of the highest rates in the world. Agriculture, however, continues as a major problem area despite a significant production increase in 1965 over the relatively poor harvest of 1964. Despite nearly a 12 per cent increase in agricultural output since the Alliance began in 1961, 11 Latin American countries had lower per capita food production in 1965 than a decade earlier.

The major endeavor of Latin American countries is to improve the livelihood of their inhabitants and with this objective in mind the various governments, with varying degrees of U.S. and international assistance, are attempting to utilize domestic resources more fully to further socioeconomic development. Two general approaches or programs are available to Latin America (and to the other underdeveloped regions as well) in their process of development: (1) increased productivity (including the application of improved technology)—the objective is to expand and improve the economic base in order to increase the volume of output of goods and services; and (2) population control—the objective is to restrict population so that per capita output will rise more rapidly and increasing productivity will not be nullified by population increases. Up to the present, Latin America has relied almost exclusively on increasing productivity and the application of improved technology as the solution to the problem of living conditions, although it would appear from recent developments that the role of population control may take on added importance.

Increased Productivity. Latin America continues to rely on the expansion of the economic base and the application of improved and more advanced methods in order to augment per capita output and, thereby, to raise the levels of living. Agriculture remains a serious impediment to rapid economic development despite significant increments in production. Much of the increase in agricultural output has been from the increase in cultivated area rather than from higher yields. In the case of maize, by far Latin America's leading crop (accounting for almost one-third of the total cultivated area), about nine-tenths of the augmented production between the 1948-52 and 1960-62 periods is attributable to the increased cultivated area. How long Latin America will be able to expand output in this fashion is questionable but increasing rural pressure on the land will force ever more farmers onto marginal and submarginal lands or into the already overcongested urban centers. Between 1950 and 1960 the urban population of Latin America increased by 5.3 per cent annually and represents one of the most rapidly urbanizing areas on earth. In 1965 the urban population of Latin America probably exceeded the rural for the first time.

Food output is currently about keeping pace with population growth and there may be increasing demands in the near future for higher levels of consumption from the 2500 calories daily per capita presently available. The crux of the problem remains: to increase land and labor productivity, and this will require considerable outlays of capital and rural credit facilities for improved seed, fertilizers, pesticides, irrigation projects, and the like, along with more widespread training of farmers in the more advanced techniques. The incentives under present conditions are inadequate to effectuate large-scale improvements due to fluctuating world commodity prices, heavy indirect taxation of agriculture, direct and indirect governmental price controls, and, the most serious of all, the land tenure system. As of about 1950, only 1.5 per cent of Latin American farms accounted for nearly two-thirds (64.9 per cent) of the total farmland while nearly three-quarters (72.6 per cent) of the farms contained only 3.7 per cent of all farmland.[21] The agrarian problem in Latin America involves both attendant problems of latifundia and minifundia. The overall changes of the land tenure system since 1950 are insignificant because, despite recent or planned legislation in twelve Latin American countries, little land has actually been redistributed.

Rural conditions contribute in a major way to the mass migrations into Latin American cities, especially the larger centers. This reduces the agricultural labor supply (in a region where mechanization is not widespread), places greater strain on the remaining farmers to supply the rapidly increasing urban population, and creates serious employment problems in the most politically explosive environment, the cities.

Agricultural output is also closely tied to another major problem

[21]Thomas F. Carroll, "The Land Reform Issue in Latin America," *Latin American Issues: Essays and Comments,* edited by Albert O. Hirschman (New York: 20th Century Fund, 1961).

sector of the Latin American economy–foreign trade. Overall foreign trade has not expanded as fast as population growth and Latin America's share of world trade has been gradually declining. The export market must expand rapidly in order to sustain a rising import demand of capital equipment so necessary for any further development. Production of agricultural commodities must thereby increase sufficiently to satisfy both the growing domestic market and the necessities of exportation.

Industrial growth appears to present less of a pressing problem although there is doubt whether this sector can expand fast enough to provide employment opportunities for the very rapidly expanding urban populace. Inadequate supplies of capital, skilled labor, raw materials, and restricted local markets will also present problems. However, governmental emphasis in development in Latin America is most frequently oriented toward industrialization and four-fifths of all U.S. direct investments are in the industrial sector (notably mining). Expansion of industrial output will also place increasing pressure on raw material production and also restrict the export trade further.

Two basic requirements necessary for the rapid increase in productivity are capital and education, and the latter is dependent (in large part) on the former. There are various sources of capital available for Latin America and all are used to varying degrees: (a) domestic savings, (b) foreign trade, (c) foreign investments, and (d) foreign assistance.

Domestic savings have traditionally been the major source of investment funds in Latin America but this source has been expanding inadequately. The annual per capita income in Latin America in 1961 was only $421 and income distribution is markedly uneven. For those countries where data are available, the top 5 per cent of the population in income account for at least one-quarter to nearly two-fifths of the total national income (in contrast to about one-fifth in the United States where income distribution is hardly ideal). The rate of fixed capital formation in most Latin American countries is 13-18 per cent and this probably is as high as can be expected considering the existing levels of living and the socioeconomic structure. The encouragement of domestic savings is seriously hampered by the fact that on a regional basis Latin America has the highest rate of inflation on earth. Although very modest tax reforms have been passed in several Latin American countries resulting in the improvement of tax collections, there still is a considerable flight of local capital to the United States and Europe. As a result, in 1964 Latin American investments in the United States alone amounted to $5.5 billion and have been increasing at a faster rate than U.S. investments in Latin America.[22]

As indicated previously, the export market has not been expanding at a very satisfactory rate to warrant encouragement for expanded sources of capital from this source in the near future.

Since Castro's accession to power, foreign investment (probably four-fifths is that of the United States) in Latin America has been disappointing and in some years U.S. direct investments have withdrawn more funds from Latin America (*e.g.*, net outflow of $32 million in 1962) than have been invested. However, U.S. investments began a very modest improvement in 1963. Latin America since the 1950's has become an increasingly less significant region for U.S. direct investments accounting for only one-fifth of the world total in 1964 (in contrast to more than one-third in 1957).

Since 1959 the annual flow of U.S. direct investments into Latin America has averaged less than one-third the Alliance objective and in 1964 it had only reached about one-half the annual target of $300 million. Consequently, U.S. assistance has become that much more important to Latin America. Economic assistance to Latin America has increased appreciably both absolutely and relatively since 1960 and amounted to more than $600 million (more than one-quarter of the world total) in 1964. This aid is concentrated in Brazil (more than one-quarter of Latin America's total) with significant proportions to Chile, Colombia, and Bolivia. However, net U.S. assistance to Latin America has been declining steadily since 1961 and more than one-tenth of this net aid is military.

Fundamental changes in long-range productivity and lessening of sociopolitical pressures due to existing conditions could be effectuated by basic structural reforms, *viz.*, agrarian reform, effective progressive tax structure, social welfare programs for redistribution of wealth, and drastic curtailment of military expenditures (one-tenth to more than one-quarter of the national budgets of practically all Latin American

[22]Samuel Pizer and Frederick Cutler, "Foreign Investments 1964–65," *Survey of Current Business,* U.S. Dept. of Commerce, XLV, No. 9 (September 1965).

countries). Some of these measures were the founding principles of the Alliance when originally conceived in 1961 but in recent years they have been relegated to a very minor role indeed.

The net overall result is that in endeavoring to follow a course of relying almost entirely upon increased productivity for the solution to its serious problem of raising levels of living and absorbing a rapidly expanding population, Latin America is beset with difficulties of the greatest magnitude. All of the pressures described above are manifested in an increasing sociopolitical instability that has already brought about serious repercussions for individual Latin American countries, the United States, and the OAS.

Population Control. The other major alternative that has virtually been unutilized in Latin America is the control of fertility (except for Argentina and Uruguay, with Chile and Cuba demonstrating a transitional stage). With the population now increasing at 2.9 per cent annually, and the prospect that the rate will increase still further with the additional reductions of mortality which appear inevitable, the pressure on available resources (despite notable economic development) is considerable and will undoubtedly increase. Barring some "miraculous" birth control device, it does not seem feasible that Latin America would be able to reduce its fertility significantly before the 1980's or 1990's and by 1980 (assuming declining fertility —which at present does not appear likely) the population of Latin America will be more than 40 per cent greater than in 1965. The Puerto Rican example, which may not be valid for Latin America generally, demonstrates that the birth rate could be reduced by one-quarter from a 1945-49 level of about 40 (equaled or exceeded currently by all Latin American countries save four) to 30 by 1963–64.

Several countries of the Orient, faced with basically the same problem and the limited alternatives, have recently begun active operating programs in the field of family planning. Because of the Latin American ethos, including religious considerations, this alternative has not yet had widespread discussion in the region, let alone support. As of 1964 family planning clinics were operating in only eight Latin American countries, but by 1965 fourteen countries had some family planning services. However, President Fernando Belaúnde Terry of Peru may have been the first Latin American chief executive to recognize publicly the formidable problem that population growth poses when he established a center for demographic study in December of 1964. The Agency for International Development (AID) had recently expanded its operations and assistance in the field of population planning although it still cannot make unsolicited recommendations and proposals. Also, numerous private organizations have been active in this field of Latin America.

Governments have endeavored to avoid this approach so far, and although the attitude of the Roman Catholic Church on mechanical and chemical methods of birth control is well known, it still must definitively state its position on oral contraceptives. There is no question that Latin American fertility will be reduced, regardless of the attitude of the Church (although it certainly could facilitate matters), for the historical example of European Catholic countries, the U.S. Catholic population, and Argentina and Uruguay is clear. The reason why the problem in the underdeveloped world is so critical is . . . population pressures on resources are already great and there is now no world region willing to accept large-scale immigration. Undoubtedly, improved education and changes wrought by the industrialization and commercialization of the economies will provide social changes that will make birth control widely accepted (even for the men).

At the heart of the struggle between population growth and economic development are basically two conflicting schools of thought: the technologists who believe that improving efficiency and technology will supply sufficient goods and services for the population (notwithstanding rapid demographic growth); and the neo-Malthusians who envision the population exceeding the available resources (despite technological innovations) with the only solution remaining that of fertility control. Latin America, of course, must decide for itself as to which approach is right or, to be safe, it can use both approaches simultaneously, but Latin America's capital and energies are (like those of all regions) limited and some decisions and some sacrifices must be made and soon.

Swan Lake

BY PAUL KRAMER

Suddenly, in the midst of revelry, a bearded magician, in human form, wearing an Oriental robe of red and yellow . . . entered the ballroom with his evil daughter Odile.

Ever since liberation, revolutions in the Caribbean have been endemic. Some have succeeded; most have failed. However, they are an important part of political life and are an activity to which prominent citizens may devote their energies without loss of dignity. Within the context of Caribbean life, the role of the revolutionary is just as honorable as that of a corporation executive in the United States or a peer in Great Britain.

This has been a continuing source of wonder and amusement to Western Europeans and Americans. The writer O. Henry based one of his most humorous series of stories, which he titled *Cabbages and Kings,* on the downfall of the Tinoco regime in Costa Rica. By the 1950's, however, many believed that such events were a thing of the past, that the Caribbean had progressed beyond the era of melodrama, that O. Henry had been guilty of fictional exaggeration, and that nothing such as that which he described could really happen anymore.

But this was not true. In April, 1959, Dame Margot Fonteyn, a British subject and the world's leading ballerina, became involved with her husband, then the Panamanian ambassador in London, in an unsuccessful plot to overthrow the established government of Panama.

This account of that attempt seems convincing evidence that the era of "grand romance" in the Caribbean is not dead—plots and revolutions can occur that surpass any of O. Henry's fictionalized accounts. Despite the intrusion of Castro and the cold war into the political life of the Caribbean, revolutionary plots are still endemic and not something that can be fully captured by Moscow and Peking in the name of Communism or suppressed by Washington in the name of stability and progress.

Paul Kramer, the author of this essay, was living in Panama when the events described occurred. He was born in Cincinnati, Ohio, in 1914. He received an A.B. degree from Princeton University in 1935, and an M.Litt. degree from Cambridge University in 1938 for his work in history under the late H. W. V. Temperley and G. P. Gooch. A specialist in Latin America, he was one of the first to join Nelson Rockefeller's staff when Rockefeller was appointed coordinator of commercial and cultural relations between the American republics in 1940. In 1943 he joined the U.S. Navy as an intelligence officer, and he served in the South Pacific and in Japan. Upon his return to the United States he worked for the newly formed Central Intelligence Agency, which he left in 1951 to become a partner in a New York Stock Exchange firm. Meanwhile, he became an officer and director of a number of industrial corporations active in Ecuador, Colombia, and Panama, where he lived for several years.

His contributions to scholarly journals include the essay "Lord Acton and Latin America," published in the *Inter American Quarterly* in January, 1963, and "The International Geophysical Year," published in *Science and the Social Studies* in 1957. In 1967 G. P. Putnam's published Kramer's *The Last Manchu,* the life story of Henry Pu Yi, the last Ch'ing Emperor of China.

DAME Margot Fonteyn as wife of the Panamanian ambassador and a hostess in London in 1958 had achieved new fame. Invitations to dinner at the Embassy became as highly prized as tickets to see her dance. She and her husband, Ambassador Roberto "Tito" Arias, had converted the Embassy on Thurloe Place into a new and exciting place.

In the past, London has had its hostesses, and each has been different and special, each a product of the times. There have been the women of great fortune and exalted title, and their names and their houses have become part of British history. Holland House, Lansdowne House, and Londonderry House have left their imprint. On the eve of the Victorian era, too, there was Caroline Norton, who entertained Lord Melbourne in her little rooms with the white curtains. And later, when England was richer, there was Lady St. Helier who entertained with such marvelous gusto that *Punch* published a cartoon depicting a man in an iron pot in the jungles of Africa asking his loin-clothed host, "Haven't we met at Lady St. Helier's?"

But this was different. Dame Margot was British, yet wife of the

Panamanian ambassador and a ballerina of world renown. If there had ever in the past been such a combination, and this is doubtful, the person herself would have been the star guest, the attraction, to be captured by the hostess to serve as a drawing card. In such a case, Dame Margot would have played the part of the star supreme, who swept arrogantly into the drawing room to give a duchess three fingers and the Prime Minister a limp hand. She would not have been a wife, a zealous partisan of her husband's career and ambitions, a hostess whose friends, should they show signs of deferring to fame and position, would be brought up short with a gentle but firm "Remember, it's me!"

The house with the Spanish loggia in Thurloe Place thus became a sort of symbol of the new England. It was at once liberal, sensitive, and, above all, modest–modest about the cultural renaissance that Dame Margot, with her art, had helped England achieve. In Dame Margot's rooms the world of royalty, diplomacy, politics, and industry could meet the world of theater, music, and art and feel at home with it, comfortable in the assurance that this new England was a power in its own right. Suez might go, and Cyprus, and the Sudan, but the ability to explain the new world and the skills by which men could be lifted out of themselves were there on Thurloe Place. The guests could thus not help leaving with a renewed feeling of assurance that with such spirit, such devotion and modesty, alive and flourishing in a changing world, change was but the confusing prelude to a happier and better time.

But were times ahead to be better for Dame Margot and her husband, Ambassador Arias? There were rumblings from abroad of a discordant note. In Bruges the shipyard building vessels for the ambassador's private shipping company had managed to finish the *Ondine* only after the greatest difficulties and delays, and now it looked doubtful that the second vessel that a banana company had already chartered would ever be completed. Delay could mean bankruptcy.

And from Panama the news was worse. Tito Arias' father had given his support to the election of President de la Guardia, Tito's brother was in the Cabinet, and Tito was ambassador in London under this new regime. Even so, things were out of joint.

It started with a legal squabble. Two giants of American industry were wrestling with one another for control of Panama's bauxite. One was represented by Tito's father; the other by President de la Guardia's brother. In a typical Latin fashion the whole thing had shifted from a purely legal-commercial squabble into a contest of Spanish pride and family power, in which the Arias lost and the De la Guardias won.

Worse, like an infection, the discord spread. For there were those–the opportunists, the idlers in the cafés, the loungers in the patios–who said: "If Arias' power is such a weak reed against the ambitions of the President's brother, now is the time to strike, to make an end of them. Let's purge ourselves of these outsiders, these liberals, these *antioligarquistas,* these *rabí-prietos* (dark-tailed doves) who cannot apologize for their exalted ancestry."

So a road was plunged through the middle of an Arias factory in the name, of course, of progress, and a strike convulsed the family's newspapers and shut them down. Then Tito's brother, Gilberto, was removed from the Cabinet and was replaced by a man who everyone knew had forbidden his sister, in her youth, to be serenaded by Tito because his family was not sufficiently blue with the blood of Spain and Goya-esque grand duchesses.

Also, there were the letters. People had begun to write to London to ask why and how. Is Panama, too, to have its John Birch, they asked? Is white supremacy to be the password to the future? Are these the reasons why your family supported Don Ernesto de la Guardia, so that we of color shall wear this crown of thorns?

Then too, there was a new madness, a new hope for the future loose in the world, a new belief that there was indeed a force that could purge Latin America of its ills and set things right. Its name was *Fidelismo.*

It is hard, now that the betrayal has been complete, to recall the earlier time when the man with the beard first came out of the hills and swept out the hated Batista. In those early days there was rejoicing in the air and happiness and laughter and hope. For there was little doubt that it all meant *revolución* in the purest sense. There were a few who wondered and who asked:

"Is he not the same who was in Bogotá when Gaitán, the liberal, the non-Communist hero of the masses, was shot?

"Is not this bearded wonder the same one who sought in Mexico to disrupt and destroy the revolution?

"And why the beard?"

For the Indian has no beard and cannot grow one. To the Indian, ever since Cortez and Alvarado, the beard has been the symbol of slavery and serfdom, the cachet of white supremacy. Maximilian, the hated Hapsburg, also had a silky beard, and he sought to oppress and to transfer to Mexico the feudalism of Central Europe until Juárez, the clean-shaven Indian came along and shot him dead.

But who was there to listen? The U.S. Department of State, the New York *Times,* the intellectual leaders? On the contrary, they all flocked to Havana to see and marvel. When Castro chose a Negro minister of war and had him crown a white girl Queen of the Carnival, hope soared higher. It was like the third act of the ballet *Swan Lake,* in which Dame Margot danced with such perfection, when suddenly, in the midst of revelry, a bearded magician, in human form, wearing an Oriental robe of red and yellow and calling himself Baron von Rothbart, enters the ballroom with his evil daughter Odile. And no one, not even the ballet's hero, Prince Siegfried, sees through the disguise and realizes that Odile is not a Swan Princess but is in fact, part of the plot by which Prince Siegfried and his beloved Odette are to be lured to their doom.

From all over Latin America the guests—the oppressed, the out of office, the starving students, the hungry—came to the festivities, and they begged and pleaded for a chance to do the same in their own country, for *revolución* with Cuban help.

From Tito Arias' country of Panama, they came, too. From the university, founded by his father, came student groups to appeal for help from the oppression of "the white-tailed doves." From bars and political cafés came Tito's cousin, Reuben Miró, Caribbean plotter par excellence. And from London came Tito and Dame Margot to be welcomed by Castro and *his* ballerina, short-necked Alicia Alonzo. It all was festive and confused; there were so many groups, so many aspirants for the blessings of the Paramount Leader.

There were discordant notes. Castro subjected Tito to one of his famous tirades. "What do you, Tito, an old man of forty-four know of politics and government?" he screamed. "It takes youth, man, youth!"

While waiting to see some high government official in the Presidencia, Dame Margot and Tito found themselves shunted into a bedroom. Here they found the ladies of the revolution engaged in a tumultuous fashion show as they showed off to one another the cut and fit of the dresses Mrs. Batista had left behind upon her hasty departure.

Still, there was hope. It was clear that if Tito and Dame Margot could seize upon the confusion so that the Paramount Leader didn't know, didn't hear, and didn't see their plan to exploit the Cuban revolution for their own, rather than the Paramount Leader's benefit, there was a chance. Of course, Castro's brother Raúl knew, the wily Lebanese Chomón, the man with whom the students dealt, also knew, and others too. The truth was that in their devious Communist hearts, they were Cubans who knew and liked what they saw. It fitted into their schemes, their future plans for the reenslavement of the just liberated.

For Urrutia–the non-Communist, the President–knew, and if–if only the whole thing would fail, would turn into a ballet bouffe while Castro was in the United States on a goodwill mission protesting non-involvement and claiming that his revolution was not for export, then perhaps. . . .

The Paramount Leader was mercurial, a little frenzied, mad perhaps. If things went wrong at the right time, it would be so easy to convince this bearded Von Rothbart that Urrutia, the honest country judge, was his special enemy. And while the resulting fit lasted, it would be easy to pack off this liberal non-Communist into some dank dungeon beneath Havana Harbor and replace him with a Muscovite, a red rubber stamp.

And Tito and Dame Margot also knew that through it all there would not be one but two enemies, two dangers: on the right, Panamanian President de la Guardia and his police, and on the left, Fidel Castro's left, his Communist hand. The one would seek to destroy and the other to corrupt the plot into something else again.

Still it seemed worth the gamble. Had not, a generation before, Tito's Uncle Arnulfo gambled and thus won for Tito's father by his plots the Presidencia and made his mother the *primera dama?*

Gaily and with hope, a network of plotting was spread through Panama, Cuba, the United States, and Canada. Dame Margot and Tito had no difficulty recruiting friends to assist them. For who was there in the postwar world who could resist high adventure?

Bill Sruta, skipper of the yacht *Edmar,* on which Tito and Dame Margot had spent their honeymoon, acted as paymaster and arranged for the shipping of a load of arms to the Canal Zone underneath the fake bottom of a water-skiing skiff. From the Zone it was delivered to lady plotters in Panama.

Judy Tatum acted as secretary and received from Roosevelt Zanders a bundle of brassards and insignia, which she merrily brought to Panama in a box of napkins. Here they were secreted inside a stuffed Panda, ready and waiting to be delivered to Dame Margot.

Guerrillas went into training in Cuban pastures. Navigators, boats, and a plane were readied for the assault. Meanwhile, Tito flitted back and forth between London, New York, Havana, and Panama, and Dame Margot ostensibly tucked in a sunny vacation between her dance engagements.

The final strategy was simple and had much to recommend it.

Students were to go to the mountains at two points--one near the Costa Rican border and another in the hills of the central provinces and arouse disaffection among the peasantry. The two areas selected overlooked Panama's most productive agricultural lands–the first, coffee; the second, sugar and cattle.

It was anticipated that these two operations would siphon off from Panama City and Colón a high percentage of the police-national guard and cause apprehension among landowners, who would fear for the safety of their coffee trees, their canefields, and their cattle herds.

Once this was accomplished, Tito, ostensibly fishing in the Bay of Panama, was to land at an abandoned fishing port named Caimito and proceed a few miles overland to a provincial town named Chorrera, where he was to cut Panama's only highway to the interior.

Meanwhile, another group, already secreted in suitable tenements about Panama, would emerge from their bedrooms to cut the town in half, thus separating the rich from the poor and bottling up the police in the old part of town with its churches and patios and plazas, so that its protection would be confined to Panama's past, rather than to its present and future.

Finally, a band being trained in Cuban pastures was to be landed on Panama's Atlantic coast near a semi-abandoned trail that led to the trans-isthmian highway. From here the revolutionaries could easily walk to a check point on the road, seize it, and thus cut the two terminal cities off, from each other. Then the various forces of revolt could join in a victory march on the capital city. After a wild night of dancing in the streets and rejoicing in the bars, they were to proclaim their new government from the plazas.

This was the plan, but events, alas, were different.

On April 3, 1959, and armed group of twenty Panamanians prematurely raided a hill village store above the provincial town of Santiago. They seized a shotgun and some shells and proclaimed that the "revolution is under way."

On April 9, Cousin Reuben Miró in Cuba announced that he was the head of a revolutionary movement in Panama.

On April 10, Dame Margot arrived in Panama. Tito was at the airport to meet her, and the next day they "went fishing" together in the bay aboard a cabin cruiser, the *Nola*.

That same day, April 11, a group of masked men cut the phone and power lines at Boquete, a provincial coffee town near Costa Rica.

These were the facts that anyone could read in the press of Panama. But beyond this, there were other things that made Tito and Dame Margot wonder as they set forth from their hotel that morning for the *Nola* and the bay, things that made their fishing trip an act of truly Edwardian bravery and aplomb.

In the hills above Santiago the police were having too easy a time, too direct a route to the rebels. Could it be that Chomón in Cuba, with his Communist network, was telling confederates in Santiago to speak in loud voices and discordant whispers of where and when and how?

And Cousin Miró? Why his proclamation of leadership when everyone knew it was not to be? Who was he serving? Castro? Chomón? Urrutia? Tito? Miró? It was hard to tell.

And why had the boat not set sail from Cuba? Why had the navigator deserted at the last minute? How could it possibly get to the Isthmus in time? Or had it sailed, and was it lurking along some palm-fringed shore?

But if that were so, why the phone call just before departure from someone who was not to know anything, yet must know everything, that all was lost save honor?

Anyway, they sailed, Dame Margot and Tito. Margot had her movie camera and Tito his briefcase; the one in trim Mediterranean white as if off to some Monegesque picnic, the others as if to some solicitor's to discuss tonnage rates or the salaries of stevedores in Hong Kong.

The weather held. The early morning mists evaporated, the sea remained calm, and the tides rose and fell; in fact, they rose so much that they dragged to the bottom the water-skiing skiff with the arms that Skipper Sruta had brought. Shrimp boats had to be called to the rescue, and now it seemed ironic that the shrimpers brought the panda with the brassards inside.

And where were the twenty-one confederates who were to join them? Only a few showed up.

Still Dame Margot busied herself with her movie-making. But there were even more disturbing notes. The boat had not yet landed on the Atlantic side. Where *were* the friends from Havana? And what was the plane doing overhead? It stuck to them like glue. Panama had no air force. It was, in fact, a Darien timber merchant's plane. It had a radio, too. Surely a merchant would not waste his gas and risk his insurance following revolution. Could it have been hired by the government to watch, to observe, to be an air force?

The truth was, the game was up as far as Tito and Dame Margot were concerned. From this point on, revolution would become opera bouffe (or ballet bouffe), as is always the case with plots that fail in Latin lands.

But just before, there was still a grand moment of truth and bravery. The *Nola's* fuel tanks were full. Tito had only to give the word, and it could head the other way, past the Pearl Islands toward Colombia and safety. This would have been the prudent thing to do.

But then, what of the caches of arms and friends ashore? With Tito and Dame Margot safe, away, the full wrath of a distressed and unhappy government would have been directed toward finding the arms and friends. But with Tito ashore, lurking and hiding in some remote gully, all the efforts of the police and government would be directed against him, and the lesser plotters and guns might be spared for future revolt.

The decision was made. Dame Margot and Tito agreed it had to be, and thus Tito left the *Nola* via a shrimp boat with the few confederates who had joined him for an uncertain future of flight and evasion within Panama.

The actual parting occurred so quietly and quickly as to disguise its import and danger. A shrimp boat with its nets held high and black against the mast came up steadily, silently, toward the *Nola*. Soft Spanish voices, which Dame Margot could not understand, drifted back and forth. The gap narrowed, and Tito and the others stepped quickly across from one deck to the other.

Dame Margot stood on the *Nola* with the bright tropic sun on her dark hair. There were no words spoken in the actual moment of parting; her chin was high and her shoulders back in an expression of brave encouragement. Then, as the pilots in the deckhouses spun their wheels to separate the two boats from their parallel courses, the space between them widened, and she waved.

The discipline of years of training supported her. There was no weeping until after the shrimper had pulled away and the distance would conceal her tears from Tito.

A moment later, she dried her eyes and ordered the boat around, back to the Balboa Yacht Club in the Canal Zone. There she could have stayed in safety on American territory until some friend found her a suite on a liner back to England. The Panamanian government could have ranted and raved, knowing she was inviolate on American soil, but she would have been safe.

Instead, alone, in the dead of the night, she left the panicked skipper of the *Nola* and went into Panama, first to her sister-in-law's for a few hours' sleep and a change of clothes and then to visit and gossip in true Latin style, as if nothing untoward had happened.

If people asked and pried, she giggled and waved her hand. "Oh, no," she said, "it's nothing like that. It's just that I found fishing such a bore, and besides it interfered with my practice routines."

The following night, tastefully gowned in a new Dior frock, she dined on La Cresta with the Galindos, and there, beside a blue-tiled pool set in a paved courtyard hung with orchids, the full comedy of Caribbean plotting exploded into an agony of family confusion.

For the sister of her host, Señor Galindo was Mrs. President de la Guardia. Her hostess, Señora Galindo, was Tito's sister. And it was at this point that President de la Guardia said she must be jailed! But his wife, the *primera dama,* the sister of Margot's host, said, "No. To seize her while at the table of my brother cannot be. To do so would be in the worst tradition of the Borgias. She must be lured elsewhere!"

And so the President's chief of secret police extended a hastily phoned invitation. It was not safe, he said, for Dame Margot to sleep that night at her hotel; Panama was too disturbed. She must sleep at his house, only two doors up the street from Señor Galindo's.

Thus, it was from the bed of the daughter of the chief of secret police–the child was off at boarding school at the time–that Dame Margot was bundled off to the local Bastille! And Panama at once became a ballet bouffe, a stage, a laughing stock, a scene of high adventure, a Graustark, a Zenda!

First of all, there were the cables that poured down on President de la Guardia's head. Reserve for us, they pleaded, a suite, a room, a cell, anything next to Dame Margot so that we can share this romance, this high adventure. Tell her, too, that we'll bring her fresh nighties and silken sheets. The wit, the uproarious mirth, the biting irony of the cables that rushed into Panama were such that the police at first thought they were in fact part of the plot, some sort of secret code designed to conceal their real intent.

Then there was the fatigued British ambassador. He, too, received cables galore, and he, poor man, was just recovering from a royal visit. For the very night that Dame Margot had pirouetted out of Panama Bay, the Duke of Edinburgh had sailed off on the royal yacht after a state visit.

But at least the ladies of the embassy were happy. It had fallen to them to rush to the El Panama Hilton and to pack Dame Margot's Dior frocks, left behind in her room. Never had the British ladies been so popular with Mme. de Hahn, the local dressmaker; they now had a foretaste of the latest Parisian styles. Mme. de Hahn must somehow lure them to her atelier, extract this knowledge, if she were to keep her clientele. As one good British lady put it: "The frocks were positively lovely. I've had dozens of calls to find out just how they were made. But, of course, I won't tell."

And soon the ridicule, the gossip, the pressure, the hilarious cables from a laughing world were too much for President Don Ernesto. The night after her arrest, Dame Margot and her frocks were hustled into a darkened car and rushed to the airport, to a plane, any plane that would take her away, out! So that the country could settle down to the hunt, the search for Tito!

Where was Tito? The police insisted he must be at Santa Clara, a dusty motel near his father's ranch of Santa Monica. They arrested the owner and carted her off to a provincial jail, where there was no accommodation for women. Thus, they could not jail her after all but had her sit in a chair until she feigned a thrombosis and got a bed in a nearby hospital.

Meanwhile, they had found Tito's briefcase, and so, once Dame Margot was gone, there were the letters.

At that time President de la Guardia published a little newspaper called *El País*. Previously it was read only by government employees who felt they had to follow the party line in order to keep their jobs. But now all was changed. The contents of Tito's briefcase were serialized in *El País*. Names like Onassis, the shipping magnate, and John Wayne, the movie hero, were mixed in a bewildering profusion with transactions involving more money than the annual budget of Panama.

No sooner were these read and gossiped about than Tito came. Out of the trunk of the car of a friendly legislator he popped into the safe air-conditioned gloom of the Brazilian Embassy, and no sooner was he safe than the invaders from Cuba came.

But they were not the invaders Tito had selected in Havana, and they came in a 50-foot boat instead of a 98-foot one that Tito had thought the smallest possible to risk the voyage. But who was there in Panama to know of this strange and unforeseen substitution? It was as if Columbus who had set forth to discover the New World in three ships had, during the course of his voyage, been transformed into Magellan and to add to the confusion, had landed in Florida instead of the Bahamas.

For the new invaders, instead of debarking near the Canal, landed on an obscure piece of coast on the Atlantic side of the Isthmus between the San Blas Islands and the historic town of Portobelo. Upon landing, they walked up the beach, unopposed, to the nearest village of Nombre de Dios. The local population welcomed them as a pleasant relief from the heat and the shortage of menfolk. Love affairs and friendships flourished in Nombre de Dios until it could be decided just what to do.

Meanwhile, in Panama the government began to clutch wildly in all directions for assistance. Its police force of 2,000 men, everyone agreed, was simply not sufficient to repel the 90 invaders. The authorities in the Canal Zone and then the U.S. Embassy were sounded out. Finally, it was decided to appeal to the Organization of American States for help and a team of distinguished ambassadors was whisked to Panama to find out what really was going on. But the Cubans already knew perfectly well what was going on. The invasion had left from their shores, had been trained in their pastures, and had been betrayed in their offices. So they sent to Panama, before anyone else could get there, two bearded army officers (one of whom had rather alarming mustachios and was known as Frenchie) to tell the invaders to come home. Or at least that is what they said they came to do.

Panamanian officials viewed the arrival of the two bearded Cubans with some misgiving. It was bad enough to have a band of *barbudos* on the beach at Nombre de Dios. But to have them in Panama itself was disturbing, if not awkward. After a heated discussion, it was decided to send them alone to Nombre de Dios. No Panamanian went with them, and it is thus doubtful that anyone will ever know what they really told the rebels.

At any event, one officer stayed with the rebels, and the one with the alarming mustachios returned to Panama. The press termed the mission a *fracaso,* and Panama's upper-class ladies sent their most trusted servants to the nearest novelty stores to buy false beards in case the invaders, who were rumored to be bearded just like Fidel Castro, arrived in Panama City!

Even in the tropics, where hirsute appendages seem to grow faster than in more temperate climates, there would hardly be time for their husbands to grow really the first-rate Sierra Maestra beards that they felt necessary to ensure their safety. Besides, with the diplomats about, it was hardly the time to go unshaved. If *they* saw the twenty leading families all growing beards, then they could not be expected to rescue Panama from the rebels. But if they failed, then clearly it was best to have a beard in the dresser if not on the face.

By the Friday following Dame Margot's arrest and sudden departure, the rebels had surrendered. For the peaceful solution, full credit should go to the OAS. Its brightly painted helicopters and black limousines seem to have had a pacifying effect. But also, credit should go to the climate, for the rains came.

Panama's dry season starts in January and lasts until about May 1. The last two weeks of April are always trying. The refreshing trade winds of January, February, and March have drifted out to sea, and April is hot and muggy. An air of nervous expectancy develops. People look anxiously skyward for rain and a cooling breeze, which never seems to come. The heat grows steadily more oppressive. Meanwhile, the parched countryside is brown and depressing. Brush fires burn in the hills day and night.

That year the rains came on schedule. Out of a black sky, water poured down on a parched and nervous land. Little fits of cool breeze filtered into the most secluded patios, and people sighed with relief. Plants would begin to grow again. This was really more important than Tito, or Dame Margot, or the rebels, or even President de la Guardia.

Then, too, there was the heritage from the days and nights of tropic madness that was good and comforting. The press could ignore it all, and the cynics could laugh and chuckle and forget their mad haste to buy beards. Panama's national pride could pretend there had never been the hilarious cartoons of shrimp boats festooned with tutus.

But there were simple people who saw and talked, who understood in terms of human emotion. One day some unknown stranger had a sign painted and lettered. It said: MARGOT LLORO AQUÍ (Here Margot

Wept.) He gave it to the skipper of the *Nola,* who fastened it to the deck for all to see.

This was really it. Dame Margot, with Tito had tried and failed, but most important, they had not taken the easy way out. Against all odds, they had fled inward, not outward, to save their arms and fellow plotters by the very aplomb of their bravery. And at the supreme moment of parting and danger, Dame Margot had wept for Tito and for the dashing of his hopes, a result of the characteristic confusion of Caribbean plotting.

Characteristically, too, there were political changes in Panama despite their failure. As a result of all the revolutionary confusion they had wrought, President de la Guardia did what he had earlier refused to do. He changed the electoral laws so that the decision on who was strong and who was weak could be made at the polls, instead of in the patios of the politicians who controlled the country's two main political parties.

Also in keeping with Caribbean revolutionary tradition, Dame Margot and Tito survived it all. The parting on the *Nola,* despite its drama, had not been final, merely a temporary separation.

When they were reunited a few months later in England's autumn sunshine, the wit of Britain's aging Sir Winston Churchill reduced their escapade to its right proportions, to an implied recognition that, after all, *revolución* is, in Latin America, endemic, that it is not something that can be captured or suppressed by either the monolithic designs of Moscow or the ambitions of Washington for stability in the name of progress.

They motored down to Chartwell for lunch. Viscount Montgomery, only recently back from China, was there, as well as a relative of Lady Churchill's. Sir Winston, who had fallen sometime before in Marrakesh, was still troubled with his hip and legs; regardless, there was an air of truly Edwardian indolence in the day. The wines were white and red and sparkling; the brandies, mellow and clear. Above all, the garden lay soft and green in the warm light of September.

After lunch, Sir Winston decided to descend with Dame Margot to his studio to the bottom of the hill, below the house, and to show his paintings. Later, perhaps enthused by Dame Margot's youthful stride, he insisted on walking her back up the hill, unaided, waving his nurse aside.

But halfway up, he puffed and stopped and shouted for the nurse.

Dame Margot hesitated. Perhaps she felt that it had been her obvious pleasure in being with Sir Winston that had caused him to overtax himself, and she glanced up toward Tito, who was strolling on the terrace with Lady Churchill, while the nurse came running down to help.

But when the nurse reached them, it became apparent that Sir Winston desired neither assistance nor medicines for a taxed heart, or an ailing hip. Instead, he wished only a whiskey and water with which to refresh himself before resuming his ascent. The stentorian summons, the anxious pause, the puffing, the uncertainty, and then, the relief had a timing that was more perfect than any actor might devise. It must have seemed to Dame Margot that Sir Winston was endeavoring, without actually saying so, to show that he, too, had within him all the discipline, the sensitivity, and the skills by which are created the magic of the theater.

Once back up the hill, Sir Winston settled in a chair on the terrace that overlooked the lawn. There Tito joined him, while Lady Churchill, Dame Margot and Viscount Montgomery went off to play croquet in the afternoon sunshine.

The two sat quietly and watched the others until the aged statesman turned to ask Tito what he planned to do now that he was no longer an ambassador and his wife was closing the house in Thurloe Place.

Tito explained that they would live in Panama.

"In that case," Churchill said, "I must warn you not to use Montgomery in any of your revolutions!"

"Really, sir? Why is that?"

"If you do, you will be a bankrupt before you start."

"A bankrupt?"

Sir Winston waved his cigar toward Lord Montgomery, who, just then, held his mallet poised to strike Dame Margot's ball out of range from the wicket passage through which they both were contesting. There were moans of mock grief from the ladies, and Churchill waited for the tap of Lord Montgomery's mallet against his ball to give emphasis to the point he was about to make.

"Yes," he repeated, at last, "a bankrupt! You can't possibly afford it. Do you know," he added slowly and with emphasis as he waved again toward Lord Montgomery, who had, by this time, sent his own ball through the wicket, "that man over there needs a minimum of thirteen divisions before he'll make a move."

Fidel Castro

By FRANK TANNENBAUM

Just why this profound tragedy has come to afflict the Cuban people . . . will always remain a matter of dispute.

Let us first consider by what steps a new government came into existence in Havana.

The old order terminated in the early morning of January 1, 1959, when Fulgencio Batista, dictator of Cuba, abandoned his government and, accompanied by his family and a few henchmen, flew to the Dominican Republic. Immediately there was no army, no police, no judiciary, and no congress in Cuba–nothing to substitute for the government that had vanished with the New Year revelry but a young man with a beard named Fidel Castro, who had been the leader of a small band of ill-armed and ill-trained rebels in a remote mountainous area. As a result of the nature of Batista's flight, all the power of the Cuban state passed in a few moments from an experienced, cynical, tired *caudillo* to a fresh new young one.

The speed of the substitution–and it is important to remember that this was Batista's doing, not Castro's–allowed no time for those with existing interests in Cuba or those desirous of acquiring new interests to establish claims on the new *caudillo* in exchange for their support or withdrawal of support from the old one. Thus, by Latin American standards, Castro's power was uncompromised by political expediency from either the right or the left. Furthermore, the charismatic attributes of the new leader were skillfully employed to fortify and consolidate his position.

Meanwhile, considerable confusion developed abroad about the nature of the new government, a confusion that was later compounded by the *caudillo's* public announcement that he was a Communist and by his negotiation with the Soviet Union of an alliance whose terms have never been made public. Also, at the time, the experience of the United States in dealing with Latin America was limited. There had been some success in Guatemala in overthrowing a Communist-oriented coalition, as a result of which expertise was thought to exist where it did not. Furthermore, the drama involved in the Castro government attracted to the area any number of doctrinaire writers, who, although they may have been experts on other parts of the world, had no experience in Latin America and thus tended to apply irrelevant doctrines of political analysis. The merit of Dr. Tannenbaum's writing on Castro is that it recognizes the indigenous characteristics of Latin American political life and reflects years of profound and penetrating study of the area.

There are, in America, few academicians with Frank Tannenbaum's depth of experience on Latin America. Virtually his entire mature life has been devoted to study of the area. By one means or another (on mule, afoot, by motor, plane, and train) he has traveled through the entire region. He has been a newspaper correspondent in Mexico and a member of various Latin American and North American governmental and private commissions.

Born in 1893, he attended Columbia College, from which he was graduated in 1921. In 1927 he received his Ph.D. degree from the Robert S. Brookings Graduate School of Economics and Government. He taught at Cornell and lectured at Yale. From 1936 until his retirement in 1961 he was professor of Latin American history at Columbia University.

His *Ten Keys to Latin America,* from which the following excerpts are taken, was published in 1962 and reflects the author's erudition and lifetime accumulation of knowledge of Latin America. Other books by Dr. Tannenbaum include *The Mexican Agrarian Revolution,* published in 1928; *Whither Latin America?,* published in 1934; and *Mexico: The Struggle for Peace and Bread,* published in 1950.

P. K.

Politics in this world we have been describing is very "political", very "pragmatic," and not at all "ideological." It is also very personal.

I remember many years ago, on a train from Vera Cruz to Mexico City, talking to a Honduran military man going into exile. "How many political parties are there in Honduras?" I asked.

"Only two: the Red and the Green. I belong to the Green Party," he replied.

"And what is the difference between them?"

After a moment's reflection he said: "Well, there is really no difference between them, only naturally I think that the Green Party is better."

I didn't in those days know enough about Latin America to appreciate the profound political lesson I had just been given. For what this man was trying to tell me was the simple and profound truth that Latin American politics were not ruled by theoretical considerations, that political parties were neither left nor right, but that they were good or bad depending upon whether they belonged to us or to our opponents. If the party belonged to us, it was good. If it belonged to our opponents, it was bad. Political differences were real enough but not for ideological reasons.

This is an oversimplification of the complexities of the political process in Latin America, but it is one way of saying that politics, political parties, and government administrations are personal. . . . The important political consideration is the leader and not the party.

There have been changes in Latin America in the last generation which have complicated and obscured the political scene without really changing its character. The spread of doctrines such as Nazism, fascism, socialism and communism and their adoption as party names have given foreigners and even some culturally Europeanized nationals the impression that something strange has happened in Latin American politics, that what had always been a personal phenomenon has become a matter of details, with the party and the ideology displacing the individual, the slogan more important than the leader, the law of greater significance than personal influence, and matters of principle taking precedence over friendship, family and political clan. Those who have let themselves believe all this have simply lost their bearings and are reading their politics out of a European book.

The one thing that has not changed has been the *caudillo,* the leader, he who has *"la suma del poder,"* who governs because he can, not because he was elected. . . . Leadership is personal. The basis of authority is customary rather than constitutional. The political unit is not the individual; it is the gang, the extended family, the community, and the Indian village, each with its own "natural" leader, each endowed with unlimited authority and each possessing the complete loyalty of his immediate followers.

The great leader, by some magic, fraud, or force, has at his disposal all this power, and he cannot divide it, delegate it, or refuse to use it. . . . The *caudillo* governs by his mere presence. Anything he says is an order, and if he refuses to say anything at all, then others will act in his name on the assumption that they are carrying out the orders he would have given, and he will be credited with them. The king would abidcate in favor of the legitimate heir to the Crown. But in Latin America the leader cannot abdicate because there is no legitimate heir to his power. When the successor appears, the power of the older leader evaporates. . . . The power cannot be shared. It is absolute or it does not exist. . . .

We have no model for this type of political leadership–although Huey Long of Louisiana came close to it–and therefore we do not understand it. The American gang represents personal leadership which has elements comparable to the *caudillo*. A better comparison is the Scottish clan. The clan was more important than the state and more important than the king. Loyalty was to the clan chieftain first and the clan would follow its leader against other clans, against the king, and against the whole world. But this example, too, is unsatisfactory because chieftainship in the clan was hereditary whereas leadership in Latin America is not.

The case of Fidel Castro is particularly revealing. Cuba is not typical of Latin America. The Indian influence is nil. The Negro, on the other hand, is important in numbers, but even more so in over-all influence. The Negro has given the Cubans a gentle, friendly, and optimistic attitude toward life. They tend to emphasize the importance of the moment. Their land is filled with music, song, and the dance. Also Cuba is close to the United States and our impact upon Cuba has been great–greater, perhaps, than either of us realize. There are, therefore, many reasons for arguing that politically Cuba should be less Latin American than it has shown itself to be. For what it has shown in Fidel Castro is that it still prefers to have a *caudillo*–one who stands above the law and the constitution because all authority, all justice and all good emanate directly from him.

The differences between Fidel Castro and Batista are many and great. But as administrators they both respond to the same demand in the same way. Batista was secretive, cruel, and selfish and acted for himself and a small clique. He depended upon the police and the army, but his power was absolute. All constitutional formulas were secondary. Fidel Castro uses the radio, television, and the secret police. The way things have gone, Castro differs from Batista in his claim that he is the first Cuban to stand for social justic and a strong free Cuba. The uses the power is put to are different, but the exclusive possession of it in a single hand is the same.

The power is put to a different use because the individual leaders are different and not because the "party" which carried them to power is different. In fact, there was no party in either Batista's or Fidel Castro's case. The Cuban people accepted Fidel Castro because they wanted him. They had Batista because they tolerated him–even perhaps, until the last two years, wanted him–not because he was "good" or constitutional, but because he was strong, because he was a *caudillo*. If they finally overthrew him–and the active fighters against him were never very numerous–it was because he had become a tyrant, because he was misusing his power beyond reason and beyond the wide tolerance of human fallibility so characteristic of Latin America. He lost what moral sanction he might have had or claimed. His overthrow was accepted as good and the leader of the new revolution was greeted with an outpouring of public joy.

The president who comes to office in Latin America has none of the assurance and strength provided by a political party that has deep roots in the thousands of communities that form the nation. That is why he has to be the architect of his own power. He has no institutional backing except the army, and the army is unpredictable. It may support the president one day and turn him out of the office the next. That is why he has to surround himself with people "*de absoluta confianza*" (of complete confidence).

This brings us back to Fidel Castro. During the days when he was in the Sierra Maestra with a handful of followers fighting to overthrow the Batista regime he had, on the report of those who knew him best, no ambitions other than the re-establishment of political freedom in Cuba. He wanted neither power nor office for himself. His task would be completed when the dictatorship had fallen and a new democratic government had taken office.

Both he and his friends should have known better. Latin Americans, as others, like to live in a make-believe world. They talked as if Cuba was a democracy with political parties and elections and as if the president was chosen by a majority of the people. The facts are quite different. The president was either himself a *caudillo* or was placed in office by one. The successor to Machado was Batista, and all of the succeeding governments were there by Batista's tolerance. The successor to Batista is Fidel Castro.

He does not have to be elected because his power would be just as unrestrained after an election as before one. What once passed for political parties have disappeared because they were not parties but groups of office seekers in search of a leader who would, by controlling the presidency, authorize their misuse of public funds for private ends. Castro has no need of them and is trying to run an honest government. The announcement that he is organizing a political party–it makes no difference whether it is called Communist or anything else–is in this case insignificant because his followers expect him to govern, to make every decision, to lead them and to impose his will on any and every one who opposes him.* If he is making a social revolution, it is because he wants to make it. If he does not make one, it is because he does not want to make one. There was certainly no popular demand for the changes he is bringing to Cuba. The people who supported him in his struggle against Batista did not do so for this purpose, and had they foreseen what would happen to them, they would not have helped him come to power.

I am not arguing the merits of his program. That is beside the point in this discussion. What is at issue is that the power, the program, and the policy are personal. He is the executive, the legislature, and the judiciary. Every statement he makes is the law of the land. When he says that a man ought to be executed, he is executed. When he gets the idea of cutting rents by 50 percent that is done. He governs by decree–that is, his wish is formalized into an official document and ordered to be enforced. It is what his followers expect. They know who their government is–Fidel Castro. They know where to go for help, whom to call upon, in whose name to enforce the law, and whom to blame if they do not like what is happening. Beyond that, Fidel Castro claims a moral sanction for his power. He destroyed the tyrant and is

*There is, of course, a great dispute on this point. It remains to be proven that any party, Communist or not, can substitute for a take-over from Castro. As long as he lives he will govern as a dictator. When he is gone there will be a revolution.

now, as he has declared, bringing justice and liberty to the people. As long as a sufficient number of his followers believe that his intent is good and that his purpose is to protect and help them, he will continue to be their hero, a veritable prince returned to rule with divine power. He is for them the king come to office again. *Yo el rey* has reappeared.

His difficulties have arisen because his actions have become suspect. He has become suspicious and arbitrary. When his remaining followers become fearful, as seems to be the case with large numbers of Cubans, he will become increasingly tyrannical and will be plotted against as Batista was. In fact this has already begun to happen.

He will find that he cannot resign his power, cannot transfer it, and cannot abandon it. To be able to transfer his power he would have had to come to office through a political party which had strong deep roots in every community, a political party that chose him but might have chosen someone else. The party would have brought him to office temporarily and, when the time came, would pass the office to another. But there is no such party, nor can it be created overnight.

Just why this profound tragedy has come to afflict the Cuban people and, in the end, Castro himself will always remain a matter of dispute. There are, however, certain visible things which can be listed. They may not explain everything that has happened, but no adequate explanation can leave them out.

There is first of all the nature of the political situation in Cuba itself. No country in the Western world has had a history of political corruption so universal and so corroding. Nothing touched by the government was untainted. Because the central government controlled all of the political activities in the land, corruption was correspondingly widespread and infected political life in all places. The political parties were merely means for distributing what could be taken from the governmental till, from private business in need of government sanction or favor, and from protected vice—gambling, smuggling and prostitution. There was in fact no responsible or honest political party in Cuba. The two presidents who preceded Batista's last coup were both civilian, "democratic," and possessed of an earlier gallant history of opposition to the tyranny of Machado, but their administrations were irresponsibly corrupt. Anyone trying to give Cuba an honest government would not have known where to turn, nor would he have had any confidence that the new "revolutionary" administration would be more trustworthy than the old "revolutionary" governments had been. This fact must be written down as one of the reasons for Castro's non-reliance upon the existing political parties. . . . Honesty may not be the most important political asset, but in Cuba the people had been so frequently disillusioned on this score that parties and political leaders had fallen into almost total contempt. Governmental integrity had become a popular aspiration. This then is one reason why the government of Fidel Castro turned its back on traditional Cuban political practices.

But a more fundamental reason lies in the nature of the attitude toward the political leader. This, as has been shown, is not only Cuban, it is Latin American. The leader has all the power of government and no one else has any. When, on the early morning of January 1, 1959, dictator Fulgencio Batista abandoned the government and, accompanied by his closest henchmen, flew to the Dominican Republic seeking personal safety and asylum, he left a political vacuum behind him. All of the power had belonged to Batista, and when he left there was no army, no police, no judiciary, and no congress. There was nothing to substitute for the government that had vanished like a dream. There was only Castro, the new leader coming out of the mountains, who suddenly found himself possessed of all the authority formerly exercised by Batista. He was now the army, the police, the judiciary, the congress, and the electorate as well. All of the power of the state had passed into his hands.

For an understanding of the revolutions in Latin America past, present, and those to come, it would be well for us to ponder the meaning of Castro's sudden rise to power. Castro had no substantial army, no political party, no support from the unions, no strong following among the rural laborers and small landholders. He had no philosophy known to or understood by the masses. Almost to the day that he found himself in possession of all the attributes of the state, he had in his following only a few hundred young people, mainly students from middle-class families. Not until Batista's disappearance could he count on even a few thousand men. The government became his by default. There was no other source of public power. The land was empty of authority until it was assumed by the leader of a small band of ill-armed and ill-trained young men.

Personal power has conditioned Latin American history since independence and is likely to be the catalytic element in the current ferment for social change. If the revolutions that are predicted by so many in and out of Latin America occur, they will come embodied in a person, not in an ideology, party, program, or political movement. They will appear in the shape of a revolutionary *caudillo* who, like Castro, will take over from a Batista or a Somoza, a Trujillo or a Perón. Political structure is fragile. A few riots have toppled the government of Ecuador. . . . Attempts against the governments of Argentina, Colombia and Venezuela have been made by young army officers. A captain or even a lieutenant with a few men repeatedly captures a radio station or telephone exchange. Loyal government forces then surround or kill the malcontents and the uprising fails. But the mere belief that the government could be overthrown by such a venture–a belief shared by many–sheds light on the frailty of governments in many parts of Latin America.

They are caught in a political dilemma from which they have not been able to extricate themselves. The centralized authoritarian tradition requires a strong personal government. When that is absent, rebellions surge up at frequent intervals until one of the numerous uprisings succeeds and brings a *caudillo* into office once again, and the cycle repeats itself. The revolutions are personal–Madero, Carranza, Pancho Villa, Obregón in Mexico, Paz Estenssoro in Bolivia, Betancourt in Venezuela, Castro in Cuba. This record holds for those who have passed across the political stage in the last 50 years, whether they have been liberals or conservatives.

If any one thing is certain, the revolutions of the next 50 years will be more like those that preceded them than like changes that have occurred in the United States. Latin America has had a rash of imitators of Mussolini and Hitler and will now have a succession of imitators of Castro. Fidelismo will, in all likelihood, become a banner for aspiring political demagogues who want to break through the crust of a static society and find a place for themselves. By its nature this static society does not allow for a political change without violence and without being embodied in a leader. If the leader happens to be like Castro, not only a national hero but a demagogue who brooks no criticism, takes no advice, and is shrewd, callous, and power-hungry, then like Castro, he will be free to make any kind of revolution he wants. It is as true for the future as it has been for the past. Castro can be driven out only by violence, as were Machado, Batista, and so many other leaders.

The decision to make this kind of revolution was Castro's by personal choice. No one else could have made it at the time. He had all the power and there was no restriction on how he used it. He could establish his own system of justice and take such lives as seemed right and proper for him to take. He could confiscate private property for public use as he wished. Until he is driven from office by violence or taken from it by death, no one will stop him.

The taking of human life at will is in the older tradition. There is nothing new about it. But the confiscating of private property for public ends, placing it in the hands of a governmental bureaucracy–that is rather new. Traditionally revolutions were justified by slogans that had a liberal ring. The new ones will be acclaimed on grounds of Marxian theory and social justice, but, like the older ones, they will be embodied in an individual.

The age-old tradition of personal leadership is so deeply imbedded that it affects every policy, program and ideology. *Personalismo* will prove one of the barriers in the way of the hopes held out for the *Alliance for Progress.*

Power and Social Change in Colombia: The Cauca Valley

By COLE BLASIER

Sporadic attention to reform by traditional groups has fallen far short of overcoming the shortcomings of the existing political and economic structure, notably its inability to meet the needs of peasant groups and the urban poor.

The following selection on power and social change in Colombia's Cauca Valley is a good example of recent interdisciplinary studies of Latin American contemporary situations. The quotation above summarizes the belief on which such studies are based—namely, that nondirected evolutionary processes will not solve existing Latin American problems. It is the belief of this school of thought that drastic change in Latin America is unavoidable, but that it can be peaceful if the full resources of modern social science are applied to the study of the problems involved and if action is taken on the resulting recommendations. In other words, a situation is studied not just because it is there, but because something should be done about it. The research study thus becomes the basis for a blueprint for action.

Various academic disciplines are brought to bear on the analysis of a region. The economy is analyzed to determine whether the existing industries are the most appropriate for the area and how they should be changed. The social effects of the existing situation, as well as the cultural barriers to possible change, are studied. Political organization and power structure are viewed as they relate to possible change in the status of the underprivileged. Within the framework of the microeconomy of a single coherent region under examination, a study is made of major Latin American problems, such as land reform, industrial development, education, and political organization. All are viewed in the local setting or by comparison with the same problems in other areas. This approach represents both the philosophy and the technique of many modern Latin Americanists and is being used in many centers of Latin American research. The consequence of the adoption of this type of activist research on Latin America by many universities has been that the results are of immediate use in the formulation of government policy. Government and academia in the Latin American field in the United States have drawn much closer together.

Professor Blasier's life is a good example of this union. Born in Michigan in 1925, he was graduated from the University of Illinois and received his M.S. and Ph.D. degrees from Columbia University in 1953 and 1955. While at Columbia, he specialized in Russian studies. Having entered the United States Foreign Service in 1955, he served in Yugoslavia, Germany, and Russia. In 1961 he left the Foreign Service and now directs the Center for Latin American Studies at the University of Pittsburgh. As a visiting professor of political science at the Universidad del Valle, Colombia, under a Rockefeller Foundation grant in 1963 and 1964, he was able to carry on the research which went into the following article.

R. E. M.

The Cauca Valley in southwest Colombia offers a good closeup view of social change, the power struggle at the grass roots, and rural and urban problems in a country whose size and strategic location make her future a matter of special concern to those who seek to avoid violent solutions to Latin America's social problems.

Colombia would seem to have better prospects for evolutionary development than several Latin American countries with less enlightened leadership and fewer democratic traditions. But Colombia's ruling groups face formidable, sometimes seemingly insoluble economic and social problems. The economy has been wobbly for years, buffeted by fiscal crises, foreign exchange shortages, quickening inflation, and urban unemployment. Also, Colombia has suffered more than any other country in this hemisphere from a species of internal war referred to locally as the *violencia*. Guerrillas, including some Communists, have been active in the country for many years and the nation has been alleged to be one of the half-dozen "main targets" of the Communist movement in the Western hemisphere.[1]

Agricultural, industrial, and financial interests have maintained fairly firm control of the Republic during much of its recent history. Except for the military dictatorship of Rojas Pinilla (1953–1957), the country has been alternately ruled during this century by the Conservative and Liberal parties. Since shortly after the fall of Rojas in 1957, the nation has had a coalition government, the National Front, in which the Conservative and Liberal leaders alternate in the presidency and divide equally legislative, executive, and judicial posts. Traditional forces–landowners, the industrialists, the Church, and the military–have not yet been unseated by the forces of the Left.

Yet, social progress has been a preoccupation of enlightened elements of the so-called oligarchy for many years. President Alfonso López introduced land, tax, labor, and other reforms during his first administration (1934–38) which have often been compared with the New Deal in the United States. Most of the leaders of both parties have long given lip service to the need for social reform and there has been a variety of programs undertaken to ameliorate the lot of the poor. Thus, some Conservative and Liberal leaders, such as the new President Carlos Lleras Restrepo, have shown a flexibility of method and grasp of reality sufficient to give hope for avoiding a bloody revolutionary upheavel.

Sporadic attention to reform by traditional groups has fallen far short of overcoming the shortcomings of the existing political and economic structure, notably its inability to meet the needs of peasant groups and urban poor. Their dissatisfactions and boiling resentments have been expressed in the *violencia,* a combination of guerrilla warfare, banditry, pillage and murder, that has wracked the nation for nearly a generation. Although the *violencia* has political causes, such as ancient local feuds between Conservatives and Liberals, it has not yet become the tool of a single leader capable of imposing his will on the nation.

The presence of the *violencia* makes it all the more difficult to effect

[1]See *Communism in Latin America.* Hearings before the Subcommittee on Inter-American Affairs of the Committee on Foreign Affairs, House of Representatives (Washington, 1965), p. 35 and *passim.*

peaceful rather than violent social change. In either case, extensive social changes require a generation or more as the Mexican and Soviet revolutions show. Castro's experience, too, indicates that the seizure of power marks only the beginning of the "revolution."

One important difference between revolution and evolution is that in the former more changes are effected from the top down, and in the latter, more from the bottom up. In an evolutionary situation, where there is some measure of representative government, local interests should have a better opportunity of influencing national policy. If so, there is utility in studying conflicts of interest and prospects of social change, including changes in the power structure at the local level, as in the Cauca Valley.

I

The politics of agriculture, perhaps the fundamental political issue in the Cauca Valley, are inextricably linked with the problems of agricultural productivity. The fact that the Valley has not produced food in quantity and quality sufficient to provide a proper diet for many of its inhabitants who suffer from hunger and malnutrition has inescapable political implications. The failure of the Valley's agriculture to meet social needs is a commonly voiced justification for land reform, whether moderate or radical. More important, low agricultural productivity and its attendant social evils are largely responsible for peasant resentment of the ruling groups and of the peasants' alienation from the existing political and social system.

The Valley's agricultural leaders are expecially vulnerable since the region's remarkable agricultural potential has never been realized. The soils of the Valley compare favorably with rich agricultural lands almost anywhere in the world. The climate is even, there is a growing season of twelve months, and the water supply from rainfall and irrigation sources, recently much improved, is good.

Despite this favorable endowment, two thirds of the rich land of the Valley were still in pasture as late as 1959.[2] Cattle breeding, the main use to which these lands have been put, is on an *extensive* basis. With

[2]Universidad del Valle, *Censo Agropecuario del Valle del Cauca, 1959* (Cali, septiembre, 1963), p. 21.

notable exceptions, most ranchers have simply let their cattle out to roam in open pastures. It is only in the last few years that there has been much experimenting with special grasses, supplemental feeding, and other intensive cattle raising methods. Ranching is often done with a minimum of effort, differing little from that of centuries ago. Beef specialists have estimated that cattle output could be at least tripled on existing lands.[3] Observers report that in some parts of the Valley, notably in the north, much land is in no use at all, or only pastures token numbers of cattle.[4]

But the problem is not only to encourage intensive cattle production. Agricultural experts believe that the most economic use of the land would require a far higher proportion in crops, rather than pasture. Presumably, the cattle could be shifted in part to the mountainous slopes on either side of the Valley. Traditional land use has shown a glaring contradiction: the rich lands of the Valley held in large plots and used extensively for cattle breeding; the rocky, uneven mountainous slopes covered with small plots and used intensively for crops by small, subsistence farmers. In recent years, however, there has been a rapid shift towards crops in the Valley, caused largely by profit opportunities. Under the threat of expropriation some large owners are planning to introduce more intensive methods, particularly in sugar cane.

What is the impact of low production? In a rich agricultural region food is scarce and dear in terms of the population needs.[5] Malnutrition is rife, particularly among children in the critical growing years. Protein shortage and disease, notably gastro-intestinal complaints, stunt physical and mental potential. Mortality rates are high and survivors enter adulthood handicapped. Hunger is widespread and begging not uncommon.

[3]Harold M. Riley, "Beef Production in Colombia" (Facultad de Agronomía, Palmira, 1962), p. 64. (Mimeographed.)

[4]José Américo Castillo, "Las relaciones hombre tierra en el panorama colombiano (1936–1963)" (unpublished *Tesis de grado,* Universidad del Valle, 1964), p. 103.

[5]See, for example, José Francisco Montoya, "Problemas principales de la agricultura vallecaucana" (unpublished ms., May 1964). Income per capita in small plots in the north of the Valley, including the value of produce consumed from the farm itself, came to only $.84 a day (farms less than one hectare), and $1.09 a day (farms less than five hectares).

These ills are often ascribed to the extremely uneven distribution of land. The rich, flat lands of the Valley are concentrated in relatively few hands. The large plots, those exceeding 50 hectares, constitute about 70 per cent of the land, and this has been held by as few as 8 per cent of the owners.[6] Moreover, many of these large holdings include the best land in the Valley, particularly in the North. Far too much of this land is worked inefficiently or little at all. The land is held for speculative purposes, often operated at a loss, the major source of income being capital gains on sales, which have seldom been taxed. The owners are able to maintain the living standards to which they are accustomed by following the traditional antiquated management methods.

At the other end of the scale are the minifundia which are really too small to support a farm family. If small plots are arbitrarily defined as less than 10 hectares in size, such plots constitute about 10 per cent of the land and are held by 70 per cent of the owners.

Thus about 80 per cent of the land is held either in large plots which many owners are disinclined to work efficiently, or in small plots which the owners do not know how to work efficiently. Only about 20 per cent of the land is held in medium size properties.

The necessity for encouraging wider distribution of land is widely accepted in public, though often deeply resented and bitterly opposed in private. In any case, the official Colombian position is that there should be some redistribution of agricultural land, particularly of inefficiently operated large holdings, as embodied in the land reform law of 1961.

This law was passed by a government dominated by large agricultural and industrial interests. Why were they prepared to support legislation aimed at dispossessing some of their members? As Hirschman has pointed out, the traditional parties needed popular social issues which would attract support at the polls, they were fearful of rural unrest and violence, and were sufficiently enlightened to prefer to introduce reforms of their own making rather than to have them imposed on them at some later date.[7] Beyond this there existed justifiable skepticism that the law, like those in the past, would result in any significant land redistribution.

[6] *Censo Agropecuario, op. cit.,* Cuadro 5. About 58% of the land was in plots exceeding 100 hectares.

[7] Albert O. Hirschman, *Journeys Toward Progress* (New York: Twentieth Century Fund, 1963), pp. 155 ff.

The Colombian Institute of Land Reform (INCORA) was established to put the 1961 law in effect. The Institute is empowered to undertake technical improvements in agriculture, including irrigation and reclamation projects, but the politically significant part of its work involves the redistribution of land. The large agricultural interests have long encouraged colonization of public lands and INCORA has made greater headway on such projects than in the more sensitive area of expropriation.

A major struggle over the implementation of the Agrarian Reform law has been taking place in the north of the Valley.[8] In fact, this region became a test of INCORA's determination to carry out the land redistribution measures of the reform in the country as a whole. In 1963 INCORA's plans called for the expropriation of some 17,000 hectares of poorly cultivated land in this region. To sweeten this bitter pill, INCORA also proposed to undertake irrigation and reclamation works in the area, the large landowners to pay their share of these costs by turning over land to INCORA. Thus, expropriated landowners, who would retain part of their original plots, were to benefit from technical improvements in the area.

The landowners of the area, supported by other members of the Society of Agriculturalists and Cattlemen, formed cooperatives in the north and took other means to oppose expropriation. The best known effort is the so-called "Sugar Plan" which called for planting this land in cane to meet the then heavy demand on world markets, thereby providing the country with much needed foreign exchange. The agriculturalists hoped that the introduction of sugar cane into the area, combined with the necessary investments in mills, would cause INCORA to drop expropriation. By mid 1965 INCORA had made little progress toward land redistribution in the area, and plummeting sugar prices later discouraged new investment.

The large landowning interests have not always made a frontal attack on land reform as such. Ostensibly, they support the work of INCORA, particularly its technical improvements on the land; nor do most oppose outright land redistribution provided their "constitutional rights" are respected. In fact, however, they have fought the land

[8]Castillo, "Las relaciones," pp. 106 ff.

reform legislation tooth and nail, usually on the grounds that it is being badly administered.[9]

The main burden of their attack on redistribution schemes is that they are not economic. They say that breaking up large estates and distributing the land to peasants in small plots—too small, they say, for efficient exploitation—is neither in the nation's nor the peasants' interest. Most Colombian peasants, they maintain, are not capable of efficient exploitation of land: they lack the technical and managerial skills required. And unfortunately, they add, the so-called "middle peasants" or family farmers who form the basis of much of agriculture in the United States and Europe are few and far between. To provide lands to the illiterate peasants, they contend, simply means increasing their misery and denying them the protection and benefit of experienced supervision. The implication of the argument is that the land should be left with its present owners, those best equipped to have it efficiently worked, and that these owners should be encouraged and provided the means for achieving its more efficient use.

The large owners are right in their allegation that Colombia has a shortage of peasants capable of managing the family farms which support their own members and provide a large marketable surplus as well. Here lies Colombian agriculture's great weakness: the shortage of entrepreneurial skills on the countryside in all classes of society. At the same time, if land expropriation continues at a snail's pace, there should not be much difficulty in finding competent men to run the small number of newly established units.

If land redistribution is to have much impact, however, it will need to be widely redistributed. This in turn could mean the creation of inefficient minifundia. What the large agricultural interests have failed to make clear is how the existing system of land tenure, which has been relatively inefficient for centuries, will suddenly prove itself capable of the steep increases in output sufficient to feed the exploding population. Nor is it clear, even if the continuation of the existing system were more efficient, that it will prove *politically feasible.* Ruling groups in Colombia are formally committed to land redistribution. If the land

[9]Raimundo Emiliani Román, *La replicación errónea de la Reforma Agraria* (Bogotá, 1963).

reform law continues to be frustrated, one can not predict how long the poorer elements in the population will remain quiescent.

Fear of the landless and the need to attract votes to gain office appear to be the major sources of motivation behind land reform. Peasants continue from time to time to sweep down from the mountains, and forcefully occupy unused lands.[10] The authorities vacillate in ejecting them, and the peasants not infrequently remain. Yet, often these very peasants do not succeed in scratching more than a bare subsistence from such lands and their titles remain forever clouded. Such incursions are a continuing source of concern and give added impetus to INCORA's work. Independent peasant republics are further evidence of the potentially explosive character of almost the entire Colombian countryside. In remote areas peasants have set up their own local government and defied central authority. Often these groups are summarily dismissed as bandits or Communists; whatever their social or political complexion, they reflect deeply entrenched malaise on the countryside. In 1964, for example, the Armed Forces only with difficulty crushed the "independent republic" of Marquetalia and the Minister of War found it expedient to travel to the area and hoist the Colombian flag as a symbol of the restitution of national authority.

Thus, Colombia's land reform can only be clearly seen in the larger context of the nation's political and social instability. With the help of the armed forces President Guillermo León Valencia made progress in bringing the *violencia* under control despite several dramatic kidnappings.

Despite the urgency which the *violencia* gives to building a healthy society, there are relatively few powerful groups in the Valley who give more than lip service to the need for agrarian reform. There appear to be no really strong organized groups behind it. Obviously, the landholding class would be the last place to look. But one sees little militancy among industrial or labor groups either. Only one of Cali's daily newspapers, which was forced through lack of advertising to close down, gave consistent support to land reform. Labor unions are not exerting much influence in favor of the reform and they, too, are only peripherally concerned with agriculture. The leading exponent of

[10]John P. Powelson, "The Land-Grabbers of Cali," *The Reporter,* January 16, 1964, p. 30.

agricultural reform, and one of its authors, the new President Carlos Lleras Restrepo, continues to support the reform. The question, however, is whether much can be achieved with consistent chipping away from all sides.

The one group which is supposed to benefit from the reform, the peasants, are not an influential source of support. Far too few have the vaguest idea of what the reform is all about. Peasant sentiment in favor of parcelization is fairly strong in the north where INCORA has publicized its work. In the south of the Valley rural workers are pitifully uninformed. Many peasants are distrustful of politicians and public measures generally; they have been disappointed so often, so long. But even if they were well informed and united in their support of land reform, it is not clear how well they would make their voices heard.

Thus land reform finds few fervent supporters in the country. The ruling groups have accepted the principle of land reform reluctantly and there are strong well organized groups opposed to more than token implementation. Thus it is not clear how any far-reaching reform with its accompanying painful wrenching of the social fabric is possible under existing circumstances.

For the immediate future the most that can be expected is probably a gradual improvement in production methods in the larger estates and a very slow widening of the base of ownership. Assuming such moderate implementation of the reform, which itself is still in jeopardy, the question arises whether gradualism, even if justifiable on purely economic grounds, will forestall an explosion on the countryside.

Peasants, who account for something less than half the population of the Valley, are for the most part unorganized. Labor unions recognize their potential importance in a perfunctory way but their main interests lie in industry. Much progress has been made, of course, in organizing workers in the sugar fields; the major mills are unionized, many by Communist-oriented unions. But sugar workers resemble industrial labor more than peasants. A few haciendas have been organized and Jesuit priests, associated with the labor federation, the Colombian Workers Union (UTC), have been active in some communities. The Communist-oriented labor federation, FEDETAV, has a secretary for peasant affairs but this does not appear to be a major union interest. The President of the FEDETAV told the author that there are some 10 to 12 FEDETAV unions of peasants, totaling about 500, but this represents a slim agricultural component for the Communist "peasant-worker alliance." The other major federations also claim a few scattered unions in some of the larger haciendas or in dairy operations, but there are few signs that this is an important part of their work. Here and there, poor peasants have banded together to seek outside help, but have had a discouraging response.

The Catholic Church appears to be among the most active in attempting to organize the peasants. The Office of Coordination of Catholic Social Action has a number of projects among the peasants. The office's main arm is the National Agrarian Federation (FANAL) which has been active in about 120 counties in the Department. FANAL, whose Department headquarters in Cali occupied a single small office, is dedicated to education of peasants to organize to meet their own local needs. FANAL works through the rural clergy. The areas where they have been most active are in the Western cordillera where clerical and Conservative influences predominate. Recently, FANAL has been focusing efforts in the Eastern cordillera areas which have tended traditionally to be of Liberal persuasion. What FANAL seeks to accomplish above all is to help the peasants learn to work together to meet their own needs. Another instrument which Catholic Social Action is using is UCONAL, an organization of credit cooperatives.

The Jesuit Fathers are also concerned about the preparation of men to lead the peasants, many of whom are semi-literate or illiterate. They have recently opened a Peasant University (Universidad Campesina) at Buga in the center of the rich agricultural lands. Its initial emphasis is to be on peasant cooperatives; six hundred students were expected to enroll, one hundred as boarders. Later the "University" will deal with trade, unionism, community development, and the study of the social sciences.

Peasants are accustomed to living and working on their own, asking little of others, receiving nothing. Collaborative efforts are not popular; their experience in this regard has been bitter. They are suspicious of external authority and organization. For the most part, peasants view their lot fatalistically. Today, they remain an amorphous, discontented mass, lacking leadership and direction. Without any systematic ways of expressing their interests and achieving their objectives, they remain passive except when accumulated tensions take violent form.

II

The industrial sector of society is usually expected to provide much of the impetus to political and economic modernization. And there can be no doubt that it has played such a role in the Cauca Valley. Less than twenty years ago Cali was a sleepy, provincial capital with a small downtown area and a few shops and offices; farms were within a few minutes' drive of the central plaza. Today, the city's mood and appearance have been radically transformed. Cali is now a bustling city with crowded sidewalks, congested traffic, and a dynamic economy. Factories, warehouses, and residential areas, many of them slums, have pushed out the borders of the city several miles from the central plaza. Cali has become the most rapidly developing urban and industrial center in Colombia.

Industrialization has changed not only Cali's appearance, but also the community's approach to social problems. Forces capable of challenging the traditional dominance of landed interests have increased. Of most immediate importance is the new group of industrialists who tend to have wider horizons in the economic and political sense than the landed aristocracy. Management's dependence on labor, especially now that it has been organized, is just one of the pressures which forces them to adjust to new social demands.

Another important and growing group is the middle class, a group which owns neither factories, nor large farms, but which has interests different from those of the peasant and industrial worker. Now that industry is no longer confined mainly to small shops, there are many employees who stand midway in the industrial hierarchy between management and labor. The growth of trade and commerce, the construction of new public and parochial schools, and expanding public employment have contributed to a sharp increase in the ranks of the middle class.

Industrial labor has grown too, with the establishment of many new factories in food processing, household and office goods, drugs, and chemicals, and automobile supplies. In the larger firms workers are relatively well paid, have numerous fringe benefits, and regulated working hours and conditions. In the higher ranks many might already be considered middle-class and there are thousands of other middle-class prospects following close behind. In a sense, the industrial workers become an elite when compared with other urban elements, such as the poorly paid in the trades, domestic help, the lower ranks of public employees, and the unemployed.

Thus, industrialization in the Cauca Valley fits the classic pattern at least in part. The rise of the middle sectors is already a familiar phenomenon.[11] What one finds most interesting in the Valley are the obstacles to adjustments in the social system, and the reasons why shifts in the power structure come slowly and hard.

Despite rapid industrialization and the social developments described above, political power in the Valley is still closely tied to agricultural interests. In the first place, much of the new industry is owned and controlled by outsiders,[12] that is, persons who are less likely and less able to participate in the local political process. These outsiders have played an important role in the industrial development of the Valley partly because of the character traits of the local resident, the *Vallecaucano* himself. Traditionally, the large landowners have lacked entrepreneurial skills and interest in industrial development. Even today, landowning, and particularly cattle raising, represents the ideal of many leading *Vallecaucanos;* men with the money and education suitable for assuming positions of leadership in industry prefer sunny skies and open fields to office or factory. Members of the landowning class are used to independence: running their own farms in their own way. The tradition of the rich cattle breeder is often that of romantic individualism ill adapted to the modern industrial corporation. The upper-class *Vallecaucano* is not naturally attracted to the technique of team work and compromise of the modern impersonal industrial corporation. As a result, he has been slow to seize his industrial opportunities. He tends to prefer the measured, less hectic life of the gentleman farmer.

The *Vallecaucano's* agricultural traditions and open outlook have helped make him hospitable to outside participation in industrial ventures. He had demonstrated less drive and entrepreneurial abilities

[11]John J. Johnson, *Political Change in Latin America: The Emergence of the Middle Sectors* (Stanford, Calif.: Stanford University Press, 1958).

[12]Everett E. Hagen, "El cambio social en Colombia," Chapter XV of *On the Theory of Social Change* (Bogotá, 1963). Professor Hagen found that in 1956 of the 44 large industrial firms in the *Valle,* 17 were founded by *Antioquenos,* 9 by persons of foreign origin, 8 by *Vallecaucanos,* 7 as branches of foreign firms, and remainder by other Colombians. See p. 64. The number of foreign-owned firms has increased sharply since 1956.

than his northern neighbors from Antioquia and Caldas, but is known for hospitable treatment of newcomers. As Colombian citizens, entrepreneurs from these two Departments are in a position to play fairly active political roles, but can not be expected to have the political weight of a local family of long standing.

Foreign control of manufacturing, especially North American, is large. A leading figure associated with the local association of manufacturers estimates that 40 per cent of local manufacturing is foreign-owned, and even this estimate may be low. Among the companies represented are: Alcan, Colgate-Palmolive, Gillette, Goodyear, Grace, Home Products, Quaker Oats and Squibb. Almost all of the top managements of these companies are North American. The managers have quite a different outlook from that of local owners of manufacturing concerns. In the first place, they take their orders from their North American headquarters, frequently New York, and ordinarily spend only a few years in Cali moving on, and hopefully up, to another of their companies' overseas operations. Even those who consider themselves "permanently" settled in Cali often do not own their own homes. Although they usually take their obligations towards their companies' Colombian employees seriously and participate in civic activities; particularly of a charitable nature, the North American managers are not especially interested, nor do they consider it fitting for them to participate, in local politics. Their social relations with Colombians are limited. Except for the immediate impact political developments may have on their business, they do not ordinarily consider themselves as having a heavy stake in the country.

The French, Germans, Swiss and Swedes have also made investments in Cali. The Lebanese have been active in the textile industry and some have remained as permanent residents. Since World War II, there also has been a large immigration of Central Europeans, particularly Germans, into small business, including trade, optics, baking, hotels, and other services.

Many local industrialists have their roots in the land. As might be expected, local capital for industrial development has often come from landed interests, notably in sugar refining and other food processing, but also in metal working and pharmaceuticals. Thus, local industrialists often continue to have large vested interest in rural real estate, and their interests are reflected in their political behavior.

Some strong evidence on the national scene in support of what might be termed industry's under-representation in politics may be found in comparing the tax burdens of the agricultural and industrial sectors. According to an analysis of taxes paid in 1959, the industrial sector paid 37 per cent of direct taxes, and agriculture paid only 14 per cent even though the contributions to the net private product was almost reversed with industry contributing about 11 per cent, and agriculture 42 per cent.[13]

Labor unions have often served as cradles for the leadership of the Left and as the organizational base of revolutionary forces. The labor movement in the Valley, however, has had only limited political impact. In recent years the largest and most influential unions have not sought radical changes in the social structure but have concentrated their efforts on collective bargaining and organizations. These efforts have achieved success because the earnings and working conditions of organized labor in the Valley have improved materially in recent years and most managers have been forced to keep alert and responsive to their employees' demands. Despite labor's economic gains, however, the local labor leaders require greater maturity, particularly in matters of negotiation and organization.

Labor's political role is restricted by the leaders' personal limitations. Lacking education, many find it difficult to compete with the experienced and well-heeled representatives of management. Some of the leaders of the traditional unions, rather than considering themselves spokesmen of the downtrodden or exhibiting much class consciousness, are proud of their achievements and enjoy their newfound influence and affluence. In some cases, too, corruption has played a role. Reliable sources point out that some labor leaders have been known to accept money from management as the price of their cooperation in wage negotiations. Also, leaders of the ruling groups have made it a practice to offer promising young leaders of the Left lucrative career opportunities that dampen their revolutionary ardor.

Labor's role is further limited because the trade unions are split among some half dozen competitive labor federations, none of which has a commanding lead. The largest is UTRAVAL, the Union of

[13]Milton C. Taylor and Raymond L. Richman, *Fiscal Survey of Colombia* (Baltimore, 1965), p. 253.

Workers of the Valle, affiliated to the *Unión de Trabajadores de Colombia.* Although many of the leaders of UTRAVAL are Liberals, the federation usually is associated with the Conservatives–a national president Tulio Cuevas, for example, is a Conservative–and with the Catholic Church. A leading figure in UTRAVAL has been the hard-driving, pragmatic Jesuit priest, Francisco Xavier Mejía, who serves in the capacity of "spiritual adviser."

Another federation which has grown rapidly, particularly at the expense of Communist groups is FESTRALVA, Federation of Free Workers of the Valle, which is frequently associated, not always correctly, with the Liberal party. FESTRALVA, affiliated with the national Confederation of Colombian Workers (CTC), has recently incorporated several sugar mill unions which were formerly Communist-dominated.

The Communist-oriented Federation of Workers of the Valle (FEDETAV) has been engaged primarily in holding operation in its competition with other federations, especially on the Right. Another Left-wing group is the *Bloque Independiente Sindical,* a militant association of various unions including those of Colgate-Palmolive and Goodyear. The *Bloque's* leadership has a syndical and political orientation closely resembling that of the Communist-oriented FEDETAV.[14] The *Bloque* may have external support, perhaps from Castro. Many of its leaders have been members of the Socialist party, persons with a Marxist orientation and vague Soviet sympathies. While the *Bloque* appears to maintain a certain independence from the international Communist movement as compared to the FEDETAV, the Communists are probably making use of the *Bloque* for their own purposes.

Both the Left-wing groups, FEDETAV and the *Bloque,* sharply attack the UTRAVAL and the FESTRAVALVA as company, government, or Church-dominated unions, essentially as traitors to working-class interests. Whatever may be one's views about this, the two traditional groups do maintain fairly close and friendly ties with management and seek to temper class antagonisms. Also they are less concerned with politics and soft-pedal appeals for radical changes in the social structure.

[14]Andrés Almarales and Marina Goenaga, *Las luchas obreras y la legislación laboral* (Cali, 1964), *passim.*

The Left-wing unions (FEDETAV and the *Bloque*) call for a trade union movement that transcends mere collective bargaining and has a revolutionary orientation. Both federations take a strong anit-American line particularly in propaganda directed against American firms. Even they, however, find limits to these activities since they cannot afford to sacrifice their following to political ends. The fact is that most of organized labor represents the elite of the working classes and many workers are not inclined to push management too far and thereby jeopardize through revolutionary adventures their hard-earned gains. As a whole, one must therefore conclude that much of the labor movement does not currently exhibit revolutionary zeal, although inflation, rapid deterioration of the economy, or a political upheaval, could alter its behavior.

III

Unlike many Latin American countries, Colombia does not have a single large city which dwarfs all others with the chief division being between the metropolis and the rest of the country. Colombia is sometimes referred to as a "Country of Cities," with strong regional centers in Medellín, Cali, Barranquilla, and elsewhere. Thus it is worthwhile to examine the government and politics of Cali and the Department which it heads to determine the prospects for local development.

Under Colombia's unitary constitution all significant legislative authority is concentrated in the national Senate and House of Representatives and the President of the Republic controls local administration throughout the country. The Department of the Valle del Cauca has its own parliamentary organs as does the Municipality of Cali and other cities within the Department, but their legislative powers are minimal. Cali's leaders brush the local legislatures off as politically insignificant and concerned almost wholly with petty administrative details. The legislatures provide a forum for the discussion of local questions and are sometimes used to launch the political careers of men whose objective is Bogotá.

One of the major reasons for the weakness of Department and Municipal legislatures is their lack of fiscal autonomy. The most productive tax sources (income, excess profits, net wealth, customs) are reserved to the nation. The Department relies principally on taxes on tobacco, alcoholic beverages, gasoline, profits from the Department's liquor monopoly, and national subsidies. Municipalities rely primarily on real estate taxes and taxes on industry and commerce. In most cases the authority to tax, and tax rates, are fixed by the national legislature so that local government has little control over its revenues, and is restricted also in their allocation. The Department and Municipality also are heavily dependent on subsidies from above.[15]

The Department and the Municipalities lack administrative autonomy in that the Governor is appointed by the President of the Republic, often on the recommendation of his senior cabinet member, the Minister of Government, to whom the governors report. The Governor in turn appoints his own cabinet, that is to say the chief executive officers of the Department, and the mayors of the Department's municipalities. The latter form their own administrative groups. Thus a change at the top frequently results in a chain reaction all the way down the line. The Mayor of Cali appears to be merely an agent of the Governor of the Department, and the latter serves at the whim of the President of the Republic. Nonetheless, Department Governors are typically sensitive to public opinion and ordinarily must maintain some measure of popular support to hold their jobs. In fact, one observer in Cali expressed the view that the Governor was selected by the President and leading local citizens for his capacity to keep the populace in line.

Appointment of all local executive officials means that there is no single elected leader of the Department. The Governor is beholden to the President, not the people, and the latter are, in a sense, denied their own elected local leadership. The elected officials of the Department are the senators and representatives whose responsibilities are legislative and whose forum is the national parliament.

As a result of the Department's fiscal and administrative dependence, the leaders of the *Valle*[16] sometimes leave the impression

[15]See, for example, David T. Geithman, *Estudio de las rentas e ingresos del presupuesto del Municipio de Cali 1955–63* (Cali, 1964) and *Presupuesto del Valle del Cauca 1964* (Cali, 1964).

[16]*Valle* refers to the *Departamento del Valle del Cauca.* This Department occupies most but not all of the Valley of the Cauca River. The "Valley" refers to the Cauca Valley which includes *Valle* and parts of the Departments of Caldas and Cauca.

that their future is not in their own hands. The tendency is to look to Bogotá for decisions and financial aid; centralization serves as a break on local initiative. Another fruit of this system is frustration and political apathy at the local level. In a sense, this varies almost inversely with the extent to which the Department has the ear of the powers that be in the center. This sense of frustration mounts as one moves away from the center. Extreme centralization lends itself readily to bitterness and charges of favoritism.

Another reason for the turning away from government is the nature of the local governments themselves. The spoils system is rife, offices are overstaffed, and politics frequently paralyzes affirmative actions. One authoritative observer has said that the payroll of the Municipality could be cut by one third and result in an improvement of public services. Salaries are low, training programs inadequate, long range planning poor or absent.

The National Front's arrangements under *paridad* mean that all local government jobs ranging from the Governor to janitor must be split evenly between Conservatives and Liberals. Applicants are forced to state their party affiliation, even though they may be of two minds about it, and such a statement can be decisive.

The paralysis in public administration is especially tragic because of the flight of poor and uneducated citizens from poverty or the *violencia* in the country to the brighter lights of Cali. The city has not been able to accommodate this vast influx and there is serious unemployment and overcrowding. Housing, sanitary facilities, streets, and public transport are absent or heavily overloaded in some areas, and perhaps half of the school children of elementary age can not be accommodated in existing schools. Immigration to Cali is probably more than 4.5 per cent a year and new births may exceed 3 per cent, so the city is growing at about 8 per cent a year.[17]

In spite of social problems of alarming proportions, local government officials have difficulty acting promptly or formulating effective long range programs to deal with these problems. Periodic efforts are made by political leaders and public spirited citizens to modernize and strengthen government services without much success. The public at large is disillusioned, pessimistic, and apathetic about

[17] *Colombia, País de Ciudades, Cali* (Santiago de Cali, 1962), p. 6 of Chapter I by Alfonso Bonilla Aragón.

public administration. The *Valle's* disappointing record in public bodies, though perhaps no worse than in many other Latin American cities, has been offset by great strides forward in autonomous public agencies, controlled privately by public spirited civic leaders.

Among the autonomous public organizations with broadest scope is *La Unidad de Acción Vallecaucana,* a civic group formed to promote the general interests of the *Valle* without respect to political party. Many leading citizens are associated with the *Unidad* which maintains a small office staff in downtown Cali. The *Unidad* has a lobbyist in Bogotá and attempts to initiate and coordinate a variety of public activities in the *Valle* without serving as an operating agency itself. One of its best publicized efforts was the acquisition of some 50 police patrol wagons for the maintenance of security and order in that city. Before the trucks were made available to the city's police forces, thievery and other violent acts were widespread, partly because police protection was meager or nil. The city had relied, as it still does in part, on private police. The introduction of the patrol trucks improved public order and traffic conditions, although many are now out of action for lack of spare parts. The *Unidad* has also campaigned for a jet airport for Cali, encouraged the construction of more elementary schools, attempted to improve the supply and control the prices of basic foods, and attempted to strengthen municipal administration.

Cali also has reason to be proud of its *Empresas Municipales,* an autonomous public utilities concern, providing telephone service, power and water to the city, as well as administering the city's markets. The enterprise is reputed to be well and efficiently run and not mired down in local political squabbles. Some thought has also been given to making similar arrangements for the management of the city's various bus lines.

The *Corporación Autonoma Regional del Cauca* (CVC) is one of the better known development corporations in Latin America, and is a Colombian counterpart of the TVA in the United States. As a result of the efforts of local citizens and with the advice of Mr. David Lilienthal, the CVC was established in 1954 to help develop the Cauca Valley. The activities of the CVC are financed mainly by a surcharge tax on real estate. The CVC's major functions have been the construction of dams for the generation of hydroelectric power, land reclamation, irrigation and flood control.

Although the CVC has a broad charter, most of its activities have been restricted to technical matters. Nonetheless, it has undertaken a number of studies related to land reform, its specialists frequently speak out privately in favor of such reform, and it has acted as an agent in the Valley of INCORA, the land reform institute. As an autonomous and nonpolitical body, however, the CVC has avoided entanglement in the land reform controversy.

A comparatively new Colombian institution is the *Junta de Acción Communal,* the Community Development Committee. These organizations have been formed under government sponsorship and the provisions of legislation passed in 1959. The Juntas are designed to encourage all sorts of community action and improvement through self-help measures, such as the construction of school and sanitation facilities, community centers, establishment of agricultural cooperatives, etc. Ordinarily, the Juntas are organized in urban residential districts or rural communities at the county level. Peace Corps Volunteers work actively with many of the Juntas in development projects. Some of the Juntas have been converted into the hollow voice of local political bosses; others have achieved remarkable results through effective community teamwork.

Another important autonomous body that merits comment is the *Universidad del Valle.* A rising center of learning in Latin America, the University is best known for its Medical School and the associated hospital but has also made great strides forward recently in other Faculties. The University's administration is closely associated with the traditional leadership, but avoids political involvement. The University aspires to leadership in the Valley, particularly in social policy; so far this has taken place mainly as the result of the work of individuals associated with the University rather than through comprehensive institutional commitments.

As a result of Colombia's unitary form of government and the important role of autonomous agencies in the *Valle,* the local electorate is not in a position to influence policy and administration directly in many important areas. Similarly, there are serious impediments to popular participation in politics.

The most obvious restrictions are the constitutional arrangements under the National Front. The fact that all executive and legislative posts in government are divided evenly between the Conservatives and the Liberals means that elections are not supposed to affect the established balance of power. And these arrangements are to continue until 1974.

The local executive officials are, of course appointed, but elections are not crucial in the selection of the President–at least as long as the National Front holds up. The crucial test is the nomination of the Party (Liberal or Conservative) which has the next turn in the presidency. The Front's candidates were elected in 1958, 1962, and 1966.

Another obstacle to a decisive turn in Colombian politics within the framework of the National Front is the traditional character of politics in the *Valle,* as well as in all of Colombia. Political life continues to be dominated at the center by the leading caudillos and their local supporters. As a result, there is extreme fractionalization in politics at almost all levels which impedes the formulation of clear political alternatives. Among the Conservatives, for example, there are still conflicts between the followers of Laureano Gómez and Mariano Ospina, both former presidents of Colombia of the pre-Rojas era. Similarly, the Liberals of the local level are split between the followers of the leading *oficialistas,* like Alberto Lleras Camargo and Carlos Lleras Restrepo, and the Liberal opposition of Alfonso López Michelsen.

What these fractions do is give the voter in *Valle* many groups from which to choose, none of which gives any good prospect of putting through a strong and creative new program of social reform. This frustrating prospect has tended to throw many voters, particularly from the urban scene, into the hands of the extremists, the Communists on the Left and the followers of Rojas Pinilla on the Right.

In the *Valle* the Communist Party has been fighting a holding action against resurgent democratic and Right-wing forces. In the elections before 1966 it had a very narrow base of support as indicated by the small vote obtained by the Liberal faction which it supported. And the Communists cannot even claim all these votes because there still appear to remain elements within this faction independent of Communist control. Probably the strongest Communist leader in the *Valle* is José Cardona Hoyas, who spent several months during 1964 behind the Iron Curtain. Another leading member is Nicolas Buenaventura, who is reputedly a large landowner.

Communist strength in the *Valle* is centered in the labor federation,

FEDETAV. This federation has had a number of setbacks in recent years through the loss of several unions in the sugar industry to the Anti-Communist FESTRALVA.

Since the Sino-Soviet conflict for control of the international Communist movement has come out into the open, there have been repercussions in the *Valle* and more widely in Colombia. Most of the established Communists in Cali have come out strongly in favor of the Soviet Union in the dispute with China. Three leaders of the FEDETAV, sometimes referred to as the Chinese wing, were expelled in 1964 for having collaborated with management and the government. The spokesmen of FEDETAV denied the charge saying that the federation refused to be led to a precipice "without considering the relation of forces which exist today in the country."[18] Younger elements in the party, too, impatient with the old guard leadership, are setting themselves up apart to pursue a more radical course. Although there is some doubt that Communist China has given these groups significant support, Chinese policies provide disaffected Communists, oriented towards violence, and ideological home.

In recent years a group of leading local industrialists has taken steps to oppose Communist infiltration, and this group is sometimes known as the Black Hand. The organization is said to use a number of unorthodox methods, including the use of force, to check Communist penetration of trade unions and other organizations and the Party's efforts to stir up the masses. Financial support has also been given to sponsor propaganda activities in favor of democracy and free enterprise and against totalitarian systems. Since this group works behind the scenes, it is difficult to verify charges that the Black Hand is fascist-tinged.

A non-Communist Left-wing group in the *Valle* is the Socialists, long associated with a leading Colombian intellectual, Antonio García. This group is distinguished more for its intellectual ingenuity than its popular following. In fact the group has not attempted to establish a mass party at all, but instead has proclaimed the necessity of establishing a *Movimiento de Integración Nacional* (MIN). The program of the MIN is an appeal for social justice "without Communism" in which an attempt is made to stand above the struggle

[18] *El Expreso* (Cali daily newspaper), April 15, 1964, p. 1.

between the United States and the Soviet Union. The question remains whether its high-sounding program will attract much support unless this group comes to grips with concrete organizational and political problems. An offshoot of the Socialists has been active in the *Bloque Sindical Independiente,* often characterized as a Castroite labor group. The latter collaborated with the Communist labor organizations and the nature of its ties with the latter were not entirely clear. The popular appeal of the Socialists has been limited because of the participation of their leader, Antonio García, in the cabinet of ex-dictator Rojas Pinilla.

Finally there is also a Christian Democratic group with its own small trade union base which maintained a small office of two or three people in the city of Cali. The local Christian Democrats there have not yet played a politically significant role. Perhaps this is because of the Church's strong ties, past and present, with the Conservative party.

Another organization of political significance which should not be overlooked is the Roman Catholic Church under the leadership locally of Archbishop Alberto Uribe Urdaneta. The Church is influential not so much because of overt political activities which are little or nil, but because it is one organization which reaches deeply into all sectors of society in the *Valle*. Politicians and businessmen, to take two examples, hesitate to take openly anti-clerical positions, not, perhaps, because of specific sanctions imposed by the clergy itself, but because of a variety of social and other penalties imposed for failure to conform.

Within the clergy there are priests and many political persuasions, from those who embrace outmoded political views to those of pronounced Leftist tinge. Archbishop Uribe Urdaneta attempts to play it down the middle: "We have a thankless and difficult task, difficult and thankless because we are attacked by the Right and we are attacked by the Left."[19] The Church is active in many social fields, such as education, public health, and community development. It administers several community centers financed by the Foundations of rich local families and works actively in local labor circles through the UTRAVAL and on the countryside in various community development projects. In a political crisis the voice of the Church carries great weight as was shown at the time of the fall of dictator Rojas

[19]*El Occidente* (Cali daily newspaper) May 1, 1964, p. 1.

Pinilla. Clearly, the Church must be looked to primarily as a stabilizing, rather than a motive social force.

The influence of the United States on life in Cali is very great indeed. Much of Cali's industrial development is attributed to North Americans and North American capital. Among the first North Americans to be active in the *Valle* was James M. Eder who led in the development of the sugar industry there in the latter half of the nineteenth century. American investment in the area has continued ever since and has been particularly marked in light manufacturing during the last ten or fifteen years. Thus a large proportion of Cali's industrial labors force work under North American management. It is estimated that well over one thousand American citizens live in Cali.

North American public funds are made available in the form of loans to Colombian-controlled firms. The United States-sponsored private investment fund for industrial development has been estimated as counting for perhaps as much as two thirds of the long-term industrial loans made in the Valle.

The U.S. Agency for International Development through the Alliance for Progress has also been responsible for many social development projects.[20] New low-cost housing units are rising rapidly on the outskirts of Cali. In one month, March 1964, nineteen new primary schools financed under the Alliance for Progress were inaugurated in the *Valle*. Several million dollars have also been set aside for extending the power grid and improving the water and sewerage facilities of the city. Loans have also been made for the construction of health centers and other public works affecting the well-being of the entire populace.

Particularly noticeable have been the activities of the Peace Corps volunteers in the *Valle*. There were some 155 Peace Corpsmen in southwestern Colombia in 1964, of whom perhaps the majority were working in or within a few hours' drive of Cali. These young men and women were teaching; building schools, health centers, bridges and roads; and working with peasants. The Peace Corps views work on community development primarily as a means of encouraging democratic initiative and cooperation rather than as small-scale engineering projects.

[20]*El Occidente,* April 14, 1964, p. 2. Text of address by U.S. Consul S. Morey Bell.

Under the Partners of the Alliance Program there has been an interesting exchange of visits and experience between the leaders of the *Valle* and Oakland County, Michigan. The *Unidad de Acción Vallecaucana* has sought to improve municipal administration, particularly budgeting and planning, with the help of the Oakland Group. Progress in these and other areas necessarily affects vested interests and complicates the role of the North American visitors. The Oakland group sent a resident representative to Cali in mid-1964 and specific projects in public administration, education and other fields were planned.

The *Universidad del Valle* has also been the focus of much American interest, particularly by the Rockefeller and Ford foundations. A number of U.S. professors have been teaching at the University, and U.S. funds, whether from local, national, or foreign sources, have been used to strengthen the University's physical plant and academic programs. Other important efforts in the cultural field have included the work of the United States-Colombian Cultural Center. The Center has a library, offers lessons in English and sponsors visits of numerous scholars and artists from the United States. For some years now, too, able U.S. consuls have played active and prominent roles in the city's life.

In their relations with the various social strata, the U.S. representatives are faced with a dilemma. On the one hand, the United States wants and needs to help strengthen the hand of moderate groups favoring social reform. The consulate's labor officer has very close relations with the leaders of FESTRALVA and UTRAVAL and the American consulate frequently makes a point of its sympathy for organized labor. Also, the United States government stresses, as often as appropriate, its aid for construction of low-cost housing and other benefits for the poorer elements. The work of the Peace Corps and the Colombo-American Cultural Center are other constructive steps in this regard.

Nonetheless, the main associations of U.S. officials in Cali are with members of the dominant upper class. These are the people with whom American officials must deal, and they are also the ones with whom the official most naturally has social contact. The newspapers tend to publicize the North Americans' more frivolous activities. In addition, heavy North American investments in industry are well known and these companies naturally tend to identify with local propertied interests. As a result, although the United States is properly credited with providing impetus for social change, North Americans are also closely associated in the public mind with the defenders of the *status quo*.

Despite the rapid social changes that have been taking place in the Valley in recent years political power is still concentrated in the hands of agricultural and industrial property owners. It is sometimes said that a half-dozen men run the Cauca Valley. Granted that such a statement may be exaggerated and oversimplified, a few leaders have an immense influence on the Valley's affairs. They include a leading industrial figure, Manuel Carvajal; the head of the CVC, Bernardo Garcés; the editors of the local newspapers both of whom are senators; the Governor; the Bishop; and the sugar producers like the late Harold Eder.

While traditional interests remain in control, several of these leaders look more to the future than to the past. And although they are not about to preside over their own liquidation, this group is giving increasing attention to the city's urgent social needs. They act partly from humanitarian reasons. No less important is the growing realization of what may happen if these needs are not met. As a result, the civic leaders of Cali have become somewhat more socially conscious and responsive to popular demands.

Many of the efforts of social improvement are essentially designed to ameliorate living conditions and *not* to change the power structure. The greatest progress has been made in technical areas: the provision of hydroelectric power, irrigation, land reclamation, housing, sanitation facilities, etc. The least progress has been made in politically significant areas like land and tax reform. Prospective changes in the power structure appear more likely under existing conditions to come about as a result of the repercussions from rapid industrialization and urbanization than through deliberately planned tinkering with the political framework.

Current efforts to improve living conditions and strengthen the social fabric, while commendable, fall far short of the Valley's needs, especially in the face of the population explosion. Living and working conditions in the country and in many urban areas are appalling.

The masses of the people lack effective means of voicing and satisfying their demands. The peasants who constitute somewhat less than one half the Department's population are scarcely organized at all; the spokesmen for the countryside are still mainly the large landowners and their political representatives. The industrial workers in the cities, an elite group in comparison with the urban poor, are fairly well organized for economic purposes but the trade union leadership has not yet played a decisive political role. The urban poor lack strong organizations and appear to shift their allegiance back and forth between old time political caudillos and the demagogic extremists on the Left and Right. The rapidly growing middle classes still prefer to follow the lead of the traditional upper class and are quick to shed their ties with the lower classes. The unitary political system and the constitutional arrangements for the National Front also serve to restrict the usefulness of elections as a means of popular control over public policy and administration.

However imperfect popular representation may be, the majority of the *Valle's* voters formally support the National Front and the traditional leadership. But it is also probably not far from the mark to state that there is seething discontent near the surface that, once focused and ignited, could blow the local social structure to bits.

In the Cauca Valley, as in most other parts of Colombia, no popular leader has arisen capable of commanding the loyalty of the broad masses of the population in an assault on the traditional leadership. Extremists on both the Left and Right have been discredited. The Communist leadership in the *Valle* has lost ground in the labor movement and is distrusted because of its foreign ties; Rojas Pinilla, who is attempting to rebuild the Radical Right, was badly discredited at the time of his downfall, especially in Cali. The only other important group opposing the National Front is the MRL of López Michelsen which is badly split and weakly led.

In a sense, the political apathy and ignorance on the countryside and disorganization and confusion in the cities made it possible for the traditional leadership to resist rapid social change. If, however, Colombia's peasants and urban poor ever manage to find a focus of their discontent, the resulting revolution and anarchy could bring the existing power structure tumbling down, and with it, recent social gains. The nation would then need a generation or two to rebuild a new society on the ruins of the old.

Cuban Students in Politics: 1956–57[1]

By JAIME SUCHLICKI

The trial and, especially, the testimony of Marquito brought to light something that otherwise would not have been known—the tactics and strategy of the Communist Party in relation with the student movement.

A continual concomitant to Latin American government has been the political activity of university students. Why this is so has been the subject of much controversy. Many reasons have been given, ranging from the supposed greater idealism of youth and its willingness to risk everything for ideas to the fact that the universities are usually strategically located in capital cities, where demonstrations and violence can have the greatest direct effect on government. The realities of this situation have been recognized by all adult political parties. Often they seek to control and subvert student movements and convert them into shock forces through which

[1]This article is a chapter of the author's unpublished M.A. thesis, entitled "The Role of the University of Havana Students in Cuban Politics, 1952–1957," written at the University of Miami in 1965. A Spanish version of this article appeared originally in the *Journal of Inter-American Studies,* January, 1967. University of Havana students were chosen for this study because of their historically important role in political developments in Cuba and specifically because of the part they played in bringing about the revolution. Although students in the other universities were also active in politics, unfortunately their role cannot be appraised within the limited scope of this essay. Prior to Castro's revolution, there were in Cuba three state-controlled universities, one private university, and several private colleges, with approximately 21,000 students. More than 17,000 students attended the University of Havana in the 1950's. After the revolution former private institutions were abolished or nationalized, and the former Catholic University, "Santo Tomás de Villanueva," in Havana was transformed into the Makarenko Institute for adult teachers. All university instruction is now offered at the universities of Havana, Oriente, or "Marta Abreu" of Las Villas. Enrollment at the University of Havana was 15,315 students in 1966.

they can advance their own political views. University politics have thus long been a training school for politicians on a national level and major national universities have been made the arena in which adults have experimented with the effectiveness of national policies. If success is won by any group or movement, the next step is to move it onto the national stage, which physically is not far away. The peculiar complex of university autonomy in Latin America, plus the relation between the university and its graduates and the members of the professions, has made a combination that has put the university students into national politics in a way very dissimilar to that of the United States. Throughout Latin America the Communists have been especially active at the student level.

Thus, in the light of Castro's revolution in Cuba, the activities of the university students prior to his takeover acquire special interest and merit some detailed attention as an example of what can happen elsewhere.

Mr. Suchlicki, the author of the following selection, was born in Havana in 1939 of a Polish father and an Argentine mother of German extraction. He was educated at the Institute of Havana and attended the University of Havana for two years, 1959–1960. He thus lived in Cuba during the period covered by this essay and witnessed many of the events he describes. Mr. Suchlicki emigrated to the United States in 1960 and received his A.B. and A.M. degrees from the University of Miami. He is now working toward a Ph.D. degree in history at Texas Christian University in Fort Worth.

R. E. M.

Cuba has a prominent tradition of student political activism. In the last decades of the nineteenth century the University of Havana became a hot bed of anti-Spanish sentiment. In the early 1930's, students participated in the struggle that overthrew Dictator Gerardo Machado's regime (1927–33) and made Ramón Grau San Martín, a University of Havana physiology professor, Cuba's Provisional President. This activism reached a high-water mark during the dictatorship of Fulgencio Batista (1952–58).

The political vacuum created by Machado's overthrow in 1933 was filled by Fulgencio Batista, an obscure army sergeant. After the downfall of Grau San Martín's revolutionary regime in January, 1934, Batista emerged as the arbiter of Cuba's destiny. Until 1940 he remained behind the scene, allowing Carlos Mendieta (1934–36), Miguel Mariano Gómez (1936), and Federico Laredo Bru (1936–40) to occupy the presidency. Batista maintained tight political control until 1940, when he officially assumed the chief executive office, securing his election through a coalition of political parties. His four-year rule ended in 1944, when he allowed free elections.

For the next eight years, the *Partido Revolucionario Cubano* (Auténtico), which had been founded by Grau in 1934, governed Cuba. In 1944, Grau won the presidency, and in 1948 his political protégé, Carlos Prío Socarrás, became Cuba's last elected President. Despite numerous accomplishments, the *Auténticos* failed to provide the country with an honest government or to diversify Cuba's one-crop agricultural economy. The reformist zeal evident during Grau's first administration had diminished considerably in the intervening decade. Grau faced, furthermore, determined opposition in Congress and from conservative elements which had joined the party. For many Cubans the Auténticos failed to fulfill the aspirations of the anti-Machado revolution, especially in the area of administrative honesty.[2]

Grau's failure to bring honesty and order to Cuba's public life and the presidential aspirations of *Auténtico* Congressman and former student leader Eduardo Chibás produced a rift in the party. Chibás and other Auténtico leaders formed the *Partido del Pueblo Cubano (Ortodoxo)* in 1947. Led by Chibás, this party became the repository of the ideals of the "frustrated revolution" and the refuge of a new generation determined to transform those ideals into reality. Although the Communists had attracted several intellectuals and some students had embraced Marxism, few Cubans were prepared to accept the particular discipline which demanded working agreements with Machado and Batista in the 1930's. The past history of opportunism and political accommodations of the Communists had discredited them in the eyes of the Cuban people.

By 1950 the *Ortodoxos* had become a formidable political force. The party's nationalistic program of economic independence, political liberty, social justice, an end to corruption, and its insistence on

[2]See Carlos González Palacios, *Revolución y seudo-revolución en Cuba* (La Habana: 1948). Writing in 1951, Professor Stokes pointed out that results of the 1948 presidential elections challenged the *Auténticos*' right to lead the revolution, and he questioned the regime's ability to win future electoral contests. See William S. Stokes, "The Cuban Revolution and the Presidential Elections of 1948," *Hispanic American Historical Review,* Vol. XXXVII, No. 1 (February, 1951), pp. 78–79.

remaining free from political pacts had won for it a considerable following, especially among University of Havana students. With its slogan *Vergüenza Contra Dinero* (Honor Against Money), Chibás, already an elected senator, pounded on the consciences of the people in his Sunday radio programs and sought to awaken their minds to the corruption of the *Auténtico* administration. Chibás monopolized the rhetoric of revolution, becoming the exponent of the frustrated old generation and the leader of a new generation bent on bringing morality and honesty to Cuban public life.

But the hopes of the people were thwarted when Chibás, in one of the most bizarre episodes of Cuban political history, shot himself at the end of what started out to be one of his routine weekly radio appeals in August, 1951. Unaware that his radio program was over, Chibás continued to speak. "Cuban people, awake!" were his last words as he pulled a revolver and shot himself in the stomach. Chibás ' "last knock on the conscience of the Cubans," as his final address came to be known, and his death several days later produced a collective feeling of hysteria among the emotional masses. His body was taken to the University of Havana, where the Cuban people and the students could mourn their immolated leader. His role as the forerunner of the Castro Revolution is still an unwritten chapter of Cuba's history. Chibás' death created a political vacuum, left the masses leaderless, produced a rift in the *Ortodoxo* party, and left the door open for Batista's coup d'état on March 10, 1952.

By the time of Chibás' death, Cuba's political life was a sad spectacle. Although Prío had attempted various reforms, his administration resembled those of his predecessors. A system of nepotism, favoritism, and gangsterism predominated. Governmental positions were used to enrich the officeholder. The prestige associated with being a student leader was used by unscrupulous individuals to further their political aspirations and obtain governmental positions for friends and relatives. The presidency of the Federation of University Students (FEU) degenerated into a stepping-stone to national politics. The organized use of force became, furthermore, one of the main characteristics of student politics. During 1949 the president and vice-president of the FEU and several students were assassinated. The activities of the *bonches* (student gangs) became so conspicuous that *El Mundo* (Havana daily) declared editorially:

> . . . Violence holds sway in the halls of the university. Professors and students are nothing but the prisoners of a few groups of desperados, who impose their will and pass their examinations at pistol point. The University Council itself has declared its inability to repress these gangs for lack of coercive power.[3]

The breakdown in morale, respect, and values came to be aggravated by Batista's interruption of constitutional government in 1952. What the Cubans believed would never happen again, the return to military rule, became a reality. At the beginning of 1952, while Cuba awaited a presidential election to be held in June of that year, candidate Batista, convinced that he had no chance to win, overthrew on March 10, 1952, the constitutionally elected regime of Carlos Prío Socarrás. Bastista justified his exploit on the pretext that he was forestalling a similar coup by President Prío. Other reasons, however, have been adduced to explain his action. Cuba's distinguished writer and historian Juan J. Remos, a personal friend of Batista's and minister of state and of education during his first administration, told this author what he considers to be some of the factors which influenced Batista's decision. Remos explains them as follows:

> The reasons for Batista's action may be found in his ambitious nature and that of those surrounding him, particularly his own wife; in his desire for popularity, and in the political maneuverings of President Prío, who bribed Batista's allies into shifting their support and thus minimized his political possibilities in the June elections.[4]

The Cubans reacted to the new situation with skepticism. Had it not been for the depressed status of Cuba's political life as evidenced by the corruption, lack of respect for political figures, and gangsterism that prevailed during the *Auténtico* administrations, perhaps the reaction

[3]*El Mundo,* September 5, 1949, p. 3.

[4]Interview with Juan J. Remos, Miami, Florida, April 30, 1965. Remos, as all other persons interviewed, participated actively in or was closely connected to the events narrated in this essay. Although these interviews provide the main substance of the data obtained, wherever possible documentary evidence has been used to supplement these accounts—*i.e.,* newspapers, magazines, pamphlets, personal letters, tape-recorded speeches, and manifestos. It is obvious that interviews vary in value because of the intense involvement of some and the faulty memories of others. All interviews have therefore been used cautiously.

to Prío's overthrow would have been more vigorous. This, together with the prevailing disunity of the *Ortodoxo* party, which split after the death of Chibás, Batista's performance in 1944 when he restored order and allowed for free elections, and his promise for an election in November, 1953, contributed to the people's acquiescence in the coup.

In spite of the apparent consent, Batista was neither popular nor accepted as the island's legitimate ruler. Strong opposition soon developed. The *Ortodoxos,* one faction of the *Auténtico* party under Grau San Martín, and most of Cuba's politicians opposed Batista through peaceful means, hoping for an honest election. Another faction of the *Auténticos,* however, followers of the deposed President, immediately went underground and began plotting insurrectionary activities.

But the active rebellion was led by the University of Havana students through their organization, the Federation of University Students. It should be pointed out that the FEU was the only student organization within the University of Havana, and it represented a majority of the student body. The federation was composed of the presidents of the thirteen student associations from each of the different faculties at the university. These were elected yearly by the students and they in turn selected the president of the federation.[5]

Several factors enhanced the importance of the University of Havana students during the 1950's. First, more than 17,000 students attended the university and were represented by only one organization. Then the location of the university in the very center of the capital city exposed the students to the shock waves of Cuba's political turmoil and placed them in an ideal situation for making their political views known. The inadequate student unions and library facilities and a part-time faculty composed of professional men who lacked a feeling of responsibility so characteristic of the North American full-time faculties diminished still further the campus' educational atmosphere. Finally, the autonomy, originally a sheltering device against the encroachment of the government, converted the university into a sanctuary for political agitators. The fact that police were not allowed to enter the campus gave the students a safe

[5]For the structure of the FEU, see José Ramón Rolando Puig y Pupo, *Apuntes sobre la escuela de Derecho y la Universidad de la Habana.* (La Habana: Imprenta de la Universidad, 1959).

emplacement from which to carry on activities against the government.[6]

The very day of the coup, while Batista was still in the military garrison at Camp Columbia, FEU leaders marched to the Presidential Palace offering Prío their help to fight the military revolt. Their efforts were in vain. Prío's indecision and the speed with which the *golpistas* controlled the situation did not allow much action, and the President sought refuge in the Mexican Embassy.[7]

The students returned to their bastion at the University of Havana and from there organized demonstrations to repudiate the new regime. Their activities during the first three years of Batista's rule (1952–54) were limited to riots and protests and lacked ideological content or a systematic order of behavior. When compared with other political developments in Cuba, such as the ineffective role of the political parties or even Fidel Castro's attack on the Moncada garrison on July 26, 1953, the actions of the students seemed less important at the time. They proved, however, historically important, as they awakened the minds of the Cubans to the nature of Batista's rule and paved the way for the insurrection that followed.

During the first few years of Batista's regime, political parties exerted considerable influence on the students. The *Ortodoxos* were particularly influential. Their political platform and uncompromising attitude toward Batista, the mystique of their immolated leader, Eduardo Chibás, and the fact that several prominent party members were professors at the University of Havana contributed to their popularity among students. Also, the National Revolutionary Movement, an offshoot of the *Ortodoxo* party, commanded strong support. This latter group, led by professor Rafael García Bárcena, succeeded in recruiting a group of students for an attack on the military camp that had given Batista the command of the army. Bárcena had no

[6]Up to 1933 the university was under government jurisdiction. Decree No. 2059 of October 6, 1933, established the university autonomy and provided for a council composed of faculty and administrative officials. Later the 1940 constitution also guaranteed the autonomy. The university, however, continued to depend financially on the government. For a brief history of the university, see Luis Felipe Le-Roy y Gálvez, *La Universidad de la Habana: síntesis histórica* (La Habana: Imprenta de la Universidad, 1960).

[7]"En Cuba," *Bohemia,* No. 52, December 28, 1952, pp. 67–68. *Bohemia* was Cuba's most popular weekly magazine, and its section "En Cuba" carried the events of the week.

program other than the reenactment of the 1940 constitution and the holding of free elections. Batista's military intelligence, however, averted the plot and arrested Bárcena and several conspirators in April, 1953. After a brutal police beating, they were tried and sentenced to prison.[8]

The relations between Batista and the FEU, which had never been cordial, deteriorated rapidly. Early in 1953, police shot and killed a University of Havana student during a demonstration in front of the school. A national student's strike followed. Disorders spread throughout the island. Demonstrations against the government were almost daily occurrences. When the regime announced the postponement of the 1953 national elections for a year, the FEU quickly accused Batista of perpetuating himself in power. The federation demanded general elections as soon as possible and a neutral government that could give all parties ample guarantees.[9]

Batista's mock elections in November, 1954, placed Cuba at a dangerous crossroads. To obtain a peaceful solution to her political difficulties, it was imperative that government and opposition reach an understanding. The opposition wanted new elections, whereas Batista insisted on remaining in power until his new term expired in 1958. Throughout 1955 numerous meetings were held in an attempt to find a compromise. The failure to reach an agreement that would satisfy both parties forced the Cubans reluctantly to follow a road that led to civil war, chaos, and revolution. Until the end of 1955 the students shared the belief in, and participated in every attempt toward, a peaceful solution. Only when they realized that the government would not relinquish power and that the greed of the governing clique was not as yet satisfied did they resort to rebellion.

At the end of 1955 a series of student riots shocked the country. On November 27 the FEU called for a commemorative ceremony to honor eight students shot by Spanish authorities in 1871. When the meeting turned into an anti-Batista rally, police arrested several of the leaders, while others had to be hospitalized as a consequence of brutal

[8]"Resolverá el Tribunal de Urgencia situación de los detenidos," *Diario de la Marina,* April 7, 1953, p. 1. See also "En Cuba," *Bohemia,* No. 16, April 19, 1953, p. 77, and No. 22, May 31, 1953, pp. 68–69.

[9]For a description and photographs of the murdered student's funeral, see *Vida Universitaria,* No. 32, March, 1953, pp. 13–14. Also, see "Interview with José Joaquin Peláez," *Bohemia,* No. 10, March 8, 1953, pp. 70–71.

police methods. Similar events, but with more dramatic results, occurred in Santiago, capital of Oriente Province, where police ruthlessly beat students who attempted to commemorate the November 27 ceremony. In protest, the FEU called a student strike which quickly spread throughout the island. All universities, colleges, and secondary schools closed. For three weeks, daily sorties were made against the police all over the country, usually under the pretext of honoring the numerous martyrs. On December 2, when students attempted to march from the University of Havana, they were stopped and beaten by the police. The new FEU president, José A. Echeverría, and vice-president, Fructuoso Rodríguez, had to be hospitalized. On December 4, during a baseball game, a group of fifteen students ran into the field and displayed banners condemning the regime. Several dozen policemen, who were waiting for the demonstrators, surrounded them and beat them brutally in front of thousands of astonished television viewers. In clashes during the following months more than thirty persons were wounded, including several policemen–many by gunfire. Finally on the pretext of searching for hidden arms, government forces entered the university, demolished the rector's office, and destroyed documents, scientific equipment, and furnishings. The action was decried as a violation of the university autonomy, and Rector Clemente Inclán suspended classes indefinitely.

While student riots and demonstrations against the government were going on, other Cubans unconnected with student activities were plotting to unseat Batista. Fidel Castro, in exile since July, 1955, was an early advocate of armed action against the government. He organized his July 26 Movement and traveled to the United States and Mexico seeking followers and funds for the revolutionary cause. In 1956 Castro vowed to overthrow Batista or to die fighting in the attempt.[10] Another group, known as *Montecristi,* plotted with army officers and attempted to overthrow the regime through a bloodless coup. Batista uncovered the conspiracy and arrested the principal military plotters in April, 1956.[11] The same month another group belong-

[10]"Carta a varios líderes políticos de Cuba," *La sierra y el llano* (La Habana: Casa de las Américas, 1961), p. 66. This book contains a collection of original accounts and documents pertaining to the anti-Batista insurrection.

[11]La Conspiración del 3 de Abril," *Bohemia,* No. 16, April 15, 1956, pp. 63–77.

ing to former President Prío's *Organización Auténtica* attacked unsuccessfully the Goicuría army barracks in Matanzas Province.[12]

The eruption of violence added a note of urgency to the need for finding a peaceful solution. Despite the opposition leaders' continuous attempts toward this end after April, 1956, skepticism grew about the willingness of the regime to relinquish power and about the opposition's ability to influence the course of events. The adherents to violence continued to grow in number. Instead of seeking to discourage rebellion by moderation, the regime encouraged it by meeting terrorism with a murderous counterterrorism that defeated its own ends.

By the end of 1955 the leaders of the FEU realized that the efforts of nonpartisan organizations to reconcile government and opposition were futile. They proposed the creation of an insurrectionary organization that could lead an active struggle against Batista until freedom was obtained. As the FEU proposal found little response among the electorally oriented politicians, the students formed their own clandestine organization–the *Directorio Revolucionario* (Revolutionary Directorate) in December, 1955. In a secret meeting at the University of Havana on February 24, 1956, FEU President Echeverría, now also *Directorio* coordinator, announced its creation.

The reasons for organizing the *Directorio* were varied. One of its founders, Félix Armando Múrias, explained to the author that the students had maintained constant contact with labor leaders who were willing to participate in coordinated actions against the regime. "There was a need to have an organization that could lead those actions," said Múrias. "Furthermore, members of the FEU who advocated an insurrection against Batista met with opposition within the federation, adding a note of urgency to the need for a separate organization."[13] Armando Fleites, also an active member of the *Directorio* since its inception and later a commander of the guerrilla forces which fought Batista, explained that during 1955 many labor and professional leaders, disappointed with the electoral negotiations and having no underground movements to which to turn, approached Echeverría to

[12]"Cuartel Goicuría, 29 de Abril," *Bohemia,* No. 24, June 10, 1956, pp. 60–65.

[13]Interview with Félix Armando Múrias, Miami, Florida, July 19, 1965. Of the eight original founders of the *Directorio,* José A. Echeverría, Fructuoso Rodríguez, Joe Westbrook, and Tirso Urdanivia died in the struggle against Batista; Faure Chomón and Rene Anillo are in Cuba supporting the revolutionary regime; Jorge Valls is in a Castro jail, and Múrias is in exile.

coordinate the armed resistance against Batista. Since the federation operated under the aegis of the university and could not incorporate these nonstudent elements, it became necessary to create an organization apart from the FEU that could lead the resistance against Batista.[14]

Out of the interviews with former *Directorio* activists, the following portrait emerges. The student leaders were admirers of Eduardo Chibás and José Martí and shared the latter's vision of an idealized *patria*, a socially united, racially harmonious, and economically independent country. They were democratic, strongly nationalistic, and opposed to Communism. "Not only were we anti-Communist," said Múrias, "but we opposed agreements with Cuban Communists, whom we considered opportunists and collaborators with Batista since the nineteen thirties."[15]

The students advocated economic reforms, such as diversification of agriculture, industrialization, and agrarian reforms. They opposed administrative corruption and other evils of Cuba's public life, and they wanted the full reestablishment of the 1940 constitution and the holding of free elections. Most of them did not aspire to political office and limited their involvement in politics to Batista's overthrow, but a few were interested in using the university as a stepping-stone for national prominence. After Batista's fall several *Directorio* leaders showed their eagerness for positions in the Castro government. In general, they were politically immature but well-intentioned and idealistic youngsters who desired the best for their country. It is significant to note that several of the FEU and *Directorio* leaders were from areas other than Havana and that they usually came from poorer or lower-middle-class homes. It seems that these students, living away from their families and exposed to the loneliness of a new environment, gravitated toward the campus and were more prone to get involved in political activities than the average city student.

Several characteristics distinguished the *Directorio* from other insurrectionary organizations fighting Batista. As far as its membership was concerned, the *Directorio* was predominantly a student organization. It was not until after the attack on the Presidential Palace and the assassination of its principal leaders in 1957 that nonstudent

[14]Interview with Armando Fleites, Miami, Florida, July 12, 1965.
[15]Interview with Félix Armando Múrias, Miami, Florida, July 19, 1965.

elements enjoyed a degree of importance and shared in the decision-making process of the organization. As far as their strategy was concerned, its leaders believed in tyrannicide and assassination as the means of overthrowing the government. They were, however, strongly opposed to indiscriminate terroristic acts, such as bombing or strafing crowds which might kill innocent people.

The plans of the *Directorio* called for establishing contact with other leaders advocating armed opposition against Batista. One of these, Fidel Castro, had been training an expeditionary force in Mexico and planned to land in Cuba at the end of 1956. Early that year, Echeverría, head of the *Directorio* and FEU president, led a student delegation to Mexico and signed an agreement with Castro known as *La Carta de México.* (The Mexican Letter). The students pledged a series of diversionary riots in Havana to coincide with Castro's landing on the other end of the island. "Since the landing date had not been set," Múrias explained, "Castro promised to advise the students as to his exact plans."[16]

In October, 1956, the *Directorio's* delegation which had signed the pact, returned to Cuba. Despite their public pronouncements and apparent enthusiasm, the students were not totally statisfied with their conversations with Castro. "Differences occurred," said Múrias, "because the operations of the *Directorio* were made to depend on Castro and his landing venture. Furthermore, when Fidel proposed the incorporation of the *Directorio* into his 26 July Movement, he met Echeverría's and the others' stern opposition."[17] Several of those returning from Mexico manifested privately their dissatisfaction with Castro's egocentric attitude. Dora Rosales, mother of Joe Westbrook, one of the leaders of the *Directorio* who attended the meeting, explained to the author that friction occurred between her son and Castro when the latter expressed himself contemptuously about Professor Rafael García Bárcena. Mrs. Rosales remembers hearing her son say, "May God prevent us from falling into the hands of Fidel. . . . He is an absolutist."[18]

Joe Westbrook was not the only one to show discontent with Castro. In another interview, Annaelis Esteva, daughter of the *Auténtico*

[16]Interview with Félix Armando Múrias, Miami, Florida, July 19, 1965.
[17]*Ibid.*
[18]Interview with Dora Rosales, Miami, Florida, May 14, 1965.

congressman Salvador Esteva Lora and a close collaborator of the *Directorio,* told the writer that Fructuoso Rodríguez, vice-president of the FEU and a participant in the conversations in Mexico, asserted that "Fidel Castro was another *caudillo.*" The only member of the delegation who showed any enthusiasm for Fidel," commented Miss Esteva, "was Juan Nuiry."[19] Although these remarks are emphasized more strongly today, there is no doubt that the students were not happy with the results of their meetings with Castro. Their common enemy at the time, however, was Batista, and the students brushed aside most of the differences that arose.

Only a few days after Echeverría's arrival, the *Directorio* undertook one of its first operations–an attempt on the life of Colonel Antonio Blanco Rico, head of the Military Intelligence Service. (SIM). On October 28, 1956 two members of the *Directorio* fired at Blanco Rico and a group of his friends in the Montmartre Nightclub in Havana, killing him and critically wounding Colonel Marcelo Tabernilla, second in command of the Cuban Air Force, and son of the commander in chief of the Army.[20] The attack on Blanco Rico undoubtedly was perpetrated in order to call the attention of the editors of Latin American newspapers attending the Inter-American Press Association (SIP) meeting in Havana, to the situation existing in Cuba. Aldo Baroni, representing *Excelsior* of Mexico City, described the scene in the glass-enclosed dining room of the nightclub, explaining that in the confusion women crashed into mirrors which they mistook for open space.[21]

In the chaos after the shootings the attackers were able to escape. At first their identities were unknown to the police, but on December 1, Dr. Armando de Cárdenas y Arangúren, a well-known Havana heart specialist, was arrested and accused of being in complicity with the assassins of Blanco Rico. Cárdenas admitted to the police that he had given refuge in his home to two students, Juan Pedro Carbó Serviá and Rolando Cubela, but that he was in no way connected with the plot that led to Blanco Rico's death.[22]

[19]Interview with Annaelis Esteva, Miami, Florida, May 11, 1965.

[20]"La muerte del Coronel Blanco Rico," *Diario de la Marina,* October 29, 1956, p. 1.

[21]"La trágica muerte del Coronel Blanco Rico," *Bohemia,* No. 45, November 4, 1956, pp. 60–66.

[22]"Arrestó el SIM al que ocultó a los matadores de Blanco Rico," *Diario de la Marina,* December 1, 1956, p. 1.

By the time of Cárdenas' arrest, Cubela had been able to escape to Miami, and Carbó Serviá had found refuge in a Havana house. The author interviewed Ada Azcarreta a *Directorio* delegate in Miami at the time that these events occurred. Mrs. Azcarreta explained that during Cubela's stay in Miami, he visited her home quite frequently. "He was deeply disturbed," she added, "by reports coming out of Cuba which portrayed him as an assassin–so much so, in fact, that he underwent psychiatric treatment here in Miami."[23]

The boldness of the attack brought censure from several sectors of society. Sensing the indignation that the assassination of Blanco Rico had produced, Castro used the incident for his own propaganda objectives. "There was no need to kill Blanco Rico," he told a reporter in Mexico in November, "others deserved to die much more than he did."[24] Still in exile, and on the eve of his landing in Cuba, Castro was attempting to project his image to the Cuban people as an advocate of a frontal struggle against Batista and as opposed to actions of the type perpetrated by the *Directorio*. Undoubtedly, Castro intended to discredit the student leaders, for he considered them rivals in the quest for power.

While these events took place in Havana, in Oriente Province, at the other end of the island, a small but well-organized July 26 underground led by Frank País, prepared for Castro's arrival. Castro set November 30, as the date of his landing. On that day commando groups attacked several military installations and touched off a wave of sabotage throughout the province. Terrorism flared; bombs exploded. Underground cells derailed trains and sabotaged power lines, blacking out towns.

In Havana, meanwhile, the leaders of the *Directorio* watched the Oriente developments, anxiously awaiting word from Castro to go into action in the capital. "Fidel's notification," said Múrias, "did not come until December second–the same day he was landing in Oriente."[25] By that time the uprising had been crushed, and most of the leaders of the July 26 Movement were either dead or in jail. Batista suspended

[23]Interview with Ada Azcarreta, Miami, Florida, May 7, 1965.

[24]"Interview with Fidel Castro in Mexico," *Bohemia,* No. 11, January 6, 1957, p. 6.

[25]Similar statements, claiming that Fidel failed to notify the *Directorio* in advance of his landing, were made in other interviews by Juan A. Rodriguez, Miami, Florida, May 7, 1965; Annaelis Esteva, Miami, Florida, May 11, 1965; and Armando Fleites, Miami, Florida, July 12, 1965.

constitutional guarantees and established total censorship of news. The dreaded military police patrolled the streets of Havana day and night and began a roundup of all suspected revolutionary elements. Castro's movement was not acclaimed by the general public or by the regular opposition parties. The army remained loyal. Fidel found refuge in the Sierra Maestra Mountains and from there began waging guerrilla warfare against the regime.

The *Directorio* leaders failed to support the Oriente uprising. Without Castro's word they wavered in confusion. Fearing that the regime might be faking a revolt to expose anti-Batista revolutionaries, they decided to wait. The speed with which Batista's repressive forces controlled the situation left very little room for action. Several years later, *Directorio* leader Faure Chomón justifying their failure to support Castro's landing said that at the time the students lacked "the necessary means" [weapons] to stage a revolt in Havana.[26]

The events in Oriente prompted the University of Havana Council to suspend classes temporarily on November 30, 1956. But as terrorism and violence continued, the council indefinitely postponed the reopening of the university, which remained closed until early in 1959.[27]

Batista and his group welcomed the closing of the university. For five years the students had been a thorn in their sides. Now that the most vociferous and persistent focus of rebellion had been closed, the government expected to neutralize student opposition. But the closing of the university threw almost 20,000 students into the vortex of Cuban politics. As time went on and the university remained closed, the impatience of the students grew and many began joining insurrectionary organizations. The need for a quick solution which would end Batista's regime became more pressing. The struggle against Machado's dictatorship in the 1930's, which resulted in the overthrow of his government, the restoration of popular elected regimes, and almost two decades of political freedom and economic progress served as a precedent to justify the fight against Batista and the belief in a similar result after his overthrow.

[26]Testimony of Faure Chomón at the trial of Marco Armando Rodríguez, *Hoy,* March 24, 1964, p. 8.

[27]"Suspenden clases en la Universidad," *Diario de la Marina,* December 1, 1956, p. 1; December 3, 1956, p. 1. Also see "Calmada la capital de Oriente después de dos jornadas de sucesos," *ibid.,* December 2, 1956, p. 1.

The students and the Cuban people in general looked at the emergence of Batista as only a temporary interruption of Cuba's democratic political development. It was considered a consequence of Batista's own ambitions for power and Prío's corrupt rule, rather than a symptom of more profound social, political, and economic problems. The reduced importance of political institutions at the local level, the reliance on *personalismo,* the widespread administrative corruption, the continuous dependence on a one-crop economy, etc., were problems that did not receive the attention they required. The elimination of Batista's dictatorship was considered the panacea that would cure all of Cuba's ills. This rather simple and politically unsophisticated approach was to serve Fidel Castro's purposes during his stay in the Sierra Maestra Mountains, when he proclaimed the overthrow of the regime as the only and immediate task, avoided as much as possible the issue of defining his movement's ideology, and advocated very few but popular reforms.

The *Directorio* began planning the overthrow of the government by assassinating Batista. Its leaders reasoned that a fast and decisive action such as the physical elimination of the dictator would produce the crumbling of the regime and prevent unnecessary loss of life in a possible civil war. Castro's denunciation and his rebuke of Echeverría, whom he accused of not fulfilling "the Mexican Letter," added a note of urgency to the students' insurrectionary activities.[28] Juan A. Rodríguez, a prominent FEU leader, points out that Echeverría felt it was a question of honor to prove his courage and the *Directorio's* determination to fight.[29]

Other groups, especially some made up of *Auténticos*, shared the *Directorio's* idea of killing Batista. Early in 1957 they all combined forces and drew plans to storm the Presidential Palace and assassinate Batista. There were various reasons for the selection of the palace as the site of an attempt on Batista's life. The secrecy surrounding any move of the President outside the palace made it impossible to pinpoint a location for an assassination attempt, and the obvious strong security deployed on such occasions made Batista almost invulnerable. Another reason was perhaps less objective. The plotters felt that by capturing the palace, where the entire

[28]Rodríguez, Fleites and Múrias all asserted that Castro blamed Echeverría for not fulfilling the pact.

[29]Interview with Juan A. Rodríguez, Miami, Florida, May 7, 1965.

governmental machinery resided, they would be able to control the reins of power. Although the plans after the attack were not totally known by those interviewed, it seems that the plotters attempted to establish a provisional government, perhaps under the presidency of a distinguished political figure, until elections could be held. One of the individuals considered by the *Directorio* to head a provisional government was *Ortodoxo* Congressman Pelayo Cuervo Navarro.

A twofold plan to overthrow Batista got under way. On March 13, 1957, a combined force of the *Directorio* and followers of former President Prío stormed the Presidential Palace and succeeded in penetrating to the second floor of the building. Despite their audacity, the strong palace defense held out. The poor quality of the attackers' armaments and the failure of reinforcements to arrive turned a possible victory into a costly defeat. The official government figure of deaths was twenty, including five members of the palace guard slain during the attack. That total, however, did not include the many conspirators who were hunted down and killed by the police after the palace assault.[30]

The attack on the Presidential Palace coincided with the takeover of a radio station. At 3:25 P.M. the station began announcing, "At this moment armed civilians are attacking the Presidential Palace! President Batista has been killed." A second announcement reported that General Francisco Tabernilla, chief of the Army, had been arrested, along with other high-ranking officers of the regime. Then José A. Echeverría spoke. "People of Havana," said the FEU leader, "the revolution is in progress. The Presidential Palace has been taken by our forces and the dictator has been executed in his den. . . ." A switch thrown in the station's control room cut his voice abruptly.[31] The events that followed were narrated to the author by Mrs. Rosales:

Echeverría, my son [Joe Westbrook], and Fructuoso Rodríguez hurried out of the building. Other armed students had been standing guard at the entrance. All of them entered three cars and sped away toward the university. A police car came into sight. Figueredo, the driver of the car in

[30]The attack on the Presidential Palace is narrated by one of the participants, Faure Chomón, in a series of three articles, entitled "El ataque al palacio presidencial el 13 de Marzo de 1957," published in *Bohemia,* No. 11, March 15, 1959; No. 12, March 22, 1959; and No. 14, April 5, 1959.

[31]Julio García Olivera, "La operación Radio Reloj," *Bohemia,* No. 11, March 15, 1959, p. 12.

which Echeverría was riding, thinking that the police had discovered them, rammed his automobile against the police vehicle, and began firing his pistol. When Echeverría tried to jump out of his car, the police shot and killed him.[32]

The other students, some of them wounded were able to escape. "Joe and Fructuoso Rodríguez," added Mrs. Rosales, "joined two companions in one of the *Directorio's* apartments at Humboldt Street, while the rest went into the various hideouts of the *Directorio* throughout the city."[33]

The bullet-ridden body of Echeverría lay there in the street, not far from the university he had loved so much and where he had demonstrated so many times against Batista. Just minutes before his death, he had written a manifesto which came to be known as his political testament. In one of its parts, Echeverría seemed to have sensed his destiny when he wrote:

> . . . We trust that the purity of our ideals will grant us the blessings of God so we may obtain the predominance of justice in our country. . . . If we fall, let our blood indicate the road toward freedom. The tremor our actions will originate, whether or not it is as successful as we expect it to be, will make us advance on the path toward victory.[34]

In his first statement made after the attack, Batista expressed his gratitude to the members of the palace guard for their courage and loyalty and added: "My life does not matter. What does matter is that the nation does not become embroiled in chaos."[35] In a meeting with the press shortly before midnight on March 13, Batista said that the attackers were "poor, mad fools, paid by people who looted the national treasury, who were carrying out directives of the Communist party."[36]

[32]Interview with Dora Rosales, Miami, Florida, May 15, 1965.
[33]*Ibid.*
[34]Echeverría's political testament has been published in several newspapers, magazines, and student publications in Cuba. The Revolutionary Student Directorate, a Cuban student organization in Miami, provided the author with a copy.
[35]Frustrado el asalto al Palacio Presidencial por un grupo de 40 hombres con numerosas armas," *Diario de la Marina,* March 14, 1957, pp. 1, 12A.
[36]"Rebel Suicide Squad Wiped Out," *The Times of Havana,* March 14, 1957, p. 1, 4.

Fidel Castro, from his hideout in the Sierra Maestra, criticized the attack. In an interview filmed in April and shown on television in the United States early in May, Castro told CBS correspondent Robert Taber that it had been "a useless waste of blood." "The life of the dictator," said Fidel, "is of no importance. . . . Here, in the Sierra Maestra is where they have to come to fight."[37]

Not only Fidel but also two of his sisters were critical of the assault on the Presidential Palace. Lydia and Emma Castro, during a brief visit to New York from Mexico, declared that all projects of the 26 July Movement were going in accordance with their brother's plans, but that in no way did these plans contemplate the assassination of President Batista or any member of his regime; the movement desired only their removal from office."[38]

Fidel Castro was in no way connected with the palace attack. Throughout his stay in the mountains, he was opposed to a military coup, the assassination of Batista, or any violent act by any group not directly under the control of his July 26 Movement that would topple the regime. The success of the March attempt would have left his small and disorganized movement in an uncomfortable situation, cutting short his struggle for total power.

Another group which spoke against the attack on the Presidential Palace was the *Partido Socialista Popular* (official name for Cuba's Communist party). The head of the party, Juan Marinello Vidaurreta, wrote to Herbert L. Matthews on March 17, 1957, explaining the official party line. "In these days," wrote Marinello, "and with reference to the assaults on barracks and expeditions from abroad–taking place without relying on popular support–our position is very clear, we are against these methods." The PSP opposed the attack on the Presidential Palace or any similar type of action. The Communists advocated, as the only correct strategy against Batista, a mass struggle based primarily on the mobilization of the proletariat and leading toward the national elections. They called for the creation of a *Frente Democrático de Liberación Nacional* (Democratic Front of National Liberation) to form a government representing the workers, peasants, urban petty bourgeoisie, and the national bourgeoisie, all under the

[37]"En Cuba," *Bohemia,* No. 28, May 28, 1957, p. 97.
[38]*Hispanic American Report,* Vol. X, No. 3 (March, 1957), p. 127.

leadership of the proletariat.[39] It is significant to note that the Communists specifically mentioned the workers and peasants but failed to mention the students who had led the struggle against Batista and had just attacked the Presidential Palace.

The PSP leaders were following a dual strategy. While publicly advocating peaceful opposition to Batista, they were secretly making overtures to the insurrectionary groups for closer collaboration. As early as December, 1955, Raúl Valdés Vivó, secretary general of the *Juventud Socialista* (Youth Branch of the PSP), held meetings with Echeverría and Fructuoso Rodríguez pressing for closer relations with the *Directorio.* Vivó also advocated a "united front" of all students, including the *Directorio,* but under the leadership of the FEU.[40] The Communists, encouraged by their success in electing Amparo Chaple, a member of the *Juventud,* to the presidency of the school of philosophy at the University of Havana in November, 1955, figured they could eventually dominate the FEU and attempted to neutralize the creation of the *Directorio* by placing it under the federation's control. Despite Communist overtures, no union emerged out of these early contacts with the students. Echeverría and other student leaders were not ready for an alliance with the Communists and went ahead with their plans for the *Directorio.* Later, in February, 1957, in a letter to the July 26 Movement, the PSP leaders also called on Castro for "closer understanding" based on a "coincidence" of strategy. They insisted that armed action was the wrong tactic and explained that they disagreed with Fidel over "methods and tactics." They noted, however, that among the different groups in Cuba the July 26 Movement "came closest" to the Communists' "strategic conception."[41]

Throughout most of Batista's rule, the Communists had enjoyed complete liberty, and several of them even held important posts in the

[39]Marinello's letter can be found in Herbert L. Matthews, *The Cuban Story* (New York: George Braziller, 1961), pp. 51–52. The original letter is in the Columbia University Library. The passages quoted in the text are from Matthews' book and from Theodore Draper, *Castroism, Theory and Practice,* (New York: Praeger, 1965), pp. 30–31.

[40]Testimony of Raúl Valdés Vivó at the trial of Marco Armando Rodríguez, *Hoy,* March 25, 1964, p. 4.

[41]Carta del Comite Nacional del Partido Socialista Popular al Movimiento 26 de Julio," February 28, 1957, quoted in Draper, *Castroism,* pp. 29–30.

government. Batista took certain measures against the PSP, principally to appease the United States government. These were minor, however, when compared with the persecution suffered by the non-Communist forces and especially the students. The PSP consistently attempted to undermine, infiltrate, and control the groups combating Batista. The importance of the *Directorio Revolucionario* as a dangerous rival organization in the quest for power and the militant anti-Communism of several of its leaders were constantly present in the minds of the top members of the party. Their attempts to infiltrate the *Directorio* became known only after Castro's rise to power.

The defeat suffered at the palace was further aggravated by the assassination a month later of the *Directorio's* remaining top leaders. On April 20, 1957, police surrounded an apartment building at Humboldt Street in Havana and massacred Fructuoso Rodríguez, acting president of the FEU, Joe Westbrook, Juan Pedro Carbó Serviá, and José Machado.[42] The brief official police communiqué issued soon after stated simply that three students, Fructuoso Rodríguez, Juan Pedro Carbó Serviá and José Machado, had opened fire against the police and were killed while attempting to escape from the building at Humboldt 7, in which they had been hiding. A fourth, Joe Westbrook, was killed inside the building. In a curious postscript, the police added that two students, Eugenio F. Pérez Cowley, and Marco Armando Rodríguez, had escaped from the building.[43] That the police were able to locate the students' hideout seemed almost impossible to the friends and family of the murdered youths. Every indication pointed toward a police informer among the students. Any investigation of the events, however, had to wait until Batista's downfall.

The Humboldt event, as this episode was later known, the failure of the attack on the Presidential Palace, and the death of Echeverría, at

[42]Interview with Dora Rosales, Miami, Florida, June 14, 1965. Mrs. Rosales, Joe Westbrook's mother, took up the fight against Batista after her son fell. She went into exile and traveled throughout Latin America denouncing Batista. After Castro came to power, she returned to Cuba and supported the revolutionary regime. When it became clear, however, that Communism had gained control in Cuba, she again went into exile and denounced Castro's betrayal of the revolution.

[43]"Police Press Search for Two Who Escaped Saturday's Gunfight," *The Times of Havana,* April 22, 1957, p. 2. A note of mystery was added to these events when the Spanish version of the police communiqué that appeared in the *Diario de la Marina* that same day, did not mention any students having escaped from Humboldt 7.

the time the most popular figure opposing Batista, left the *Directorio* leaderless and disorganized. Almost a year was to go by before the organization recovered from that blow, and even then it did not regain the prestige and importance it had enjoyed prior to the palace assault. This period of decline of the *Directorio* marked the rise of the July 26 Movement. Unchallenged in the mountains, Fidel Castro gained in prestige, strength, and following. His movement gained adherents in the cities and won over many discontented elements who, despite their differences with the July 26 Movement, found no other insurrectionary organization to join.

The remaining *Directorio* leaders went into exile and began reorganizing under the direction of Faure Chomón. In a speech in Miami on October 20, 1957, Chomón advocated unity among the revolutionary groups, called for "a nationalistic united party of the revolution," and attacked the United States for selling arms to Batista.[44] Chomón also supported the unity efforts of representatives from seven anti-Batista organizations, including the *Directorio* and the July 26 Movement, who had gathered in Miami following Castro's July, 1957, "Manifesto of the Sierra Maestra" calling for a united front to overthrow Batista.[45] Out of that meeting, on November 1, 1957, a unity pact was signed, a *Junta de Liberación Cubana* (Cuban Liberation Council) was organized, and a provisional president was appointed to take over after the overthrow of Batista's regime.[46]

The junta, however, was short-lived, for Castro soon denounced the pact. In a letter sent to members of the junta on December 14, 1957, Castro explained that he opposed the unity pact because it failed "to reject foreign [U.S.] intervention in Cuba's internal affairs and to repudiate a military junta after Batista's downfall." Castro wrote, furthermore, that the junta's pretensions "to approve or disapprove of the Provisional President's appointment of cabinet members and to incorporate all revolutionary forces into the armed forces after victory" were unacceptable. "The July 26 Movement," asserted Fidel,

[44]A tape of Chomón's original speech was supplied to the author by Ada Azcarreta in Miami, Florida, on May 7, 1965.

[45]A copy of the "Manifesto" can be found in Fidel Castro, *La Revolución Cubana,* edited by Gregorio Selser (Buenos Aires: Editorial Palestra, 1960), pp. 119–24. This book contains documents, letters, and speeches pertaining to the insurrectionary and revolutionary eras.

[46]For the main provisions of the unity pact, see *ibid.,* pp. 125–26.

"claims for itself the functions of directing the revolutionary struggle and of reorganizing the armed forces of the nation."[47]

This attack and the withdrawal of the July 26 Movement from the junta shattered all attempts at unity. Evidently Fidel's change of tactics since July, when he had called for such a united front, was motivated primarily by his fear that the junta would reduce his authority, thus limiting his ambition for total power. After Batista's overthrow, Castro disclosed that he had opposed unity in December, 1957, because he was not strong enough to dominate the united groups.[48] Also, the junta's selection of the distinguished economist Felipe Pazos as provisional president displeased Castro. Aware, perhaps, that Pazos would be difficult to influence, Castro in his letter proposed Dr. Manuel Urrutia to head the provisional government.[49] Finally, the spontaneous strike that occurred in the three easternmost provinces of Cuba following the assassination of the July 26 Movement underground leader Frank País by Batista's police on July 30, 1957, strengthened Castro's conviction that a general strike, organized by the July 26 Movement, could topple the regime. From that time on, all his efforts were directed toward that end, until the ill-fated April 9, 1958, general strike heightened the need for unity. In a speech in Havana at the cultural society *Nuestro Tiempo* (a front organization of the PSP) in January, 1959, Che Guevara revealed that the strike after Frank País' death produced a tactical turn, and the July 26 Movement began organizing the workers for a general strike. "The failure of the April 9 strike," Che continued, "provoked an ideological struggle in our movement that led to a radical change in our focusing of the country's conditions and of its action groups. We learned that the Revolution did not belong to one group."[50] Presumably the struggle was over whether or not to form an alliance with the Communists. The PSP had sent representatives to the Sierra prior to the April strike.[51] Apparently, however, no formal agreement had been reached with Fidel since the Communists failed to sup-

[47]The full text of the letter can be found in *ibid.,* pp. 127–40.

[48]*Revolución,* December 1, 1961.

[49]Dr. Manuel Urrutia, a distinguished Cuban judge, presided over the tribunal that tried some *Granma* expeditionaries and the revolutionaries involved in the November 30, 1956, uprising in Santiago de Cuba. After proclaiming in a dissenting opinion that "armed action by the accused men was legitimate because it was an attempt to end oppression in Cuba," Urrutia went into exile, becoming Castro's candidate to head a provisional government.

[50]Guevara's speech is found in Castro, *La Revolución Cubana,* pp. 427–36.

[51]Hirán Prats, an organizer of the University Bureau, PSP group that worked

port the April 9 strike. The PSP blamed the failure of the strike on the July 26 Movement's "unilateral call without counting on the rest of the opposition or the workers themselves."[52]

Meanwhile, the *Directorio* leaders prepared to resume their struggle against Batista. Early in 1958 they organized a small expedition that sailed from Miami, landed in Cuba, and started guerrilla activities in the mountains of central Cuba. Following Castro's invitation for new unity talks, the *Directorio* sent delegates to the Sierra Maestra in mid-1958.[53] In July, representatives from several anti-Batista organizations, including the *Directorio* and the July 26 Movement, but excluding the PSP, met in Venezuela and signed a new unity pact known as the "Caracas Letter." This time not only was Fidel's candidate for the presidency, Dr. Urrutia, accepted, but also the broad and vague provisions of the pact left Castro's hands free.[54]

---

within the University of Havana, testified at the trial of Marco Armando Rodríguez (*Hoy,* March 25, 1964, p. 5) that he was ordered "in 1957 to go to the Sierra del Escambray to join Guevara," Prats' statement, however, if printed accurately by the newspaper, is contradictory. Since Che Guevara did not arrive in the Escambray Mountains until late in 1958 and since Prats went to the Sierra Maestra (see Draper, *Castroism,* p. 31), evidently he could not have been ordered in 1957 to go to the Sierra del Escambray to join Guevara, in which case he confused both the date and the mountain range. Or perhaps he meant that he was ordered "in 1957 to go to the Sierra Maestra Mountains to join Guevara," in which case his statement is indeed significant, for it would indicate a PSP understanding with the July 26 Movement, or with Guevara alone, earlier than 1958, the year advanced by Draper and other writers for the Castro-Communist alliance.

[52]See "Declaraciones del PSP: Las mentiras del Gobierno sobre la huelga y la situación," PSP leaflet of April 12, 1958, quoted in Draper, *Castroism,* p. 32.

[53]Testimony of Carlos Rafael Rodríguez at the trial of Marco Armando Rodríguez, *Hoy,* March 26, 1964. PSP leader Carlos Rafael Rodríguez also went to the Sierra Maestra at the same time.

[54]The "Caracas Letter" of July 28, 1958, called for "a common strategy of armed insurrection, a brief provisional government that would guide the country back to normality through constitutional and democratic means, and a minimum government program guaranteeing the punishment of the guilty, workers' rights, order, peace, freedom, the fulfillment of international agreements and the economic, social and institutional progress of the Cuban people." For the text of the pact, see Castro, *La Revolución Cubana,* pp. 152–55. Owing to the opposition of the several groups represented in the unity pact, the Communists were excluded. Fidel, however, was holding parallel talks with PSP leaders at the time, and one of the party's top theoreticians, Carlos Rafael Rodríguez, visited Castro in the mountains in July, 1958. Draper claims in his book *Castroism,* pp. 32–34, that Fidel surreptitiously negotiated a second unity pact with the Communists, and a Castro-Communist alliance was realized in 1958.

In the meantime, differences arose between *Directorio* forces in the mountains. One group commanded by Faure Chomón and claiming that the correct strategy was to *golpear arriba* (strike at the top) advocated moving to Havana to reorganize their underground and to assassinate Batista. Another, led by Eloy Gutiérrez Menoyo and Armando Fleites, urged a continuation of guerrilla warfare. Menoyo and Chomón, furthermore, clashed over who should direct the military operations and over Chomón's decision to send a quantity of badly needed weapons to Havana. In mid-1958 the two factions finally split. Fleites explained to the writer that his group, later known as the Second Front of the Escambray, continued to fight Batista, and followed a line of political independence opposing alliances with the July 26 Movement or any other organization, and attained toward the end of 1958, a force of about 1,000 men, mostly farmers and residents of the area. "When in August, 1958," said Fleites, "a PSP representative, Ovidio Díaz, visited our headquarters and proposed unity, he met with our stern opposition to any pacts with the Communists."[55] Of the remaining members of the *Directorio,* some, led by Chomón, moved to Havana and began rebuilding their underground organization, while others, commanded by Rolando Cubela, carried on small guerrilla operations in the mountains. Finally, faced with mounting repression in the capital, Chomón returned to the mountains and the *Directorio* joined Che Guevara's forces three months prior to Batista's downfall.[56]

After the Humboldt event, several questions remained unanswered in the minds of the leaders of the *Directorio* and of the relatives of the murdered students. If only a small group knew of the apartment in Humboldt, how were the police able to discover the student's hideout? Furthermore, if the four students in the apartment were murdered without being questioned, how were the police able to identify two students as having escaped? Everything pointed in the direction of a police informant. But who was to be blamed for it? Naturally, the first suspects were the two students mentioned by the police as having escaped. For many of the relatives and other students, the innocence of

[55]Interview with Armando Fleites, Miami, Florida, July 12, 1955.

[56]Interview with Lázaro Fariñas, Miami, Florida, July 2, 1965, Fariñas, a *Directorio* member, fought under Cubela in the Escambray Mountains.

Marco Armando Rodríguez, known as "Marquito," was beyond question, particularly in view of his friendship with Joe Westbrook, one of the murdered youths. On April 23, 1957, he and Pérez Cowley, the second student mentioned in the police communiqué, sought asylum in the Brazilian Embassy and several days later left for Latin America. Any investigation, therefore, had to be postponed until the end of Batista's rule.

As soon as Castro came to power, the *Directorio* requested an investigation of the Humboldt event, which revealed that Marco Armando Rodríguez (Marquito) had denounced the student's hideout to Captain Esteban Ventura. This investigation coincided with the arrest in January, 1959, of two agents of Ventura's–Alfaro and José de Jesús Mirabal. Both of them identified Marquito as the person who had visited Ventura in April, 1957, and told him of the Humboldt 7 apartment. The accused, who had returned to Cuba after the downfall of Batista, was immediately arrested. The two agents, however, were executed shortly thereafter, and Marquito was freed because of "lack of evidence."[57] The other student, Pérez Cowley, who had established residence in Guatemala, traveled to Cuba in 1959 to submit himself to a similiar investigation, was cleared from any suspicion, and returned to Guatemala.[58]

The question lagged until January 1, 1961, when the Cuban government requested Marquito's arrest in Prague, Czechoslovakia, where he had been studying and working at the Cuban Embassy. Deported to Cuba shortly after, Marquito remained in jail until his trial in March, 1964. While in jail, Marquito confessed having informed the police about the four students and disclosed that he was a member of the *Juventud Socialista* (Youth Branch of Cuba's Communist party), had worked in the cultural society *Nuestro Tiempo,* a front

[57]"Statement of Marta Jiménez during the trial of Marco Armando Rodríguez," *Hoy,* March 24, 1964, p. 4. *Hoy* was the official newspaper of the PSP. It merged with *Revolución* in 1966 to form *Granma,* the present official newspaper of Cuba's Communist party. For the Marquito affair, see Suchlicki, *University of Havana Students in Cuban Politics,* pp. 152–63. Also, see *Humboldt y el Communismo Cubano* (Panamá: Directorio Revolucionario Estudiantil, n. d.) and Janette Habel, "Le Procès de Marcos Rodríguez et les Problèmes de l'unité du Mouvement Révolutionnaire à Cuba," *Les Temps modernes,* No. 219–220 (September, 1964), pp. 491–531.

[58]*Ibid.*

organization of the *Partido Socialista Popular,* and was a close friend of several of the top leaders of the PSP.[59]

During the three years that Marquito remained in jail, several interesting developments occurred in Cuba. The *Directorio Revolucionario* was incorporated into the United Party of the Socialist Revolution (PURS) and Faure Chomón became a staunch supporter of Fidel Castro, serving for two years as Cuban ambassador to the Soviet Union. A power struggle developed, furthermore, between the neo-Marxists–i.e., the two Castros, Chomón, Armando Hart, etc.–and the old guard of Cuba's PSP, followers of the Soviet Union line–i.e., Blas Roca, Marinello, Carlos Rafael Rodríguez, Aníbal Escalante, Joaquín Ordoqui, etc. A third faction, under the leadership of Che Guevara and following the Chinese line, also developed. Apparently, Marquito was caught up in this power struggle. Castro awaited the right time to bring out his case and use it to reassert his own personal power.

In March, 1964, Marquito was tried and sentenced to death. The uproar caused by the trial and the fact that parts of Faure Chomón's testimony, in which he hinted that the Communist party had ordered Marquito to denounce the students' hideout to Batista's police, were not published in the press forced Castro to intervene. On March 21, Fidel sent a letter to Blas Roca, editor of the newspaper *Hoy* (official Communist party organ) asking him to publish Chomón's testimony and informing him that he would request that the appeal made by the accused to the Supreme Court be made public and witnesses be called to testify again.[60] The trial, broadcast on radio and television throughout Cuba, began on March 23. The court ratified the death sentence, and on April 19, 1964, Marco Armando Rodríguez was executed.[61]

The trial, especially the testimony of Marquito, shed much light on a very important and perhaps otherwise unknown subject; the tactics and strategy of the Communist party in dealing with the student movement

[59]Texto del juicio al delator de los mártires de Humboldt 7," *Hoy,* March 24, 1964, p. 4.

[60]"Se abrirá a nueva prueba el juicio al delator de Humboldt 7," *Hoy,* March 21, 1964, p. 1.

[61]"Ejecutado el delator de Humboldt," *Hoy,* April 20, 1964, p. 1. For the official transcript of the trial, see *ibid.,* March 24, 25, 26, and 27, 1964.

during the 1955–57 period. At first, during 1955, the Communists attempted to infiltrate the *Directorio.* Marquito explained that the Youth Branch of the PSP ordered him to concentrate on intelligence work within the *Directorio.* "All information," said the accused, "was transmitted to the University Bureau [PSP group that worked within the University of Havana] from where it would be sent to its final destination . . . the Party."[62] Later on, in 1956, the Communists, realizing the impossibility of infiltrating and gaining control of the *Directorio,* attempted to influence the creation of a United Student Front composed of delegates from the *Directorio,* the 26 July Movement, and the Communist party. The Communists reasoned that any such front would reduce the *Directorio*'s strength and would eventually fall under their control. Marquito narrated the failure of that attempt and the differences that arose between the three factions. Finally, the accused explained the refusal of the *Directorio* to allow his participation in the plans for the Presidential Palace attack. "On March 13," said Marquito, "Joe [Westbrook] and I were standing downstairs in the building where Mercedes Blanca Mesa lived in Vedado. Joe told me that he was sorry to say that when he proposed my participation, he was told that there was no room for the 'red dye.' "[63]

After admitting his guilt and explaining the meeting he had with Captain Ventura, in which he informed him of the exact location where the leaders of the *Directorio* had been hiding, Marquito narrated the events of his exile and added:

> . . . The Directorio summoned me and Pérez Cowley to a meeting in Mexico. However, he didn't show up and nothing could be explained. After that, I felt very bad, and I trusted the secret to Edith [García Buchaca, wife of Joaquín Ordoqui, one of the top leaders of the PSP]. I told her everything the way it was. She was perplexed, and didn't know what to do. She promised not to say anything. She explained to me that she knew of cases similar to mine in the Republic of China. . . . The Czechoslovakian Embassy in Mexico offered five fellowships to study in that country. The

[62]"La Revolución no ha de ser ni tolerante ni implacable," *Hoy,* March 27, 1964, p. 6. Marquito's confession and all the details connected with his activities and contacts with the Communist party were made public by Castro in his four-and-one-half-hour witness deposition during the trial.

[63]*Ibid.*

Party decided that I should take one. When I accepted, Joaquín [Ordoqui] accompanied and introduced me. . . .[64]

Faure Chomón also testified against Marquito in this second trial. During his deposition, he explained that on September 10, 1962, Marquito wrote a letter to Joaquín Ordoqui, one of the top members of the PSP. In that letter Marquito requested Ordoqui to intervene with the government on his behalf in order to save him. Furthermore, in the last paragraph of the letter, he threatened Ordoqui, and aware that the knowledge he possessed could be of a very embarrassing nature to the Communist party if revealed, he hinted that this disclosures would produce the same effect "as the explosion of a nuclear device." Chomón had received a copy of that letter, and he read it at the trial. "Why must I be the one," wrote Marquito, "who is precisely pointed out as the traitor of Humboldt? . . . Two opposed types of information should not be confused. . . . The first one is watchful of every road that leads to revolution; the second destroys all the roads that lead to it . . . the difference between the man that offers information to his party and the man that offers information to the police should be clearly established."[65]

The trial of Marco Armando Rodríguez brought into the open the struggle for power in Cuba between Fidel and his neo-Marxists, on the one side, and the old guard of the PSP, on the other. Castro used the occasion to reassert his own power. He tried Marquito and took advantage of that opportunity to put the Communist party on the bench of the accused. All the top members of the PSP testified at the trial and everyone took pains to deny the accused's membership in the *Juventud Socialista* or his connection with the Communist party. Nevertheless, Marquito's close contact with the Communist party and the continuous protection that organization had offered him were clearly demonstrated. Toward the end of the trial, Fidel, perhaps aware of his economic dependence on, and fearful of provoking the wrath of, the Soviet Union, exonerated the PSP from any guilt in the Humboldt event. Whether Marquito acted on his own initiative, or he followed the

[64]*Ibid.*

[65]For Chomón's testimony and the full text of the letter, see "Texto de la declaración del Comandante Faure Chomón en el juicio seguido al delator de los Mártires de Humboldt 7," *Hoy,* March 21, 1964, p. 5.

directives of the party, is not known. It became clear, however, that the Communists used him in their efforts to undermine the non-Communist revolutionary forces, and especially the *Directorio*. The insidious maneuverings of the Cuban Communist party came into the open, as did the struggle for control of power in Cuba.[66]

The issues discussed at and the revelations learned from the trial present a unique opportunity to study the tactics and strategy of Communism. The activities of the PSP to subvert the democratic student movement in Cuba during 1956–57 are only a small-scale example of the operations of Communists throughout Latin America.

[66]Only a few months after the trial, Joaquín Ordoqui was arrested and accused of "political crimes." Edith García Buchaca was relieved of her post at the department of culture. On February 15, 1965, Fidel Castro purged Carlos Rafael Rodríguez as director of the National Institute of Agrarian Reform (INRA) and appointed himself to that position. Other old PSP leaders were scorned and attacked by Castro's press.

Mexican Machismo: *Politics and Value Orientations*

By EVELYN P. STEVENS

Contrary to the misconception prevalent in popular non-Latin literature, the distinguishing characteristic of machismo *is not violence but intransigence. . . .*

Undoubtedly the value systems of a people have a direct effect on their political activities. Different peoples react to a given stimulus in terms of their beliefs, prejudices, and ideas of what is proper, admirable, and worthy of being imitated. Frequently the response to a given set of circumstances is completely automatic, and nonresponse raises the question whether an individual is a worthy member of the culture group. Political scientists in recent years have attempted to correlate the findings of modern psychology and anthropology with studies of the principles and conduct of government. The selection that follows is an attempt to relate political attitudes in Mexico with the culture complex referred to as *machismo*. The importance of this article is derived not only from the subject matter–for an awareness of *machismo* is important to understand the Latin American–but also from its methodology. Although the application of Freudian and anthropological techniques to political science is relatively new, no modern survey of a geographic area would be complete without a recognition of their use.

The concept of *machismo* has never been out of style in Latin America. Until recently, however, it was considered too strong a word for use in mixed company and hence did not appear in print. While difficult to define, it is recognizable as a form of male pride that combines courage, the essential element in establishing the *machismo,* with an aggressive maleness that also may take the prestigious form of the successful pursuit of women.

Probably there are two main original elements in *machismo*. First is the Hispanic sense of the dignity of the individual, which, as Angel Ganivet says, is the diamond axis on which the Hispanic philosophy of life revolves. The honor or public dignity of the Spaniard must be guarded, if necessary, from the slightest affront or even oral aspersion by the risk, if necessary, of life itself. This attitude was carried to extremes in the Renaissance pundonor, in which the feminine members of the family were custodians of the family honor. An affront to them had to be erased with blood. The extravagances of the plays of the "cape and the sword" of sixteenth-century Spain dramatized this attitude and made it known to the world as typically Spanish.

The second original element in *machismo* is the Spanish point of pride or vanity, the Don Juan complex by which individuals tried to convince themselves and others that they were irresistible conquerors of women. The pursuit and amatory conquest of all available women constituted a principal activity of the gentlemen of the time, and their status depended greatly on public opinion of their ability. At the same time the aggrieved brothers, fathers, or husbands of the conquered beauties had to recur to dueling or some form of violent revenge to save their own public image of private honor.

These elements have been incorporated into Latin American political life which requires of its participants outward manifestations of personal bravery. Doubts in this respect can lead to loss of face and concomitant political defeat. Therefore, a politician must embody uncompromising maleness and courage, and the need for these attributes often requires that the Latin American politician assume a public air of intransigence. Political campaigning in Latin America is often accompanied by public debate on the maleness of the opposition. In Latin America there seems to be a high correlation between those successful in politics and those with a strong public image as *machos*. Complementary reputation as a Don Juan can add to this favorable image. All this, however, does not seem to mean that Latin American political situations are necessarily a byproduct of *machismo*. As Miss Stevens points out in her study of Mexico, the Mexican political system is neither a product of nor explicable by the "culture" of Mexico as seen in its personality systems and social system.

The author of this selection, Miss Evelyn P. Stevens, was born in Chicago, studied at the universities of Puerto Rico and California and at the Institut d'Etudes Politiques of France and is a candidate for a doctoral degree in political science at the University of California in Berkeley. She has held fellowships from the Falk Foundation and the Fulbright Commission and is a specialist on Mexican politics. She now lives in Cleveland, Ohio.

R. E. M.

> *What is the strongest and most intimate wish of the Mexican? He would like to be a man who predominates over all others in courage and power . . . he tries to fill a vacuum with the only value within his reach: that of his maleness.*[1]

NOTE: I am indebted to Drs. David Apter (Political Science), May N. Díaz (Anthropology) and Carlos Fernández (Psychiatry) for fruitful discussions which clarified many points in this article.

This is one of the most explicit statements to be found concerning a wide spread phenomenon which appears under many guises in the personality systems and social systems of Latin American countries. To the Latin Americans themselves, this phenomenon is known as *machismo;* it is all about them and is as familiar as the air they breathe. Foreign observers call it "the cult of virility," and almost anyone who has lived for some time in Latin America includes its many manifestations in a list of distinguishing characteristics of the region.

Passing mention has been made of the subject by some investigators,[2] but a search of social science literature fails to reveal a full-scale treatment of it. One of the most recently published books in English has this to say: ". . . considerable emphasis is placed by most observers on the role of *machismo* in the Mexican culture. Described in different ways by different writers, the concept almost invariably projects the picture of the aggressive male protagonist, alone and withdrawn—constantly preoccupied with the image he is conveying, constantly concerned to create the impression of masculinity and courage, invulnerability and indifference to the attacks of others."[3]

[1]Samuel Ramos, *El perfil del hombre y la cultura en México* (Buenos Aires, 1951), pp. 55–61.

[2]See, for example, Oscar Lewis, *Five Families* (New York: Basic Books, 1959, and J. Mayone Stycos, *Family and Fertility in Puerto Rico: A Study of the Lower Income Group* (New York: Columbia U. Press, 1955), pp. 19, 34–35, 42–44, and 105.

[3]Raymond Vernon, *The Dilemma of Mexico's Development* (Cambridge: Harvard U. Press, 1963, p. 159.

Ramos notes that Mexicans equate virility with exaggerated aggressiveness and with intransigence. Faced with a threat, a Mexican male will often react by shouting, "I am a *macho*" (gesticulating toward his external genitalia), and will impute feminine characteristics to his adversary. Mexican novels and films abound in references to *machismo;* most notably in the latter category, *El Sietemachos* and *Animas Trujano* come to mind. Octavio Paz's *The Labyrinth of Solitude* (New York: Grove Press, 1962) is a powerful literary treatment of the same theme.

In an attempt to get "some feeling for the Mexican ethos," one investigator recently undertook a small-scale survey and concluded that the salient "hero type" is a "man who is *muy macho* (strong, virile, valiente, stubborn, fuerte) . . . described as 'a real man, good drinker, lover, singer, fighter, brave and willing to defend what he believes in.' "[4]

What connection, if any, can there be between the cult of virility and the Mexican political system? An attempt to answer this question will be made in the following pages.

Virility is a cultural symbol; to be understood in the context of an action system, it must be translated into a "way of orienting." We are told that "The outcome of defeat is bondage or death. There is no middle ground: if a man does not wish to be victor, he must needs be loser. Ultimately, all means are legitimate in this battle for personal control of people and things, even violence and death."[5]

In Mexico, as in other parts of Latin America, politics is considered to be "the business of men"– a sphere of activity peculiarly appropriate to males. This is not to say that women do not participate in political activity; a small number of them do, but they are the exception rather than the rule. There is now a "woman's sector" in the *Partido Revolucionario Institucional,* corresponding to the extension of woman suffrage to the national elections in 1958. But in the main, politics remains a "man's world" and male values are regarded as appropriate. Role expectations in politics, as in other spheres of action, require that a man must get his own way; he may brook no opposition

[4]Orrin Klapp, "Mexican Social Types," *American Journal of Sociology,* 69 (January 1964), 404–14.

[5]Eric Wolf, *Sons of the Shaking Earth* (Chicago: U. of Chicago Press, 1959), p. 239.

nor share his power with anyone else.[6] To do so would be to show traits of femininity, of submissiveness and of passivity. As one observer has expressed it,

> Any kind of gentleness or refinement of attitude, any kind of moderation in action, will be censured as being feminine. Of the gentle or timid man, he (the other man) will say, "he is an old woman," whereas *he* (the speaker) is "very much a man." This he is always willing to demonstrate, bragging about a series of supposed virtues of masculinity. . . . The boasts of the *macho* are classic and appear frequently in Mexican songs. . . . Mexican life is full of anecdotes in which it is easy to recognize the presence of the *macho* element.[7]

Above all, the Mexican value system requires that politicians must *tener pantalones* (wear the pants, show who is boss).

Contrary to the misconception prevalent in popular non-Latin literature, the distinguishing characteristic of *machismo* is not violence but intransigence. Each man is convinced that there is only one right way of doing things: his way. If his way is challenged by someone else, he may, of course, have to resort to violence to impose his criterion. But men customarily take precautions against this eventuality by avoiding intimacy with others, abstaining from discussing controversial matters and leading a rather lonely life. Although intransigence at the individual level may often be preserved without violence, with the consequent impoverishment of interpersonal relations, such a solution is not always effective at the group level.

Must we then expect to find Mexican politics characterized by violence and intransigence? If we were to accept the hypothesis that politics reflects the dominant value patterns of the social system, we might anticipate that in this case the political system would conform to one of the following models:

Absolute authoritarianism. One man or group of men will establish complete control over all political activity and will maintain this control by repressive measures which will when necessary include the

[6]May Nordquist Díaz, *Tonalá: A Mexican Peasant Town in Transition* (Ph.D. dissertation, U. of California, Berkeley, 1963), p. 202.

[7]Angelina C. de Moreleón, "Algunas formas del valor y de la cobardía en el Mexicano," *Filosofía y Letras,* 23 (enero-junio de 1952), 165–74.

extensive use of physical violence (carried out by the military forces) against all challenges. Intrigue will be endemic and potential rivals, alert for the smallest sign of weakness, will seize the first opportunity and use physical violence to eliminate the authoritarian figure. His successor will find it necessary to employ the same methods in order to stay in power.

Anarchy or near anarchy. Each man or group of men who are active in politics will try to become as powerful as possible, while at the same time refusing to recognize the authority of other contenders for power. Physical violence, equated with male aggressiveness, will be used to eliminate rivals, and this violence may include assassination as well as guerrilla warfare. Armed bands, accepting as leaders only the strongest figures, will roam the country, extending their control over as wide an area as possible, until checked by clashes with other armed bands.

Totalitarianism. This will develop under the rule of a charismatic leader who effectively symbolizes the values of *machismo.* Total allegiance will be demanded by this leader in the name of some ideology such as nationalism, communism, or religion, and will be rendered to him as long as he continues to represent himself convincingly as the epitome of virility and to act out the need-disposition of aggressiveness. In the absence of a charismatic leader, a dedicated single-minded elite may perform the same role.

THE RECORD: PORFIRIATO AND REVOLUTION

In 1876, General Porfirio Díaz seized the reins of government in Mexico, holding fast to them until 1910. Sometimes he occupied the presidential chair himself; at other times he placed a puppet on it, but at all times during the period, he was the absolute and undisputed ruler of the nation.[8]

After thirty-four years of absolutism, the Díaz regime collapsed under the impact of armed uprisings in widely separated parts of the country. In Chihuahua, Pascual Orozco, Doroteo Arango (Pancho Villa) and Abraham González carried on a guerrilla war, while to the

[8]For an extended treatment of this period in Mexican history see, for example, Frank Tannenbaum, *Mexico: The Struggle for Peace and Bread* (New York: Knopf, 1950).

south in Morelos, Emiliano Zapata gathered another "army" and carried on his own campaign.[9]

In 1911 Francisco Madero, a middle-class intellectual, became the first post-Porfirian president of Mexico, but he proved timid and indecisive, lacking in *pantalones,* and unable to put a stop to the warfare raging in the countryside. From his exile in Texas, Pancho Villa (Mexico's *macho* hero *par excellence*) counseled Madero, "all you have to do is to hitch up your pants and be a man."[10] After fifteen months in office, Madero was murdered, less than a month after he received Villa's letter. His successor was forced into exile and the next president was assassinated.

During the period 1916–28 there were five major political parties contending for national office, as well as an almost interminable list of regionally based groupings, some of which managed to muster considerable support, both electoral and military.[11] The most notable characteristic of party activity at that time was the pervading influence of *caciquismo* (satrapies), typified by "the strong individual, posing as the father image and spreading his figurative mantle of protection . . . demanding unquestioning loyalty."[12] Physical violence was still accepted as a mode of reacting to political problems, as evidenced by the fact that in 1928 the three presidential candidates–Gómez, Serrano and Obregón–were killed.

Organization and Development of the Revolutionary Party

Plutarco Elías Calles, president of Mexico from 1924 to 1928, and not-so-grey eminence for several years after that, is generally recognized as having been responsible for the founding of the

[9]A description of the activities of the guerrilla armies is contained in Mariano Azuela's novel, translated into English as *The Underdogs* (New York: Brentano's, 1929).

[10]Letter from Pancho Villa to President Madero dated January 20, 1913 (Department of Historical Research, Instituto Nacional de Antropología e Historia, Document No. 429336).

[11]For an exhaustive listing and description of the most important of these groups, see Vicente Fuentes Díaz, "Partidos y corrientes politicas," *Mexico: cincuenta anos de Revolución* (Mexico, 1961).

[12]Vernon, *op. cit.,* p. 159.

Revolutionary party.[13] It came into being on March 4, 1929, in a constituent assembly held in Querétaro, and was named the *Partido Nacional Revolucionario,* thus preempting the only symbol of legitimacy to emerge from the chaos of the previous eighteen years.

The PNR was created "from the top down," that is, by presidential fiat.[14] After two reorganizations (in 1938 and in 1946) it assumed its present structure, under the new name of *Partido Revolucionario Institucional.*[15] Independent observers estimate that the PRI carried 85 per cent of the total votes cast in the 1958 elections.[16] Other parties do exist, in an electoral limbo from which there is no expectation that they will emerge.

A Mexican sociologist has classified the existing parties in three groups: "Those created and supported wholly or mainly by the government or by government officials (PRI, PNM and PARM); those which receive or have received government subsidies or have benefited from posts as advisers to the government or to decentralized institutions (PAN and PPS); and those which live and have [always] lived in opposition to the government (PC and POCM)."[17]

If we assume that the dominant orientational modes observable in Mexican personality and society will operate inflexibly to produce a corresponding type of activity in political affairs, the scope of development will of necessity be confined to the kinds of political systems described earlier in this essay.

We can see that the period of Porfiriato, from 1876 to 1910, fits neatly into the frame of absolute authoritarianism, and the category of anarchy or near anarchy adequately describes the period from 1910 to about 1925. But what can we say about the subsequent period, continuing to the present time? The process which has been taking place cannot accurately be described by calling it anarchical or totalitarian, or unadulterated authoritarian.

[13]A detailed account of the founding of the party is contained in Frank Brandenburg's *Mexico: An Experiment in One-Party Democracy* (Ph.D. dissertation, University of Pennsylvania, 1955).

[14]Vicente Fuentes Díaz, *op. cit.,* p. 392.

[15]Robert E. Scott, *Mexican Government in Transition* (Urbana: U. of Ill. Press, 1959), *passim.*

[16]Gabriel A. Almond and Sidney Verba, *The Civic Culture* (Princeton: Princeton U. Press, 1963), p. 292.

[17]Héctor Solís Quiroga, *Los partidos politicos en México* (Mexico, D. F.: Editorial Orión, 1961).

Through a process as yet imperfectly understood, because of the paucity of empirical data, political objectives are apparently being attained through a process of bargaining, maneuvering, and settling for the "best possible deal." No one interest gets all that it wants, yet the major organized interests, both the "official" groups which form part of the party organization, and the "unofficial" interests which are excluded from the party by the Constitution (notably the business organizations) have in the past had many of their needs recognized and satisfied.[18] When sufficiently powerful new groups form, they are either "bought off" with partial satisfaction of their "petitions" (Mexicans do not conceive of the process as one of formulating "demands" on the government) or they are co-opted into the party structure.

There is little evidence which might indicate that the party serves functions of interest aggregation or interest articulation except in a nominal sense. In fact, it has been suggested that the main function of the PRI is the mobilization of support for government policies which are decided in the "inner circle" of advisors close to the President.[19] Unlike the President of the United States, the Mexican Chief Executive does not have to share power with the legislature, nor does he run the risk of seeing his decisions nullified by the judiciary. But to conclude that he therefore enjoys complete and unchecked authority or that he and his advisors operate within an information vacuum would be to ignore the record of Mexican politics during the past three decades. Until more explicit information is available, speculation must be satisfied with the observation that "the Mexican president must be constantly aware of the margins of toleration of the components of the Revolutionary coalition, for his power is ultimately dependent on the maintenance of that coalition; but in comparision with his United States counterpart, he can count on greater leeway. . . ."[20]

[18]But see Pablo González Casanova, "México: desarrollo y subdesarrollo," III Desarrollo Económico, Nums. 1–2 (Abril–Septembre, 1963), pp. 285–302, for the view that the most "neglected" sector of the nation in recent years has been the agrarian population. The *campesinos* represent a hard core of poverty which has not been dissolved by previous efforts at redistribution of land nor by the more recent increasing pace of industrialization.

[19]Charles W. Anderson, "Bankers as Revolutionaries: Politics and Development Banking in Mexico," in William P. Glade, Jr., and Charles W. Anderson, *The Political Economy of Mexico* (Madison: U. of Wis. Press, 1963), p. 131. See also Frank Brandenburg, *The Making of Modern Mexico* (Englewood Cliffs: Prentice Hall, 1964), for a description of the "Revolutionary Family."

[20]Anderson, *op. cit.*, p. 133.

It is precisely at this point that there occurs a hiatus in the empirical data. Thus it becomes impossible at the present time to trace the formulation of policy from the initial stages of articulation of interest through the final making of a decision, in the shape of a presidential decree. From the evidence already at hand, however, it seems probable that when such case studies become available, the Mexican political system will be found to contain many elements of a "reconciliation system," characterized by the "high value it places on compromises between groups which express prevailing political objectives."[21]

By contrast with the aggressiveness, intransigence, and physical violence which was described earlier in this essay, the current practices of "petitioning" and maneuvering behind the scenes would seem to display characteristics of what is regarded as feminine behavior. We can thus observe the realm of political action a way of behaving which is directly at variance with a predominant value orientation of the prevailing personality system and the social system of Mexico. How can we explain this? A clue can be discovered in the statement that "this form of organization, divided and sub-divided *ad infinitum* . . . is the product of the post-revolutionary conditions that saw the foundations of the PRI in 1928. After the assassination of Alvaro Obregón, the revolutionary leader, it became evident that there was a need for a majority party that would both embody the Revolution and yet, through self-cancelling internal structures, would prevent a 'struggle for power' among the *caudillos.*"[22]

The signifiance of the Revolution (the use of the capital letter distinguishes the 1910 revolution from prior ones) as a unifying symbol can hardly be overstressed. In attempting to explicate the very marked discrepancy between Mexicans' sense of political competence and satisfaction and the actual performance of the political system, one team of analysts has stated, ". . . the ordinary citizen's awareness of politics and, indeed, of his membership in a nation probably derived from the dramatic upheavals of the Mexican Revolution. . . . And the symbolic importance of the Revolution in Mexican politics has persisted to the present day."[23]

[21]David Apter, "System, Process and the Politics of Economic Development," in Bert F. Hoselitz and Wilbert E. Moore (eds.), *Industrialization and Society* (UNESCO, 1963), p. 140.

[22]Keith Botsford, "Mexico's 'Parti Unique,'" *The New Leader,* October 28, 1963, pp. 13–16.

[23]Almond and Verba, *op. cit.,* p. 252.

When it is remembered that the Revolution began in 1910 and that the most "dramatic upheavals" had subsided by 1928, it becomes clear that many of the respondents in the survey referred to above must have had, at best, only hearsay knowledge of the most violent phase of the conflict itself. What remains is a collective revulsion against the now almost legendary accounts of violence, senseless bloodshed and social, political, and economic disintegration of the revolutionary period.

It has been postulated by some observers that the Spanish people, who share many of the attitudes toward virility which prevail in Mexico, look upon their Civil War in the same light. But it is evident that Spain, where anarchic movements flourished more vigorously and persisted longer than in other parts of Europe, has accepted an unmitigated authoritarian system since 1939.

It is suggested that in the case of Mexico the dominant PRI, with its hierarchical structure and its virtual monopoly of effective political activity, its overwhelming victories at the polls and its control of elective and appointive offices, provides an emotionally satisfying symbol of masculine aggressiveness and omnipotence. Individuals and groups can identify their need-dispositions of aggressiveness with the outward appearance and behavior of the PRI, and can feel reassured that political affairs are being conducted in an appropriately virile (or revolutionary) way.

At the pinnacle of the political structure stands the President, who behaves in a fashion satisfactorily reminiscent of the Mexican stereotype of the *macho*: powerful, intransigent, at times capricious, but usually just. In connection with this, it is interesting to note that the members of the President's cabinet are fair game for scapegoating but the figure of the President is considered above reproach.[24] Witness a rather typical manifestation of the virile stereotype in a recent periodical: "The Government of the Republic is now the government of a single man—a man with a team—determined to sustain the rhythm of growth, to carry out the plans for development, and to bring to fruition the programs of the government. . . . And the people will continue to pronounce implacable, unmerciful judgment against those who

[24]Francisco González Pineda, *El Mexicano: su dinámica psicosocial* (Mexico, Editorial Pax, 1959), pp. 35–38 and 53–54.

interfere, or say that they will interfere, with the management of national affairs."[25]

But as we have seen, there are intimations that behind this façade of toughness there is enough flexibility, enough "give and take," and yet enough built-in limitation on unbridled aggressiveness to prevent a relapse into bloody warfare or anarchy. An anthropologist gives us some insight into the manipulation of stereotypes. Describing a family situation in Mexico, the observer indicates that the women achieve their objectives by maneuvering the men—"by appealing to the formal structure . . . put in terms of the easily understood cultural symbol of who wears the pants. . . . One is left," concludes the writer, "with the impression that the women are maneuvering busily while the men really do not understand what is happening."[26] This is what seems to be taking place at the level of the national political process, with male politicians playing the role of "feminine" maneuverers.

Our quick overview of eighty-eight years of Mexican political history would seem to indicate that the political system of that nation has undergone a series of metamorphoses, from authoritarianism to anarchy, to something which incorporates some of the features of a "reconciliation" system. Present-day reality includes a party which has no exact counterpart anywhere in the world and a political *modus operandi* which has only occasional—and even then but tangential—correspondence to the written constitution enshrined in a floodlighted glass case in the National Historical Museum in Chapultepec Park.

Psychology, Culture and Politics

In an interesting study of Burmese politicians, Pye has indicated that there is an observable relationship between child training, dominant cultural values, and adult political behavior in that country. He suggests two general ways in which the "latent psychological restraints to effective development" may be dissolved. These are ". . . the grand ideological solution in which some leader, out of the depths of his own personal experience, is able to give his people an understanding of the new sentiments and values necessary for national development. . . .

[25]*Siempre!* (Mexico, D.F.), December 11, 1963 (editorial), p. 19.
[26]May Nordquist Díaz, *op. cit.*, p. 177.

Fundamentally, this is the quest of the charismatic leader. . . . The second broad approach [is] through mastery of demanding skills."[27]

Some other recent area studies have employed a similar approach to the problem of change. One author, for example, has employed massive documentation from the field of psychiatric theory, coupled with social psychology data drawn from numerous countries to demonstrate his thesis that early childhood experiences such as toilet training have a profound effect on the future of a nation.[28]

It would be unfortunate if such valuable area studies as these were to be interpreted as indicating that the avenues of change are limited to a narrow range of possibilities consonant with the prevailing personal and social modes of orienting. The student of comparative politics might thus be tempted to follow the primrose path of predicting political events exclusively on the basis of "national character," without taking other variables into account.[29]

The first section of the present article demonstrates the dangers inherent in the exclusive use of cultural or psychological data to predict political behavior. If by "national development" is meant the employment of rational means for the achievement of rational ends, then Mexico's shift from fratricidal intransigence to widespread support of the government program of economic development would seem to fit that category. However, we were unable to correlate actual present political behavior with the dominant value orientation of *machismo*. Thus, if our analysis of the present state of Mexico's political system corresponds to reality, it may prove advisable to regard the political development of other societies as open-ended. We need not regard other Latin American nations whose people share the *machismo* value orientation as doomed by "latent psychological restraints" to conform to patterns of anarchy, authoritarianism or totalitarianism.

No attempt is made here to discredit the use of psychoanalytic insights to explicate historical developments. But the utility of such a method as a tool for prediction is, at the very least, doubtful. The historian can always find, *ex post facto,* an appropriate value orientation on which to base his explanation. Numerous case studies

[27]Lucian Pye, *Politics, Personality, and Nation Building* (New Haven: Yale U. Press, 1962), pp. 287–89.

[28]Everett Hagen, *On the Theory of Social Change: How Economic Development Begins* (Homewood: Dorsey, 1962), Part II, especially pp. 123–60.

[29]See the discussion of national character in David Potter, *People of Plenty* Chicago: U. of Chicago Press, 1954), chaps. I and II.

have shown that both the social system and the personality system are shot through with ambivalence. For every dominant value orientation which disposes an individual or a society to act in a certain way, there exists an alternate value orientation which struggles for an outlet.

Recognition of this datum multiplies the possibilities of choice so enormously that an attempt to predict the outcome on the basis of value orientation alone may produce little better than chance correlation. The political pundit who stakes his reputation on personality formation to the exclusion of other variables would do well to couch his predictions in Delphic terms. One critic of the psychoanalytic approach has pointed out that "it is necessary to treat motivational problems in the context of their relation to structure, and to raise dynamic problems in terms of the *balance of forces* operating to maintain or alter a given structure."[30]

The example of Mexico's political development during the past three decades indicates that politics can and does make creative use of alternate value orientations to devise new and more satisfactory approachs to the solution of old problems. If it can be inferred that the old approach was consonant with the predominant value orientation of society, it may be assumed that the appraisal of that approach as "unsatisfactory" for political activity involved in a choice of values different from the then prevailing ones. The problems involved in Mexico's case was one which was concerned with methods of resolving inter-group conflict. The choice made by Mexico was not the same as that made by Spain, nor the choices made by other Latin American nations.

What is suggested here is that the political system may be that part of the social system which has as its principal concern the problem of making choices amongst alternatives affecting the maintenance or alteration of structure—"the authoritative allocation of values," as Easton has claimed.[31]

Myth and symbol can be manipulated to achieve results quite at variance with those one might be led to expect from a study of cultural or psychiatric data alone. Today, as in the past, no self-respecting Mexican would admit to being anything but a *macho completo* (100

[30]Talcott Parsons, "Psychoanalysis and Social Structure," in *Psychoanalysis and Social Science,* ed. Henrik M. Ruitenbeek (New York: Dutton, 1962), p. 48 (italics added).

[31]David Easton, *The Political System* (New York: Knopf, 1953), p. 129.

per cent male). But because of decisions politically made and politically implemented, he is free to conduct certain crucial activities according to other, more rational criteria.

"In this respect," we are told, "modern Mexico has been quite distinct in reducing the debilitating, bitterly partisan factionalism so much in evidence in other Latin American countries. . . . In providing such a mystique the Revolution has been able to work part of the way toward the transmutation of the motivation for individual achievement into cooperation for group and national achievement. In the process, it has probably mitigated the contra-productive aspects of Hispanic individualism and personalism."[32]

The "great man" theory of history, in which change is attributed to the intervention of a charismatic figure, is not helpful in understanding political developments in Mexico during the past thirty-six years. During that time, the nation has had no truly charismatic leader who carried the whole country with him by the force of his personality.[33] The founding and institutionalization of the *Partido Revolucionario* was the work of many people; no one knows how many, nor is it important for the present discussion to know.

A recent writer has stated: ". . . men are rather more the masters of their destiny than ever before . . . No longer must we wait only on the slow grinding of economic mills or the accidental appearance of great men to erect the 'bases' upon which other social changes build themselves. The political and social functions of men, instead of being dependent upon other presumably more basic circumstances, assume importance as engines of fundamental choice in themselves."[34]

The course of development as outlined in the previous pages contains some factors which would suggest that the political system, as an analytical concept, is neither a product of nor explicable by the "culture" of a country as seen in its personality systems and social system. It would instead seem to have properties which make it a subject for study in its own right.

[32]William P. Glade, Jr., in Glade and Anderson, *op. cit.*, pp. 43–44.

[33]This statement is made with full knowledge that some observers have called Lázaro Cárdenas a "charismatic figure." Such a view is rejected here, but limitations of space prevent a full discussion.

[34]K. H. Silvert, "The Strategy of the Study of Nationalism," in *Expectant Peoples,* ed. K. H. Silvert (New York, 1963), p. 7. See also Norton Long, "The Political Act as an Act of Will," *American Journal of Sociology,* 69 (July 1963), 1–6.